FREEDOM OF EXPRESSION
A Critical Analysis

MARTIN H. REDISH
Professor of Law
Northwestern University

THE MICHIE COMPANY
Law Publishers
CHARLOTTESVILLE, VIRGINIA

Copyright © 1984
BY
The Michie Company

Library of Congress Catalog Card No. 84-61656
ISBN 0-87215-822-5

All rights reserved.

For
Caren, Jessica and Sylvia Redish

PREFACE

This book is the product of several years of thought about various aspects of first amendment theory. All of the essays have appeared as separately published articles in one or more of the following journals: The California Law Review, the Northwestern Law Review, the Stanford Law Review, the University of Pennsylvania Law Review and the Virginia Law Review. In certain instances, however, the material has been expanded or rearranged for purposes of this book. In addition, introductory and concluding sections have been added, in order to demonstrate how the five essays are linked on a broader theoretical level.

The book would not have been possible without substantial assistance from numerous sources. Initially, the Northwestern University School of Law has provided significant research support, for which I am sincerely grateful. Also a number of past and present law students at Northwestern proved extremely helpful as research assistants: Yvette Ehr, Mark Litvack, Andrea Sussman, Maxine Wolfe and Karen Zulauf. A number of my colleagues at Northwestern — Robert Bennett, Victor Goldberg, Frank Haiman, Thomas Merrill and Michael Perry — provided valuable comments on various drafts. Kent Greenawalt of Columbia and Matthew Spitzer of Southern California also assisted by commenting on portions of the book. As is usually the case, however, all of the views expressed, as well as any mistakes, are my own. A special thanks goes to my secretary, Martha Koning, who has had the unenviable task of typing all of my manuscripts for the last five years, and without whom I would no doubt be lost. Finally, the special people in my life, to whom this book is dedicated, have, in one sense or another, made important contributions to this product, as well as to all other aspects of my life.

Martin H. Redish
Chicago, Illinois

November, 1984

SUMMARY TABLE OF CONTENTS

	Page
Introduction	1
Chapter I. The Value of Free Speech	9
Chapter II. The Content Distinction in First Amendment Analysis	87
Chapter III. The Proper Role of the Prior Restraint Doctrine's Role in First Amendment Theory	127
Chapter IV. Advocacy of Unlawful Conduct and the Clear and Present Danger Test	173
Chapter V. The Warren Court, the Burger Court and the First Amendment Overbreadth Doctrine	213
Conclusion	259
Table of Cases	265
Index	269

TABLE OF CONTENTS

	Page
Introduction	1
CHAPTER I. THE VALUE OF FREE SPEECH	9
I. Self-Realization and the Democratic Process: Ascertaining the Ultimate Value of Free Speech	14
A. The "Democratic Process" Value	14
B. Deriving the Ultimate Value	19
1. Collective Self-Rule and Individual Autonomy	22
2. The Impact of the Elitist Theorists and the Definition of "Political"	26
C. Scholarly Criticism of the Self-Realization Theory	29
II. Separating Value from Subvalue: An Inquiry into the Alternative Goals of Free Speech	40
A. The Checking Value	41
B. The Marketplace-of-Ideas Concept	45
C. The "Liberty" Model	49
III. The Self-Realization Value and the Balancing of First Amendment Interests	52
IV. Acceptance of the Self-Realization Value: Implications for Constitutional Construction	55
A. Commercial Speech	60
B. Obscenity	68
C. Defamation	76
D. Advocacy of Unlawful Conduct	81
V. Conclusion	86
CHAPTER II. THE CONTENT DISTINCTION IN FIRST AMENDMENT ANALYSIS	87
I. The Nature of the Content Distinction	88
A. Definitional Questions	88
B. Implications of the Content Distinction	93
II. The Content Distinction in the Supreme Court	95
III. A Theoretical Critique	102
IV. Practical Difficulties in Applying the Content Distinction	114
V. Abandoning the Content Distinction	116
VI. Conclusion	125
CHAPTER III. THE PROPER ROLE OF THE PRIOR RESTRAINT DOCTRINE IN FIRST AMENDMENT THEORY	127
I. Introduction	127
II. The Traditional Justifications for the Prior Restraint Doctrine: Rationale and Critique	132
A. Inhibition of the Marketplace of Ideas	132
B. Overuse	134

TABLE OF CONTENTS

	Page
C. Difference in the Level of Procedural Protections	136
D. Abstract Determinations	139
E. Impact on Audience Reception	142
F. Improper Division State and Individual Authority	144
III. Determining the Proper Role of the Prior Restraint Doctrine	147
A. Assessing the True Theoretical Rationale	147
B. Practical Implications of the Theoretical Rationale	155
1. Demonstrations	155
2. National Security	157
C. Differentiating Among Forms of Judicial Restraint	158
IV. Nonjudicial Prior Restraints and Subsequent Punishment Contrasted	161
V. Implications for the Collateral Bar Rule	164
VI. Conclusion	170

CHAPTER IV. ADVOCACY OF UNLAWFUL CONDUCT AND THE CLEAR AND PRESENT DANGER TEST 173

I. The Clear and Present Danger Test: History, Theory, Criticisms and Alternatives	175
A. History	175
B. Proposed Structure	186
1. The Role of Intent	187
2. Direct v. Indirect Incitements	188
3. Types of Substantive Evil Threatened	189
4. Imminence	190
C. Defense and Criticisms	191
1. The Case for Clear and Present Danger	191
2. Ely's Search for a Categorical Rule: A Look at *Brandenburg* and *Masses*	193
3. Professor Emerson and the Speech-Action Dichotomy	201
4. Alexander Meiklejohn and the "Absolute" Alternative	204
5. Criticisms from the Opposite Direction: the Charge that Clear and Present Danger is Overprotective	206
II. Conclusion	211

CHAPTER V. THE WARREN COURT, THE BURGER COURT AND THE FIRST AMENDMENT OVERBREADTH DOCTRINE 213

I. Introduction	213
II. The Overbreadth Doctrine: Definition and Consequences	216
A. Defining the Doctrine	216
B. Consequences of the Doctrine's Use	221

TABLE OF CONTENTS

                        Page

III. The Warren Court and the Overbreadth Doctrine: an Exercise in Balancing the Unbalanceable 226
  A. Ad Hoc Balancing and Free Expression 226
  B. The Application of Overbreadth in *Robel* 227
  C. Reluctance to Evaluate Less Restrictive Alternatives as an Avoidance of Balancing 230
  D. Reluctance to Evaluate Less Restrictive Alternatives as a Limitation of the Judicial Function 233
  E. Analyzing the "Risk of the Wrong Guess" 235
IV. Suggested Alternatives for Overbreadth Analysis: the Continued Search for Categorical Alternatives 237
V. The Burger Court and the Overbreadth Doctrine: Retrenchment and Reaction 241
  A. The "Expressive Conduct" Limitation 243
  B. The "Substantiality" Requirement 250
VI. Conclusion: The Overbreadth Doctrine and the Categorization Debate in First Amendment Analysis 255

Conclusion 259

Table of Cases 265

Index 269

INTRODUCTION

Shortly after the turn of the century, the first amendment right of free expression[1] emerged from its long-held state of benign judicial neglect.[2] To be sure, it would be difficult to characterize many of the cases decided in that early period as especially protective of that constitutional right.[3] But at least certain members of the judicial branch[4] were beginning to struggle with many of the controversial free speech issues that continue to occupy the efforts of scholars and jurists today: What are the purposes of protecting the right of free expression? Are there certain forms of purely expressive activity not worthy of that protection? When, if ever, should expression clearly falling within the broad boundaries of the constitutional right be properly subject to government regulation? Should it matter what form that regulation takes? How do we conceptually distinguish protected expression from unprotected conduct? Is there any reason why expression should receive greater constitutional protection than conduct?

---

1. The term, "free expression" is employed, though the word "expression" appears nowhere on the face of the first amendment, because it summarizes all forms of protected activity: speech, press, assembly, and the satellite communicative activities that have been wisely included within the amendment's reach — association, art and music. Use of the term is well accepted in the literature. *See, e.g.,* T. EMERSON, THE SYSTEM OF FREEDOM OF EXPRESSION (1970). In recent years, use of the term has come under attack. *See* F. SCHAUER, FREE SPEECH: A PHILOSOPHICAL ENQUIRY 50-52 (1982). Basically, Schauer contends that "[w]hen speech is considered merely as one form of self-expression, nothing special is said about speech. Because virtually any activity may be a form of self-expression, a theory that does not isolate speech from this vast range of other conduct causes freedom of speech to collapse into a principle of general liberty." *Id.* at 52. However, for reasons explored in detail in Chapter I, this criticism is totally unfounded: There exists absolutely no value served *exclusively* by speech, rather than other forms of liberty, and at no point does Schauer even attempt to suggest one. In any event, the term "expression" could be employed, simply as a shorthand for the freedoms of press and assembly, as well as that of speech, all three of which are equally protected by the terms of the first amendment.

2. It was primarily in the World War I Espionage Act cases in the Supreme Court, concerning the level of constitutional protection to be given advocacy of unlawful conduct, in which first amendment theory began to take shape, particularly in the opinions of Justices Holmes and Brandeis. *See, e.g.,* Schenck v. United States, 249 U.S. 47 (1919); Abrams v. United States, 250 U.S. 616, 628 (1919) (Holmes, J., dissenting); Gitlow v. New York, 268 U.S. 652, 672-73 (1925) (Holmes, J., dissenting); Whitney v. California, 274 U.S. 357, 373 (1927) (Brandeis, J., concurring).

3. *See* the discussion in Chapter IV *infra* at 175-79. While many of the opinions cited in note 2 have traditionally been deemed protectionist, most of them did not speak for the Court.

4. In particular, this refers to Justices Holmes and Brandeis. *See* the opinions cited in note 2.

The issues presented by these questions are of enormous practical and intellectual appeal, and it is therefore not surprising that they have occupied the time and effort of numerous scholars of law and philosophy. What may be somewhat surprising, however, is the relatively recent date of much of that scholarly activity. While the early giants — Chafee[5] and Meiklejohn[6] — authored their pathbreaking work in the 1940's and another scholar of equal magnitude produced many of his important insights in the early 1960's,[7] much of the most important scholarly work in free speech theory has been produced within the last fifteen years.[8] A majority of this literature has been characterized by attempts to develop coherent, easily applied approaches to first amendment construction.[9] The apparent concern of many of these commentators has been the historic manipulability that has pervaded judicial construction of the first amendment, and the resultant reduction in protection of expression in times of crisis. It is only through the creation of rigid lines of demarcation in first amendment interpretation, they reason, that we can be reasonably assured of a consistent level of judicial protection.[10] In part for this

---

5. Z. CHAFEE, FREE SPEECH IN THE UNITED STATES (1941).

6. A. MEIKLEJOHN, POLITICAL FREEDOM (1960). *See also* Meiklejohn, *The First Amendment Is an Absolute*, 1961 SUP. CT. REV. 245. Professor Meiklejohn's book was an expanded version of his FREE SPEECH AND ITS RELATION TO SELF-GOVERNMENT, first published in 1948.

7. T. EMERSON, TOWARD A GENERAL THEORY OF THE FIRST AMENDMENT (1963). Professor Kalven also did much of his most significant work in the 1960's. *See* H. KALVEN, THE NEGRO AND THE FIRST AMENDMENT (1965).

8. *See, e.g.,* Baker, *Scope of the First Amendment Freedom of Speech*, 25 U.C.L.A. L. REV. 964 (1978); BeVier, *The First Amendment and Political Speech: An Inquiry Into the Substance and Limits of Principle*, 30 STAN. L. REV. 200 (1978); Blasi, *The Checking Value in First Amendment Theory*, 1977 AM. B. FOUND. RESEARCH J. 521; Bork, *Neutral Principles and Some First Amendment Problems*, 47 IND. L.J. 1 (1971); Ely, *Flag Desecration: A Case Study in the Roles of Categorization and Balancing in First Amendment Analysis*, 88 HARV. L. REV. 1482 (1975); Greenawalt, *Speech and Crime*, 1980 AM. B. FOUND. RESEARCH J. 645; Karst, *Equality as a Central Principle in the First Amendment*, 43 U. CHI. L. REV. 20 (1975); Shiffrin, *Defamatory Non-Media Speech and First Amendment Methodology*, 25 U.C.L.A. L. REV. 915 (1978); Stone, *Restrictions of Speech Because of Its Content: The Peculiar Case of Subject-Matter Restrictions*, 46 U. CHI. L. REV. 81 (1978). *See also* F. SCHAUER, FREE SPEECH: A PHILOSOPHICAL ENQUIRY (1982); F. HAIMAN, SPEECH AND LAW IN A FREE SOCIETY (1981); J. BARRON & C. DIENES, HANDBOOK OF FREE SPEECH AND PRESS (1979); M. YUDOF, WHEN GOVERNMENT SPEAKS: POLITICS, LAW, AND GOVERNMENT EXPRESSION IN AMERICA (1983); Van Alstyne, *A Graphic Review of the Free Speech Clause*, 70 CALIF. L. REV. 107 (1982).

9. This is particularly true of the works of Ely, Tribe, Emerson, Meiklejohn, Blasi, Bork and Baker.

10. *See* particularly the discussion in Chapter IV *infra* at 193-206.

INTRODUCTION

reason and perhaps in part because of an understandable desire to replace chaos with order, these scholars have sought to introduce relatively hard-line distinctions into first amendment construction. This tendency can be found both in the literature concerning what types of expression serve the values intended to be fostered by the first amendment[11] and in commentary about the extent to which normally protected expression should be outbalanced by competing social needs.[12] In addition, the Supreme Court itself has often sought resolution of difficult first amendment problems by means of deceptively simple formulas and easily-applied distinctions.[13]

In my view, first amendment interests are generally not furthered by these attempts to resolve complex and difficult issues by means of rigid, hard-line distinctions and categorizations. Of course, to leave the judiciary with absolutely no guidance in its interpretation of the first amendment would be to invite disaster. But the issue is one of degree: the alternatives are not merely total, unguided chaos on the one hand and rigid, unbending lines of demarcation on the other. Instead, we must seek general guidelines of interpretation that simultaneously provide the strong deference to free speech interests that the language and the policies of the first amendment command while allowing the judiciary the case-by-case flexibility necessary to reconcile those interests with truly compelling and conflicting societal concerns. The primary goal of this book is to fashion such standards in a number of important structural and theoretical issues of first amendment interpretation.

A few words are required to explain the scope and limits of the chapters that follow. The book in no way purports to serve as a definitive treatise on all subjects of first amendment interpretation.[14] Rather, the book consists of five distinct essays on separate issues of first amendment construction. Each could be viewed as an independent analysis of a particular first amendment issue of substantial current and historical concern.[15] Yet all five are linked on one or more levels.

---

11. *See* the works of Meiklejohn, Bork, Baker and Blasi cited in note 8. *See generally* Chapter I.

12. See the works of Emerson, Tribe and Ely cited in note 8. *See generally* Chapters II, IV and V.

13. *See generally* Chapter V.

14. The pathbreaking theoretical work that did approach such a comprehensive analysis was the book by Professor Emerson. T. EMERSON, *supra* note 2. More recently, two excellent books have appeared: F. HAIMAN, *supra* note 8, and J. BARRON & C. DIENES, *supra* note 8.

15. In fact, each has appeared — sometimes in modified form — as individually published articles over the last four years. Each is published here with the permission

First, each deals primarily with what I label "theoretical" or "structural" issues. In other words, their primary purpose is not to critique and describe the state of the law concerning the first amendment's application to a specific type of expression, or to consider how the first amendment is to be reconciled with a specific competing societal interest. In varying degrees, they do in fact undertake such examinations.[16] But whenever such inquiries into the specific application of the first amendment are made, it is largely for the purpose of making a point about a broader issue of first amendment construction that pervades many or all potential applications of the free speech guarantee. Second, each criticizes and rejects one or more judicial or scholarly attempts to seek rigid, unbending answers to issues too complex for such solutions, and attempts to replace them with more flexible guidelines that, I submit, both foster the value served by free speech more fully and reconcile competing social interests more effectively.

The first chapter deals with the broad theoretical question of what value or values the protection of free speech appropriately serves, and the implications of that question for specific types of expression. I attempt to demonstrate here that those commentators who believe that the values of free speech are served only by one type of expression — for example, political information and opinion — or who believe that certain forms of expression — for example, obscenity or commercial speech — are beneath first amendment concerns are mistakenly drawing distinctions that are not justified by a proper analysis of first amendment values. For such an analysis reveals that all forms of purely communicative activity[17] serve the same ultimate value —

---

of the journal in which the essay appeared. Chapter I is a modification and combination — as well as an expansion — of three of my previously-published articles: *The Value of Free Speech*, 130 U. PA. L. REV. 591 (1982); *Self-Realization, Democracy, and Freedom of Expression: A Reply to Professor Baker*, 130 U. PA. L. REV. 678 (1982), and *Advocacy of Unlawful Conduct and the First Amendment: In Defense of Clear and Present Danger*, 70 CALIF. L. REV. 1159 (1982). Chapter II is a slightly modified version of *The Content Distinction in First Amendment Analysis*, 34 STAN. L. REV. 113 (1981). Chapter III is based on *The Proper Role of the Prior Restraint Doctrine in First Amendment Theory*, 70 VA. L. REV. 53 (1984). Chapter IV is derived from *Advocacy of Unlawful Conduct, supra*. Chapter V appeared as *The Warren Court, the Burger Court, and the First Amendment Overbreadth Doctrine*, 78 NW. U.L. REV. 1031 (1983).

16. Chapter IV, dealing with regulation of advocacy of unlawful conduct, does so the most. In addition, Chapter I considers the applicability of the theory developed there to the areas of commercial speech, obscenity, defamation, and unlawful advocacy. Chapter II also applies the theory developed there to a number of previously-decided cases.

17. To a certain extent, physical conduct can also have a communicative element,

what I label "self-realization" — and that a government determination that one type of expression fosters this value better than another is itself a rejection of the self-realization principle, premised on the value of individual choice and intellectual development.

It might be suggested that my exclusive reliance on the self-realization principle is itself an illustration of an improper emphasis on an overly simplistic "code word" in first amendment analysis. In reality, however, it is just the opposite. For my development of the self-realization principle is designed to undermine the rigid, simplistic distinctions among different subjects of expression that courts and commentators have superimposed on the first amendment guarantee. Development of the self-realization principle, then, demonstrates that those who have asserted these distinctions have failed to examine the ultimate purposes for protecting the particular subject matter that they have exalted. Thus, the self-realization principle is designed to recognize the broad range of expressive activity that fosters the values of the first amendment, and to reject narrow and artificial distinctions among various subjects of such activity.

The second and third chapters consider judicial and scholarly attempts to gradate the level of constitutional protection of speech on the basis of the nature of the governmental regulation sought to be imposed. Chapter II attacks the well-established dichotomy between governmental regulation of the content of expression and those which, though having a negative impact on expression, regulate on the basis of some factor other than the substance of what is said.[18] Traditionally, regulation of content has been subjected to a high degree of judicial scrutiny, while regulations that are "content-neutral" have been subjected to a considerably weaker level of review. My analysis concludes that harm to the values served by free speech protection may be as undermined by so-called content-neutral regulation as by content-based regulation. The chapter therefore suggests that the rigid dichotomy be replaced by a standard that demands a truly compelling justification for all regulation of expression.

Chapter III concerns perhaps the most venerated of all first amendment theories: the prior restraint doctrine. Under this principle, expression which could constitutionally be subjected to regulation in

---

often presenting difficult definitional line-drawing problems in determining the scope of the first amendment protection. Though this difficult issue does not provide the central focus of any of the chapters, the question is considered in Chapter I *infra* at 17-19 and 34-35, and in Chapter IV *infra* at 201-06. *See also* note 1 in the Conclusion.

18. *See* discussion *infra* at 87-126.

the form of "subsequent punishment" (i.e. criminal or civil penalties following dissemination) generally may not be regulated by means of a governmental restraint prior to dissemination.[19] In this chapter, I explore the asserted justifications for this strong presumption against prior restraints and conclude that many of those who have considered the question have improperly equated the harms of all forms of such restraints, whether judicially or administratively issued. The chapter takes the position that it is only the non-judicial forms of such restraint that are deserving of special disdain, and that the dangers of judicially-imposed prior restraints are either irrelevant to first amendment concerns or are equally true of subsequent punishment systems, and therefore do not justify the traditional disdain given prior restraints. Ultimately, emphasis on the nature of the regulatory method has prevented the Court from dealing effectively with important and difficult issues of the substantive scope of first amendment protection. Moreover, the Court has, ironically, allowed certain forms of non-judicial restraint on expression without ever inquiring whether such regulation is justified by a truly compelling governmental interest, in situations in which those restraints actually do present a unique threat to first amendment concerns. I therefore attempt to demonstrate that the issue of prior restraint — like so many other issues of first amendment structural interpretation — is too complex to lend itself to the use of simple code words and formulas that have characterized the judicial development of that doctrine.

The final two chapters discuss what I call lessons in the dangers of a categorization approach to first amendment analysis. In Chapter IV, I have selected one of the most troubling issues of first amendment application: the degree of protection to be afforded advocacy of unlawful conduct. Primarily, the chapter examines the "clear and present danger" test, a controversial judicial method of determining when such advocacy is to be protected. After considering the test's historical development and suggesting my own version of how the test ought to be defined, I discuss and attempt to refute the many criticisms that have been levelled at the test over the years. Much of that criticism has been premised on what has been deemed the test's unduly flexible scope, and the resultant invitation to judicial manipulation, particularly in times of social or political crisis. The danger is a real one, and I make no claim that the clear and present danger test is free from defect. However, an examination of all alternative approaches that attempt to confine case-by-case judicial flexibility demonstrates

---

19. *See* discussion *infra* at 127-32.

their inadequacy. This results primarily from the very fact that these tests remove case-by-case flexibility, for they ultimately prove too clumsy to provide the proper level of constitutional protection in individual cases.

The final chapter considers the first amendment overbreadth doctrine. Under this principle, laws regulating expression are held unconstitutional when they go further than is necessary to achieve a legitimate governmental goal. By its nature, the doctrine calls upon the judiciary to strike a careful balance in each application between first amendment interests and competing governmental concerns. For in each case, the court will have to determine whether the additional burdens resulting to the government because it is required to employ a more restricted method of achieving its legitimate goal are justified by the relevant free speech interests. Yet, perhaps because of its traditional aversion to a case-by-case balancing process, the Supreme Court of the 1960's attempted to confine the overbreadth doctrine by refusing to consider in individual cases whether the government's goal could in fact be achieved through less invasive means. The Supreme Court of the 1970's, on the other hand, reacted to this far-reaching doctrine by imposing rigid categorical limitations on its use — limitations that generally appear to have no rhyme or reason, other than that they have the effect of confining the overbreadth doctrine's reach. Both Courts mistakenly attempted to restrict by use of broad categorical limitations a doctrine that inherently requires a substantial degree of case-by-case flexibility. As a result, in many cases, the doctrine serves the interests of neither the first amendment nor of the government seeking to regulate expression.

Throughout these five chapters, I adopt a largely protective approach to free expression, one that recognizes the overriding importance that our society's traditions and values place on the first amendment right. Thus, I extend the reach of the first amendment protection further than does virtually any other commentator,[20] and, for reasons developed in Chapter I, propose that the authority of the judiciary to gradate first amendment protection on the basis of the relative value of the challenged expression be severely restricted: this is a judgment the philosophy of the first amendment vests in the individual, not in an external governmental body. But unlike many of the protectionist scholars — for example, Meiklejohn, Emerson, Baker — who purport to provide some sort of absolute protection to the freedom of speech,[21] I reject any such attempt. Such approaches are either practicably

---

20. *See* discussion *infra* at 55-68.
21. See the discussion in Chapter I *infra* at 53-55; Chapter IV *infra* at 201-06.

unworkable or effectively amount to little more than disguised forms of balancing. The problem with such approaches is that they do not avoid balancing; they simply transform that balancing process into a less refined, less candid procedure. Thus, I frankly recognize the need for the judiciary to reconcile the free speech right with competing governmental interests. To be sure, we must direct the courts to place a supreme value on the right of free expression and to limit it only in the presence of a truly compelling governmental interest. In certain instances, this broad directive may be transformed into a more narrow directive that applies the compelling interest analysis to specific issues of first amendment application. But even in these situations, it would be unwise — and often impossible — to deny to the courts a substantial amount of flexibility to reconcile competing interests in a specific case.

The book purports to provide no easy answers to the complex issues of first amendment analysis. Indeed, I believe that it is the mistaken desire to find such solutions and answers that has caused so much difficulty for both Court and commentators. Thus, none of the approaches suggested here is totally free from question, and it is quite conceivable that difficulties and ambiguities in their application would arise in individual cases. But if the book can provide at least some guidelines of construction in specific areas of first amendment application that simultaneously place a strong emphasis on the value of free expression and recognize the power of the government to undermine that value only in instances that present a truly serious threat to a vital interest, it will have attained an important part of its goal. If it can further establish that ultimately we cannot expect in such a complex area solutions which draw neat distinctions and which purport to provide correct answers for all time and every case, it will have accomplished its remaining purpose.

CHAPTER I
THE VALUE OF FREE SPEECH

Commentators and jurists have long searched for an explanation of the true value served by the first amendment's protection of free speech. This issue certainly has considerable intellectual appeal, and the practical stakes are also high. For the answer we give to the question, what value does free speech serve, may well determine the extent of constitutional protection to be given to such forms of expression as literature, art, science, commercial speech, and speech related to the political process.

There seems to be general agreement that the Supreme Court has failed in its attempts to devise a coherent theory of free expression.[1] These efforts have been characterized by "a pattern of aborted doctrines, shifting rationales, and frequent changes of position by individual Justices."[2] Commentators, by contrast, have been eager to elaborate upon their unified theories of the value of free speech. Professor Emerson, probably the leading modern theorist of free speech, has recognized four separate values served by the first amendment's protection of expression: (1) "assuring individual self-fulfillment;"[3] (2) "advancing knowledge and discovering truth;"[4] (3) "provid[ing] for participation in decisionmaking by all members of society;"[5] and (4) "achieving a more adaptable and hence a more stable community, ... maintaining the precarious balance between healthy cleavage and necessary consensus."[6] Although Emerson sees these as distinct values, he believes that "[e]ach is necessary, but not in itself sufficient, for the four of them are interdependent."[7]

Other scholars have culled from the values suggested by Emerson, concluding either that the first amendment is designed to foster or protect only one of them, or that it protects a hierarchy of these

---

1. *See, e.g.,* T. EMERSON, THE SYSTEM OF FREEDOM OF EXPRESSION 15 (1970) ("The outstanding fact about the First Amendment today is that the Supreme Court has never developed any comprehensive theory of what that constitutional guarantee means and how it should be applied in concrete cases."); *see also* Bloustein, *The Origin, Validity, and Interrelationships of the Political Values Served by Freedom of Expression,* 33 RUTGERS L. REV. 372 (1981).
2. Blasi, *The Checking Value in First Amendment Theory,* 1977 AM. B. FOUND. RESEARCH J. 521, 526.
3. T. EMERSON, *supra* note 1, at 6.
4. *Id.*
5. *Id.* at 7.
6. *Id.*
7. Emerson, *First Amendment Doctrine and the Burger Court,* 68 CALIF. L. REV. 422, 423 (1980).

different values, with the constitutional protection given to various forms of expression to be adjusted accordingly. Professor Meiklejohn, for example, spoke eloquently of the value of free speech to the political process.[8] In order to prevent the protection of such speech from being reduced to a matter of "proximity and degree,"[9] he urged exclusion from the first amendment guarantee of all speech that did not relate to this self-government value.[10]

Although Meiklejohn in later years appeared to soften the rigidity of his lines of demarcation by effectively extending his doctrine — in a somewhat less than persuasive manner — to many forms of apparently nonpolitical speech,[11] other commentators have adopted his initial premise and kept within its logical limits. Judge Bork, now the leading exponent of the government-process school of thought, has concluded that the sole purpose served by the constitutional guarantee is to aid the political process, and that absolutely no other form of expression can logically be considered to fall within it.[12] Professor Blasi, although not rejecting all other asserted values of free expression, has urged recognition of what he labels the "checking value" as the primary purpose of the first amendment.[13] Under this analysis, speech relating to official misconduct would receive the greatest degree of constitutional protection.[14] Other commentators have selected various forms of an "individual development" model as the touchstone of first amendment protection,[15] and have structured their constitutional interpretation accordingly. Finally, there exists the "marketplace-of-ideas" approach (long associated with the famous dissent of Justice Holmes in *Abrams v. United States*[16]), which posits that the primary function of free speech is as a catalyst to the discovery of truth.[17]

---

8. *See* A. MEIKLEJOHN, POLITICAL FREEDOM (1960) (expanded version of Meiklejohn's FREE SPEECH & ITS RELATION TO SELF-GOVERNMENT (1948)).
9. *Id.* at 55.
10. *See infra* notes 28-32 and accompanying text.
11. Meiklejohn, *The First Amendment Is an Absolute,* 1961 SUP. CT. REV. 245; *see infra* text accompanying notes 32-33.
12. Bork, *Neutral Principles and Some First Amendment Problems,* 47 IND. L.J. 1 (1971); *see also* BeVier, *The First Amendment and Political Speech: An Inquiry Into the Substance and Limits of Principle,* 30 STAN. L. REV. 299 (1978).
13. Blasi, *supra* note 2.
14. *See* discussion *infra* at 41-44.
15. Baker, *Scope of the First Amendment Freedom of Speech,* 25 U.C.L.A. L. REV. 964 (1978) ("liberty"); Scanlon, *A Theory of Freedom of Expression,* 1 PHIL. & PUB. AFF. 204 (1972) ("autonomy").
16. 250 U.S. 616, 630 (1919) (Holmes, J., dissenting).
17. *See* discussion *infra* at 45-48.

Although many respected scholars have appraised this myriad of free speech theories, it is time for a major reassessment of the subject, for each of these theories is, I believe, flawed in result, or structure, or both. Many first amendment theorists have failed to return to first principles in determining the value served by free speech, whereas others who may well be approaching an analysis of true first principles have neglected to examine the logical implications flowing therefrom. The result in virtually all cases is an unduly narrow description of the category of communication that is deserving of full constitutional protection.

The position taken here is that the constitutional guarantee of free speech ultimately serves only one true value, which I have labeled "individual self-realization." This term has been chosen largely because of its ambiguity: it can be interpreted to refer either to development of the individuals' powers and abilities — an individual "realizes" his or her full potential — or to the individual's control of his or her own destiny through making life-affecting decisions — an individual "realizes" the goals in life that he or she has set. In using the term, I intend to include both interpretations. I have, therefore, chosen it instead of such other options as "liberty" or "autonomy," on the one hand, and "individual self-fulfillment" or "human development," on the other. The former pair of alternatives arguably may be limited to the decisionmaking value,[18] whereas the latter could be interpreted reasonably as confined to the individual development concept.

That the first amendment serves only one ultimate value, however, does not mean that the majority of values thought by others to be fostered by free speech — the "political process," "checking," and "marketplace-of-ideas" values — are invalid. I have not chosen from a list of mutually exclusive possibilities, nor do I argue that the value that I have selected supersedes these alternatives. My contention is that these other values, though perfectly legitimate, are in reality

---

18. One authority interprets "autonomy" to mean:

> making one's own choices. A person is not autonomous whose choices are dictated "from outside" at gunpoint or, perhaps, through hypnosis .... On the other hand, full deliberative rationality is not required for autonomy. Spontaneous or ill-considered decisions can be just as much *my* decisions, and that is the touchstone as I understand autonomy.

L. CROCKER, POSITIVE LIBERTY 114 (1980).

Professor Baker also adopts the term "liberty" to describe his operative model of free speech, yet appears to be referring to the concept of individual self-fulfillment. *See* Baker, *supra* note 15, at 990-96.

subvalues of self-realization. To the extent that they are legitimate, each can be explained by — and only by — reference to the primary value: individual self-realization. It therefore is inaccurate to suggest that "the commitment to free expression embodie[s] a complex of values."[19]

In this Chapter, I attempt to establish that the first principle — individual self-realization — can be proven, not merely by reference to some unsupportable, conclusory assertions of moral value,[20] but by reasoning from what we in this nation take as given: our democratic system of government.[21] It demonstrates that the moral norms inherent in the choice of our specific form of democracy logically imply the broader value, self-realization. It then concludes that all forms of expression that further the self-realization value,[22] which justifies the democratic system as well as free speech's role in it, are deserving of full constitutional protection.

An analysis of the self-realization value must avoid giving it an unduly restrictive interpretation.[23] Any external determination that certain expression fosters self-realization more than any other is itself a violation of the individual's free will, recognition of which is inherent in the self-realization principle. I therefore argue that the Supreme Court should not determine the level of constitutional protection by comparing the relative values of different types of speech,[24] as is the current practice.[25]

---

19. Blasi, *supra* note 2, at 538.
20. Professor Baker, for example, attempts to establish the correctness of his "liberty" model by reasoning in the following manner: "Obligation exists only in relationships of respect. To justify legal obligation, the community must respect individuals as equal, rational and autonomous moral beings. For the community legitimately to expect individuals to respect collective decisions, i.e. legal rules, the community must respect the dignity and equal worth of its members." Baker, *supra* note 15, at 991. Although I personally might accept Professor Baker's moral assertion, I — and, I expect, Professor Baker — would have a difficult time responding to someone who denied that an individual's obligation to obey the law has anything to do with government's respect for the individual, other than to say, "Oh, yes it does."
21. *See* discussion *infra* at 19-29.
22. For an analysis of exactly how expression may be thought to foster the self-realization value, see *infra* at 21-29.
23. Professor Baker's analysis is flawed in this respect. *See infra* at 49-52.
24. *See infra* at 55-60.
25. *See, e.g.*, FCC v. Pacifica Found., 438 U.S. 726 (1978). The argument has been made that this point is invalid because the government gradates on the basis of the relative value of expression on numerous occasions, for example, in establishing the content of public school curricula and in selecting books for public libraries. *See, e.g.*, Shiffrin, *The First Amendment and Economic Regulation: Away From a General Theory of The First Amendment*, 78 Nw. U.L. Rev. 1212 (1978). However, as I argue

This chapter then proceeds to discuss briefly the appropriate role of "balancing" in first amendment analysis. Although recognition of the self-realization value leads to the view that all forms of expression are equally valuable for constitutional purposes, this does not necessarily imply that all forms of expression must receive absolute, or even equal, protection in all cases. Protestations of a number of commentators to the contrary notwithstanding,[26] there is no inconsistency in recognizing that individual self-realization is the sole value furthered by free speech and simultaneously acknowledging that, at least in extreme cases, full constitutional protection of free expression may be forced to give way to competing social concerns.

In summary, then, my thesis rejects those authorities (1) who believe that the first amendment is multivalued, whether they superimpose a hierarchy upon those values or recognize them as interdependent coequals; (2) who argue that the first amendment is single-valued, with that value being something other than individual self-realization; (3) who, although accepting the self-realization value or its rough equivalent as the sole determinant of free speech, refuse to acknowledge one or more of the various subvalues that derive from it; and (4) who believe that total reliance on something akin to the self-realization value is inconsistent with any form of constitutional balancing process with regard to free speech.

After detailing the sources and parameters of the self-realization value[27] and demonstrating how each legitimate subvalue is

---

later *(see* discussion *infra* at 59), these are instances in which the government itself rather than the private individual, is engaging in expression. Those who make this argument quite probably reject any governmental attempt to make such value judgments in deciding what books a private bookstore owner may sell or a private individual may have in his library. Moreover, curricular decisions and public library selections may be justified because *somebody* must make these choices, if chaos is not to prevail. This amounts to a compelling interest.

26. See *infra* at 52-53.

27. A word should be said at this point about the nature of my reasoning process. My argument is essentially a logical one, reasoning from what I take to be widely held premises. I make only brief and tangential reference to the history of the first amendment and the intent of the amendment's framers. See *infra* note 54. My theory, therefore may be attacked by those who believe that historical analysis is the only appropriate method of constitutional interpretation.

Few, if any, of the commentators analyzing the value of free speech, however, place significant reliance on the intent of the framers. This is primarily because, as Judge Bork states, "[t]he framers seem to have had no coherent theory of free speech and appear not to have been overly concerned with the subject." Bork, *supra* note 12, at 22. To the extent that any consensus did exist, it appears to have been on an extremely narrow and technical conception of free expression. *See generally* L. LEVY, LEGACY OF SUPPRESSION (1960). It is therefore not surprising that historical reference has been of limited value in first amendment analysis.

explainable only as a manifestation of that principle, I consider how acceptance of these theoretical precepts would affect the level and form of constitutional protection given to four categories of expression: commercial speech, defamation, obscenity, and advocacy of unlawful conduct.

I. Self-Realization and the Democratic Process: Ascertaining the Ultimate Value of Free Speech

A. The "Democratic Process" Value

An appropriate way to begin analysis of the self-realization value is, ironically, with a discussion of the theory of free speech perhaps furthest in practical result from that value: the view that the sole purpose of the free speech guarantee is to facilitate operation of the democratic process. Advocates of this position are logically required to establish two propositions: first, that the first amendment facilitates the political process, and second, that the first amendment does not foster any value other than conduct of the political process. Examination of the writings of those expounding this view reveals that they have established the former with considerably greater force than they have established the latter.

As already noted, the original exponent of such a theory was Professor Meiklejohn. He began with the premise that "[g]overnments ... derive their just powers from the consent of the governed. If that consent be lacking, governments have no just powers."[28] Because government officials in a democracy are merely agents of the electorate, the electorate needs as much information as possible to aid it in performing its governing function in the voting booth.[29] Therefore, "[t]he principle of the freedom of speech springs from the necessities of the program of self government.... It is a deduction from the basic American agreement that public issues shall be decided by universal suffrage."[30]

Few would argue with Meiklejohn's logic to this point. If the electoral decisions made by the voters are to be based on anything more than emotive hunches, they need a free flow of information that will inform them not only about the candidates but also about the day-to-day issues of government.[31] But what seemed counterintuitive to

---

28. A. Meiklejohn, *supra* note 8, at 9.
29. Meiklejohn, *supra* note 11, at 255.
30. A. Meiklejohn, *supra* note 8, at 27.
31. *Cf.* B. Berelson, P. Lazarsfeld & W. McPhee, Voting 307 (1954) ("if there is one characteristic for a democratic system (besides the ballot itself) that is theoretically required, it is the capacity for and the practice of discussion").

some was the apparent implication of Meiklejohn's theory that such "nonpolitical" forms of speech as art, literature, science, and education were not protected by the first amendment.[32] Meiklejohn himself ultimately concluded "that the people do need novels and dramas and paintings and poems, 'because they will be called upon to vote.'"[33] He thus included within the category of "political" speech numerous forms of expression that do not appear to have any direct — or arguably even indirect — impact upon the political process. He would presumably give full first amendment protection to both the author and the reader who profess absolutely no interest in the political system, and who have never voted and never will, but who simply enjoy writing or reading good fiction. For this extension of his theory, Meiklejohn has been attacked both by those who believe that the first amendment has no special political basis[34] and by political "purists" who accept Meiklejohn's initial premise about the relationship between the first amendment and the political process, but question the logic of his extension.[35]

Judge Bork begins his analysis with this same premise about the political process, but rigidly limits his conclusion to such speech, thus escaping the attack levelled at Professor Meiklejohn. Judge Bork, however, has great difficulty explaining why the first amendment should be read to protect only political expression.

Judge Bork's first amendment analysis flows from his concern that constitutional interpretation be premised on "neutral principles."[36] The decisions of the Supreme Court "must be controlled by principle,"[37] which may be defined as " 'reasons with respect to all the issues in a case, reasons that in their generality and their neutrality transcend any immediate result that is involved.'"[38] Judge Bork concludes that

---

32. *See* Kalven, *The Metaphysics of the Law of Obscenity,* 1960 SUP. CT. REV. 1, 15-16; Chafee, Book Review, 62 HARV. L. REV. 891, 896 (1949).

33. Meiklejohn, *supra* note 11, at 263.

34. I include myself within this category. *See* Redish, *The First Amendment in the Marketplace: Commercial Speech and the Values of Free Expression,* 39 GEO. WASH. L. REV. 429, 437-38 (1971).

35. According to Professor BeVier, "[t]he essential problem with accepting Meiklejohn's analogies is that one cannot know in principle which forms of thought and expression contribute to 'the capacity for sure and objective judgment.'" BeVier, *supra* note 12, at 317.

36. Bork, *supra* note 12, at 1-20. In so doing, he draws upon the famous work of Professor Wechsler. Wechsler, *Toward Neutral Principles of Constitutional Law,* 73 HARV. L. REV. 1 (1959).

37. Bork, *supra* note 12, at 2 (footnote omitted).

38. *Id.* (quoting, with a minor error, Wechsler, *supra* note 36, at 19).

only speech serving the political process can be deemed "principled."[39]

The method by which Judge Bork reaches this conclusion may be described as a lesson in the limits of the "neutral principles" concept. It demonstrates all too clearly that if the selection of premises is flawed, "neutral principles" will not prevent a doctrine from being applied in a similarly flawed — albeit "principled" and consistent — manner. Judge Bork begins his analysis by quoting the well-known concurrence of Justice Brandeis in *Whitney v. California*.[40] Brandeis identified what Bork has distilled into four benefits provided by the free speech guarantee: "[t]he development of the faculties of the individual; [t]he provisions of a safety value [sic] for society; and [t]he discovery and spread of political truth."[41] Bork then proceeds to explain why the first three values cannot be considered values of the first amendment under a "principled" analysis.

Since Justice Brandeis's first category is the closest to the concept of individual self-realization urged here, it is most relevant to determine why Judge Bork concludes that this value cannot be thought to lie behind the constitutional guarantee. Although Bork does not deny that free speech may develop individual faculties,[42] he nevertheless believes that the development of an individual's faculties and the happiness derived from engaging in speech

> do not distinguish speech from any other human activity. An individual may develop his faculties ... from trading on the stock market, following his profession as a river-port pilot, working as a barmaid, engaging in sexual activity, playing tennis, rigging prices or in any of thousands of endeavors .... These functions or benefits of speech are, therefore, to the principled judge, indistinguishable from the functions or benefits of all other human activity.[43]

Judge Bork ultimately concludes that Justice Brandeis's fourth category — the search for "political truth" — is the only legitimate ground of the first amendment. This conclusion in turn leads him to adopt a first amendment construction that is quite probably the most narrowly confined protection of speech ever supported by a modern jurist or academic: "Constitutional protection should be accorded only to speech that is explicitly political. There is no basis for judicial intervention to protect any other form of expression, be it scientific,

---

39. Bork, *supra* note 12, at 26.
40. 274 U.S. 357, 375 (1927) (Brandeis, J., concurring).
41. Bork, *supra* note 12, at 25.
42. *Id.*
43. *Id.* a similar argument is fashioned by Professor BeVier. BeVier, *supra* note 12, at 313-14.

literary or that variety of expression we call obscene or pornographic."[44]

Judge Bork's rationale for including political speech and excluding nonpolitical forms of expression, even if they further the value of self-fulfillment, is that it is logically possible to limit the value served by political speech to "speech." Self-fulfillment, on the other hand, cannot logically be limited to "speech," but must also be taken to include countless forms of action. Judge Bork's conclusion that political speech should be protected is, however, inconsistent with his belief that any acceptable rationale for free speech must be logically unique to speech. For there are countless actions — such as a bombing by the FALN to protest oppression of Puerto Rico, an assassination of a foreign political leader because of human rights violations in his country, and the breaking of windows at the Iranian Consulate to protest the treatment of Americans in Iran — that can be thought to convey very significant political messages. Those who undertake such activities could argue with a fair degree of persuasiveness that the public attention attracted to such acts is geometrically greater than that which would be received by public statements or pickets. Even if we rejected this argument, however, the issue for Judge Bork is not whether the value in question can be furthered by speech, as well as by conduct, but whether it can *only* be furthered by speech. Bork otherwise could not exclude nonpolitical speech that aids individual self-fulfillment on the ground that conduct may also aid such a goal. It is, therefore, difficult to understand how he can protect political speech, when countless forms of political action could achieve similar results.[45]

Political actions, unlike some of the faculty-developing activities referred to by Judge Bork, have as an essential part of their purpose a

---

44. Bork, *supra* note 12, at 20. "Moreover, within that category of speech we ordinarily call political, there should be no constitutional obstruction to laws making criminal any speech that advocates forcible overthrow of the government or the violation of any law." *Id.*

45. One might argue that these actions standing alone do not effectively convey any message. Rather, there also must be some oral or written communication by the perpetrators of the act describing their motivation. Assuming this to be true, the point in no way undermines the conclusion that the act is an essential aspect of the attempt to convey political truth, since the statement of motivation would make little sense without performance of the act.

Professor BeVier, arguing in support of Judge Bork's position, reasons that "beliefs and opinions are often most effectively communicated by forms of conduct other than verbal expression." BeVier, *supra* note 12, at 319 (footnote omitted). My point is, simply, that the exact same thing can be said about political speech, the only category of expression that Judge Bork and Professor BeVier believe deserves constitutional protection.

communicative aspect. But it is unlikely that Bork would be satisfied with a distinction based on communicative purpose, since he leaves little doubt that he would not choose to protect such actions. In any event, there are numerous non-communicative, nonspeech activities that may be thought to aid in the attainment of political truth. For example, working as a farmer could help one understand the problems and benefits of farm price supports; working as a doctor could do the same with respect to socialized medicine; living in a large urban area and taking public transportation might convince one of the need for greater federal aid to cities and mass transit. Thus, nonspeech activities could aid attainment of knowledge of political truth as much as does any political discourse. Bork's logic therefore must be rejected, because it inescapably results in the content of speech protected by the first amendment being a null set: there is no category of expression that furthers a value or values unique to speech.

If one were to look for an appropriate basis for limiting the protection of the first amendment to "speech," the natural starting place would seem to be the language of the amendment itself, which says nothing about protecting only political speech.[46] What the language does refer to is "speech," and not action. Thus, we need not find a logical distinction between the value served by speech and the value served by conduct in order to justify protecting only speech, for the framers have already drawn the distinction. Whether or not the constitutional language must be read to provide absolute protection to speech,[47] there can be little doubt that it was intended to provide greater protection to speech than to conduct, which is relegated to the fifth amendment's protection against deprivation of "liberty" without "due process of law." Indeed, that the framers deemed it necessary to create a first amendment at all, rather than merely include speech within the other forms of liberty protected by the fifth amendment, indicates that speech is to receive a constitutional status above and beyond that given to conduct.

It is not hard to understand why constitutional protection of speech would be greater than that of conduct. The first amendment may be viewed as a recognition of the overriding importance of developing the uniquely human abilities to think, reason and appreciate. It is true

---

46. One would think that any attempt to develop a "principled" interpretation of a constitutional provision would not begin by inserting limitations that are not even hinted at in the constitutional language, and that indeed appear to depart from a natural reading of the words. The first amendment refers simply to "the freedom of speech, and of the press."

47. This issue has been the subject of endless debate. *See infra* notes 112-116.

that on occasion non-communicative conduct may develop these intellectual faculties, and that speech at times may cause harm. But if we were to draw a rough distinction — the kind that must necessarily have been drawn by the framers — we could reasonably decide that speech is less likely to cause direct or immediate harm to the interests of others[48] and more likely to develop the individuals' mental faculties than is purely physical conduct, and that speech thus deserves a greater degree of constitutional protection than does conduct. Bork's assumption that any principled first amendment theory must rely solely on values that are *uniquely* protected by speech effectively removes all categories of speech from the amendment's protection.

B. Deriving the Ultimate Value

The primary flaw in the analysis of Bork and Meiklejohn is that they never attempt to ascertain what basic value or values the democratic process was designed to serve. Examination of the "process" values inherent in our nation's adoption of a democratic system reveals an implicit belief in the worth of the individual that has first amendment implications extending well beyond the borders of the political world. Indeed, political democracy is merely a means to — or, in another sense, a logical outgrowth of — the much broader value of individual self-realization. The mistake of Bork and Meiklejohn, then, is that they have confused one means of obtaining the ultimate value with the value itself.

The logic employed by Meiklejohn and Bork to reach their conclusion that the protection of speech was designed to aid the political process would have absolutely no relevance except in a democratic system. For a monarchy or dictatorship to function politically, it of course is not necessary that the general public be able to speak freely or receive information about pressing political questions, because private individuals will have no say in decisions. Even a benevolent dictator would be more likely to allow free expression in traditionally nonpolitical areas such as art, literature, and music than in the

---

48. Dean Wellington has correctly noted that "speech often hurts. It can offend, injure reputation, fan prejudice or passion, and ignite the world. Moreover, a great deal of other conduct that the state regulates has less harmful potential." Wellington, *On Freedom of Expression,* 88 Yale L.J. 1105, 1106-07 (1979) (footnote omitted). He cites, as one example of the latter, laws prohibiting certain forms of sexual relations between consenting adults. *Id.* at 1107. But (as noted in the text), in establishing a constitutional rule that is to provide a guide for future generations, it is impossible to enumerate the specific instances that deserve a greater degree of protection and those that deserve a lesser degree. It is almost certainly true in the overwhelming majority of cases that speech is less immediately dangerous than conduct.

political realm. The free speech value emphasized by Meiklejohn and Bork, then, is inherently linked to a democratic form of government.

Democracy is by no means the only system that could have been chosen when our nation was founded. Indeed, it is probably safe to say that the overwhelming majority of organized societies throughout history have not chosen it, even in its most diluted form. It would seem, then, that there must be some values that the founding fathers believed to be uniquely fostered by a democracy, values that succeeding generations of political leaders presumably have shared, since there has been little or no effort to alter substantially our system of government by constitutional processes.

One conceivable value is "consequentialist" in nature: efficiency. One could believe that the results of a democratic system are somehow better than any other system's. Such an argument, however, would be very difficult to prove for several reasons. Initially, it would probably be difficult to obtain agreement on the criteria for measuring results. How are we to decide what is "better"? Higher gross national product? More international influence? And better for whom? Elites? A majority? Oppressed minorities? Secondly, it is doubtful that we could establish empirically that throughout history democracies have fared better than other forms of government. After all, we do know that the trains ran on time in Mussolini's Italy; can the Chicago Transit Authority make the same claim? Moreover, it may well be counterintuitive to believe, especially in a modern, highly technological society, that decisions made by the masses or their elected representatives — who are rarely chosen because of any degree of real expertise — would be either the wisest or the most efficient. Finally, it is doubtful that many of us would be anxious to discard democracy even if it were established definitely that an alternative political system was more efficient. It is likely, then, that the values inherent in a democratic system are "process-oriented," rather than related to some objective standard of governmental efficiency.

These "process" values seem to translate into two forms: an "intrinsic" value and an "instrumental" value. The "intrinsic" value is one that is achieved by the very existence of a democratic system. It is the value of having individuals control their own destinies. For if one does not accept the morality of such a proposition, why bother to select a democratic system in the first place? As Meiklejohn said, "[i]f men are to be governed, we say, then that governing must be done, not by others, but by themselves. So far, therefore, as our own affairs are concerned, we refuse to submit to alien control."[49] The point is so

---

49. A. MEIKLEJOHN, *supra* note 8, at 9.

obvious that it requires no further elaboration, except to say that the core concept of "self-rule" appears to have formed the cornerstone of every theory of democracy to date.[50] It would seem to be so as a matter of definition.

The second value of a democratic system is labeled "instrumental," because it is a goal to which a democratic system is designed to lead, rather than one that is attained definitionally by the adoption of a democratic system. It is a goal that is associated primarily with "classical" (fully participatory) democracy: development of the individual's human faculties. In the words of a leading authority:

> The most distinctive feature, and the principal orienting value, of classical democratic theory was its emphasis on individual participation in the development of public policy .... Although the classical theorists accepted the basic framework of Lockean democracy, with its emphasis on limited government, they were *not* primarily concerned with the *policies* which might be produced in a democracy; above all else they were concerned with *human development,* the opportunities which existed in political activity to realize the untapped potentials of men ....[51]

My thesis is that: (1) although the democratic process is a means of achieving both the intrinsic and instrumental values, it is only one means of doing so; (2) both values (which, as noted previously,[52] may be grouped under the broader heading of "self-realization") may be achieved by and for individuals in countless nonpolitical, and often wholly private, activities; and (3) the concept of free speech facilitates the development of these values by directly fostering the instrumental value and indirectly fostering the intrinsic value. Free speech fosters the former goal *directly* in that the very exercise on one's freedom to speak, write, create, appreciate, or learn represents a use, and therefore a development, of an individual's uniquely human faculties.

---

50. In the words of Professor Bachrach, "[d]emocratic participation ... is a process in which persons formulate, discuss, and decide public issues that are important to them and directly affect their lives." Bachrach, *Interest, Participation, and Democratic Theory,* in PARTICIPATION IN POLITICS: NOMOS XVI, at 39 (J. Pennock & J. Chapman eds. 1975).

51. Walker, *A Critique of the Elitist Theory of Democracy,* 60 AM. POL. SCI. REV. 285, 288 (1966) (emphasis in original); *see also* C. MACPHERSON, THE LIFE AND TIMES OF LIBERAL DEMOCRACY 51 (1977) ("[D]emocracy drew the people into the operations of government by giving them all a practical interest, an interest which could bring down a government. Democracy would thus make people more active, more energetic; it would advance them 'in intellect, in virtue, and in practical activity and efficiency'."). John Stuart Mill is often associated with this "developmental" value of democracy. *See* Walker, *supra* at 285; *see also* J. MILL, ON LIBERTY (1947) (1st ed. London 1859).

52. *See supra* text preceding note 18.

It fosters the latter value *indirectly* because the very exercise of one's right of free speech does not in itself constitute an exercise of one's ability to make life-affecting decisions as much as it *facilitates* the making of such decisions.

This conceptual framework indicates that the appropriate scope of the first amendment protection is much broader than Bork or Meiklejohn would have it. Free speech aids all life-affecting decisionmaking, no matter how personally limited, in much the same manner in which it rids the political process. Just as individuals need an open flow of information and opinion to aid them in making their electoral and governmental decisions, they similarly need a free flow of information and opinion to guide them in making other life-affecting decisions. There thus is no logical basis for distinguishing the role speech plays in the political process. Although we definitely need protection of speech to aid us in making political judgments, we need it no less whenever free speech will aid development of the broader values that the democratic system is designed to foster.

Before this thesis can be accepted, however, each of its two prongs must confront significant counterarguments:

> (1) The moral value of "self-rule" intrinsic in adoption of a democratic system is not transferable to the private sphere, because that we value society's collective ability to control its destiny does not necessarily imply that we place an equal value upon individuals' power to direct their personal lives. Individual and collective self-determination are very different conceptually, and indeed are often in conflict.
>
> (2) Although classical theorists of democracy may have believed that human development would result from mass political participation, modern theorists — the "elitists" or "revisionists" — have totally undermined the basis for this belief. Furthermore, that such human development could be gained from participation in the political process would not imply that similar benefits would derive from individuals' control over their private lives, because an essential premise of the classical theorists' belief was that this benefit stemmed from individuals extending themselves beyond narrow self-interest to concern about the common good.

Although each of these arguments deserves a detailed response, it is my contention that neither invalidates my thesis.

1. Collective Self-Rule and Individual Autonomy

One can argue that there is a conceptual difference between the value of collective self-rule and that of individual self-rule. In a democracy, numerous conflicts may develop between the majority's will and the desires of the individual. A "tyranny of the majority," under which there is little or no room for the exercise of individual autonomy, is readily imaginable.[53] But my purpose in this discussion is not to establish that the concept of collective self-rule necessarily implies an impenetrable sphere of individual autonomy (although the form of democracy established in this nation, both historically and morally, does include the existence of such a sphere).[54] My point, rather, concerns the level of constitutional protection to be given to speech that is related to whatever decisionmaking the collective society does allow the individual to make. I intend to show only that the logic employed by Meiklejohn and Bork to justify first amendment protection for speech relevant to political decisionmaking dictates a similar level of protection for speech related to whatever decisions actually are allowed to the individual.

The point may be understood by analyzing the logic of the majoritarian principle. We may begin with the valid assumption that

---

53. *See generally* THE FEDERALIST NOS. 10 & 51 (J. Madison); 1 A. DE TOCQUEVILLE, DEMOCRACY IN AMERICA 241-54 (1966) (1st ed. Bruxelles 1835); J. MILL, *supra* note 51, at 1-14.

54. The ideological father of the American Revolution is generally thought to be John Locke. *See* L. LEVY, *supra* note 27, at 100; J. ROCHE, COURTS AND RIGHTS 9-10 (1961); *see also* G. WOOD, THE CREATION OF THE AMERICAN REPUBLIC, 1776-1787, at 14, 283-84 (1969). Locke is widely thought of as a libertarian who

> assumed ... that there ought to exist a certain minimum area of personal freedom which must on no account be violated; for if it is overstepped, the individual will find himself in an area too narrow for even that minimum development of his natural faculties which alone makes it possible to pursue, and even to conceive, the various ends which men hold good or right or sacred.

I. BERLIN, FOUR ESSAYS ON LIBERTY 124 (1977); *see also* G. PARRY, JOHN LOCKE 158-60 (1978).

It may well be, as Professor Roche suggests, that only "[a] careless reading of Locke's *Second Treatise* suggests that he was a militant defender of the rights of the citizen against government in general." J. ROCHE, *supra*, at 9; *see also* L. LEVY, *supra* note 27, at 103-04. However, Locke was undoubtedly a libertarian relative to his contemporaries, *see id.* 100-01, and, as Roche acknowledges, the image (perhaps mythical) of Locke as a strong believer in individual rights "had an enormous impact, particularly in the American Colonies." J. ROCHE, *supra*, at 9. *See also* G. WOOD, *supra*, at 283-84. In any event, there can be little question that the form of democracy that we have adopted imposes constitutional enclaves to protect the individual's autonomy from majoritarian interference.

For an alternative interpretation of the ideological origins of the American Revolution — one that de-emphasizes the role of Locke and substantiates the influence of the moral-sense philosophy of the Enlightenment — see G. WILLS, INVENTING AMERICA (1978). Wills' interpretation provides a historical and intellectual background that is consistent with the theory of individual self-realization advanced in this book.

no society could function if every individual were allowed total self-determination. This is true, even if we were to place great moral value on the ability of an individual to control his or her destiny. But if we simultaneously value individual self-determination yet recognize the practical impossibility of such a principle in a collective setting, the next best alternative is self-determination by the majority. For under such a structure, as many individuals as realistically possible are receiving the benefits of self-determination without sacrificing the essential societal need for collective action in many areas of day-to-day existence. This, in short, is the logic of majoritarian democracy. Ultimately, the system's moral premise is the desirability of having individuals control decisions that affect their lives. In those situations in which society (either by means of legislative decision or through the imposition of a constitutional structure) has determined that the exercise of individual choice is more important than the negative societal impact of such a choice, it cedes to the individual this total decisionmaking power. But whether society makes the choice for the individual by majority rule or cedes to the individual total control, it is ultimately the same moral value at work: the belief in self-determination for as many individuals as practical. For society, it should be recalled, is nothing more than a collection of individuals; in a democratic society, it is, ultimately, the will of these individuals (albeit in the aggregate) that is given priority.

The point may be illustrated by means of an example. Let us imagine a hypothetical democratic society premised solely on the utilitarian belief in the greatest good for the greatest number, and with no moral or political regard for the individual as such, except assurances that every individual will have a say (a vote) in decisionmaking. Assume further that in this society *every* decision affecting individuals — including decisions about dinner menus, hair styles, entertainment activities, and bedtimes — is made by a collective vote. Although in concept such a society is democratic, it of course removes from the individual more choices than does virtually any authoritarian regime. Nevertheless, the inherent value on which the system is premised is (collective) self-rule.

Under Meiklejohnian logic, debate and information about every one of these decisions, no matter how trivial, would presumably have to receive full constitutional protection, because the individuals that make up this society are in fact their own "governors," and therefore need open communication to aid them in their "political" decisionmaking. This logic applies to speech of the minority as well as the majority, because we presumably cannot determine before the actual vote who will be in each group. Therefore, every voter must have the right to hear and learn every factor that might influence the final vote.

Now assume a slight alteration in the arrangement of this society: instead of collectively voting on every conceivable life-affecting decision, the members of the society vote periodically for specific governors, who make each life-affecting decision for the entire society. Under Meiklejohnian logic, here, too, we need full protection of information for society's members about each of the issues that the governors will decide, because the underlying moral precept of the society is still self-rule. The individuals therefore need to know how the competing candidates for office will decide these issues — for example, whether they will order chicken or steak for dinner — so that they can choose the governors whose views coincide most closely with the individuals' personal preferences. Moreover, if the price of steak should rise during the governors' term of office, under Meiklejohnian logic the society's members would need the constitutional right to tell each other about it, so that they might better judge the dinner choices made by their governing agents. Simply put, Meiklejohn and Bork would protect only speech related to the political process, but the term "political" does not include a set category of specific substantive issues. Rather, it applies to whatever issues a society decides collectively, whether by direct popular vote or through elected agents.

Now assume that, whether because of moral concern about individual autonomy or simply because it does not wish to be bothered with so many decisions, the collective society cedes to each individual full decisionmaking power, much as our own democratic society does, on such questions as what to eat for dinner, what commercial products to buy, whom and whether to marry, what career to choose, and where and whether to go to college — decisions that previously were made by the collective or its agents and that therefore were "political." At this point, the individual has more than an indirect say in how these decisions are to be made; he now has full authority to make them, as well as commensurate responsibility for their consequences.

Once these decisions have been removed from collective authority and completely given over to individual will, presumably Meiklejohn and Bork would say that the individual no longer has a constitutional right to information that will help him make them, because they are no longer part of the political process. Their logic, however, leaves us with an untenable situation: when an individual only has an indirect say in governing his life, either by voting on particular questions or by selecting governing agents who will make the decisions, he has a right to information that will enable him to exercise his power more effectively; but when the individual has full and total authority to make the very same decisions, his right to the information mysteriously vanishes. Reason would seem to dictate, however, that the individual has at least as great a need for a free flow of information and opinion related to life-affecting decisions that he makes solely for himself. For whether the decisions are made collectively or by the individual, in a democracy we assume the moral value of self-rule. Thus, the first amendment guarantee of free expression is designed to play an important role in the exercise of that decisionmaking power at either level.

2. The Impact of the Elitist Theorists and the Definition of "Political"

A critique based on the findings and conclusions of the so-called "elitist"[55] or "revisionist"[56] democratic theorists — who have come into prominence mostly within the last forty years[57] — is aimed at the "instrumental" value of a democratic system: the development of individual abilities and faculties thought by classical theorists to flow from participation in the political process.[58] The argument, put simply, is that it is today unrealistic to expect the common masses to gain such benefits, because it is unrealistic to expect them to have both the interests and the ability to involve themselves on a significant scale in day-to-day political affairs. The pulls of work and family, Professor Lipset tells us, are too great to expect the individual to bother with the complexities of political affairs, especially when he sees the impact of those matters on his life as remote.[59] Professor Dahl writes that "neither by instincts nor by learning is [man] necessarily a political animal."[60]

---

55. *See, e.g.*, P. BACHRACH, THE THEORY OF DEMOCRATIC ELITISM: A CRITIQUE (1967); Walker, *supra* note 51.

56. Although the term "elitist" was apparently coined by one of the theory's proponents, *see* Lipset, *Introduction* to R. MICHELS, POLITICAL PARTIES 33 (1962), at least one of the theorists who is often thought to fall into this grouping rejects the term, because it is inaccurate and "even more so because in our language and in our society it is unavoidably ... a pejorative, even a polemical epithet." Dahl, *Further Reflections on "The Elitist Theory of Democracy,"* 60 AM. POL. SCI. REV. 296, 297 n.7 (1966). The term "revisionism" is applied to this type of democratic theory in Keim, *Participation in Contemporary Democratic Theories,* in PARTICIPATION IN POLITICS: NOMOS XVI, at 1 (J. Pennock & R. Chapman eds. 1975).

57. The origin of the theory of democratic elitism is contained in the later chapters of G. MOSCA, THE RULING CLASS (1939). *See* P. BACHRACH, *supra* note 55, at 10.

58. *See supra* text preceding note 51.

59. Lipset, *supra* note 56, at 17; *see also* P. BACHRACH, *supra* note 55.

60. R. DAHL, MODERN POLITICAL ANALYSIS 55-56 (1963).

Well-known empirical studies describing the average American voter's shocking lack of knowledge underscore this judgment.[61] Revisionists have therefore presented a vision of democracy in which more-involved elites compete for the allegiance of the masses at election time, but in which most individuals have no significant role beyond exercising a periodic choice through election, or occasionally through other formalized procedures.[62] Such data and theories may seem to make the instrumental value of classical democracy a museum piece. If so, it might be argued that the implications I have drawn from my theory about the broader value of individual self-realization are inaccurate. This, however, is not the case.

First, it should be noted that the impact of the elitists' argument goes at most to the instrumental value of democracy, and in no way challenges the *intrinsic* value of allowing individuals to maintain self-rule.[63] More importantly, the elitist theorists do not seem to question the *normative* imperative recognized by classical theorists, but rather

---

61. *See, e.g.*, B. BERELSON, P. LAZARSFELD & W. MCPHEE, VOTING (1954); A. CAMPBELL, P. CONVERSE, W. MILLER & D. STOKES, THE AMERICAN VOTER (1960). *But see* N. NIE, S. VERBA & J. PETROCIK, THE CHANGING AMERICAN VOTER 123-73, 319-44 (1979). This more recent analysis suggests that the indicia of voter awareness, issue consistency, and issue voting have demonstrated a marked increase in voter awareness between 1956 (the terminal year of the Campbell, Converse, Miller and Stokes study) and 1976. However, Nie, Verba, and Petrocik add this cautionary note to their data: "This is not to say that the mass citizenry now has patterns of attitude consistency equal to that of a group of political Elites such as congressional candidates."*Id.* at 137.

Note that these studies dealt only with the lack of knowledge of *voters*; the implications about the many who do not even perform that minimal civic function are all too clear. Dahl has suggested an explanation for such behavior:

> The explanation, no doubt, lies in the fact that man is not by instinct a reasonable, reasoning, civic-minded being. Many of our most imperious desires and the source of many of our most powerful gratifications can be traced to ancient and persistent biological and physiological drives, needs, and wants. Organized political life arrived late in man's evolution; today man learns how to behave as a political participant with the aid, and often with the hindrance, of instinctive equipment that is the product of a long development. To avoid pain, discomfort, and hunger, to satisfy drives for sexual gratification, love, security, and respect are insistent and primordial needs. The means of satisfying them quickly and concretely generally lie outside political life.

R. DAHL, *supra* note 60, at 103-04. If Dahl is correct, the problem is not that the classical theories are outmoded in modern society, but rather that they were unrealistic from their inception. In any case, the problem remains with us.

62. *See* Keim, *supra* note 56, at 7 ("[Under revisionist theory, h]*omo civicus* is constrained to a mode of participation characterized by the binomic 'yes' or 'no.' Participation is effectively reduced to the approval or disapproval of the performance of elected official and lobbyist.").

63. *Id.*

only its attainability. Indeed, the impact of the findings of the elitist theorists is arguably to shift the emphasis from attaining this goal through the political process to its achievement through individual involvement in the private sector. Modern theorists have redefined the concept of the "political" to include decisionmaking within areas such as the work place, where decisions are likely to have a more immediately recognizable impact on the individual's daily life.[64] Therefore, the elitist theory can be seen as being totally compatible with the thesis asserted here; democratic political control is only one means of achieving the values inherent in a democratic system, and it is therefore necessary to recognize that free speech may aid attainment of those values in nonpolitical settings.

Elitist thinking, then, does not undermine — indeed, it may facilitate — the extension of Meiklejohn's reasoning about the role of free speech to such nonpolitical activities as various kinds of community groups, as well as to the workplace.[65] What remains unclear, however, is whether this logic may be extended as well to such purely private decisions as commercial purchases or an individual's choice of friends. The difficulty is that it has been generally assumed, since democracy's origins in ancient Athens, that the moral benefits to the individual derived from being forced to look beyond his or her own narrow interests and to work with others to attain the common good.[66] It is perhaps for this reason that Professor Bachrach, the leading exponent of the redefined "political" sphere, believed it necessary to stay within the bounds of the "political," no matter how strained his definition of the term.[67] But whatever unique benefits one derives from involvement in organizations that look to the common, as opposed to the individual, good, it is impossible to deny that many of the developmental values — particularly the intellectual benefits — that are thought to result from participation in the political process also may be obtained from private self-government. After all, the elitists

---

64. *See* P. BACHRACH, *supra* note 55, at 102-03. *See generally* R. PHANGER, THE ECLIPSE OF CITIZENSHIP (1968).

65. *See* P. BACHRACH, *supra* note 55, at 96 & n.2; *see also* Mansbridge, *The Limits of Friendship*, in PARTICIPATION IN POLITICS: NOMOS XVI, at 246 (J. Pennock & J. Chapman eds. 1975). The constitutional requirement of state or federal action, however would probably limit the first amendment's reach into these nonpolitical or private areas to restricting *governmental* interference with the exercise of free speech.

66. *See* G. SABINE & T. THORSON, A HISTORY OF POLITICAL THEORY 64-66, 539-44 (4th ed. 1973).

67. The political scientist must recognize, Bachrach says, "that large areas within existing so-called private centers of power are political and therefore potentially open to a wide and democratic sharing in decision-making." P. BACHRACH, *supra* note 55, at 102; *see also* Keim, *supra* note 56, at 13.

tell us that "[p]olitical participation constitutes an effort to protect threatened interests,"[68] and by adopting a democratic system we are expressing a belief that presumably individuals are capable of deciding what is best for them. There is therefore no basis to believe that development can be derived solely from common, as opposed to individual, activity.

In any event, one may seriously question whether much political decisionmaking in modern society has a great deal to do with collaborative efforts. Modern campaigning is done largely through the media, and governmental decisionmaking is today a far cry from the New England town meeting.

A final, related argument is that speech concerning the political process is simply more important than speech concerning private decisionmaking, because it affects many more lives. One may question, however, whether this is true of all activity within the political process; one can imagine town council elections in miniscule hamlets, which, I assume, both Meiklejohn and Bork would include in their definition of "political," even though relatively few people would be affected. In any event, the argument is misleading, because it fails to recognize that, when we value private decisionmaking, we are referring to such decisionmaking on the part of *all* individuals.

C. Scholarly Criticism of the Self-Realization Theory

Since the first amendment theory developed in this chapter was first expressed,[69] a number of scholars have attempted to point out what

---

68. Keim, *supra* note 56, at 7. The interesting insights of political scientist Jane Mansbridge about the nature of democratic theory support my conclusion that moral benefits derived from working for the common good, as opposed to the individual's selfish interests, were not inherent in the type of democratic theory adopted by the framers. According to Professor Mansbridge, the form of democracy adopted by the framers for the nation was "adversary" democracy, "built on self-interest." "In current adversary theory," she writes, "there is no common good or public interest. Voters pursue their individual interests by making demands on the political system in proportion to the intensity of their feelings.... From the interchange between self-interested voters and self-interested brokers emerge decisions that come as close as possible to a balanced aggregation of individual interests." J. Mansbridge, Beyond Adversary Democracy 16-17 (1980). While Professor Mansbridge does argue that the values of so-called "unitary" democracy — a pursuit of the common good through consensus — may be attainable in certain smaller modern settings, it is not feasible to attain such values in the national political system, which, after all, is the origin of modern American democracy.

69. As noted in the introduction to this book, the self-realization theory described in this chapter was first expressed in my article, *The Value of Free Speech*, 130 U. Pa. L. Rev. 591 (1982).

they deem to be its flaws.[70] It is therefore appropriate at this point to respond to these arguments.

The most detailed of the critiques has come from Professor Baker.[71] Baker begins his comment by correctly noting our significant difference over the outcome in *First National Bank of Boston v. Bellotti*,[72] in which the Court struck down a state law regulating corporate political expenditures; I believe it was rightly decided, whereas he believes the decision was wrong.[73] This difference flows from our respective beliefs concerning the relevance for first amendment purposes of the *receipt*, as opposed to merely the expression, of information, opinion, and thought. Because I firmly believe that the value of self-realization, as I define it, may be fostered as much by the receipt of expression as by the act of expressing, I conclude that the source or motivation of the expression is largely irrelevant. Baker, on the other hand, believes that the source is all important.[74] Baker apparently believes that this difference of opinion flows from the differing ways in which we structure and develop the self-realization value, and therefore that he can establish that his emphasis on the source of expression is the more appropriate approach by demonstrating that my structural analysis is inaccurate or unfounded.[75]

Unlike Baker, who supports his normative assertions about the value of self-realization with little more than conclusory contentions,[76] I attempt to justify recognition of its centrality by reasoning from the existence of our democratic system. Democracy, I argue, is not an end in itself; it is, rather, a means of achieving broader values. After considering and rejecting certain conceivable values thought to be fostered by a democratic system, I settle upon two — the inherent value in allowing individuals to control their own destiny, and the instrumental value in developing individuals' mental faculties so that they may reach their full intellectual potential — and group these two values under the broader heading of "self-realization." Because speech unrelated to the actual conduct of democracy may aid self-realization as well as speech that concerns the operation of the political process, I

---

70. *See* Schauer, *Codifying the First Amendment: New York v. Ferber,* 1982 SUP. CT. REV. 285; Baker, *Realizing Self-Realization: Corporate Political Expenditures and Redish's* The Value of Free Speech, 130 U. PA. L. REV. 646 (1982).
71. *Id.* Baker, *supra* note 70.
72. 435 U.S. 765 (1978).
73. *See* Baker, *supra* note 70, at 655-58.
74. *See* discussion *infra* at 49-52.
75. *See* discussion *infra* at 31-34.
76. *See* discussion *infra* at 49-52.

conclude that the reach of the first amendment must be considerably broader than that suggested by such scholars as Bork, Blasi, and Meiklejohn.

Baker's criticism takes the following course. First, he rejects my conclusion that democracy is designed to foster the development-of-faculties value. Then, having left me only the self-rule value, he concludes that, although self-rule is indeed a value of a democratic system, my method of viewing free speech as a means of fostering that value is improper.[77]

> Although democracy may further the "development of the individual's human faculties," a concern with self-development does not in any obvious way require a democratic political order. More relevantly..., one might accept democracy for reasons other than a concern for individuals' development of their faculties — for example, because of the importance we place on self-rule.[78]

In this statement, Baker effectively asserts that democracy is not needed for self-development, and that self-development is not needed for democracy. Whatever the merits of the latter comment, the former is, I believe, plainly incorrect. As Mill argued, any development of mental faculties in a nondemocratic setting is inherently and fatally incomplete.[79] Even in the most benevolent dictatorship, in which individuals might be free to express themselves through art, music, or literature, the inherent limitation on the individual's ability to employ these devices as a means of attacking the government and to take part in collective decisionmaking would inescapably stunt full and free development. Mill wrote, in the final paragraph of *On Liberty*, that:

> The worth of a State, in the long run, is the worth of the individuals composing it; and a State which postpones the interests of *their* mental expansion and elevation, ... a State which dwarfs its men, in order that they may be more docile instruments in its hands even for beneficial purposes — will find that with small men no great thing can really be accomplished ....[80]

For believers in realization of an individual's intellectual potential, then, Mill was certainly correct when he argued that a "benevolent dictatorship" is a contradiction in terms.[81]

---

77. *See* Baker, *supra* note 70 at 660-68.
78. *Id.* at 660 (footnote omitted).
79. J. MILL, CONSIDERATIONS ON REPRESENTATIVE GOVERNMENT 62-63, 69-80 (1882).
80. J. MILL, *supra* note 51, at 62-63 (emphasis in original).
81. J. MILL, *supra* note 79, at 62-63.

As to Baker's second point, it is true, I suppose, that one could choose to adopt a democratic system without concern for the intellectual development of the individual — although, as Baker recognizes, such a benefit will inherently flow from use of such a political system, whether intended or not. But whether or not one *could* logically choose to adopt a democratic system without concern for individual development, classical democratic theorists have long recognized the resulting benefits for individual mental, intellectual, and human development as one of the primary values of democracy.[82] This normative principle is so ingrained in traditional democratic theory that it is reasonable to suggest that it be deemed a value behind the longest living democratic system of modern times.[83] Moreover, because the effective functioning of a democracy requires that individuals employ their mental faculties in making political choices, it is not a significant leap to suggest that adoption of a democratic system implies a belief in the value of individual mental development. There is no reason to suppose — as Baker implies — that the values of self-rule and self-realization are in any way mutually exclusive as justifications for our adoption of a democratic system.

Once Baker believes that he has disposed of the self-development value, he attempts to demonstrate that my link between the self-rule value and the free dissemination of information is unfounded. My theory is, simply, that performance of the function of self-rule is fostered by the receipt of information that enables the individual to make life-affecting decisions in a more informed fashion. Free dissemination of information, in other words, helps inform the individual of the possible benefits and risks of each of the courses of action that he or she can take. The concept of self-rule definitionally implies that at every turn an individual may make one of several choices in governing his or her life, and information relevant to those various options can only foster the effective use of the individual's decisionmaking power.[84]

---

82. As Professor Bachrach argues, "[c]lassical [democratic] theory ... is based on the supposition that man's dignity, and indeed his growth and development as a functioning and responsive individual in a free society, is dependent upon an opportunity to participate actively in decisions that significantly affect him." P. BACHRACH, *supra* note 55, at 98. Bachrach cites "the belief of Rousseau, Kant, Mill, Lindsay, and others, that man's development as a human being is closely dependent upon his opportunity to contribute to the solution of problems relating to his own actions." *Id.* at 99.
83. *See* discussion *supra* at 20-22.
84. *See* 1 M. ADLER, THE IDEA OF FREEDOM 112 (1958).

Baker offers three criticisms of my theory: (1) that "self-rule and democracy can and do operate without full or complete information";[85] (2) that, "even if supplying information to the listener usually promotes self-rule, this 'indirect' support does not distinguish the information's contribution from the contribution made by various other resources and opportunities, such as food, shelter, health care, and employment and educational options," or a right of access to government-held information,[86] and (3) that "it remains an open empirical and normative question whether this additional information [provided by corporate speech] actually promotes rational, intelligent self-rule."[87] Baker even suggests that such widespread protection of the dissemination of information "might in fact detract from self-rule by contributing to information overload, by supplying an ideologically unbalanced and distorted background, or by promoting simplistic thinking."[88] None of these points, however, effectively impairs recognition of the importance of free speech protection to the goal of self-rule.

Baker's first point is quite probably the least persuasive of the three. That democracy or self-rule can operate without complete information is beside the point. The questions that Baker should — but does not — ask are whether self-rule's operation is likely to be improved by an increase in the flow of relevant information, and whether, correspondingly, that operation is likely to be impaired by a decrease in information flow. In the political realm, leading commentators[89] and the Supreme Court[90] have assumed that people's decision in the voting booth are impaired to the extent that they are unable to obtain information about the candidates, such as their stands on the issues. The accuracy of this conclusion easily can be seen by imagining an election in which no one, including the candidates themselves, was allowed to say anything about the relative qualifications or positions of the competing office seekers. The public's performance of the democratic function in such an election would be a mockery. Although I suppose that the level of information could never be "complete," that does not mean that the performance of the self-rule function would not

---

85. Baker, *supra* note 70, at 661.
86. *Id.* at 662.
87. *Id.* at 663.
88. *Id.*
89. *See, e.g.*, A. MEIKLEJOHN, *supra* note 8.
90. *See, e.g.*, Monitor Patriot Co. v. Roy, 401 U.S. 265 (1971); New York Times Co. v. Sullivan, 376 U.S. 254 (1964).

be significantly undermined if we reduced protection for the dissemination of whatever information is available.[91]

Baker's second point — that other resources can contribute to self-rule — sounds vaguely reminiscent of the argument of Judge Bork that there is no rational means to distinguish the values derived from protection of most forms of expression and many forms of conduct.[92] The answer I would make to Baker is similar to the answer I gave to Bork: the primary basis of the distinction is that the framers chose to draw one, by framing the first amendment to protect only speech, and thereby relegating the liberty to undertake other forms of activity to the considerably reduced protection of the fifth amendment's due process clause.[93] I also suggested that such a decision made good practical sense, because the potential harm flowing from speech generally is considerably less direct and acute than is the danger from action, and because speech and communicative activities are in general more likely to develop individuals' mental faculties.[94]

---

91. Baker argues that "[a]s long as the first amendment protects a free press and the individual's right to speak, most information and argument that the corporation would subsidize will be made available anyway ...." Baker, *supra* note 70, at 663. But we can never be certain that "enough" information has been made available, since we can never be sure how and when people obtain their information. The Supreme Court has generally been unmoved by arguments that a particular restriction on expression still leaves room for most communication. *See, e.g.,* Mills v. Alabama, 384 U.S. 214 (1966); Schneider v. State, 308 U.S. 147 (1939). In any event, if one accepts that protecting both the dissemination and the receipt of information is a valid and important function of the first amendment, Baker's suggestion that denying protection to profit-oriented speech would leave most information available is irrelevant. The same could be said of a rule that people with red hair may not speak, or that a particular demonstration is not allowed. The question that must be asked is whether the distinction that Baker draws makes any sense. If we agree that the receipt of information serves a valuable first amendment interest and that even profit-oriented speech may further this value, there is no rational basis upon which to distinguish such speech; it is therefore no answer that such a limitation would leave "most" information available.

92. *See* discussion *supra* at 15-17.

93. *See* discussion *supra* at 18.

94. Baker's second point ultimately goes much further than Bork, in that Baker fails to distinguish not only among different forms of liberty, but also between freedom from governmental restraint and the right to a governmental subsidy. The framers quite probably never considered providing constitutional rights to education, food, or shelter, but if they had considered it, they could easily have distinguished those means of fostering self-rule from freedom of expression. Each of those methods requires affirmative governmental assistance; protection of free expression, on the other hand, simply requires the government not to act. The financial and administrative burdens that would be caused by constitutional protection for the items suggested by Baker would no doubt be substantial.

Baker's response is that, "[a]lthough there is an explicit constitutional judgment concerning the importance of freedom of speech, ... [t]he text of the Constitution does not itself show whether the first amendment's focus is on the provision of information or on the individual's freedom."[95] But Baker's second criticism does not really go to that issue, because the same argument could be directed at Baker's own model: without food or shelter, a right of self-expression — or of anything else, for that matter — is meaningless. In structuring his own theory, Baker actually includes within the first amendment guarantee activity that is admittedly "conduct" and cannot rationally be defined as "speech," even though the explicit language of the amendment that he purports to interpret could not make it more clear that the protection is limited to "speech." Yet not even Baker extends the first amendment's protection to an obligation of governmental support. Although I might well agree with Baker that effective self-rule requires access to government-held information, education, food, and shelter,[96] the need for such rights is totally irrelevant to the meaning and interpretation of the first amendment's guarantee of free speech. Rights to information, education, food and shelter would each require an additional constitutional amendment. But that, for whatever reason,[97] the framers chose not to provide constitutional protection for every conceivable means of fostering self-rule does not imply that we should fail to recognize the importance to self-rule of the activity that they did choose to protect so thoroughly.

Baker's third criticism — that the additional information may not advance "rational, intelligent self-rule" — is no more persuasive. Baker's fallacy on this point is his assumption that the value of self-rule is limited to whatever he would label "rational, intelligent self-rule."[98] But such a limitation would totally undermine the concept, for to allow individuals to choose only what some external force determines is "rational" and "intelligent" is effectively to deprive them of self-rule.[99] As for Baker's fear of an "information overload," if there

---

95. Baker, *supra* note 70, at 662.
96. *Id.* at 665.
97. *See* note 94 *supra.*
98. Baker, *supra* note 70, at 663.
99. It is, of course, true that for many activities the state may, and often does, constitutionally limit an individual's power of self-rule. But, as I have argued, the relevant point for first amendment purposes is that, at least for those activities in which we do allow the individual to make life-affecting decisions, it hardly makes sense to say that individuals have the authority to decide for themselves, but that we will allow or encourage only those decisions that are externally deemed "rational" or "intelligent."

could ever be such a thing, my only response is that I simply do not feel comfortable in deciding — or in having anyone else decide — at what point such an "overload" has been reached. Since we can never really know when "enough" information has been made available, I, for one, would much prefer to risk "too much" information than too little.

Professor Schauer has also expressed general disagreement with exclusive reliance on the self-realization value. One of his difficulties concerns the necessarily broad and abstract nature that any single principle purporting to rationalize all of free expression must have. In his words, "[u]se of a single principle to deal with all of our problems produces application that is more likely to be conclusory than principled."[100] This is because "[a]n abstract single principle will be able to accommodate almost any foreseeable and unforeseeable change in the nature of First Amendment problems,"[101] and "that very flexibility is a crippling weakness, for unitary abstract principles can also accommodate any more particularized intuition of the designer or applier of the principle."[102]

Professor Schauer, uncharacteristically, has missed the point. The overriding goal of my exclusive reliance on the self-realization principle was to prevent the very kind of arbitrary shifting among first amendment rationales that Schauer decries. Recognition of the underlying self-realization value as the ultimate normative source for all of the other conceivable sub-values logically precludes choosing among these various sub-values in seeking the true rationale of free speech protection. For example, under the self-realization analysis as I have developed it, neither Bork nor Meiklejohn could assert that the first amendment is concerned only with political speech; nor could Blasi assert that the so-called "checking" function was supreme; nor could any jurist or scholar suggest that only expression contributing to the "marketplace of ideas" was deserving of protection. Understanding that the ultimate value served by protecting expression in each of these categories is no different from that served by protecting such traditionally disdained forms of expression, as commercial speech,[103] private defamation,[104] so-called "obscenity"[105] or even advocacy of unlawful conduct[106] renders totally illogical attempts to distinguish

---

100. Schauer, *supra* note 70, at 312.
101. *Id.* at 311-12.
102. *Id.* at 312.
103. *See* discussion *infra* at 60-68.
104. *See* discussion *infra* at 76-81.
105. *See* discussion *infra* at 68-76.
106. *See* discussion *infra* at 81-86.

among these forms of expression in terms of their relative value.[107] Thus, the self-realization theory actually does just the opposite of what Professor Schauer accuses it of doing: rather than invite manipulation of first amendment values to justify whatever narrower principle the creator desires, it logically precludes this very practice.

To support his assertion about the undue maleability of the self-realization theory, Schauer points to *New York v. Ferber*,[108] where the Court upheld a state statute making criminal the use of minors in pornographic but non-obscene performances, and to *Gertz v. Robert Welch, Inc.*,[109] upholding state defamation laws when invoked by non-public figures.[110] In the former case, he asserts, self-realization could lead to opposite results, "varying with whether we focused on the self-realization of the children or the producers."[111] In the latter, the results of a self-realization theory turns "on the effect of self-realization or ... on the self-realization of the defamer in being unfettered in his communicative acts."[112] But in both examples, Schauer erroneously contrasts self-realization achieved through expressive activity on the one hand with self-realization — of a sort — achieved through non-expressive activity (not participating in pornographic performances, or not being the subject of defamatory statements). Since neither of these latter activities constitute expressive activity within the bounds of the first amendment, they simply do not attain the protection of the constitutional command. Thus, reliance on the self-realization principle in *Ferber* and *Gertz* does not lead to potentially conflicting results; under the terms of the first amendment, only that activity promoting self-realization that can be characterized as "expression" is deserving of constitutional recognition. It should be recalled, however, that under my analysis in extreme cases, non-speech interests can on occasion outbalance free speech values. But this is not because of the lesser value of the speech in question in comparison to other forms of expression, but simply because of its danger. Schauer would be correct in suggesting that such an analysis contains a troubling degree of indeterminacy, but the same would be true of *any* balancing process, regardless of what value or values speech was thought to serve. The

---

107. As I argue elsewhere, however, it is conceivable that gradations in speech protection may be made on grounds other than relative value, such as relative danger of harm. *See* discussion *infra* at 65.
108. 458 U.S. 747 (1983).
109. 418 U.S. 323 (1974).
110. Schauer, *supra* note 70, at 312.
111. *Id.*
112. *Id.*

argument, then, goes to the broad issue of balancing (dealt with elsewhere in these pages),[113] not to the advisability of the self-realization rationale.

Ultimately, much of Schauer's difficulty with the unitary self-realization value is not so much that it is premised on the value of self-realization, but that it is unitary. "But why must we assume that the First Amendment has a unitary essence," he asks.[114]

> The First Amendment might instead be the simplifying rubric under which a number of different values are subserved. We wish to prevent government from silencing its critics, but we wish as well to prevent an imposed uniformity in literary and artistic taste, to preserve open inquiry in the sciences and other academic fields, and to foster wide-ranging argument on moral, religious, and ethical questions. This list is representative rather than exhaustive, but it shows that the concept of freedom of speech may not have one central core.[115]

Of course, the entire point of my analysis has been to demonstrate that it shows nothing of the sort. Schauer makes absolutely no attempt to refute my arguments that all of these seeming values are in reality nothing more than sub-values of the broader self-realization principle.

In his earlier work, Schauer implicitly[116] attacked the self-realization rationale on another ground. I have acknowledged that the self-realization value is not uniquely fostered by expressive activity.[117] As both Bork[118] and Baker[119] have correctly noted, many of the same benefits — even to intellectual development — may come from activity that cannot be deemed "speech" for purposes of the first amendment, either conceptually or practically. In a manner reminiscent of Bork, Schauer argues that "if there is no principle of free speech independent of a more general liberty, then free speech is more a platitude than a principle."[120] He then suggests that "[i]n order to keep this distinction to the fore, I will hereafter refer to the hypothesized independent principle as the Free Speech Principle",[121] a principle "independent of

---

113. *See* discussion *infra* at 52-55.
114. Schauer, *supra* note 70, at 313.
115. *Id.* (footnote omitted).
116. Professor Schauer's book was written prior to publication of the original version of my work on the self-realization theory.
117. *See* discussion *supra* at 16-19.
118. Bork, *supra* note 12.
119. Baker, *supra* note 70.
120. F. SCHAUER, FREE SPEECH: A PHILOSOPHICAL ENQUIRY 6 (1982).
121. Professor Schauer writes:

principles of general liberty."[122] But one may search the rest of Professor Schauer's book in vain for anything approaching a detailed explanation of exactly what unique value speech may be thought to serve. Schauer's ultimate justification for an independent "free speech principle" turns not on some unique value which speech is thought to serve, but rather on what Schauer perceives as a unique *danger* to the speech interest deriving from governmental regulation — one he does not see present in governmental regulation of a broader liberty. In Schauer's words:

> Even if there is nothing especially good about speech compared to other conduct, the state may have less ability to regulate speech than it has to regulate other forms of conduct, or the attempt to regulate speech may entail special harms or special dangers not present in regulation of other conduct.
>
> ....
>
> One reason may be the bias or self-interest of those entrusted with the task of regulating speech....
>
> This desire to suppress, this longing for a consensus, may be stronger in reference to other forms of conduct.... If there is this special urge to suppress, then a Free Speech Principle may be necessary merely to counter the tendency towards over-regulation.[123]

Schauer acknowledges, however, that there exists no empirical basis to support these "conjectures," and it is by no means intuitively clear that a government jealous of its power is more likely to suppress speech than conduct. A police state is likely to regulate all aspects of an individual's life, threatening interests of privacy and liberty of movement as much as those of speech. Even a democratic government may feel at least as threatened by physical conduct (for example, what

---

The hypothesized Free Speech Principle is a principle of free speech independent of principles of general liberty. But, although independent of broader conceptions of liberty, it may still be a component of a principle of rationality, of democracy, or of equality, for example .... Because free speech is a liberty, it is *necessarily* part of most broader conceptions of liberty. But liberty to speak has less of a logical relationship to concepts other than liberty, although such other concepts may provide powerful arguments for recognizing a principle of free speech. This distinction — between free speech as part of freedom and free speech as part of anything else — justifies reference to the hypothesized Free Speech Principle as independent, even if it is not and could not be completely independent of all other political and legal principles.

Id. at 6 (footnote omitted). However, at no point in this passage does Professor Schauer explain exactly what value or values "independent of principles of general liberty" that free speech serves.

122. *Id.* at 6.
123. F. Schauer, *supra* note 120 at 81-83.

it deems actual attempt to overthrow) as by speech (for example, advocacy of overthrow). Moreover, as the Japanese Relocation cases of the 1940's illustrate, a government in a state of fear from its citizens is as likely to respond to such threats by suppressing freedom of movement as by suppressing freedom of speech. In any event, it is clear that Schauer asserts no *value* uniquely served by protection of free speech.

Schauer's later work [124] argues that there is no single value served by protection of free speech, but only a conglomeration of traditionally accepted values.[125] None of those values is fostered exclusively by expressive activity falling conceptually within the first amendment's boundaries; each could just as easily be viewed as fostering a value "of a more general liberty."[126] Yet, as Schauer seems implicitly to concede, that fact has never been thought to disqualify them as rationales for free speech protection. This is because, as I have previously noted,[127] there simply is no value that is fostered exclusively by speech, rather than conduct.

II. Separating Value from Subvalue: An Inquiry into the Alternative Goals of Free Speech

This chapter so far has established that values inherent in the democratic process extend the benefit of free speech well beyond the confines of the "political." The original claim made, however, was

---

124. Schauer, *supra* note 70, at 313.

125. The values to which Schauer refers are "to prevent government from silencing its critics, ... to prevent an imposed uniformity in literary and artistic taste, to preserve open inquiry in the sciences and other academic fields, and to foster wide-ranging argument on moral, religious, and ethical questions." *Id.*

126. For example, the "value" of preventing silencing government's critics would be a most hollow goal, if government were simultaneously free to deny all other forms of liberty. We prevent government from silencing its critics, primarily as a means of insuring that government may not interfere with our broader liberties. For what good would the power of free and open criticism be, if government still retains the absolute right to take away all of our personal liberty? Preventing uniformity in literary and artistic tastes is not itself a "value," but merely a means of preserving a broader individuality, the same value undermined by governmental denial of all forms of non-expressive liberty. Preserving open scientific inquiry would be significantly undermined if government were allowed to regulate all liberty of conduct, for in a technical or conceptual sense, much scientific inquiry necessarily involves physical conduct, as much or more than it involves expression. Finally, non-communicative conduct — such as travel, work experience, or simply day-to-day life experience — may also "foster wide-ranging argument on moral, religious, and ethical questions." *See* discussion *supra* at 17-18.

127. *See* discussion *supra* at 18.

considerably more ambitious: that all of the so-called "values" of free speech, to the extent that they are to be accepted, derive ultimately from the single value of self-realization. Such a demonstration would preclude future theorists from asserting that although they believe in the concept of free speech, they will select a value other than self-realization as the guiding force. The argument here is that, to the extent one accepts the value of free speech at all, one must necessarily accept the self-realization value, for there is no other. In addition, for the thesis to be complete, it must be established that those who do accept the self-realization value cannot logically escape acceptance of these "subvalues" as well. It is to these issues that we now turn.

A. THE CHECKING VALUE

Perhaps the asserted value most closely analogous to the "democratic process" value is Professor Blasi's "checking value." Blasi believes that speech concerning misconduct by government officials deserves special constitutional protection.[128]

The first question about Blasi's checking value concerns the precise scope of the speech included within it. At different points, Blasi refers to speech concerning "abuse of power," the misuse of official power," and "breaches of trust by public officials,"[129] implying that these are the operative terms. But the meaning of these terms is by no means self-evident. A natural starting point would seem to be illegal conduct on the part of public officials, such as taking bribes, and Blasi unquestionably intends to include such activity.[130] But he does not stop there, nor could he without all but trivializing the free speech guarantee. If we are to understand where his theory is to apply, we must know exactly what, in addition to illegal conduct, Blasi would include under the heading of "misconduct." In attempting to define "a

---

128. In Blasi's words, "if one had to identify the single value that was uppermost in the minds of the persons who drafted and ratified the First Amendment, this checking value would be the most likely candidate." Blasi, *supra* note 2, at 527. Although Blasi at one point asserts that "the checking value is to be viewed as a possible supplement to, not a substitute for, the values that have been at the center of twentieth-century thinking about the First Amendment," *id.* at 528, he later asserts that speech related to the checking function "should ... be accorded a level of constitutional protection higher than that given any other type of communication," because "the particular evil of official misconduct is of a special order." *Id.* at 558.

129. *Id.* at 527.

130. *See id.* at 543. ("Behavior in violation of the applicable criminal code such as embezzlement or the acceptance of a bribe might provide a starting point for such a concept.")

viable concept of official 'misconduct', that does not simply collapse into 'unwisdom' or 'unpopularity,'"[131] Blasi provides some illustrations:

> Some governmental actions such as the deliberate bombing of civilians during wartime, the assassination of foreign political figures, or less extreme examples of improper involvement in the domestic affairs of another nation might also be regarded as so in violation of shared standards of morality as to fall within a distinctive concept of misconduct.[132]

So described, Blasi's first amendment theory degenerates into little more than a means of fostering one individual's — presumably Professor Blasi's — political philosophy and foreign policy.[133] What about the individual who believes that *not* bombing civilians in the Vietnam War would have been "misconduct" — someone who would assert that "if we are going to fight a war, let's win it; it's immoral to have our boys die in a limited war" — or who believes that assassinating certain foreign political figures — perhaps Castro or Hitler or Idi Amin — is morally dictated? Are only those who share the views on these issues described by Professor Blasi to receive the special protection given speech concerning the checking function? Such a result-oriented, content-based approach to free speech must of course be rejected, yet it seems to be the implication of Professor Blasi's description of "official misconduct," for Professor Blasi's theory by its terms refers to conduct, rather than issues. Moreover, what about discussion of official conduct that, although perhaps not offensive to Professor Blasi, is considered by many to be so? Is it "misconduct" for the government to allow abortions? To pay welfare? Again, to deny the inclusion of speech concerning such official actions would constitute a wholly unacceptable interpretation of the first amendment on the basis of political or social viewpoint, for if the first amendment means anything it is that the level of constitutional protection cannot vary on the basis of differing viewpoints.[134]

---

131. *Id.*
132. *Id.*
133. At the outset of his article, Professor Blasi notes the impact that public outcries had on limiting the Asian war policies of Presidents Johnson and Nixon. *Id.* at 527; *see also id.* at 640. ("[T]he communication achieved by the wave of draft-card burnings at the height of the United States involvement in Vietnam represents a paradigm example of the 'speech' with which the First Amendment is concerned.")
134. I have argued elsewhere that it is improper to provide stricter constitutional scrutiny to regulation of expression based on content than to regulation that is imposed equally on all speech. *See* Chapter II *infra*. However, this was not intended to imply that *less* scrutiny should be given to viewpoint regulation, but rather that *greater* scrutiny should be given to neutral regulation.

Perhaps Professor Blasi did not intend to establish such a solipsistic view of the first amendment. At one point, he states that "[u]nder the checking value, that determination [of what actions can be considered misconduct] must be made by each citizen in deciding when the actions of government so transcend the bounds of decency that active opposition becomes a civic duty."[135] But Blasi's distinction of speech concerning official "misconduct" from speech about general governmental action collapses if the determination of what is official misconduct is to be left to the individual citizen. For how effective a limit would it be if any individual could render governmental action or inaction "misconduct" for first amendment purposes merely by characterizing it as such?

At least in a broad sense, however, it is accurate to recognize the value of speech, as Professor Blasi does, as a means of controlling governmental actions.[136] The question for discussion, then is whether this value is independent of the self-realization value or, instead, as contended here, is merely derivative.

Professor Blasi describes the purposes thought to be served by the checking function. He argues primarily that "a proponent of the checking value views speech of a certain content as important because of its *consequences:* alerting the polity to the facts or implications of official behavior, presumably triggering responses that will mitigate the ill effects of such behavior."[137] If Blasi is correct in characterizing the checking function as fostering the consequential value of producing "good results," the value would in fact be distinct from the "process" goals inherent in the self-realization value. But closer examination of the reasoning behind the checking function reveals that this value can be sustained only on the basis of process, rather, than consequential values. To view the checking function as having a consequential value logically requires us to adopt the following reasoning: if government officials believe that it is correct to do "*A*" — a particular course of action or policy decision — and some or many members of the public

---

135. Blasi, *supra* note 2, at 543 (footnote omitted).

136. As restructured, Professor Blasi's "checking function" appears strikingly similar to the "democratic process" value of Meiklejohn, notwithstanding Professor Blasi's statements to the contrary, *see id.* at 558.

137. *Id.* at 546 (emphasis in original). This emphasis on consequences is what Professor Blasi believes primarily distinguishes the checking function from what he describes as the "autonomy" value. *Id.* At another point, underscoring his "consequentialist" approach, he states that the evil of government misconduct "is so antithetical to the entire political arrangement, is so harmful to individual people, and also is so likely to occur, that its prevention and containment is a goal that takes precedence over all other goals of the political system." *Id.* at 558 (footnote omitted).

believe that doing *A* would constitute "misconduct" and instead prefer that the officials do "*B*," we know that *B* will produce "better" — less evil or more beneficial — results than *A* will. But this conclusion surely does not follow as a matter of logic, and may well be counterintuitive in light of the empirical evidence obtained by elitist theorists of a tremendous lack of political interest and knowledge on the part of the large mass of private citizens.[138]

Of course, if we were to read Professor Blasi to suggest that there is a set category of political actions that are to be objectively deemed "misconduct,"[139] then we would be able to conclude that speech by private citizens criticizing such activity would produce "better" results. But, as already noted,[140] such an unprincipled construction of the first amendment, providing greater protection to speech urging results with which one agrees, is totally unacceptable. Therefore, we must assume, as Blasi states at another point, that it is the individual citizen's subjective characterization of official action as "misconduct" that is determinative.[141] Given that premise, we cannot support the checking value on consequential grounds, for we cannot be sure that the official policies thought by particular individuals to constitute "misconduct" necessarily would be more evil than the alternative policies urged by the private individuals.

To the extent that there is an important value behind the checking function, then, it must be a process value. And it is not difficult to determine what that value is; it is the intrinsic democratic value that individuals should have a say in the policies of their government, because their government, in a democracy, is acting on their behalf. As democratic theorist Edmond Cahn has stated, democracy requires "examining, judging, and assuming responsibility for what our representatives do in our name and by our authority, the unjust and evil acts as well as the beneficient and good."[142] Indeed, to the extent that Professor Blasi relies on the proposition that "the general populace must be the ultimate judge of the behavior of public officials,"[143] he, too, is viewing the checking function as merely one manifestation of the intrinsic democratic value.[144] Because the

---

138. *See supra* note 61 and accompanying text. According to Professor Walker, "[a]t the heart of the elitist theory is a clear presumption of the average citizen's inadequacies." Walker, *supra* note 51, at 286.
139. *See supra* text accompanying notes 41-42.
140. *See supra* text accompanying note 42.
141. Blasi, *supra* note 2, at 543.
142. E. CAHN, THE PREDICAMENT OF DEMOCRATIC MAN 29 (1961).
143. Blasi, *supra* note 2, at 542.
144. Blasi acknowledges that "the checking value grows out of democratic theory,

checking function ultimately derives from the principle of democratic self-rule, and because that principle in turn follows from the self-realization value,[145] the checking function is merely one concrete manifestation of the much broader self-realization value.[146]

B. THE MARKETPLACE-OF-IDEAS CONCEPT

"[T]he ultimate good desired," wrote Justice Holmes in his *Abrams* dissent, "is better reached by free trade in ideas — ... the best test of truth is the power of the thought to get itself accepted in the

---

but it is the democratic theory of John Locke and Joseph Schumpeter, not that of Alexander Meiklejohn." *Id.* His reference to Schumpeter, however, is puzzling. Blasi asserts that, under Schumpeter's view, "the role of the ordinary citizen is not so much to contribute on a continuing basis to the formation of public policy as to retain a veto power to be employed when the decisions of officials pass certain bounds." *Id.* (footnote omitted). However, Schumpeter actually raised serious doubts about the individual citizen's ability to question the specific policies of government. *See* J. SCHUMPETER, CAPITALISM, SOCIALISM AND DEMOCRACY 261 (3d ed. 1950); *see also* C. PATEMAN, PARTICIPATION AND DEMOCRATIC THEORY 3-4 (1970). Schumpeter urged an extremely limited role for private citizens, primarily that of "accepting or refusing the men who are to rule them." J. SCHUMPETER, *supra*, at 285. It is doubtful that this philosophy is consistent with Professor Blasi's view that private citizens have authority to determine for themselves what actions of public officials constitute misconduct. Blasi, *supra* note 2, at 543.

Blasi is probably much closer to Meiklejohn than he is to Schumpeter, for essential to Meiklejohn's philosophy was the belief that "[a] government of free men can properly be controlled only by itself. Who else could be trusted by us to hold our political institutions in check?" A. MEIKLEJOHN, *supra* note 8, at 16. Although Meiklejohn believed that the people were truly the "governors" and that elected officials were merely their agents, he did not advocate a system of direct democracy. Rather, he believed that citizens needed information and opinion, so that they could better perform their governing function *in the voting booth.* Meiklejohn, *supra* note 11, at 255-56.

Blasi asserts that "[t]he self-government value [of Meiklejohn] appears to place slightly more emphasis on argumentation (as contrasted with information) than does the checking value." Blasi, *supra* note 2, at 563. However, if Blasi believes that the activities of antiwar protestors (including draft card burning) constitute a classic example of how the checking function operates, *see id.* at 554, it is difficult to accept his information-opinion distinction. For were not the primary activities of the antiwar movement more a matter of expressing opinion than of conveying information?

145. *See supra* text accompanying notes 50-68.
146. Blasi expends considerable effort in an attempt to establish a historical link between the checking value and the origins of the first amendment. Blasi, *supra* note 2, at 529-38. But most of the historical sources to which he refers were concerned primarily with ensuring the liberty of citizens — the intrinsic democratic value — and saw the checking of government not as an end in itself or as a means of assuring "better results," but as a means of assuring that government would not interfere with the individual's exercise of his liberty.

competition of the market. ... That at any rate is the theory of our Constitution."[147] The theory, derived originally from John Stuart Mill,[148] posits, in the accurate description of one of its critics, that:

> [C]ompetition among ideas strengthens the truth and roots out error; the repeated effort to defend one's convictions serves to keep their justification alive in our minds and guards against the twin dangers of falsehood and fanaticism; to stifle a voice is to deprive mankind of its message, which, we must acknowledge, might possibly be more true than our own deeply held convictions .... Just as an unfettered competition among commodities guarantees that the good products sell while the bad gather dust on the shelf, so in the intellectual marketplace the several competing ideas will be tested by us, the consumers, and the best of them will be purchased.[149]

The "marketplace-of-ideas" concept, in its use as a defense of free speech, has often been subjected to savage attack,[150] and to a certain extent the attacks have been entirely valid. In one sense, the theory appears to suffer from an internal contradiction: the theory's goal is the attainment of truth, yet it posits that we can never really know the truth,[151] so we must keep looking. But, if we can never attain the truth, why bother to continue the fruitless search? More importantly, any theory positing that the value of free speech is the search for truth creates a great danger that someone will decide that he finally has attained knowledge of the truth. At that point, that individual (or society) may feel fully justified, as a matter of both morality and logic, in shutting off expression of any views that are contrary to this "truth." To be sure, Mill would not have accepted such reasoning. He believed that even views that we know to be false deserve protection, because their expression makes the truth appear even stronger by contrast.[152] But acceptance of Mill's initial premise that the goal of free speech is

---

147. Abrams v. United States, 250 U.S. 616, 630 (1919) (Holmes, J., dissenting).

148. J. MILL, *supra* note 51. According to Professor Baker, Mill provides the "marketplace-of-ideas" theory's "best formulation." Baker, *supra* note 15, at 968 n.9; *see also* R. WOLFF, THE POVERTY OF LIBERALISM 11-12 (1968).

149. R. WOLFF, *supra* note 148, at 11-12; *see also* Baker, *supra* note 15, at 967.

150. *See, e.g.,* R. WOLFF, *supra* note 89, at 12-19; Baker, *supra* note 15, at 974-81. According to Professor Dworkin, "John Stuart Mill's famous essay *On Liberty* has on the whole served conservatives better than liberals .... [C]ritics of liberalism have been pleased to cite the essay as the most cogent philosophical defense of that theory, and then, by noticing the defects in its argument, argue that liberalism is flawed." R. DWORKIN, TAKING RIGHTS SERIOUSLY 259 (1977).

151. *See* I. BERLIN, *supra* note 54, at 188 ("[Mill's] argument is plausible only on the assumption ... that human knowledge was in principle never complete, and always fallible; that there was no single, universally visible, truth ....").

152. J. MILL, *supra* note 51, at 34-45.

the ultimate attainment of truth does not necessitate acceptance of this second premise. For, as Dean Wellington has argued, "[i]t is naive to think that truth will *always* prevail over falsehood in a free and open encounter, for too many false ideas have captured the imagination of man."[153] Therefore, if the only value of free speech were the attainment of truth, we might persuasively argue that the view that the Earth is the center of the Universe does not deserve constitutional protection, because we know the truth to be different. Perhaps we could further conclude that constitutional protection should not be given to the assertion that cigarette smoking does not cause cancer, because the Surgeon General has already discovered the truth about this subject; the same could be said about the view that certain races are genetically inferior, since we know that all men are created equal. The danger — one that Mill would undoubtedly neither expect nor condone — should by now be clear.

It does not necessarily follow, however, that the marketplace-of-ideas concept must be discarded. To the contrary: if viewed as merely a means by which the ultimate value of self-realization is facilitated, the concept may prove quite valuable in determining what speech is deserving of constitutional protection. In other words, it could be argued that, if the intrinsic aspect of the self-realization value[154] is to be maintained, the individual needs an uninhibited flow of information and opinion to aid him or her in making life-affecting decisions, in governing his or her own life. Since the concept of self-realization by its very nature does not permit external forces to determine what is a wise decision for the individual to make, it is no more appropriate for external forces to censor what information or opinion the individual may receive in reaching those decisions. Thus, an individual presumably has the right[155] not to associate with people of different races in the privacy of his home, and may decide to exercise that right because he believes those who contend other races are genetically inferior.[156] That is his choice, and he may reach it on whatever basis he

---

153. Wellington, *supra* note 48, at 1130 (emphasis in original). *See also* I. BERLIN, *supra* note 54, at 187.

154. *See supra* text following note 49.

155. In using the term "right" in this context, I do not intend to limit its meaning to a constitutional, or even a statutory right, although in certain instances it could conceivably be either of these. I mean, rather, the absence of a governmental prohibition.

156. An individual of course would not be allowed to decide on the basis of this information to kill members of these races, or to refuse to associate with them in public accommodations. These are situations in which society has decided to limit the individual's freedom of action.

chooses, no matter how irrational it may seem to others. Because individuals constantly make life-affecting decisions — from the significant to the trivial — each day of their lives, there is probably no expression of opinion or information that would not potentially affect some such decision at some point in time. Therefore, the marketplace-of-ideas concept as a protector of all such expression makes perfect sense.[157]

So revised, the marketplace-of-ideas concept can be successfully defended against another attack: Baker's contentions that the theory "requires that people be able to use their rational capacities to eliminate distortion caused by the form and frequency of message presentation and to find the core of relevant information or argument," and that "[t]his assumption cannot be accepted [because e]motional or 'irrational' appeals have great impact."[158] If we accepted the attainment of truth as the theory's goal, Professor Baker's point would be well taken. But the point becomes irrelevant if we instead view the theory simply as a means of facilitating the value of self-realization. For if an individual wishes to buy a car because he believes it will make him look masculine, or to vote for a candidate because the candidate looks good with his tie loosened and his jacket slung over his shoulder, who are we to tell him that these are improper acts? We may prefer that he make his judgments (at least as to the candidate, if not the car) on more traditionally "rational" grounds, and hope that appeals made on such grounds will be heard. But in these areas society has left the ultimate right to decide to the individual, and this would not be much of a right if we prescribed how it was to be used.[159]

---

157. Although I will deal with the point in detail in subsequent discussion, *see infra* at 52-55, it is perhaps necessary to emphasize here that I am referring only to the issue of what speech rightfully belongs within the first amendment's umbrella of constitutional protection. Since I am not a believer in construing the first amendment to provide absolute protection to speech, the conclusion that speech falls within the first amendment does not necessarily imply that it will outbalance all competing social concerns.

158. Baker, *supra* note 15, at 976. According to Baker, "[t]he assumptions on which the classic marketplace of ideas theory rests are almost universally rejected today." *Id.* at 974. However, there may be some inconsistency in Baker's analysis. On the one hand, he attacks the marketplace-of-ideas concept because it is premised on a presumption of individual rationality that is unrealistic. Yet Baker's own theory of free speech is based on the view that individuals must be respected as "equal, *rational* and autonomous moral beings." *Id.* at 991 (emphasis added). He rejects limitations on free speech that are designed "to protect people from harms that result because the listener adopts certain perceptions or attitudes," because to do so "disrespects the responsibility and freedom of the listener." *Id.* at 998.

159. It might be argued that the marketplace-of-ideas theory is unrealistic in

C. The "Liberty" Model

Although Professor Baker's primary attack on the marketplace-of-ideas theory is premised on the inability of the system to produce rational results, the essential elements of his own theory of free expression, if accepted, logically lead to a rejection of even the revised version described here. Professor Baker adopts as the center of his theory of free speech the "liberty model,"[160] under which respect for individual autonomy leads us to protect communication that defines, develops, or expresses "the self."[161] "[T]he values supported or functions performed by protected speech," he writes, "result from that speech being a manifestation of individual freedom and choice."[162] Therefore, he concludes, speech that "does not represent an attempt to create or affect the world in a way which can be expected to represent anyone's private or personal wishes" is not deserving of constitutional protection.[163] It is for this reason that Baker would give no constitutional protection to commercial speech.[164] Because there is presumably a considerable amount of information or opinion flowing to individuals from corporations and others who are motivated by economic considerations, Baker would not be likely to accept even the revised rationale for the marketplace-of-ideas theory. Although Baker correctly recognizes the self-realization value lying behind the protection given free speech, he has so narrowly confined this concept

---

assuming that, absent government regulation, individual decisionmakers will receive an unbiased flow of information because certain groups, holding particular viewpoints, control the media and exclude unpopular opinions from the information stream. Many who have recognized this difficulty have urged increased right of access to the communications media. *See, e.g.,* Red Lion Broadcasting Co. v. FCC, 395 U.S. 367 (1969); Barron, *Access to the Press — A New First Amendment Right,* 80 HARV. L. REV. 1641 (1967). Such an access theory faces serious constitutional questions itself, see Miami Hearld Publishing Co. v. Tornillo, 418 U.S. 241 (1974), but, at least under certain circumstances, provides an answer to this criticism. In any event, even if this criticism were accepted, it does not imply that the marketplace-of-ideas theory is useless, but merely that it is not perfect. Thus, this argument offers no support for any efforts to further impede the flow of information.

160. Baker, *supra* note 15, at 990.
161. *Id.* 992.
162. Baker, *Commercial Speech: A Problem in the Theory of Freedom,* 62 IOWA L. REV. 1, 3 (1976) (footnote omitted).
163. *Id.* Baker elsewhere has argued that "if it is not a manifestation of the speaker's values, even though the speech may cause change or advance knowledge, it does not serve this liberty value and is not protected," Baker, *supra* note 15, at 991 n.86, and that "to the extent that speech is involuntary, is not chosen by the speaker, the speech act does not involve the *self*-realization or *self*-fulfillment of the speaker," *id.* at 996 (emphasis in original).
164. Baker, *supra* note 162, at 3.

that he has effectively excluded significant amounts of expression that could substantially foster the self-realization value.

Baker's adoption of an extremely narrow view of how the self-realization value can be fostered apparently results from his acceptance of a truncated version of the value itself. The form of self-realization that he seems to be describing is limited to the "instrumental" value referred to previously: the value of having individuals develop their faculties.[165] Even with this truncated version, Baker has failed to acknowledge that individuals may develop their personal and intellectual faculties by *receiving,* as well as by expressing.[166] Once this is recognized we can see that the motivation of the speaker may be irrelevant, as long as the individual's faculties are developed by the *receipt* of information, whether it be opinion or fact. For example, that an author is writing primarily to make money, rather than to express his personality, does not diminish the potential development of the reader. More important, however, is Baker's refusal to recognize the correlative principle to self-fulfillment's instrumental value: the intrinsic value, self-rule. Thus, if an individual is given the opportunity to control his or her destiny, at least within certain bounds, he or she needs all possible information that might aid in making these life-affecting decisions. Because Baker fails to include this vital aspect of the self-realization concept, he develops a theory of free speech that is correspondingly incomplete.

Even if we were to accept Baker's unduly narrow conception of self-realization, his theory fails to deal adequately with the inseparability of the profit motive from the desire for self-expression. The problem arises because many people make a living by means of self-expressive work. Should the creative advertiser or commercial artist not be

---

165. Baker notes that, "[o]n the liberty theory, the purpose of the first amendment is not to guarantee adequate information." Baker, *supra* note 15, at 1007. He also writes, however, that "[s]elf-expressive and creative uses of speech more fully and uniformly promote the two key first amendment values, self-fulfillment and participation in both societal decisionmaking and culture building, than does speech which communicates propositions and attitudes." *Id.* at 995 (emphasis omitted).

166. At one point, Baker acknowledges that "[t]he listener uses speech for self-realization or change purposes and these uses provide the basis of the listener's constitutional right." *Id.* at 1007. He adds, however, that "the constitutional analysis of any restriction must be in terms of who is restricted — the speaker or the listener. Both parties have separate constitutional claims. Only if the restricted party does not have a constitutional claim is the government restriction permissible." *Id.* Thus, since Baker does not believe that those motivated by profit incentives, rather than self-expression, have a constitutional right, he must believe that these "speakers" can be constitutionally restricted, even though the listeners' ability to gain fulfillment may well suffer as a result.

recognized for their "self-expression," merely because they are doing it to make money? Baker responds that "even if the speech happens to correspond to the speaker's values, the content is determined by the structure of the market and is not chosen by the speaker."[167] But surely within the dictates of the market structure the advertiser has a range of selection; there is never merely a single possible way to sell a product. Thus, can we can not say that within that range the advertiser has exercised his or her self-expression? Moreover, if we accept Baker's analysis, what protection do we give to the political candidate who tailors his public positions to what he thinks will lead to his election, to the magazine or newspaper that chooses to publish what sells, or to the author who writes what he believes his audience will buy? Are *their* efforts not to receive first amendment protection? And what would Baker say about the level of first amendment protection to be given to welfare or social security recipients who picket to protest insufficient government aids? Is not *their* expression also dictated by the needs of the market?

Baker has responded in detail to the question raised about political candidates. His answer is that:

> First, for many, if not most, political actors' [sic] political activity is not primarily and, more importantly, is not necessarily determined by the need to maximize either electoral support or economic profit .... Thus, no structure requires that the speaker choose increased chances of election (which is not even an option for minor parties) over increased advocacy of their values. Second, unlike the economic sphere ... , many politicians and most defenders of the political process argue that, here, it is highly praiseworthy to truthfully and forcefully state, explain, and advocate one's own visions or understanding of the public good.[168]

Baker provides no statistical support for his first assertion, and it certainly seems counterintuitive to me, at least, to think that most candidates for office do not have election as their primary goal. Nor am I convinced of the accuracy of his second assertion, but even if it were true it is irrelevant. That honesty may be "praiseworthy" does not mean that many candidates actually practice it, no matter how much they may purport to do so. Most importantly, what would Baker do if he could be convinced that ninety-nine percent of candidates were actually motivated more by the desire for election than by the desire to express their values? Would he urge no first amendment protection for their speeches? His logic would seem to lead to that conclusion. Baker's

---

167. *Id.* at 966 n.102.
168. *Id.*

fundamental assumptions thus appear to be both pragmatically unrealistic and theoretically dubious.

Baker has unsuccessfully attempted to respond to my attack on his theoretical structure.[169] His example of the worker whom, Baker suggests, "the market does not compel ... to seek more",[170] even if accurate, is not analogous to the individual who is totally dependent on entitlement programs that have been reduced or eliminated. In such a situation, the content of the individual's expression is as much dictated by "market forces" as is the advertising of a commercial enterprise; the former is no more likely to urge further cuts than the latter is to urge customers to purchase a competitor's product. Yet Baker would not deny protection to the speech of the welfare or social security recipient, as well as should not. He analogizes my example of the creative advertiser to "the pianist who ... has a right to engage in her activity but no right to demand an economic arrangement that pays for her expressive activities."[171] But this comment views the situation in reverse. No one is arguing that the first amendment somehow gives the pianist the right to demand an economic arrangement; the point, rather, is that the mere fact that one has entered into an economic arrangement should not automatically forfeit her — or her listeners' — right of free expression and self-development.

This discussion is designed to underscore the artificiality of the distinction that Baker attempts to draw. But Baker's greatest mistake is his assumption that anything should turn on the distinction, even if it could be drawn. This is because it makes no difference logically what the source of the expression is; whatever the source, the individuals who receive that information can put it to good use in exercising their "self-rule" function.

III. The Self-Realization Value and the Balancing of First Amendment Interests

Professor Blasi writes that:

> The concept of human autonomy is largely irreducible. The libertarian argument from autonomy rests on the proposition that unless individuals retain a basic minimum of choice-making capability, they cease to be "individuals" at all. It is no accident, therefore, that claims based on the value of individual autonomy tend to be absolute in nature; they concern not interests to be promoted against competing regulatory interests but rather

---

169. *See* Baker, *supra* note 70.
170. *Id.* at 672 n.87.
171. *Id.*

constitutive elements the integrity of which must be respected if the whole edifice of constitutional limitations is to remain coherent.[172]

Professor Baker makes a similar point,[173] but it is difficult to understand. The concept of individual autonomy certainly has never been thought to lead to absolute protection for conduct, yet we may still maintain a belief in such an autonomy value. Why should our recognition of something akin to that value as the underlying force behind the protection of speech necessarily lead to any greater degree of absoluteness? There is, then, no logically necessary link between a belief in individual self-realization and a so-called "absolute" construction of the first amendment. In fact, the issue of absoluteness appears to present the same questions and to give rise to the same conflicting arguments, whatever values are thought to be fostered by the free speech guarantee.

It is not my goal here to rehash the competing contentions on this issue, nor to consider the nuances of the various absolutist and balancing-test theories that have been suggested over the years. Those matters are explored elsewhere in this book. The primary goal at this stage has been to delimit the scope of the category of communication and expression that is to fall within the constitutional protection in the first place. But, in light of this suggested logical link, it is necessary to provide at least a brief explanation of why an absolute construction cannot be accepted, even if self-realization is recognized as the ultimate value underlying the first amendment.

The answer is simply that an absolute construction is (1) not required by the language of the amendment, (2) not dictated by the intent of the framers, and (3) impossible in practice. As to the issue of language, the phrase "freedom of speech" is not necessarily the same as "speech," and is certainly not self-defining. As to the intent of the framers, what little evidence there is suggests that, to the extent they thought about it at all, they intended an extremely narrow construction of the first amendment,[174] and certainly not an absolute construction. Finally, I simply refuse to believe that anything in first amendment language or policy requires us to protect the statement of a

---

172. Blasi, *supra* note 2, at 547; *see also* BeVier, *supra* note 12, at 320.
173. Baker, *supra* note 15, at 1009. Note, however, that Baker does not believe in "absolute" protection for speech (even though he does include certain types of conduct within the constitutional guarantee), since he excludes speech dictated by the market structure. *See id.* at 996 & n.102.
174. *See* L. LEVY, *supra* note 27, at 247-48.

mob leader, outside a poorly defended prison, urging his torch-carrying compatriots to lynch a prisoner inside.[175] Once it is acknowledged that the free speech interest must give way in such a situation to a competing social interest, acceptance of at least *some* form of balancing process is established. The question is simply where and how to draw the line.

The concept of balancing gained a bad name among civil libertarians during its heyday in the 1950's, because it was usually used simply as a code word for substituting legislative determinations for judicial review.[176] However, if we define "balancing" to include definitional balancing, as well as the ad hoc variety, we can see that the concept has gained wide acceptance,[177] for any general rule of first amendment interpretation that chooses not to afford absolute protection to speech because of competing social concerns is, in reality, a form of balancing.

---

175. It appears that Professor Baker's construction of the first amendment would protect such expression. Although Baker believes that "[r]espect for individual autonomy hardly requires protection of speech when the listener is coerced," he also asserts that "outlawing acts of the speaker in order to protect people from harms that result because the listener adopts certain perceptions or attitudes disrespects the responsibility and freedom of the listener." Baker, *supra* note 15, at 998. Speech is protected because "it depends for its power on increasing the speaker's own awareness or on the voluntary acceptance of listeners." *Id.* at 999. Because the harm in the lynching hypothetical results from "the voluntary acceptance of listeners," the conclusion seems inescapable that Baker would protect such speech.

176. *See, e.g.,* Frantz, *The First Amendment in the Balance,* 71 YALE L.J. 1424, 1444 (1962) ("[I]t must be regarded as very nearly inevitable that a court which clings to the balancing test will sooner or later adopt a corollary that the balance struck by Congress is not only presumed correct, but is to be accorded extreme, almost total, judicial deference."); Mendelson, *On the Meaning of the First Amendment: Absolutes in the Balance,* 50 CALIF. L. REV. 831, 826 (1962) ("Above all, the open balancing technique is calculated to leave 'the sovereign prerogative of choice' to the people — with the least interference that is compatible with our tradition of judicial review."); *see also* Dennis v. United States, 341 U.S. 494, 525 (1951) (Frankfurter, J., concurring).

177. It is not my purpose here to debate the relative merits of *ad hoc* and definitional balancing (also referred to as "categorization"). *See generally* Ely, *Flag Desecration: A Case Study in the Roles of Categorization and Balancing in First Amendment Analysis,* 88 HARV. L. REV. 1482 (1975); Nimmer, *The Right to Speak From Times to Time: First Amendment Theory Applied to Libel and Misapplied to Privacy,* 56 CALIF. L. REV. 935 (1968). That issue is considered extensively in Chapters II, IV and V. My point is simply that one need not be an absolutist if one relies on self-realization as the ultimate value of free speech. What form of "balancing" one adopts at that stage is beyond this chapter's scope. The only point to be underscored is that, in the broad sense of the term at least, the categorizers, too, are engaged in "balancing," in that they reject an absolutist approach in favor of an analysis that in certain cases allows fully protected speech to be superseded by overriding social interests.

The point, however, is to balance with "a thumb on the scales" in favor of speech.[178] Although the first amendment cannot practically be interpreted to provide absolute protection, the constitutional language and our political and social traditions dictate that the first amendment right must give way only in the presence of a truly compelling governmental interest.[179] To be sure, such an analysis places a good deal of faith in the ability of judges to exercise their authority with wisdom and discretion, both in establishing and applying general rules of first amendment construction, and where necessary,[180] in engaging in *ad hoc* balancing. But, after all, that is what they are there for, and in any event we appear to have little choice.

IV. Acceptance of the Self-Realization Value: Implications for Constitutional Construction

If the self-realization value were accepted as the guiding force behind constitutional protection of free speech, it is likely that the Court's approach to numerous issues of first amendment construction would have to change. Initially the "two-level" concept of speech derived from *Chaplinsky v. New Hampshire*,[181] which recognizes a sublevel of speech that is unworthy of constitutional protection, would have to be abandoned. That doctrine posits that:

> There are certain well-defined and narrowly limited classes of speech, the prevention and punishment of which have never been thought to raise any Constitutional problem. These include the lewd and obscene, the profane, the libelous, and the insulting or "fighting words" — those which by their very utterance inflict injury or tend to incite an immediate breach of peace. It has been well observed that such utterances are no essential part of any exposition of ideas, and are of such slight social value as a step to truth that any benefit that may be derived from them is clearly outweighed by the social interest in order and morality.[182]

The theoretical fallacy in the *Chaplinsky* doctrine is the assumption that the value of free speech is as a means to attain truth. Once one recognizes that the primary value of free speech is as a means of fostering individual development and aiding the making of life-

---

178. Frantz acknowledges that "it is conceivable that a court might apply the balancing test, yet attach so high a value to freedom of speech that the balance would nearly always be struck in its favor." Frantz, *supra* note 176, at 1440.
179. I discuss the application of a "compelling interest test" as a measure of free speech protection in Chapter II *infra* at 117-26.
180. *See* Chapter II, *infra* at 119-20.
181. 315 U.S. 568 (1942); *see also* Beuharnais v. Illinois, 343 U.S. 250 (1952).
182. 315 U.S. at 571-72 (footnotes omitted).

affecting decisions, the inappropriateness of distinguishing between the value of different types of speech becomes clear. Although subsequent sections[183] deal explicitly with the categories of libel and obscenity to which the Court referred in *Chaplinsky,* the doctrine's problems can be seen clearly in its application to the type of speech actually at issue in that case: "fighting words."

In *Chaplinsky,* a Jehovah's Witness distributing literature was involved in a disturbance and was taken into police custody. On the way to the police station, he confronted the City Marshall and allegedly called him "a God damned racketeer" and "a damned Fascist."[184] He was convicted pursuant to a state statute that made it an offense to address "any offensive, derisive or annoying word to any other person who is lawfully in any street or other public place."[185] Why not view Chaplinsky's comments as a personal catharsis, as a means to vent his frustration at a system he deemed — whether rightly or wrongly — to be oppressive? Is it not a mark of individuality to be able to attack a society viewed as oppressing the individual? Under this analysis, so-called "fighting words" represent a significant means of self-realization, whether or not they can be considered a means of attaining some elusive "truth."

This is not to suggest that fighting words should receive absolute protection, any more than any other form of expression deserves such a guarantee of freedom.[186] The point, rather, is that fighting words should not be deemed constitutionally regulable per se. If, in particular circumstances, such words are likely to have the effect of starting a riot or significantly and immediately disturbing the peace, their use can of course be subjected to penalty. But in *Chaplinsky* itself no such showing was even attempted, and, given the facts, it is unlikely that one could have been made. For the words were not spoken to militant armed opponents of Jehovah's Witnesses in the street, but to an apparently oversensitive city official on the way to the police station. Other than a slight ruffling of the official's feathers, Mr. Chaplinsky's colorful language did not cause any harm. Hence, if the Court had recognized the legitimate first amendment value in the use of such language, it would have been required to engage in a careful weighing of competing interests, an endeavor it seemingly found not to be worth the effort.

---

183. *See* discussion *infra* at 76-81, 68-76.
184. 315 U.S. at 569.
185. *Id.*
186. *See* discussion *supra* at 52-55.

The discussion of the level of constitutional protection to be given so-called "fighting words" raises a broader issue: whether there is *any* form of pure expression that does not foster self-realization, and that therefore is not worthy of first amendment protection. In answering this question, it is necessary to recall the two different aspects of self-realization: self-governance and the development of one's human faculties.[187] As to the former, there is clearly a wide variety of speech that is irrelevant, for this branch of the self-realization value is furthered only by expression that provides information or opinion that will aid an individual in making decisions about how his or her life will be conducted. Thus, advocacy of unlawful conduct cannot be deemed relevant, because the individual is not allowed to undertake the conduct urged by that form of expression. Nor is the dissemination of undisputedly false factual information a valid means of aiding private self-government, since such information cannot be thought to provide legitimate guidance to individual decisionmaking.[188] A mere stream of obscenities must also be deemed irrelevant to the goal of private self-government.

There is more to self-realization, however, than private self-government. For it is highly doubtful that fine art, ballet, or literature can be thought to aid one in making concrete life-affecting decisions, yet all three seem deserving of full first amendment protection. This is because of the other branch of self-realization: the development of one's human faculties, recognized as an end in itself. Once this form of self-realization is acknowledged, it becomes significantly more difficult to exclude many of the categories of expression deemed irrelevant to the private self-government branch.

Of course, we might conclude that, whereas art, literature, and ballet are proper means of developing one's mental faculties, a mere stream of obscenities or advocacy of crime is not. But, although it may well be appropriate to distinguish among different forms of expression on the ground that some of them present greater danger of harming society,[189] it is considerably more doubtful that an arm of the state should have the authority to decide for the individual that certain means of mental development are better than others. If two consenting

---

187. *See* discussion *supra* at 21-22.

188. There may still be a problem about suppressing certain false factual assertions, because of the potential chilling effect on expression of true factual statements. *See* New York Times Co. v. Sullivan, 376 U.S. 254 (1964).

189. *See* discussion *supra* at 52-55.

individuals wish to engage in a conversation consisting of little more than a stream of obscenities, assuming no harm to others,[190] it is dangerous to provide the state with the power to prohibit such activity on the ground that such discourse is not "valuable."[191] For, if the state can make that decision, what is logically to prevent it from deciding that the works of Henry Miller are not "valuable" because of their constant use of obscenities? Or why could not the state similarly set up an administrative board to decide that certain works of literature, art, dance, or music are not as "valuable" as others, and can therefore be suppressed? Most of us would no doubt find such a process intuitively repugnant, presumably even if we agreed with the censor about the lack of quality of a particular book, movie, or performance. We would explain this feeling of repugnance, I suppose, by reasoning that it is simply not the state's business to decide for each individual what books, movies, or shows are "valuable"; that is a decision for the individual to make for himself or herself. But once we have gone that far, how could we rationally distinguish the stream of obscenities between consenting adults? There, too, we would have to reason that perhaps that particular form of discourse is not our cup of tea, but that this gives the state no more inherent right to suppress it than it would have to suppress a particular book or movie we found distasteful. A stream of obscenities may not develop one's *intellectual* abilities (though it could conceivably increase one's vocabulary), but neither does music, art, or dance. An individual's "mental" processes cannot be limited to the receipt and digestion of cold, hard theories and facts, for there is also an emotional element that is uniquely human and that can be "developed" by such "non-rational" forms of communication. Perhaps a protectionist reading this who still feels awkward about bringing the stream of obscenities within the bounds of the first amendment should simply transform the hypothetical into a Lenny Bruce- or George Carlin-type comedian,[192] who at various points in his act employs a string of obscenities. I would imagine that a protectionist would be most uncomfortable in totally excluding such expression from

---

190. Even if a "stream of obscenities" were fully protected by the first amendment, legitimate "time, place, and manner" regulations could be imposed. For example, it would probably be legitimate to prohibit such a discussion on a public street corner, unless the people talking could establish somehow that it was essential that their discussion take place at that location.

191. *Cf.* Cohen v. California, 403 U.S. 15 (1971) (state cannot prohibit display of "Fuck the Draft" on a jacket, because it is the individual's choice how to convey his substantive message).

192. *Cf.* FCC v. Pacifica Found., 438 U.S. 726 (1978) (regulation of broadcast of George Carlin's "Filthy Words" monologue).

the first amendment. A conversation between consenting individuals composed exclusively of obscenities raises no additional problems.

A possible response to this line of argument is that governmental judgment of the relative value of various types of thought is a commonly-accepted practice in schools, where agents of the government — whether they be board of education members, school administrators, or teachers — make countless judgments of this type every day, simply by deciding what books or theories to teach and which not to teach, and in public libraries, where government agents choose which books are worthy of purchase. While of course such practices are well accepted, they really do not undermine my broad conclusion that governmental gradations of first amendment protection on the basis of the relative value of communications is repugnant to our system. Initially, in regard to the example of schools, it has long been accepted that the first amendment rights of children are on a level lower than of adults. Such a principle is not necessarily inconsistent with the theory developed here, since common sense and experience dictate that the individual's intellectual processes must undergo some form of maturation process in the early years of life. Secondly, the ability of governmental agents to make such judgments in preparation of school curricula may be justified by the obvious compelling interest that *somebody* has to make these judgments if the educational process is not to be reduced to chaos. A similar point could be made about library acquisitions. Thirdly, despite these obvious differences between the school setting and other situations, it is highly doubtful that a school board would be constitutionally authorized to prohibit the teaching of communism in the public schools, or to require that teachers state that Republicans are smarter than Democrats. Even in the school context, then, the courts would quite probably impose outer limitations on the extent of school officials' authority to impose intellectual orthodoxy on students. Similarly, it is doubtful that a public librarian could constitutionally refuse to purchase any books taking an ideological position with which he or she disagrees. Finally, it is difficult to imagine that even one who rejected the self-realization theory developed here would accept the conclusion that governmental authority to make value judgments on different types of thought in the school or public library contexts logically leads to a similar authority to control the shelves of bookstores and private libraries.

There may, of course, be some forms of expression that could be thought to fall beyond the outer fringes of even this relaxed realm of faculty development. A "primal scream," at least if not used to communicate a need for help, might be thought to be so lacking in communicative value as to fall outside the range of self-realization in the sense contemplated by the first amendment. But such a purely academic question[193] need not detain us for long. For however the question is ultimately answered, both the courts and the commentators are a long way from the primal scream in their unduly narrow classification of expression deserving of full first amendment protection.[194]

Some might deem it the height of absurdity to equate the value of a stream of obscenities with great literature or eloquent political discourse. But, of course, not all literature or political discourse is of such a high order. There is much political speech that many of us find nonsensical, stupid, vile, and repulsive, yet we take it as given that we cannot gradate first amendment protection on the basis of how vile or stupid a court or legislature finds the particular political expression to be.[195] The same holds true for literature, at least outside of the realm of obscenity. Again, the reason presumably is that we have construed the first amendment to leave to the individual final say as to how valuable the particular expression is.

This broad discussion has been designed to demonstrate how constitutional analysis should be generally altered to reflect acceptance of the self-realization value as the guiding philosophy of the first amendment. The following discussions are designed to indicate the specific alterations needed in three important areas of first amendment application: commercial speech, obscenity, and defamation.

A. Commercial Speech

The impact of the self-realization value on the protection to be given commercial speech is not difficult to determine. My comment on the issue some thirteen years ago is, I believe equally applicable today:

> When the individual is presented with rational grounds for preferring one product or brand over another, he is encouraged to consider the competing information, weigh it mentally in the light of the goals of personal satisfaction he has set for himself, counterbalance his conclusions with possible price differentials, and in so

---

193. The issue is largely academic, because it is difficult to conceive of a reason why the state would have an interest in regulating a primal scream other than in the form of traditionally accepted time, place, and manner regulations, which could be employed even if the actual speech were fully protected by the first amendment. *Cf.* Kovacs v. Cooper, 336 U.S. 77 (1949) (upholding neutral limits on the use of sound trucks).

194. *See* discussion *supra* at 14-19; 41-55.

195. *See* Police Dep't v. Mosley, 408 U.S. 92, 95 (1972) ("[A]bove all else, the First Amendment means that government has no power to restrict expression because of its message, its ideas, its subject matter, or its content.").

doing exercise his abilities to reason and think; this aids him towards the intangible goal of rational self-fulfillment.[196]

To this should be added that information and opinion about competing commercial products and services undoubtedly aid the individual in making countless life-affecting decisions, and therefore can be seen as fostering both elements of the self-realization value.[197]

Although the Supreme Court for many years casually dismissed even the most minimal level of constitutional protection for commercial speech,[198] in 1976 the Court finally recognized this form of expression as falling within the constitutional guarantee, in *Virginia State Board of Pharmacy v. Virginia Citizens Consumer Council, Inc.*[199] The Court's analysis in reaching this conclusion, however, contained the seeds of its own destruction. It is therefore not surprising that only a few years later commercial speech is perhaps only marginally better off than it was in the years prior to *Virginia Board*.[200]

In *Virginia Board,* the Court advanced two grounds for providing constitutional protection to commercial speech, neither of which represented recognition of a true first amendment value in that form of expression. The first was more a concrete economic consideration than a first amendment value. The case concerned a prohibition on advertising of prescription drug prices, and the Court noted that "[t]hose whom the suppression of prescription drug price information hits the hardest are the poor, the sick, and particularly the aged."[201]

---

196. Redish, *supra* note 34, at 443-44.

197. In my earlier writing, I argued that commercial advertising that conveys significant factual information that will be of real service to the consumer should perhaps receive greater constitutional protection than its more "persuasional" counterpart. *Id.* at 447. Under the analysis developed in this chapter, however, such a distinction is unacceptable. Recognition of the individual's unencumbered right to make life-affecting decisions logically precludes the determination by external forces that certain grounds upon which to make such decisions are better than or preferable to others.

198. *See, e.g.,* Valentine v. Chrestensen, 316 U.S. 52, 54 (1942). For a discussion of the early history of the commercial speech doctrine, see Rotunda, *The Commercial Speech Doctrine in the Supreme Court,* 1976 U. ILL. L.F. 1080; *see also* Redish, *supra* note 34, at 448-58.

199. 425 U.S. 748 (1976).

200. *See, e.g.,* Friedman v. Rogers, 440 U.S. 1 (1979); Ohralik v. Ohio State Bar Ass'n, 436 U.S. 447 (1978). Occasionally, however, the Court does still provide a significant degree of constitutional protection to commercial speech. *See* Carey v. Population Servs. Int'l, 431 U.S. 678 (1977); Linmark Assocs., Inc. v. Willingboro, 431 U.S. 85 (1977).

201. 425 U.S. at 763.

Information as to drug prices "could mean the alleviation of physical pain or the enjoyment of basic necessities."[202] Because of its focus on the immediate material benefits that flow from commercial advertising and on how governmental regulation impedes such benefits, the Court's analysis seems closer to the logic of the economic due process cases than it does to traditional first amendment doctrine.[203]

The second ground recognized by the Court was an indirect benefit of commercial speech: "Even an individual advertisement, though entirely 'commercial,' may be of general public interest."[204] The pharmacist affected by *Virginia Board*, for example, "could cast himself as a commentator on store-to-store disparities in drug prices, giving his own and those of a competitor as proof."[205] Advertising might well be "indispensable to the formation of intelligent opinions as to how that system ought to be regulated."[206] The primary first amendment value of commercial speech, in other words, is that it will lead individuals to think about not merely what purchasing decisions are personally best for them, but also about what level of political regulation of the economic system would be appropriate. The Court appeared unwilling to acknowledge that commercial speech might benefit individuals in the exact same ways that political speech does: by developing their individual faculties and aiding them in making life-affecting decisions.

Because it selected indirect and diluted first amendment values to rationalize protection of commerical speech in *Virginia Board*, the

---

202. *Id.* at 764. The Court stated also that:

> Advertising, however tasteless and excessive it sometimes may seem, is nonetheless dissemination of information as to who is producing and selling what product, for what reason, and at what price. So long as we preserve a predominantly free enterprise economy, the allocation of our resources in large measure will be made through numerous private economic decisions. It is a matter of public interest that those decisions, in the aggregate, be intelligent and well informed.

Id. at 765.

203. *See* Comment, *First Amendment Protection for Commercial Advertising: The New Constitutional Doctrine*, 44 U. CHI. L. REV. 205, 216 n.75 (1976) ("The Court's ruling that the microeconomic functions performed by commercial speech constitute interests protected by the first amendment is a novel addition to the list of interests traditionally thought to have first amendment protection. ... [T]he Court's recognition of resource allocation as a constitutionally protected interest, at least when 'speech' is involved, portends a partial return to *Lockner's* [sic] substantive due process review of business regulation.").

204. 425 U.S. at 764.
205. *Id.* at 764-65.
206. *Id.* at 765.

Court was conveniently able in subsequent decisions to afford "commercial speech a limited measure of protection, commensurate with its subordinate position in the scale of First Amendment values," while allowing modes of regulation that might be impermissible in the realm of noncommercial expression.[207] Thus, the Court has felt free to allow regulation of commercial speech when it is shown merely that damage "may" occur,[208] or that harm is "likely,"[209] or that there is a "possibility" of harm.[210] These standards are clearly unacceptable in virtually any other area of first amendment application. Recognition that protection of commercial and political speech derives from the same ultimate value — as well as that they are equally capable of causing serious harm — would have led the Court to provide them with a comparable level of constitutional protection.

The difficulty that gave the Court the greatest trouble in providing even the slightest degree of protection to commercial speech was the regulation of false and misleading advertising. The Court in *Virginia Board* suggested two bases on which to distinguish commercial speech from other forms of expression in order to validate such regulation: that "[t]he truth of commercial speech ... may be more easily verifiable by its disseminator than ... news reporting or political commentary,"[211] and that, "[s]ince advertising is the *sine qua non* of commercial profits, there is little likelihood of its being chilled by proper regulation."[212] To these reasons, Justice Stewart, concurring, added that commercial advertisers do not suffer from the burdens of "the press, which must often attempt to assemble the true facts from sketchy and sometimes conflicting sources under the pressure of publication deadlines."[213]

To the extent that these assertions are accurate, they may properly influence first amendment analysis under the theoretical constructs established in this chapter. For they are distinctions premised not on a difference in the relative values of different categories of expression, but rather on regulation's differing *effects* on these types of expression. There are serious reasons, though, for doubting the accuracy of the Court's suggested distinctions.

---

207. Ohralik v. Ohio State Bar Ass'n, 436 U.S. 447, 456 (1978).
208. *Id.* at 457.
209. *Id.* at 464.
210. Friedman v. Rogers, 440 U.S. 1, 13 (1979). See also the diluted standard of protection outlined in Central Hudson Gas & Elec. Corp. v. Public Serv. Comm'n, 447 U.S. 557, 564 (1980).
211. 425 U.S. at 772 n.24.
212. *Id.*
213. *Id.* at 777 (Stewart, J., concurring).

First, it is questionable whether, in general, the truth of commercial claims is more easily verifiable than the truth of political assertions. The Court's contention that "[u]nder the First Amendment there is no such thing as a false idea"[214] is correct if one is comparing statements of political ideology with commercial assertions. But many statements made in the course of political debate — particularly by the press — are simply assertions of fact, which are presumably verifiable. Moreover, it must be recalled that many claims about commercial products are, in reality, assertions of scientific fact, since many commerical products are chemical compounds or physical devices that may or may not perform the functions or have the effects claimed for them by scientists. If a consumer organization is constitutionally protected in asserting that a certain product does not do what is claimed, why should the product's manufacturer not be similarly protected in contending that it does?[215]

Second, it is also incorrect to distinguish commercial from political expression on the ground that the former is somehow hardier because of the inherent profit motive. It could just as easily be said that we need not fear that commercial magazines and newspapers will cease publication for fear of governmental regulation, because they are in business for profit. Of course, the proper response to this contention is that our concern in not *whether* they will publish, but *what* they will publish: fear of regulation might deter them from dealing with controversial subjects. But the same could be said of the commercial advertiser. The possibility of regulation would not deter him entirely from advertising, but it might deter him from making certain controversial claims for his product.

Finally, the argument concerning deadline pressure is similarly not accurate in all cases. For stories of long-range interest or for some infrequently published journals, the deadline pressure is not great. For some advertisers who are attempting to defeat a competitor or to gain first entry into a new market, timing may be critical. Time pressure is relevant to deciding the reasonableness of an assertion that later proves to have been inaccurate, whether made by an advertiser or by the press. It appears irrelevant, however, to a general attempt to distinguish the two.

It does not necessarily follow, however, that false or misleading advertising must go unregulated. Even in the area of commentary on

---

214. Gertz v. Robert Welch, Inc., 418 U.S. 323, 339 (1974).

215. One possible distinction is the speaker's motivation, as in Professor Baker's theory; however, as noted previously, this argument does not hold up under proper analysis. *See* discussion *supra* at 49-52.

the conduct of public officials, which is considered by many to be of central importance to first amendment values,[216] the Supreme Court has recognized that consciously false assertions may constitutionally be punished as libelous.[217] It would not undermine recognition of the full first amendment value of commercial speech, then, to allow regulation of consciously false or misleading assertions about commercial products or services. Of course, under this analysis, the infliction of a penalty could only be justified by a showing that such assertions were consciously or recklessly false, but it is unlikely that this requirement would preclude the bulk of existing regulation. If the regulation were limited to a cessation of the advertising, rather than imposition of a penalty for past conduct, it is possible that the danger of a chilling effect would be sufficiently reduced to justify regulation even absent a showing of knowledge or intent.

It is even conceivable that differences would remain under this approach in the levels of constitutional protection given commercial and political speech. We might reject automatically the existence of a governmental board to review each political speech or newspaper article and to censor those found to be misleading. But, again, the difference appears to derive not from a difference in the relative values of the forms of expression, but from the relative dangers of regulation. We presumably find such regulation in the political process so abhorent not because we wish to condone misleading political claims, but rather because of the dangers inherent in allowing the government to regulate on the basis of the misleading nature of assertions made in the political process. The fear is that those in power will use such authority as a weapon with which to intimidate or defeat the political opposition, a result that has been all too common in our political history. For, in the words of the noted social commentator, Bret Maverick, "the dealer always cheats."[218] In contrast, there is no reason to believe that much regulation of misleading advertising is similarly motivated.

Even though this analysis may justify many forms of governmental regulation of false and misleading advertising, it does not support attempts to draw additional distinctions between commercial and other forms of expression.[219] Although regulation and free expression

---

216. *See* Kalven, *The New York Times Case: A Note on "The Central Meaning of the First Amendment,"* 1964 SUP. CT. REV. 191; *see also* discussion *supra* at 14-18.

217. New York Times Co. v. Sullivan, 376 U.S. 254, 279-80 (1964).

218. As quoted in J. ROCHE, *supra* note 54, at 130.

219. *Compare* Ohralik v. Ohio State Bar Ass'n, 436 U.S. 447 (1978) *with* In re Primus, 436 U.S. 412 (1978).

Of course, it might be argued that the suspect nature of *any* regulation of political

must be carefully balanced, if balancing leads to different levels of regulation for different forms of speech, it cannot be because some forms are deemed to be more valuable than others.

In an often cited article,[220] Professors Jackson and Jeffries summarily conclude that commercial speech is beneath all first amendment concern. They assert that

> The first amendment guarantee of freedom of speech and press protects only certain identifiable values. Chief among them is effective self-government. Additionally, the first amendment may protect the opportunity for individual self-fulfillment through free expression. Neither value is implicated by governmental regulation of commercial speech.[221]

Perhaps the most serious flaw in the Jackson-Jeffries analysis is their extremely limited, unambitious approach to the study of first amendment values. They openly acknowledge that "[d]erivation of general principles for protecting the freedom of speech far exceeds the ambition of this piece."[222] This failure has precluded them from grasping that both political and commercial speech may serve the same life-directing function. One does so for society, the other does so for the individual in controlling his or her life, but, as I have argued, ultimately the same value is at work.

At no point do Jackson and Jeffries ever attempt to respond to this form of argument. Instead, they rely on the conceptually unsatisfying postulate that "the irrelevance of commercial speech to the political speech principle is a mere truism, at least from the speaker's standpoint, because 'commercial speech' is defined in part by the absence of political significance."[223] Once again, their argument fails because of its limited scope. Because they never consider why we wish to protect political speech in the first place, they are reduced to reliance on empty linguistic distinctions and circular reasoning. Such a narrow

---

expression justifies providing greater protection to all political speech. But the suspect nature of the regulation of political speech is most acute when imposed during the course of a political campaign and on such vague grounds as the misleading nature of the expression. More importantly, whereas the presence of an improper legislative motive for a regulation of speech will justify a finding of unconstitutionality, it in no way follows that legislative or administrative good faith automatically justifies regulation of speech. *See generally* Chapter II *infra* at 102-14.

220. Jackson & Jeffries, *Commercial Speech: Economic Due Process and the First Amendment,* 65 VA. L. REV. 1 (1979).

221. *Id.* at 7-8.

222. *Id.* at 9.

223. *Id.* at 15 (footnote omitted).

theoretical focus is most unhelpful to the development of first amendment analysis.

Even more dubious is their logic in concluding that "commercial speech has no apparent connection with the idea of individual self-fulfillment."[224] To support this conclusion, Jackson and Jeffries simply assert that "[w]hatever else it may mean, the concept of a first amendment right of personal autonomy in matters of belief and expression stops short of a seller hawking his wares."[225] This statement effectively replaces reason with rhetoric. They never consider whether commercial speech may help an individual make important life-affecting decisions and thus function as a catalyst in the fulfillment of the individual's personal goals; they never consider whether commercial speech may help develop the individual's intellectual capacities by aiding the personal decisionmaking process; they never consider whether commercial speech may constitute an exercise of the advertiser's intellectual or artistic creative powers. Instead, they support their assertion merely by noting that "Professor Emerson himself asserts that commercial soliciting and similar activities 'fall within the system of commercial enterprise and are outside the system of freedom of expression.'"[226] Their choice of wording seems to imply that we should somehow consider their reference to Emerson's rejection of first amendment protection for commercial speech to be dispositive. But Emerson's statement is no less conclusory than is the original assertion of Jackson and Jeffries on the issue. It is therefore difficult to understand why this blind appeal to supposedly higher scholarly authority is supposed to substitute for even the feeblest attempt at logic or reason.

Jackson and Jeffries also point to the failure of the Court in *Virginia Board* to rely on a self-fulfillment theory to support its decision to protect commercial speech.[227] But as already noted, the Court's reasoning in that decision was substantially less than compelling. To be sure, the Court concluded that "the advertiser's interest is a purely economic one."[228] But neither the Court nor Jackson and Jeffries even attempt to explain why a creative advertiser is to be distinguished from a newspaper publisher or professional author or artist or pianist — all of whom are not disqualified from first amendment protection because of their substantial economic motivation. Jackson and Jeffries

---

224. *Id.* at 14.
225. *Id.*
226. *Id.*
227. *Id.* at 14-15.
228. 425 U.S. at 762.

correctly note that the Court in *Virginia Board* "reconstituted the [substantive due process] values of *Lochner v. New York* as components of free speech,"[229] but they fail to recognize that this fact merely underscores the inadequacy of the Court's logic; it in no way undermines the ultimate conclusion that commercial speech is deserving of first amendment protection.

B. Obscenity

In light of the significant amount of existing scholarship on the subject,[230] it is neither necessary nor advisable to engage in an extended commentary on the various doctrines of obscenity regulation that have pervaded Supreme Court opinions over the last twenty-five years.[231] Instead, this critique will examine the rationales offered for the Court's total exclusion of obscenity from the first amendment in the light of the theoretical analysis of free speech adopted here. For whatever difficulties the Court may face in defining obscenity, it continues to exclude obscenity from any constitutional protection.

---

229. Jackson & Jeffries, *supra* note 220, at 30-31 (footnote omitted).

230. *See, e.g.*, J. Nowak, R. Rotunda & J. Young, Handbook on Constitutional Law (1978); F. Schauer, The Law of Obscenity (1976); Daniels, *The Supreme Court and Obscenity: An Exercise in Empirical Constitutional Policy-Making*, 17 San Diego L. Rev. 757 (1980); Engdahl, *Requiem for Roth: Obscenity Doctrine Is Changing*, 68 Mich. L. Rev. 185 (1969); Henkin, *Morals and the Constitution: The Sin of Obscenity*, 63 Colum. L. Rev. 391 (1963); Kalven, *The Metaphysics of the Law of Obscenity*, 1960 Sup. Ct. Rev. 1; Katz, *Privacy and Pornography: Stanley v. Georgia*, 1969 Sup. Ct. Rev. 203; Lockhart & McClure, *Literature, the Law of Obscenity, and the Constitution*, 38 Minn. L. Rev. 295 (1954); Richards, *Free Speech and Obscenity Law: Toward a Moral Theory of the First Amendment*, 123 U. Pa. L. Rev. 45 (1974); Schauer, *Response: Pornography and the First Amendment*, 40 U. Pitt. L. Rev. 605 (1979).

231. Young v. American Mini Theatres, Inc., 427 U.S. 50 (1976) (holding zoning ordinances regulating locations of adult movie theatres permissible); Paris Adult Theatre I v. Slaton, 413 U.S. 49 (1973) (holding expert testimony on obscenity of films unnecessary when films available as evidence, and that states have legitimate interest in regulating use of obscene material in local commerce); Miller v. California, 413 U.S. 15 (1973) (enumerating basic guidelines for triers of fact in obscenity cases); United States v. Reidel, 402 U.S. 351 (1971) (holding statute prohibiting distribution of obscene materials through the mail — even to willing adult recipients — constitutional because commerce in obscene material is unprotected by any constitutional doctrine of privacy); United States v. Thirty-Seven (37) Photographs, 402 U.S. 363 (1971) (holding statute prohibiting importation of obscene material constitutional on same grounds as in *Reidel*); Stanley v. Georgia, 394 U.S. 557 (1969) (holding individual has right to possess pornographic films in privacy of home); A Book Named "John Cleland's Memoirs of a Woman of Pleasure" v. Attorney Gen., 383 U.S. 413 (1966) (defining obscene material); Roth v. United States, 354 U.S. 476 (1957) (holding obscenity not within the area of constitutionally protected speech or press).

The Court's initial exposition of the rationale for excluding obscenity from first amendment protection came in *Roth v. United States*,[232] where Justice Brennan in part relied, unconvincingly,[233] on historical considerations. More significant was his statement that "[t]he protection given speech and press was fashioned to assure unfettered interchange of ideas for the bringing about of political and social changes desired by the people .... But implicit in the history of the First Amendment is the rejection of obscenity as utterly without redeeming social importance."[234] Justice Brennan then made reference to *Chaplinsky*'s "two-level" theory of free speech.[235] Thus, the Court, employing a variation of the "search-for-truth" analysis, concluded that on this subject at least, it had discovered the "truth" and knew that obscenity was not related to it.

Even under a "search-for-truth" analysis, the Court's conclusion in *Roth* is subject to criticism, for regulation of obscenity can be seen as a means of rejecting whatever life style such expression may implicitly urge.[236] But the Court's greater fallacy is to believe that the primary — or even secondary — purpose of the free speech guarantee is as a means of attaining truth. If the centrality of the self-realization value were recognized, the Court would necessarily acknowledge that it is not for external forces — Congress, state legislatures, or the Court itself — to determine what communications or forms of expression are

---

232. 354 U.S. 476 (1957).

233. Justice Brennan's historical evidence was that "[t]hirteen of the 14 States [which had ratified the Constitution by 1792] provided for the prosecution of libel, and all of those States made either blasphemy or profanity, or both, statutory crimes. As early as 1712, Massachusetts made it criminal to publish any filthy, obscene, or profane song, pamphlet, libel or mock sermon in imitation or mimicking of religious services." *Id.* 482-83 (citations omitted). This is hardly strong support for a historical obscenity doctrine. As Professor Richards has written:

> Colonial legislatures in America appear to have been either unprovoked by or indifferent to obscenity. Justice Brennan cited only one example of pre-constitutional obscenity law: an early Massachusetts law forbidding obscene or profane mockery of religious services. This law, however, is more properly viewed as a religious establishment law than as a law against obscene literature or art in general ....

Richards, *supra* note 230, at 75 (footnotes omitted). Indeed, Justice Brennan's historical reference to the Massachusetts law may prove too much, since there can be little doubt that today such a law would be declared unconstitutional, regardless of its historical status. Why, then, should obscenity's possible historical foundation preclude it from receiving better modern treatment?

234. 354 U.S. at 484.

235. *Id.* at 485.

236. *See* Richards, *supra* note 230, at 78-79.

of value to the individual; how the individual is to develop his or her faculties is a choice for the individual to make.

In more recent decisions, the Court has attempted either to expand upon or revise its rationale for excluding obscenity from the constitutional guarantees. In *Paris Adult Theatre I v. Slaton*,[237] Chief Justice Burger, speaking for the Court, reasoned:

> If we accept the unprovable assumption that a complete education requires the reading of certain books, ... and the well nigh universal belief that good books, plays and art lift the spirit, improve the mind, enrich the human personality, and develop character, can we then say that a state legislature may not act on the corollary assumption that commerce in obscene books, or public exhibitions focused on obscene conduct, have a tendency to exert a corrupting and debasing impact leading to antisocial behavior?[238]

Burger's logic fails. That we assume that good books are good for people does not necessitate our believing that bad books are bad for people.[239] Burger's erroneous reasoning may perhaps be forgiven, since he was apparently suffering from thinly-veiled irritation at those *literati* who readily assume — without any real empirical support — the practical value of good literature, yet denounce those who would restrict obscenity as harmful without any statistical foundation for their assertions. The Chief Justice failed to understand, however, that the former assertion does not need empirical support because no issue of constitutional interpretation turns on it. The same, of course, cannot be said of the latter. More importantly, the Chief Justice assumed that he, a state legislature, a city council, or a censor board is somehow morally entitled to determine for other individuals which movies and literary works are and are not "debasing."

Many of the arguments employed to justify regulation of obscenity are not confined to the worthlessness of the expression. Rather, it is

---

237. 413 U.S. 49 (1973).

238. *Id.* at 63 (citations omitted).

239. The latter assertion is the inverse of the former. As a matter of pure logic, the inverse of a statement does not necessarily flow from acceptance of the statement itself, as Burger would have us believe. The *only* statement that does flow logically from acceptance of the statement itself is the contrapositive, the converse of the inverse. Thus, if we were to accept the primary statement, "if people read good books, they will become better people," the only other statement that is necessarily proven is that "if people have not become better people, they have not read good books." This has absolutely no relevance to the possible effect of so-called "bad" books.

contended that such speech, in addition to being worthless, is harmful in that it may lead to increases in the levels of sex-related crimes.[240] Under the first amendment analysis suggested here, regulation of speech may be justified, in rare cases, on a showing of harm to competing social interests.[241] But this argument cannot of its own weight justify an exclusion of obscenity from the scope of the first amendment. Initially, the harmful effect alleged is so speculative that in no area of protected speech would such a showing justify regulation.[242] If such a showing were sufficient, government could constitutionally regulate nonobscene movies or books that contained detailed depictions or even the slightest approval of violent acts, since these might result in some harm.[243] But this is clearly not the case,[244] so some other distinction must be thought to exist between obscenity and other forms of expression. This brings the analysis back full circle, to the contention that obscenity is inherently worthless. The argument for excluding obscenity from the first amendment's scope therefore necessarily relies on its assumed lack of social value.

The final method that the Court has employed to justify the exclusion of obscenity is simply to resort to rhetorical devices. "[T]o equate the free and robust exchange of ideas and political debate with commercial exploitation of obscene material," wrote Chief Justice Burger in *Miller v. California*,[245] "demeans the grand conception of the First Amendment and its high purposes in the historic struggle for freedom."[246] In *Young v. American Mini Theatres, Inc.*, Justice Stevens, speaking for the Court, added that "few of us would march our

---

240. The Chief Justice's opinion in *Paris Theatre*, for example, noted that "[t]he Hill-Link Minority Report of the Commission on Obscenity and Pornography indicates that there is at least an arguable correlation between obscene material and crime." 413 U.S. at 58.

241. *See* discussion *supra* at 52-55.

242. *See, e.g.*, Brandenburg v. Ohio, 395 U.S. 444 (1969). Even under the heavily criticized version of the "clear and present danger" test of Dennis v. United States, 341 U.S. 494, 505 (1951), the Court required a substantially greater showing before allowing regulation of speech advocating violence. *See* Chapter IV, *infra* at 180-83.

243. In fact, much pornography may in no way directly encourage crime, as violent movies might be thought to, since it can consist of relations between fully consenting adults. *See* Yaffe, *The Law Relating to Pornography: A Psychological Overview*, 20 MED., SCI. & L. 20 (1980); *see also* Cochrane, *Sex Crimes and Pornography Revisited*, 6 INT'L J. CRIMINOLOGY & PENOLOGY 307 (1978).

244. *See supra* note 242.

245. 413 U.S. 15 (1973).

246. *Id.* at 34.

sons and daughters off to war to preserve the citizen's right to see 'Specified Sexual Activities' exhibited in the theaters of our choice,"[247] and that "society's interest in protecting this type of expression is of a wholly different, and lesser, magnitude than the interest in untrammeled political debate."[248] By contrasting pornography in a demeaning or negative way with exalted political speech, the Court precludes, rather than contributes to debate. But, if we are to deal in such rhetorical terms, I suppose that the appropriate response to Justice Stevens is that we are willing to send our sons and daughters off to war, presumably to protect the right of each individual to decide what books he or she will read and what movies he or she will see, free from the state's power to determine that such forms of communication are "worthless." For such freedom is an important element of the freedoms of self-rule and self-fulfillment, the very same principles of autonomy from which ultimately derives the freedom to choose our political leaders.

Recently, Professor Schauer put forward an interesting theory to justify the broad exclusion of obscenity from the bounds of the first amendment. Unlike those who argue that obscenity does not contribute to the marketplace of ideas, Schauer goes further and contends that obscenity cannot even be properly considered communicative activity at all. "[A] refusal to treat hard core pornography as speech in the technical sense", he writes, "is grounded in the belief that the prototypical pornographic item shares more of the characteristics of sexual activity than of communication. The pornographic item is a sexual surrogate. It takes pictorial or linguistic

---

247. 427 U.S. 50, 70 (1976).
248. *Id.* at 70. Justice Stevens was not even referring to material that was legally defined as obscene. It was, rather, in a sort of constitutional twilight zone: not extreme enough to meet constitutional standards of obscenity, but nevertheless predominantly erotic in tone. *Id.*
The actual holding in *Young* may well have been correct. The Court held that zoning ordinances regulating the location of adult theatres were permissible:

> Since what is ultimately at stake is nothing more than a limitation on the place where adult films may be exhibited, even though the determination of whether a particular film fits that characterization turns on the nature of its content, we conclude that the city's interest in the present and future character of its neighborhoods adequately supports its classification of motion pictures.

Id. at 71-72 (footnote omitted). In a footnote, the Court added: "The situation would be quite different if the ordinance had the effect of suppressing, or greatly restricting access to, lawful speech." *Id.* at 71 n.35. In a recent decision, the Court, in invalidating a local ordinance that excluded similar expression, distinguished *Young* on just such grounds. *See* Schad v. Borough of Mount Ephraim, 452 U.S. 61, 71 n.10 (1981).

form only because some individuals achieve sexual gratification in that way."[249]

He supports his contention by pointing to examples:

> Imagine a person going to a house of prostitution and, in accord with his particular sexual preferences, requesting that two prostitutes engage in sexual activity with each other while he becomes aroused. Having achieved sexual satisfaction in this manner, he pays his money and leaves, never having touched either of the prostitutes. Or imagine a person who asks that a leather-clad prostitute crack a whip within an inch of his ear.[250]

"These are hardly free speech cases", Schauer asserts, because "[d]espite the fact that eyes and ears are used, these incidents are no more communicative than any other experience with a prostitute. This is physical activity, the lack of physical contact notwithstanding."[251] He then reasons that presenting the same activity on film renders the activity no more communicative nor less physical. He therefore concludes that "much pornography is more accurately treated as a physical rather than a mental experience."[252]

As persuasive as Schauer's argument may at first appear, it is fundamentally flawed in several important respects. Initially, even if we were to assume the correctness of all of his contentions, it is unlikely that his approach would prove especially helpful in justifying regulation of much activity today deemed legally obscene. For if his "hard core" distinction were adopted by the courts, it is easy to imagine every film containing explicit sexual contact having added to it sprinklings of dialogue and perhaps a brief, superficial examination of an important social issue (for example, "sexual frustrations of modern housewives in suburbia", or "the traumatic emotional impact of rape"). Once this arguably extraneous material is added, Schauer's analysis faces a dilemma: either it attempts to "unmask" such efforts as thinly-disguised hard core pornography (in which event it invites the courts to make fruitless inquiries into motivation of the speakers and/or become literary or film critics), or it accepts at face value the conclusion that such efforts are, in fact, to be deemed "communicative" and therefore protected (in which event it renders itself useless because of the ease of circumvention).

Schauer has recognized the problem, but apparently fails to recognize that at the very least, it renders his theory a rather empty

---

249. F. SCHAUER, *supra* note 120, at 181.
250. *Id.*
251. *Id.* at 181-82.
252. *Id.* at 182.

academic exercise. He acknowledges that "if we were to construct the legal rule in a way that duplicates as best we can that abstract distinction between what should be regulated and what should not be regulated, mistakes would still occur,"[253] and that "recognition and adoption of a Free Speech Principle entails the conclusion that the mistake of over-regulation must be treated as a more serious mistake than the mistake of under-regulation."[254] He therefore concludes that "[i]n order to avoid this error, we must ... create a legal rule that in practice protects some hard core pornography."[255] The problem, however, is that he fails to specify how we are actually to determine which hard core pornography is to be protected and which is not. Is it simply a matter of whether the pornographer attempts to disguise his or her work as culture? If so, he has failed completely to avoid the problem of total and easy circumvention. Yet if that is not to be the dividing line, no other basis suggests itself — and Schauer suggests none, either — for drawing the protected-unprotected distinction.

My difficulties with Professor Schauer's analysis, however, are conceptually much more fundamental than the already fatal defects in practical application. For I believe Professor Schauer has imposed on pornography definitional standards neither he nor virtually anyone else places on other subjects of communicative activity. Surely, much protected communicative activity can have an impact that is significantly or even primarily emotive and nonintellectual. The widespread reaction of non-stop uproarious laughter at a Marx Brothers movie is undoubtedly primarily emotive, and indeed may differ little from the purely physical effects of tickling or of a whoopee cushion. I hardly think that fact intuitively removes those films from the protections of the first amendment.

Here, too, Schauer — at least in part — acknowledges the problem:

> It has been argued, however, that serious literature as well as hard core pornography may evoke the same type of physical or quasi-physical arousal. No doubt many people have been aroused by *Lady Chatterly's Lover,* and there are probably people somewhere who are aroused sexually by the plays of Shakespeare, by the *Kinsey Report,* or even by Bambi. People may become sexually excited by art or music; it is said that Hitler's speeches had the effect of arousing some of his listeners. I do not dispute any of this, but it misconceives the issue. It is not the presence of a physical effect that triggers the exclusion from coverage of that which would otherwise cause them to be covered by the principle of

---

253. *Id.* at 186.
254. *Id.*
255. *Id.*

free speech. Rather, it is that some pornographic items contain *none* of the elements that would cause them to be covered in the first instance. The basis of the exclusion of hard core pornography from the coverage of the Free Speech Principle is not that it has a physical effect, *but that it has nothing else.*[256]

One problem with Schauer's response — indeed, with his entire framework — is that he never really explains the technical difference between "physical" effects and whatever the opposite is. In the sense that a viewer of pornography may have glandular responses indicating sexual arousal, Schauer is of course correct in suggesting that pornography has a "physical" effect (though logically, his reasoning seems to lead to the questionable conclusion that pornography may actually be protected for those viewers who *fail* to become aroused by it, since then it would have no "physical" impact). But before the viewer may manifest a physical response, he or she must first "intellectually" (i.e. through use of the mind) have processed what he or she has just witnessed. In that sense, viewing pornography is clearly distinguishable, for first amendment purposes, from a vibrator, just as the whoopee cushion is distinguishable from the Marx Brothers movie. In each of the two examples, one method of attaining the physical response (sexual arousal or laughter) requires the use of intellectual processes, while the other is physical in every respect — the mental processes have been totally circumvented. Since, as even Schauer appears to concede, one of the touchstones of first amendment protection is the use of the uniquely human mental or emotional processes, there exists no logical basis for either excluding pornography from the first amendment or equating the viewing of pornography with purely physical means of sexual gratification.

That Schauer's distinction fails is demonstrated by his implicit concession that art and music are appropriate subjects of first amendment protection. True, Schauer contends that pornography contains *nothing but* a physical impact, while art and music, like literature, do something other than physically arouse. But at no point does he explain exactly what conceptual or intellectual element art and music contain that pornography does not. Indeed, one might reasonably argue that much pornography, even of the "hard core" variety, requires greater use of one's intellectual processes than does listening to music.

Of course, it might be responded that arguably art and music could be excluded from the first amendment in their entirety, in which event

---

256. *Id.* at 182 (emphasis in original).

much of the basis for my argument in favor of protecting hard core pornography would fall. But I do not believe that art or music should be excluded, for reasons already discussed, and in any event, I think it doubtful that many first amendment experts would wish to exclude pornography from the constitutional protection at the logical cost of simultaneously excluding art and music.

Ultimately, Professor Schauer's analysis fails because it attempts to insert unjustifiable and artificial distinctions between the "physical" and non-physical impact of communicative activity. No such hard line exists in reality; individuals will react to auditory or optical impacts on their senses with varying degrees of physical, emotional and intellectual reactions. But the three are often inseparable, because intellectual reactions may often produce both emotional and physical effects. It is therefore improper to exclude pornography from the bounds of the free speech guarantee on the basis of the physical responses which it may induce.

C. Defamation

Professor Meiklejohn reportedly declared that the decision in *New York Times Co. v. Sullivan*[257] was an occasion for dancing in the streets.[258] Such a reaction on his part is not difficult to understand. In *New York Times,* the Court held that a state could impose penalties for libel of public officials only upon a showing of "actual malice," defined to include knowledge of falsity or reckless disregard for the truth.[259] Although the Court declined to provide the absolute protection urged by Meiklejohn, and made no direct reference to his writings, his influence was clear.[260] Indeed, that the Court limited its holding to protection of libels against public officials about their official conduct underscores the "political speech" influence of Meiklejohn. For if the voters are the true "governors," they need an uninhibited flow of information and opinions about the conduct of their "agents." As the Court stated in *Garrison v. Louisiana*[261] (another public official libel case) shortly after its decision in *New York Times,* "speech concerning

---

257. 376 U.S. 254 (1964).
258. Kalven, *supra* note 230, at 221 n.125.
259. 376 U.S. at 280.
260. Justice Brennan, author of the Court's opinion in *New York Times,* is also the author of an article discussing Meiklejohn's philosophy of free speech. Brennan, *The Supreme Court and the Meiklejohn Interpretation of the First Amendment,* 79 Harv. L. Rev. 1 (1965).
261. 379 U.S. 64 (1964).

VALUE OF FREE SPEECH

public affairs is more than self-expression; it is the essence of self-government."[262]

In subsequent years, the Court came to face many of the logical difficulties encountered by Meiklejohn himself.[263] In particular, the Court was not able to limit the special protection of the *New York Times* doctrine to public officials, since numerous technically private individuals might well have a significant impact upon the course of political decisionmaking. Therefore, the doctrine was extended to apply also to "public figures."[264] In the closely related area of privacy "false light" cases,[265] the Court applied logic similar to that of *New York Times* to suits both by a family that had been held hostage by escaped convicts and later made the subject of a fictionalized play,[266] and by a star baseball pitcher who was the subject of an unauthorized, fictionalized biography.[267]

---

262. *Id.* at 74-75.
263. *See* discussion *supra* at 14-15.
264. Curtis Publishing Co. v. Butts, 388 U.S. 130 (1967). Justice Harlan and three other Justices would have adopted a more easily met standard of liability in defamation cases involving public figures; under this standard, public figures could recover damages upon "a showing of highly unreasonable conduct constituting an extreme departure from the standards of investigation and reporting ordinarily adhered to by responsible publishers." *Id.* at 55. However, Chief Justice Warren, joined by Justices Brennan and White, favored the *New York Times* standard, and Justices Black and Douglas argued for absolute protection, as they had done in *New York Times*. Thus, a majority of the Court desired to impose at least as stringent a protection as that imposed in *New York Times*. *See* Kalven, *The Reasonable Man and the First Amendment: Hill, Butts, and Walker,* 1967 SUP. CT. REV. 267.

As was the case with my discussion of obscenity, see discussion *supra* note 230, this analysis of defamation is not intended to supply a detailed description of the relevant case law. The goal, rather, is to analyze the state of the law in terms of the theory of free speech described earlier. For a description of the case development, see J. NOWAK, R. ROTUNDA & J. YOUNG, *supra* note 230, at 943-53.

265. According to Dean Prosser, the tort of invasion of privacy breaks down analytically into four categories: intrusion, revelation of private facts, commercial use of one's name or face, and holding someone up to the public eye in a "false light." W. PROSSER, HANDBOOK OF THE LAW OF TORTS § 117 (4th ed. 1971). It is conceptually difficult to understand why the "false light" cases are part of the privacy tort. It appears that the doctrine actually arose indirectly. Under New York's statutory right against commercialization of name or face, the courts accepted as a defense (used primarily by newspapers and magazines) that the use was in the public interest. An exception to that defense then developed for fictionalized or false description. *See, e.g.,* Time, Inc. v. Hill, 14 N.Y.2d 986, 207 N.E.2d 604, 260 N.Y.S.2d 7 (1965), *rev'd,* 385 U.S. 374 (1967); Julian Messner, Inc. v. Spahn, 18 N.Y.2d 324, 221 N.E.2d 543, 274 N.Y.S.2d 877 (1966), *vacated,* 387 U.S. 239 (1967). From this background, Dean Prosser apparently conceived a separate category of the invasion-of-privacy tort.

266. Time, Inc. v. Hill, 385 U.S. 374 (1967).
267. Julian Messner, Inc. v. Spahn, 387 U.S. 239 (1967) (per curiam). The Court

One may question whether the apparent underlying premise of *New York Times* — that speech about the conduct of public officials is "the essence of self-government" — justifies the Court's extension of the doctrine to cases involving fictionalized stories about a family held captive or about baseball players. Apparently recognizing the logical difficulty of this extension, Justice Brennan's opinion for the Court in *Time, Inc. v. Hill* emphasized that:

> The guarantees for speech and press are not the preserve of political expression or comment upon public affairs, essential as those are to healthy government. One need only pick up any newspaper or magazine to comprehend the vast range of published matter which exposes persons to public view, both private citizens and public officials. Exposure of the self to others in varying degrees is a concomitant of life in a civilized community. The risk of this exposure is an essential incident of life in a society which places a primary value on freedom of speech and of press .... We have no doubt that the subject of the Life article, the opening of a new play linked to an actual incident, is a matter of public interest.[268]

Justice Brennan's statement fails to explain either why our society "places a primary value on freedom of speech," or what limits, if any, remain on the extension of the *New York Times* logic. Having begun in *New York Times* by justifying the potential imposition of significant harm to individuals on eloquently described precepts derived from the concept of self-government, the Court in *Time* retreated to some vague notion of "public interest." And in doing so, the Court neglected to explain whether the "public interest" concept was a descriptive or normative principle. If the latter, it remains unclear what that normative principle is, what there is about particular stories such that the public will benefit from reading them. If the former, it remains unclear why the first amendment should be construed to allow the imposition of harm on an individual merely to satisfy the public's idle curiosity. What began as an attempt at a coherent theory of the value of free speech thus rapidly dissipated into a collection of vague and unsupported assertions.

---

vacated and remanded the New York Court of Appeals judgment in Spahn v. Julian Messner, Inc., 18 N.Y.2d 324, 221 N.E.2d 543, 274 N.Y.S.2d 877 (1966), in light of the *Time* decision. The state court had granted damages for the unauthorized publication of a fictitious biography of a baseball player.

268. 385 U.S. at 388 (citations omitted).

The absence of any coherent underlying first amendment theory was even more evident in *Gertz v. Robert Welch, Inc.*[269] In *Gertz*, the Court rejected the "public interest" concept[270] on two grounds: that it "would abridge [a] legitimate state interest[271] to a degree that we find unacceptable";[272] and that "it would occasion the additional difficulty of forcing state and federal judges to decide on an *ad hoc* basis which publications address issues of 'general or public interest' and which do not."[273] The *Gertz* majority instead applied the "actual malice" standard of liability only to suits by "public figures." The Court left to the states the task of defining the standard of liability for suits concerning "private" individuals involved in an issue of "public interest," but with the caveat that they "not impose liability without fault."[274] Two factors that were to influence the determination whether a defamation plaintiff is a "public figure" were "evidence of general fame or notoriety" and the extent to which the plaintiff had voluntarily thrust himself into the public eye.[275] The Court's emphasis on public officials' access to opportunities for effective rebuttal[276] indicates the importance of this factor in defining "public figure."

Although the Court thus has curtailed significantly the level of constitutional protection given to defamatory statements, it has also substantially expanded that protection in other respects. The Court held in *Gertz* that a state could not constitutionally impose a standard of absolute liability[277] or allow damages to be presumed[278] in defamation cases, even though both were well established practices at common law.[279] The Court was necessarily imposing these limitations under the first amendment; no other constitutional provision was

---

269. 418 U.S. 323 (1974).

270. In Rosenbloom v. Metromedia, Inc., 403 U.S. 29 (1971), Justice Brennan's plurality opinion had adopted a "public interest" test as the guiding principle for determining application of the *New York Times* principle in defamation cases.

271. This "legitimate state interest" reference is to the Court's conclusion "that the States should retain substantial latitude in their efforts to enforce a legal remedy for defamatory falsehood injurious to the reputation of a private individual." *Gertz*, 418 U.S. at 345-46.

272. *Id.* at 346.

273. *Id.*

274. *Id.* at 347.

275. *Id.* at 351-52.

276. *Id.* at 344.

277. *Id.* at 347.

278. *Id.* at 349. The Court qualified this latter prohibition, however, by adding: "at least when liability is not based on a showing of knowledge of falsity or reckless disregard for the truth." *Id.*

279. *See* W. PROSSER, *supra* note 265, at § 113.

mentioned, and certainly the Court has no authority to invalidate state common law or statutory practice without a finding of unconstitutionality. Yet the Court failed to point to any theory of free speech that justified imposing constitutional limitations on wholly private defamation.[280]

The Court was left, then, with a seemingly unprincipled crazy quilt of first amendment theory as it applied to defamation. On the one hand, the guiding principle of "public interest" was rejected, and the Court's emphasis on "voluntary" entry into the public eye was wholly irrelevant to the Meiklejohnian reasoning from which the Court had implicitly begun in *New York Times*. For if the operative norm of the first amendment for Meiklejohn was the need for voters to receive information related to the political process, it would make no difference that that information concerned someone who had not voluntarily thrust himself into the public eye. The Court seemed to rely upon a tort concept rather than a theory of free speech. On the other hand, the Court was willing to use the first amendment as a means of limiting state choices in adjudicating private defamation suits.

Although it is almost certain that no member of the Court consciously applied the concept, it is quite possible to employ the self-realization principle developed here to rationalize many of the Court's conclusions in *Gertz*. First, under this rationale of the first amendment, it is not necessary to find a broad "public interest" in speech prior to providing it with significant constitutional protection: any speech that may aid in the making of private self-governance decisions is deserving of first amendment protection. Comments about a private individual may be relevant to numerous life-affecting decisions of others, such as whether they should deal with him socially, enter into a business arrangement with him, or buy in his store. And imposition of either a strict liability standard or presumed damages might well deter many defamatory comments. Thus, the self-realization principle allows us to fashion an arguable rationale for providing at least a certain level of first amendment protection even to wholly private defamations.

The self-realization principle cannot be employed so easily as a rationale for the remaining distinctions among public and private defamations drawn by the Court in *Gertz*. For it should be recalled that, although the Court gave a certain degree of constitutional

---

280. Although a totally absolute interpretation of the first amendment would lead to this conclusion, the earlier portion of the Court's opinion made clear that it was not adopting such an interpretation. *See* 418 U.S. at 339-40.

protection to defamation about entirely private individuals, it retained use of *New York Times'* "actual malice" standard only for defamation of public officials and public figures. But, as noted previously,[281] recognition of the self-realization value does not preclude balancing the interest of free speech against competing social values. Under a balancing concept, we could accept on a theoretical level the equal value of different types of speech, yet still decide that the different areas of expression may be treated differently because of external considerations. Hence, the Court could arguably conclude that the social harm of defamation of an individual who has voluntarily entered the public arena is more tolerable than similar harm inflicted upon one who has assumed no risk, even though all types of defamation — at least in the absence of "actual malice" — may be thought to foster the self-realization value. Application of the theory developed here, combined with a form of categorical balancing,[282] thus could well lead to the complex structure of constitutional protection for defamatory statements adopted — albeit without much supporting explanation — in *Gertz*.

D. Advocacy of Unlawful Conduct

It is tempting to argue that advocacy of unlawful conduct — at least in its direct form — is so inherently harmful and so lacking in traditional first amendment values that it is never worthy of constitutional protection. Indeed, respected jurists and scholars have so urged.[283] There can be little doubt that such advocacy may lead to the commission of criminal acts. Even if in a particular instance the advocacy does not cause the commission of a punishable offense, why should society take the risk that inheres in allowing advocacy of acts it has deemed undesirable?

Free speech scholars have given several answers to this question. First, one might rely on the traditionally accepted "marketplace of ideas" theory,[284] which posits that even "false" speech should be protected as part of the societal discourse, because it will serve to accentuate the superiority of speech that contains truth.[285] There are, however, analytical flaws in this intuitively appealing argument.

---

281. *See* discussion *supra* at 52-55.
282. The *Gertz* Court was undoubtedly engaged in a "balancing" process, in that it declined to give speech absolute protection.
283. *See, e.g.,* Masses Publishing Co. v. Patten, 244 F. 535 (S.D.N.Y.) (L. Hand, J.), *rev'd,* 246 F. 24 (2d Cir. 1917), discussed *infra* at 197-200; Bork, *supra* note 12, at 31.
284. *See* Abrams v. United States, 250 U.S. 616, 630 (1919) (Holmes, J., dissenting); discussion *supra* at 45-48.
285. *See* J. Mill, *supra* note 51, at 34-35.

First, the basic assumption that exposure to the so-called "false" speech will help society to discover and appreciate "true" speech is empirically dubious.[286] There may be inadequate time or opportunity for response, the "false" speech may be more persuasively phrased, or the audience may simply not be sufficiently sophisticated or sufficiently interested to ascertain the difference. Second, there is a logical flaw in relying upon the "marketplace" model, because the assumption of that model is that the listeners will be afforded the opportunity to make their choice in the marketplace. Yet in the case of unlawful advocacy, by hypothesis the listeners are not allowed to make their own choice: if they heed the advice of the speaker and commit the crime, they will of course be subject to prosecution. If unlawful advocacy is to receive constitutional protection, then, it must be for some other reason.

One arguable alternative is the "safety valve" rationale for free speech, which posits that the first amendment helps to achieve a stable society by providing the cathartic opportunity to those who are displeased with society.[287] If people were not allowed to consider or discuss their beliefs that the current laws of society should be disregarded, their dissatisfaction would increase and would be further exacerbated by suppression. Open revolt could be the result of such pressure. This argument, however, is flawed as well.

If avoiding societal instability is the major reason for protecting free speech, it is by no means clear, either empirically or intuitively, that the best method of achieving that goal is protection of free and open discussion, including direct advocacy of unlawful conduct. A society could easily conclude that the immediately visible stability achieved by the suppression of unlawful advocacy is far preferable to whatever speculative future stability might be engendered by its protection. Such a judgment would be difficult to refute, as long as the only value of free speech under consideration is the achievement of societal stability. The argument that stability is a major goal of the free speech clause, then, backfires: if stability is paramount, the first amendment could be construed to give no protection to unlawful advocacy.

A third rationale for protecting the freedom of speech is advanced by theorists who premise their concept of free speech to be exclusively the facilitation of the political process. These theorists could reason that, at least when the crime urged deals with the overthrow of government, unlawful advocacy is deserving of protection. Indeed, Alexander Meiklejohn believed such advocacy deserved what he called "absolute"

---

286. Wellington, *supra* note 48, at 1130.
287. T. EMERSON, *supra* note 1, at 7. Shiffrin, *Defamatory Non-Media Speech and First Amendment Methodology*, 25 U.C.L.A. L. REV. 915, 949 (1978).

protection, which in reality meant only that the advocacy could never be regulated because of its dangerousness.[288] The argument here is that, although members of society will be punished if they act upon another's exhortation to overthrow the government, those who urge such action will usually have one or more reasons for so urging, and the political process may benefit from learning the nature of their grievances.[289] But such an argument appears strained, for it is difficult to see why aggrieved speakers cannot complain of social ills without directly advocating illegal acts. Denying first amendment protection to the unlawful advocacy need not stifle the expression of grievances.

In light of the foregoing analysis, it is doubtful that a distinction should be drawn in the level of constitutional protection given to so-called "ideological" advocacy and the non-ideological variety, as Professor Greenawalt has suggested.[290] He argues that non-ideological illegal advocacy is "far removed from what the framers had in mind when they prized expression"[291] and that though "the urging to commit the crime may be an outlet of self-expression for A ... if he may not enjoy the 'outlet' of committing the act himself, no substantial reason exists for assuring his right to enjoy the outlet of deliberately trying to convince someone else to commit the act."[292] But these arguments, even if accepted, cannot be logically limited to excluding protection for non-ideological illegal advocacy. Initially, reliance on the framers' intent is questionable, since no one has a definitive conception of what the framers actually intended,[293] and to the extent it is thought that an understanding of their goals does exist, it appears that it was such a narrow conception that it is unlikely it would have protected ideologically motivated illegal advocacy, either.[294] As to Professor Greenawalt's second point, it would seem that the exact same logic could be applied to ideological advocacy: if an individual does not have a right actually to overthrow the government, why should he have the

---

288. *See* A. MEIKLEJOHN, *supra* note 8, at 26-27. Meiklejohn's "absolutism" is very different from a common understanding of the term. *See* the discussion in Chapter IV *infra* at 204-06.

289. This theory differs from the "marketplace of ideas" model in that the latter sees unlawful advocacy as good only insofar as it invites refutation. The political process idea, on the other hand, sees the unlawful advocacy itself as a necessary process preserved by the Constitution.

290. Greenawalt, *Speech and Crime*, 1980 AM. B. FOUND. RESEARCH J. 645, 748.
291. *Id.*
292. *Id.* at 749.
293. *See* Bork, *supra* note 12, at 22.
294. *See* L. LEVY, *supra* note 4, at 176-248 (1960).

right to urge others to do so? Professor Greenawalt's logic, then, proves considerably more than he intended to prove.

The greatest difficulty in drawing this dichotomy is the impossibility of obtaining a consensus definition on the meaning of "ideological." The problem is that one person's "freedom fighter" is another person's criminal. Such a distinction would also invite manufactured ideological motivation to mask simple criminal intent. True, it is difficult to engender a significant degree of enthusiasm for protecting one man's urging another to commit murder for pay. But "non-ideological" crimes may also include such relatively innocuous activities as nudity or the smoking of marijuana. Moreover, it is no more intuitively attractive to protect an urging to "rid" society of Blacks, Jews, or some other group because of their allegedly harmful effect on society, or to protect an urging of the bombing of innocent people at an airport or restaurant to protest governmental oppression. Yet a dichotomy premised on the basis of ideology would logically lead to providing greater protection to such expression.

None of these theories, then, justifies protecting unlawful advocacy. The marketplace rationale, the stability rationale, and the political process rationale are all insufficient to explain such protection, nor does it seem that ideological content should make a difference. It still remains unclear, therefore, exactly why unlawful advocacy should come within the first amendment's protection.

What is left is the value inherent in allowing individuals to think and discuss freely. Such freedom is valuable because it enables individuals to develop their mental faculties to the fullest. To be sure, if in a specific instance such speech presents danger of serious harm we may conclude that the value of such free and open discussion will be forced to give way. But that is not the threshold question. The question, rather, is whether — wholly apart from any degree of actual danger presented by the expression — advocacy of unlawful conduct is ever deserving of constitutional protection. The answer is that, assuming no such danger, it is simply not appropriate for society to censor free and open discourse. For while particular thoughts or suggestions may ultimately be rejected, there is independent value in allowing people to explore all possibilities to think through the comparative advantages and disadvantages of various options. This is not merely because it will aid them in making decisions (for as already noted, when a particular course of action is criminal, society does not allow that choice to be adopted), but because it stimulates intellectual development. Having to edit one's own speech for fear of government interference can always retard one's intellectual development, and unlawful advocacy should therefore be suppressed only if the government can demonstrate the existence of a real threat of harm.

The propriety of protecting some unlawful advocacy is reinforced by a consideration of the effects of denying constitutional protection to all such speech. A total ban on even the most frivolous forms of unlawful advocacy would have a great impact on daily discourse. Statements such as, "I wouldn't bother paying that parking ticket," or "a little marijuana never hurt anyone," could be grounds for constitutionally permissible prosecutions. Former Chicago White Sox broadcaster Jimmy Piersall could be jailed for his comment several years ago that slugger Greg Luzinski "oughta be shot" for not running out a ground ball.[295] Such constraints on normal, harmless statements are unacceptable, even if the statements are "unlawful advocacy." If the first amendment means anything, it represents a value judgment that the interchange of ideas, information and suggestions is to be kept free and open, at least if the interchange presents no real threat of harm to society. The meaning of the first amendment would be severely truncated if people were driven to self-censorship by fears that innocent comments could be construed as unlawful advocacy.

Thus, it is not difficult to accept that a blanket exclusion of unlawful advocacy from the first amendment's scope is improper. It does not follow, however, that *all* unlawful advocacy is to receive absolute protection. Several commentators have suggested such a result,[296] but it seems unwarranted by either the language or history[297] of the first amendment. As is the case with all of the previously discussed subject

---

295. Of course, it might be suggested that Piersall's comment was mere hyperbole, rather than actual unlawful advocacy. *Cf.* Watts v. United States, 394 U.S. 705, 708 (1969) (per curiam) (suggestion of shooting the President mere hyperbole). The line between hyperbole and incitement, however, is not easy to draw. Indeed, in an earlier game the umpires complained that Piersall was actually inciting a fan riot at Comiskey Park against the umpires by means of hand gestures from the broadcast booth. The allegation may have been somewhat extreme, but whether a particular comment will ultimately be hyperbole is a risk many would rationally choose not to take.

296. *See* A. MEIKLEJOHN, *supra* note 8. Neither of these commentators is a "pure" absolutist. Professor Meiklejohn believes that certain restrictions may be imposed on the timing and location of speech, as well as on the basis of a type of "Robert's Rules of Order" principle. A. MEIKLEJOHN, *supra* note 8, at 24-26. He also excludes protection for speech unrelated to the governing process, and is somewhat inconsistent on the issue of protection for unlawful advocacy. *See* Chapter IV *infra* at 204-06. Professor Baker provides no protection to certain categories of expression, such as commercial speech or coercive speech. Baker, *supra* note 15, at 996 & n.102, 1009. However, neither would allow suppression of speech merely on the grounds of the speech's danger.

297. There can be little doubt that whatever the framers intended, it was not absolute protection. Certainly no historical evidence has ever been cited to support

areas, neither extreme of absolute protection or total exclusion is appropriate.[298]

V. Conclusion

This chapter has presented both a critique of preexisting first amendment theory and a new approach to the issue. Although each of the existing theories is correct as far as it goes, none sufficiently extends the scope of the constitutional protection. None of these theories recognizes that the values they advocate are manifestations of the broader principle of individual self-realization. Once this conclusion is reached, the values recognized in specific categories of expression will be seen to be no greater than the benefits of other forms of expression that in turn foster individual self-realization.

---

such an assertion. In fact, the most detailed historical analysis suggests that the framers intended an extremely narrow, technical version of speech protection. *See generally* L. LEVY, *supra* note 27.

298. *See* discussion *supra* at 52-55.

CHAPTER II
THE CONTENT DISTINCTION IN FIRST AMENDMENT ANALYSIS

The construction and application of the first amendment guarantee of free expression presents difficulties as complex as those existing in any area of constitutional law. To bring a degree of order to this chaos, several commentators have either recognized or urged adoption of a distinction in both the manner and degree of judicial review given to two different types of governmental regulation of expression.[1] Under this distinction, restrictions that turn on the content of expression are subjected to a strict form of judicial review, while those concerned with matters other than content receive more limited examination.[2] With only minor aberrations, the Supreme Court has adhered to this distinction in a series of recent decisions.[3]

Although no commentator to have considered the issue in detail has expressed serious concern about the use of this "content distinction,"[4] it is both theoretically questionable[5] and difficult to apply.[6] Those endorsing such a distinction labor under two misconceptions. The first is that the interests and values of free expression are necessarily more seriously threatened by governmental regulations aimed at content than those which are not; the second is that it is always possible to draw a conceptual distinction between content-based and content-

---

1. L. TRIBE, AMERICAN CONSTITUTIONAL LAW §§ 12-2 to 12-7, 12-20; Ely, *Flag Desecration: A Case Study in the Roles of Categorization and Balancing in First Amendment Analysis,* 88 HARV. L. REV. 1482 (1975); Farber, *Content Regulation and the First Amendment: A Revisionist View,* 68 GEO. L.J. 727 (1980); Karst, *Equality as a Central Principle in the First Amendment,* 43 U. CHI. L. REV. 20 (1975); Stone, *Restrictions of Speech Because of its Content: The Peculiar Case of Subject-Matter Restrictions,* 46 U. CHI. L. REV. 81 (1978).

2. *See* text accompanying notes 41-52 *infra.*

3. *Compare* Erznoznik v. City of Jacksonville, 422 U.S. 205 (1975) *and* Police Dep't v. Mosley, 408 U.S. 92 (1972) (close scrutiny for content-based regulations), *with* Greer v. Spock, 424 U.S. 828 (1976); United States Civil Serv. Comm'n v. National Ass'n of Letter Carriers, 413 U.S. 548 (1973); *and* United States v. O'Brien, 391 U.S. 367 (1968) (reduced scrutiny for content-neutral regulations).

4. Only Professor Emerson expresses concern about the distinction, though his consideration of the question is relatively brief. *See* Emerson, *First Amendment Doctrine and the Burger Court,* 68 CALIF. L. REV. 422, 472 n.116 (1980) ("[T]he basic issue goes to the actual effect of the government regulation on expression — and ... the basic first amendment doctrine is that the government cannot achieve other social interests by 'abridging' expression.").

5. *See* text accompanying notes 103-113 *infra.*

6. *See* text accompanying notes 163-175 *infra.*

neutral regulations. It is therefore time to rethink, and ultimately to abandon, the content distinction.

This chapter first explores both the nature of the content distinction and its implications for the level and form of judicial review. Part II then describes the development of the content distinction in Supreme Court decisions. Parts III and IV critique the theoretical bases of the distinction and discuss the conceptual difficulties inherent in its use. Finally, the chapter suggests a unitary mode of judicial review for all governmental regulation of expression and considers the consequences of this development for particular first amendment cases.

I. The Nature of the Content Distinction

An explanation of what is meant by "content-based" and "content-neutral" must precede any critique of the content distinction. It is also necessary to understand the practical implications that classifying regulation in terms of the content distinction has for the manner or degree of judicial review given to regulation of expression. This section examines both issues.

A. Definitional Questions

Before discussing the difference between content-based and content-neutral speech regulations, it is important to explain what the difference is *not*. The distinction is not, for example, between regulations concerned with the "time, place, and manner of expression"[7] and those concerned with something more.[8] Many "time-place-manner" regulations depend on the content of expression, and content-neutral restrictions may prohibit expression under any circumstances, and thus regulate considerably more than time, place, or manner. Several classic decisions applying the content distinction fall within the former category. In *Police Department v. Mosley*,[9] the Supreme Court invalidated a local ordinance prohibiting all picketing,

---

7. *See* J. Barron & C. Dienes, Handbook of Free Speech and Free Press 93-114 (1979); J. Nowak, R. Rotunda & J. Young, Constitutional Law 973-88 (2d ed. 1983).

8. Ely notes that the state often controls the time, place, and manner of expression out of concern for the likely effect of the communication on its audience. Ely, *supra* note 1, at 1498. He further concludes that labelling a regulation a time, place, and manner restriction or one concerned with "content" is both "irrelevant" and "unintelligible," the critical question being whether the state has acted to control dangers that flow solely from the message conveyed. *Id.* Tribe makes the same point: "[G]overnment will ordinarily defend a restriction on free expression by reference to some danger beyond the speech itself — often, by invoking the permissive talisman of 'time, place, or manner' regulation." L. Tribe, *supra* note 1, § 12-3, at 585.

9. 408 U.S. 92 (1972).

CONTENT DISTINCTION IN FIRST AMENDMENT ANALYSIS

except labor picketing, near a school. Emphasizing that the ordinance discriminated on the basis of content,[10] the Court concluded that a law containing such an exemption is unconstitutional.[11] Yet, since the ordinance regulated the manner and place of the expression (i.e. picketing near a school), it was a classic time, place, and manner regulation. Similarly, in *Erznoznik v. City of Jacksonville*,[12] the Court invalidated a municipal ordinance prohibiting the showing of films containing nudity if the theater screen was visible from a street or other public place.[13] Though such an ordinance regulated the place and manner of exhibiting such movies, the Court nonetheless categorized the regulation as content-related.[14]

By contrast, some statutes regulate expression without concern for content by imposing absolute prohibitions. For example, the federal legislation upheld in *United States Civil Service Commission v. National Association of Letter Carriers*,[15] prohibiting public employees from expressing opinions "'on public affairs, personalities and matters of public interest'" if directed "'toward party success'"[16] regulated more than time, place, or manner. Unlike the plaintiffs in *Mosley* and *Erznoznik*, the federal employees in *Letter Carriers* were completely barred from undertaking the prohibited activities. Yet the Court, emphasizing the content-neutral nature of the regulation, upheld it with a minimal degree of scrutiny.[17]

The opposite of a time-place-manner restriction, then, is not a content-based regulation; it is an absolute prohibition on expression. The reason that time-place-manner regulations are generally unobjectionable is that they presume the existence of alternative avenues of expression,[18] alternatives that are by definition unavailable in the case of absolute regulation.[19]

---

10. *Id.* at 99. The Court made clear its opposition to regulations discriminating on the basis of content: "[A]bove all else, the First Amendment means that government has no power to restrict expression because of its message, its ideas, its subject matter, or its content." *Id.* at 95 (citations omitted).
11. *Id.* at 101-02.
12. 422 U.S. 205 (1975).
13. *Id.* at 215-17.
14. *Id.* at 211-12.
15. 413 U.S. 548 (1973).
16. *Id.* at 556 (quoting United Public Workers v. Mitchell, 330 U.S. 75, 100 (1947)).
17. *Id.*
18. *Compare* Young v. American Mini Theatres, Inc., 427 U.S. 50 (1976) (time-place-manner regulation of adult movie theater valid because those who wish to view adult movies will still have access to them), *with* Schad v. Borough of Mount Ephraim, 452 U.S. 61 (1981) (absolute ban on form of adult entertainment is unconstitutional).
19. Limitations on campaign spending and financing are also examples of

Nor does the content distinction necessarily turn on the government's motivation for regulating expression. While restrictions on speech because of governmental disagreement with the views expressed would undoubtedly be characterized as content-based,[20] regulations that turn on the substance of what is being said can be motivated by goals wholly apart from the state's distaste for the message communicated.[21] The government may, for example, act to prevent the expression of certain unpopular views out of a desire to avoid violence.

It is more difficult to describe what the content distinction *is*. Both Dean John Ely[22] and Professor Laurence Tribe[23] argue that the distinction turns on whether the purpose of the regulation is to impede the "communicative impact" of the expression.[24] Ely suggests that a possible guide in drawing the distinction is to ask, "[h]ad [the] audience been unable to read English, [would there] have been an occasion for the regulation?"[25] But while emphasizing the regulation's concern with "communicative impact" seems appropriate for analyzing the nature of the content distinction,[26] the term is not free from

---

regulations of speech unconcerned with content which go beyond time, place, and manner. Despite the neutrality of the limits on campaign expenditures by candidates, the Supreme Court invalidated them on first amendment grounds in Buckley v. Valeo, 424 U.S. 1 (1976). In reaching its decision, the Court emphasized the absolute reduction in the level of expression that the restrictions would entail. *Id.* at 19. The lower court, however, had upheld the limits, in part because of their content neutrality. *See* Buckley v. Valeo, 519 F.2d 821-42 (D.C. Cir. 1975).

20. *See* text accompanying notes 34-39 *infra*.
21. *See* text accompanying notes 126-128 *infra*.
22. Ely, *supra* note 1.
23. L. TRIBE, *supra* note 1.
24. Neither Ely nor Tribe explicitly characterizes the distinction as turning on "content" (though Tribe does use the term in his section headings). However, both theories are strikingly similar to the traditional content distinction, and to the extent they provide us with a rationale, it is also similar to that traditionally employed to justify use of the content distinction. *See* notes 41-52 *infra* and accompanying text. Other scholars dealing specifically with the "content" issue have characterized both Tribe and Ely as supporters of the distinction. *See, e.g.,* Farber, *supra* note 1, at 742 & n.75.

Ely describes the distinction in the following way: "The critical question would therefore seem to be whether the harm that the state is seeking to avert is one that grows out of the fact that the defendant is communicating, and more particularly out of the way people can be expected to react to his message, or rather would arise even if the defendant's conduct had no communicative significance whatever." Ely, *supra* note 1, at 1497 (footnote omitted).

25. Ely, *supra* note 1, at 1498.
26. *But see* Farber, *supra* note 1, at 745-46.

ambiguity. If content-based regulations are those which "restrict communication because of the message conveyed"[27] — and this definition seems consistent with the "communicative impact" concept — it is not clear that a regulation is content-based merely because there would be no point to it if the audience did not understand English. The government might argue that it is not regulating expression "because of the message conveyed" when it penalizes or prohibits the use of profanity in public discourse, claiming that all views are equally restrained.[28]

Another ambiguity of the content distinction concerns the degree to which it applies to subject matter categorizations.[29] The classic content-based regulation is one that prohibits the expression of a particular point of view. The first amendment does not tolerate governmental regulation based on disagreement with the substance of speech. Yet some[30] have viewed legislation imposing restrictions on commercial advertising[31] or obscenity[32] as content-based. The obscenity cases best illustrate the distinction between viewpoint and subject matter regulation. The Supreme Court has consistently held that obscenity — however that category is defined — enjoys no first amendment protection, even though it unquestionably requires subject matter categorization.[33] It may not be surprising, therefore, that the Court often declines explicitly to assimilate subject matter regulations under the rubric of content-based restrictions. Instead, it reserves its closest scrutiny for laws distinguishing between the expression of

---

27. Stone, *supra* note 1, at 81.
28. This is the problem presented in Cohen v. California, 403 U.S. 15 (1971). *See* text accompanying notes 164-169 *infra*. One commentator who endorses use of the content distinction challenges the emphasis on communicative impact, largely because of "the lack of any justification for subjecting such a broad range of statutes to [the] stringent scrutiny" traditionally associated with content-based regulations. Farber, *supra* note 1, at 745. Professor Farber also notes that "[u]nder [the 'communicative impact'] definition, a regulation that affects all speech equally can still be considered a form of content regulation if the justification for the regulation relates to communicative impact." *Id.* at 747. "It seems more fruitful," he states, "to restrict our definition of content regulation to cover only regulations that discriminate on the basis of content." *Id.* Professor Farber's definition of a content-regulating statute is one whose "applicability depends on the message, symbols, or images used by the communicator." *Id.*
29. *See generally* Karst, *supra* note 1; Stone, *supra* note 1.
30. *See, e.g.*, Karst, *supra* note 1, at 29-35.
31. *See, e.g.*, Virginia State Bd. of Pharmacy v. Virginia Citizens Consumer Council, Inc., 425 U.S. 748 (1976).
32. *See, e.g.*, Miller v. California, 413 U.S. 15 (1973).
33. *See, e.g.*, Roth v. United States, 354 U.S. 476 (1957).

particular viewpoints. In *Kingsley International Pictures Corp. v. Regents*,[34] for example, the Court invalidated New York State's refusal to license the exhibition of the movie "Lady Chatterley's Lover" pursuant to a statute banning films that present "'acts of sexual immorality ... as desirable, acceptable or proper patterns of behavior.'"[35] Since the regulation limited the expression of a particular viewpoint, the Court held it unconstitutional.[36] Based on *Kingsley,* one might conclude that the concern of the content distinction is primarily with viewpoint regulations, rather than subject matter categorizations.

Other decisions of the Court support this conclusion. The government has discriminated on the basis of subject matter in a number of cases where the Court, finding no viewpoint discrimination, has treated the regulations with the limited review traditionally reserved for content-neutral regulations.[37] On the other hand, *Mosley,* in which the Court emphasized the dangers of content regulation,[38] involved nothing more than a classic subject matter categorization: Labor picketing was allowed while nonlabor picketing was prohibited. The nonlabor picketer's viewpoint was totally irrelevant to the ordinance's scope. The Supreme Court, therefore, provided no answer to the question whether subject matter categorizations are to be deemed content-based regulations for purposes of the content distinction.[39] However, since my primary goal is to critique the distinction between content-based and content-neutral restrictions, and since the strongest case supporting the distinction focuses on the inherent dangers of viewpoint regulation, I will generally refer only to viewpoint regulations when discussing so-called "content-based" restrictions on expression.[40]

---

34. 360 U.S. 684 (1959).
35. *Id.* at 685 (quoting N.Y. Educ. Law § 122-a (McKinney Supp. 1958).
36. *Id.* at 688.
37. *See, e.g.,* Greer v. Spock, 424 U.S. 828 (1976); United States Civil Serv. Comm'n v. National Ass'n of Letter Carriers, 413 U.S. 548 (1973).
38. *See* text accompanying notes 80-85 *infra*.
39. According to Professor Stone, "the Court has in some cases treated the subject-matter restriction as if it were indistinguishable from other sorts of content-based restrictions, while in others it has effectively disregarded the subject-matter restriction entirely and thus analyzed the challenged legislation or regulation as if it were content-neutral." Stone, *supra* note 1, at 115.
40. The one striking exception is the inclusion of *Mosley* as a case of content regulation, even though the regulation involved only subject matter categorization. Erznoznik v. City of Jacksonville, 422 U.S. 205 (1975), involving regulation of nudity in movies, arguably also involves subject matter distinctions. However, since the Court

B. Implications of the Content Distinction

In addition to the ambiguity about the meaning of the content distinction, the implications of the distinction as applied are subject to doubt. The foremost proponents of the content distinction, Ely and Tribe, suggest that the distinction is more one of the *method* than of the *scope* or *degree* of judicial review.

Professor Tribe distinguishes between regulations aimed at curtailing the communicative impact of expression — "track one" — and those directed at the noncommunicative result of an act, but which nonetheless may have adverse effects on first amendment freedoms — "track two." Under his first analysis, regulating expression is invalid unless the message constitutes a clear and present danger, a defamatory falsehood, or "otherwise falls on the unprotected side of one of the lines the Court has drawn to distinguish those expressive acts privileged by the first amendment from those open to government regulation with only minimal due process scrutiny."[41] Under his second analysis, regulations are constitutional as long as they do not "unduly constrict the flow of information and ideas."[42]

The difference between "track one" and "track two" treatment is that the latter employs case-by-case balancing while the former uses a type of categorization or definitional balancing.[43] Dean Ely earlier suggested a similar distinction,[44] finding a balancing approach appropriate where the evil the state seeks to avert does not stem from the message being expressed, but advocating "categorization" for

---

centered most of the analysis in these cases on the issue of regulation of content, I have included them in my discussion of the Court's approach to regulation of content. *See* text accompanying notes 73-85 *infra*.

41. L. TRIBE, *supra* note 1, § 12-2, at 582.

42. *Id.* Professor Tribe may not give even expression subject to "track one" regulation all that much protection, since he is willing to exclude wholesale certain categories of expression. *Id.*

43. L. TRIBE, *supra* note 1, § 12-2, at 582; *see* Nimmer, *The Right to Speak From Times to Time: First Amendment Theory Applied to Libel and Misapplied to Privacy*, 56 CALIF. L. REV. 935 (1968). Nimmer uses New York Times Co. v. Sullivan, 376 U.S. 254 (1964), where the Court held that defamatory speech against a "public official" is protected by the first amendment unless knowingly or recklessly uttered, to illustrate definitional balancing. There, the Court employed balancing not to determine which litigant in the particular circumstances presented deserved to prevail, but to define which forms of speech are within the first amendment. *Id.* at 942.

44. Ely, *supra* note 1. "[W]here messages are proscribed because they are dangerous, balancing tests inevitably become intertwined with the ideological predispositions of those doing the balancing — or if not that, at least with the relative confidence or paranoia of the age in which they are doing it ...." *Id.* at 1501.

regulations motivated by state-perceived dangers in the communication itself.

Regardless of its accuracy,[45] the Tribe-Ely approach to the content distinction contemplates significant differences in the degree of judicial scrutiny, as well as in the method of review. While Professor Tribe believes that even a "track two" regulation "may be invalid if it leaves too little breathing space for communicative activity, or leaves people with too little access to channels of communication,"[46] he acknowledges that "track two" analysis involves a "relaxed scrutiny," a practice he finds generally "unobjectionable."[47] Similarly, Dean Ely characterizes one type of review given to content-neutral regulations as "the weak, nay useless, 'no gratuitous inhibition' approach,"[48] and another as a "stronger"[49] balancing approach, but even this test he

---

45. Whether the Court has drawn this dichotomy in method of review is questionable. Examining some of the relevant decisions shows merely that the Court often employs a considerably stricter standard of review when the regulation is content-based than when it is content-neutral. *See, e.g.,* NAACP v. Button, 371 U.S. 415, 438 (1963) ("compelling" interest required); Bates v. City of Little Rock, 361 U.S. 516, 524 (1960) ("cogent"); Thomas v. Collins, 323 U.S. 516, 530 (1945) ("paramount"). The consequence of the content distinction, then, may simply be a difference in the degree of review, rather than in the method. Professor Ely acknowledges that one decision which invalidated what could be characterized as a content-based regulation, Tinker v. Des Moines School Dist., 393 U.S. 503 (1969), "does not employ a categorization approach." Ely, *supra* note 1, at 1492 n.39. Instead, "it starts with an unmistakable presumption that the regulation involved is unconstitutional and sticks with it despite some far from trivial arguments on the other side." *Id.* As characterized by Professor Ely, then, the difference would often seem to be merely a matter of degree of review, rather than method of review.

46. L. TRIBE, *supra* note 1, § 12-20, at 682-83.

47. *Id.* at 685. Professor Tribe suggests that if a "track two" inhibition takes place in a "public forum," stricter scrutiny is dictated. *Id.* at 684. But this analysis avoids the significant preliminary task of determining what is meant by "public," a term that describes a conclusion, rather than aids in analysis. *See, e.g.,* Greer v. Spock, 424 U.S. 828 (1976); text accompanying notes 93-95 *infra.* He also suggests that "whenever it can be demonstrated that the result of the government's rule or policy is to limit in some significant degree the ease or effectiveness with which a speaker can reach a specific audience with a particular message, the government should lose the case unless it can establish that an important public objective unrelated to the message would be sacrificed by any less restrictive alternative." L. TRIBE, *supra* note 1, § 12-20, at 686. But Professor Tribe does not explain how lenient the Court should be in accepting the government's characterization of "importance." Moreover, to the extent Professor Tribe actually intends to impose a significant burden on the state in such cases, he would seem to have all but obliterated any practical distinction between his "track one" and "track two" analyses.

48. Ely, *supra* note 1, at 1488-89.

49. *Id.* at 1486.

acknowledges has been "notoriously unreliable."[50] Content-based regulations, on the other hand, require "rigorous definition of the limited categories of expression that are unprotected by the first amendment."[51] Thus, whatever technical labels one uses, the proponents of the content distinction advocate considerably stricter levels of judicial review for content-based than for content-neutral regulations.[52]

II. The Content Distinction in the Supreme Court

In the earlier years of the Supreme Court's development of the first amendment, there was little concern over whether a restriction on speech was content-based or content-neutral. Indeed, the Court reserved much of its rhetoric about the values of free expression for cases invalidating content-neutral restrictions. In *Hague v. CIO*,[53] Justice Roberts's plurality opinion stated that "[w]herever the title of streets and parks may rest, they have immemorially been held in trust for the use of the public and, time out of mind, have been used for purposes of assembly, communicating thoughts between citizens, and discussing public questions."[54] Nothing in the statement implied a special concern with regulations directed at content. On the contrary, the implication seems to be that, regardless of the nature of a

---

50. *Id.* at 1490.
51. *Id.* at 1501. There appears to be some confusion in Professor Ely's attempted distinction between regulations which are subject to a categorization approach, and those that fall under a balancing test. Professor Ely believes that the advantage of a categorization approach is that it "asks only 'What was he saying?' ... A clear and present danger or ad hoc balancing approach, in contrast, would regard that question as nondispositive: a given message will be sometimes protected and sometimes not, depending on the actual or projected behavior of the audience in response to it." *Id.* at 1493 n.44. Yet Professor Ely cites Brandenburg v. Ohio, 395 U.S. 444 (1969), where the Court prohibited a state from proscribing advocacy of unlawful conduct "except where such advocacy is directed to inciting or producing imminent lawless action and is likely to incite or produce such action," *id.* at 447 (footnote omitted), as an example of his categorization approach. Ely, *supra* note 1, at 1492. But while the first portion of the *Brandenburg* test looks only to the question of "what was he saying?", the second part — the inquiry whether such speech "is likely to incite or produce" unlawful action — does consider "the likely effect of the communication." This is the very thing Ely believes a categorization approach does not do. This point is considered further in Chapter IV *infra* at 193-200.
52. *Accord* Note, *The First Amendment Overbreadth Doctrine*, 83 HARV. L. REV. 844, 918 (1970) (overbreadth doctrine should be used more freely for laws which "burden the advocacy of definable viewpoints on matters of public concern").
53. 307 U.S. 496 (1939).
54. *Id.* at 515.

regulation, the concern is with its effect on the dissemination of expression.[55] Though the statement was dictum since the case ultimately turned on what amounted to a classic regulation of content,[56] it has been widely quoted as representing a philosophy of free expression independent of issues of content regulation.[57]

Shortly after *Hague,* Justice Roberts reiterated the unimportance of the content factor in first amendment analysis in *Schneider v. State.*[58] *Schneider* invalidated several municipal ordinances prohibiting or severely restricting the distribution of handbills or circulars. The municipalities' interest in safety, health, welfare, or convenience, Justice Roberts reasoned, could not justify abridging the individual liberty to circulate information or opinion.[59]

That the ordinances applied equally to *all* handbills (there apparently being no allegations of selective enforcement) and that their asserted justification — avoiding litter — in no way turned on the content of the handbills was apparently irrelevant; that the ordinances impeded the expression of *all* viewpoints made the interference with first amendment rights no less harmful. Justice Roberts concluded that keeping the streets clean could not justify prohibiting the distribution of literature to one willing to receive it.[60] Roberts did engage in a form of balancing, but it was "a balancing approach with the scales tipped markedly in favor of First Amendment rights."[61] Administrative

---

55. Justice Roberts did note that the right "is not absolute, but relative, and must be exercised in subordination to the general comfort and convenience, and in consonance with peace and good order," but added that "it must not, in the guise of regulation, be abridged or denied." *Id.* at 516.

56. The regulation invalidated in *Hague* gave state officials wide discretion in issuing permits for meetings on public property. *Id.*

57. *See* Kalven, *The Concept of the Public Forum:* Cox v. Louisiana, 1965 SUP. CT. REV. 1, 13; Stone, *Fora Americana: Speech in Public Places,* 1974 SUP. CT. REV. 233, 238-39. Professor Stone points out that the *Hague* dictum draws a distinction between public property used since "time out of mind" for speech and assembly and other kinds of public property which cannot satisfy the "time out of mind" requirement. *Id.* We cannot be sure, then, what Justice Roberts' feeling would have been about content-neutral regulation of expression in non-traditional public forums.

58. 308 U.S. 147 (1939).

59. *Id.* at 160. Of course, "a person could not exercise this liberty by taking his stand in the middle of a crowded street, contrary to traffic regulations, and maintain his position to the stoppage of all traffic ...." *Id.* But while "[m]ere legislative preferences or beliefs respecting matters of public convenience may well support regulation directed at other personal activities ... [they may] be insufficient to justify [diminishing] the exercise of rights so vital to the maintenance of democratic institutions." *Id.* at 161.

60. *Id.* at 162.

61. Stone, *supra* note 57, at 240.

convenience could no more justify abridging expression than could governmental distrust for the views expressed.[62]

It was not until *Cox v. Louisiana*[63] that the Court expressed significant doubts about applying such close scrutiny when regulation of expression does not turn on content. In *Cox*, the Court overturned the conviction of a leader of a peaceful civil rights demonstration, primarily because city officials had previously allowed other meetings at that location.[64] But Justice Goldberg's opinion emphasized that the Court was not required "to consider the constitutionality of the uniform, consistent, and nondiscriminatory application of a statute forbidding all access to streets and other public facilities for parades and meetings."[65] *Cox* thus signalled a shift away from a concern with possible impediments to the dissemination of *any* information and opinion to a concern primarily with equal treatment in the regulation of differing viewpoints.

While the case law from the mid-1960's to the present has not been entirely consistent,[66] a distinct dichotomy has developed in the Court's attitude towards the two types of governmental regulation of speech. In decisions such an *Mosley*,[67] *Erznoznik*,[68] and *Schacht v. United States*,[69] the Court has expressed serious concern with governmental attempts to regulate on the basis of what the Court calls content, and usually invalidates such regulations without detailed analysis. On the other hand, when a regulation purports to affect all equally and is designed to avoid harms unrelated to the content of expression, as in *Greer v. Spock*,[70] *Letter Carriers*,[71] and *United States v. O'Brien*,[72] the Court has engaged in extremely limited scrutiny.

---

62. In later years, the Court did uphold a number of regulations not aimed at content in situations where it presumably would have invalidated the same regulation if it had discriminated on the basis of content. But such cases involved ordinances arguably supported by compelling noncontent justifications. *See, e.g.*, Kovacs v. Cooper, 336 U.S. 77 (1949) (upholding neutral limits on the use of sound trucks).
63. 379 U.S. 536 (1965).
64. *Id.* at 556-57.
65. *Id.* at 555.
66. *See* note 102 *infra* and accompanying text.
67. Police Dep't v. Mosley, 408 U.S. 92 (1972).
68. Erznoznik v. City of Jacksonville, 422 U.S. 205 (1975).
69. 398 U.S. 58 (1970). In *Schacht,* the Court invalidated a congressional ban on the unauthorized wearing of American military uniforms in a manner calculated to discredit the armed forces. *See also* Hudgens v. NLRB, 424 U.S. 507, 520 (1976).
70. 424 U.S. 828 (1976).
71. United States Civil Serv. Comm'n v. National Ass'n of Letter Carriers, 413 U.S. 548 (1973).
72. 391 U.S. 367 (1968).

Erznoznik and *Mosley* illustrate the former attitude. *Erznoznik* invalidated a local ordinance prohibiting the exhibition of any motion picture displaying nudity if the screen was visible from any public street or public place.[73] In doing so, the Court emphasized that the first amendment severely restricts governmental attempts to protect the public from certain kinds of speech because one kind may be more offensive than others.[74] Only when individuals cannot avoid invasions of their privacy, said the Court, can such restrictions be upheld.[75] The Court further concluded that the ordinance was overbroad as an attempt to protect children, since not all nudity was necessarily obscene, even for minors.[76] Nor could the ordinance be validated on the ground that it presented a hazard to traffic, since many contemporary movie screens without nudity might be just as distracting to passing motorists.[77] It was true, the Court acknowledged, that it had in the past "upheld underinclusive classifications on the sound theory that a legislature may deal with one part of a problem without addressing all of it."[78] But it noted that "even a traffic regulation cannot discriminate on the basis of content unless there are clear reasons for the distinctions."[79]

Mosley, upon which the *Erznoznik* Court partially relied,[80] is more complex since Justice Marshall's opinion invalidating an ordinance prohibiting all but labor picketing near public schools was based on the equal protection clause, while simultaneously emphasizing first amendment theory.[81] Justice Marshall emphasized the dangers of content-based regulation, reasoning that all viewpoints must enjoy an equal opportunity to be heard under the first amendment, and that government may not justify or base selective exclusions from the public forum on content alone.[82] At no point did the Court refer to the important first amendment values[83] served by uninhibited access to

---

73. 422 U.S. at 215-17.
74. *Id.* at 208-10.
75. *Id.* at 209.
76. *Id.* at 213.
77. *Id.* at 214-15.
78. *Id.* at 215.
79. *Id.*
80. *Id.* at 209, 215.
81. "Because Chicago treats some picketing differently from others, we analyze this ordinance in terms of the Equal Protection Clause of the Fourteenth Amendment. Of course, the equal protection claim in this case is closely intertwined with First Amendment interests ...." 408 U.S. at 94-95 (footnote omitted).
82. *Id.* at 96.
83. *See* text accompanying note 54 *supra*.

the public forum,[84] or to the conclusions of those decisions that even content-neutral state interests are insufficient to justify restrictions on expression unless the state interests are truly compelling. Of course, Justice Marshall did not need to reach these issues since he could invalidate the ordinance on the alternative basis of equal protection. But one can easily reverse the argument: Why bother to consider the discrimination issue if a total ban on picketing (rather than, for example, a ban only of noisy picketing[85]) violates the first amendment? Marshall's decision to rely on the discriminatory nature of the ordinance, rather than on its broad impact on expression, could also be taken to imply that if the city of Chicago had chosen to ban labor picketing as well, the Court would have sustained the ordinance without difficulty.

The high level of scrutiny given to content-based regulations stands in stark contrast to the Court's recent ambivalence toward restrictions that it deems to be content-neutral. A brief review of three of these decisions should illustrate the point.

In *Letter Carriers,* the Court upheld the Hatch Act's prohibition against federal employees assuming "an active part in political management or in political campaigns."[86] The plaintiffs claimed that the Act was facially invalid as a violation of their first amendment rights of free expression and assembly. The Court rejected the challenge, emphasizing the government's interest in regulating the conduct of its own employees,[87] and noting that the restrictions were not aimed at particular parties, groups, or viewpoints. The prohibition, in other words, was content-neutral. Because of this, the Court engaged in only the most cursory review of the sweeping means used by Congress to avoid undue political influence on government employees.[88] Absent were the Court's overbreadth or "less drastic means" doctrines, despite the undeniable limiting effect of the legislation on the political expression of thousands of individuals. Justice White's opinion contained not a single sentence about the difficult nature of the Court's task; nor did the opinion discuss the importance of free and open political activity and association to our governmental system.[89] Only the dissent recognized that "[w]e deal

---

84. *See* note 59 *supra.*
85. *Cf.* Grayned v. City of Rockford, 408 U.S. 104 (1972) (upholding an ordinance prohibiting noisy picketing near a school because it did not punish the expression of unpopular views).
86. 5 U.S.C. § 7324(a) (2) (1976).
87. 413 U.S. at 557.
88. *See* text accompanying notes 105-106 *infra.*
89. The Court's only reference to the first amendment interests involved was the

here with a First Amendment right to speak, to propose, to publish, to petition Government, to assemble,"[90] and that "[f]ree discussion of governmental affairs is basic in our constitutional system."[91]

The contrast between the Court's attitude toward the regulation involved in *Erznoznik* and those discussed in *Letter Carriers* is striking.[92] While the governmental purpose served by the regulation in *Letter Carriers* may have been considerably more compelling than that involved in *Erznoznik*, the total prohibition of partisan political activity by government employees represents at least as egregious an invasion of first amendment interests as a restriction on the showing of movies containing nudity. Yet because the Court saw a content-based regulation in *Erznoznik* but not in *Letter Carriers*, it reserved its rhetorical flourishes about the value of free expression, as well as its power of invalidation, for the former.

The Court's casual approach to content-neutral regulations is also evident in *Greer*. In that case, a third-party presidential candidate sought to enjoin military officials from preventing his entry onto an army base to distribute campaign literature and to discuss election issues with military personnel and their dependents.[93] Noting that there was no claim that military officials discriminated among candidates on the basis of their particular political views,[94] the Supreme Court rejected the first amendment claim.[95]

Perhaps the most troubling illustration of the Court's modern approach to content-neutral restrictions is *United States v. O'Brien*.[96] *O'Brien* upheld the application of a law prohibiting the destruction of

---

following statement: "Neither the right to associate nor the right to participate in political activities is absolute in any event." 413 U.S. at 567. Earlier, the Court had summarily concluded that " neither the First Amendment nor any other provision of the Constitution invalidates a law barring this kind of partisan political conduct by federal employees." *Id.* at 556.

90. *Id.* at 597 (Douglas, J., dissenting).
91. *Id.* at 598 (Douglas, J., dissenting).
92. The difference between the Court's attitude in *Letter Carriers* and Keyishian v. Board of Regents, 385 U.S. 589 (1967), is also striking. In *Keyishian,* the Court held invalid a New York State statute which disqualified for work as a public school teacher any individual who uttered "treasonable" or "seditious" language, or who joined any society advocating such doctrine. The Court reached this result even though the complainants — much like the plaintiffs in *Letter Carriers* — were never forced to accept government employment. For another decision indicating that the overbreadth doctrine is to play a lesser role in review of content-neutral regulation, see Broadrick v. Oklahoma, 413 U.S. 601 (1973). *See generally* Chapter V.
93. 424 U.S. at 832.
94. *Id.* at 838-39.
95. *Id.* at 840.
96. 391 U.S. 367 (1968).

draft cards to an individual who burned his card as part of an anti-war protest.[97] The Court reasoned:

> [W]e think it clear that a government regulation is sufficiently justified if it is within the constitutional power of the Government; if it furthers an important or substantial governmental interest; if the governmental interest is unrelated to the suppression of free expression; and if the incidental restriction on alleged First Amendment freedoms is no greater than is essential to the furtherance of that interest.[98]

By requiring that "the governmental interest [be] unrelated to the suppression of free expression," the Court made it clear that the remainder of its analysis was intended solely for content-neutral restrictions. For those restrictions (such as the seemingly neutral prohibition of draft card destruction), the Court required relatively little to justify a governmental limitation on expression. The test nowhere asks whether the asserted governmental interest is sufficiently "substantial" to justify the "incidental" impact on free expression. Under these conditions, it is practically inconceivable that an asserted governmental purpose will not qualify.[99] While the test does require the government to establish that the impact on expression is no greater than necessary to achieve the purpose, it takes the validity of attaining that purpose — regardless of how narrowly the government has defined the purpose or how much its attainment invades first amendment rights — as given. Moreover, the test does not make clear whether a chosen means of attaining the government's purpose has no greater impact on free speech than is "essential" if the government can establish that the increased cost of less restrictive methods will be more than nominal.[100] Ultimately, the *O'Brien* test for content-neutral regulations requires nothing more than what Dean Ely characterizes as "no gratuitous inhibition"[101] on speech, a protection which he correctly suggests is all but useless.[102]

---

97. *Id.* at 372.
98. *Id.* at 377.
99. *See* Ely, *supra* note 1, at 1485-86.
100. *See id.* at 1486-87.
101. *Id.* at 1488.
102. *Id.* Professor Tribe finds such an approach "unobjectionable" as long as the motive behind the regulation was not suppression of a particular viewpoint. L. TRIBE, *supra* note 1, § 12-20, at 685.

On at least two occasions, the Court has applied a fairly strict level of scrutiny to content-neutral regulations. In Mills v. Alabama, 384 U.S. 214 (1966), the publisher of a newspaper was convicted of violating a state law prohibiting vote solicitation on election day by publishing on that day an editorial on the election. The asserted purpose of the statute was to prevent voter confusion that might result from last-

III. A Theoretical Critique

The most puzzling aspect of the distinction between content-based and content-neutral restrictions is that either restriction reduces the sum total of information or opinion disseminated. That governmental regulation impedes all forms of speech, rather than only selected viewpoints or subjects, does not alter the fact that the regulation impairs the free flow of expression. Thus, one need not accept the self-

---

minute electioneering. In overturning the conviction, the Court failed to mention the apparent content neutrality of the statute. Of course, the Court might have interpreted the statute as containing a "content" distinction because it turned on subject matter. *See* text accompanying notes 29-40 *supra*.

Similarly, in Buckley v. Valeo, 424 U.S. 1 (1976) (per curiam), the Court invalidated federal election spending limitations even though such limitations in no way turned on the views of the particular candidates. The *Buckley* Court did uphold the contribution disclosure provisions of the Campaign Act, but made it clear that it had done so only after strict scrutiny had revealed sufficiently important governmental interests to outweigh the possibility of infringement. *Id.* at 66.

At least two decisions could be deemed aberrations in the other direction — cases which apply a relaxed level of review to what might be characterized as content-based distinctions. *See* Young v. American Mini Theatres, 427 U.S. 50 (1976); Lehman v. City of Shaker Heights, 418 U.S. 298 (1974). However, both of these cases involved subject matter categorization, rather than direct viewpoint regulation. To the extent such categorizations may be deemed content-based, they are — to a believer in the content distinction — probably less deserving of a strict standard of review than are viewpoint regulations. *See* Farber, *supra* note 1, at 735; Stone, *supra* note 1, at 108-15.

In Metromedia, Inc. v. City of San Diego, 453 U.S. 490 (1981), the Court also invalidated a restriction on expression that did not turn on viewpoint, despite the Chief Justice's impassioned dissent. The city had imposed severe restrictions on the use of billboards, and the Court held it unconstitutional "[b]ecause the ... ordinance reaches too far into the realm of protected speech ...." *Id.* at 521. However, it is significant that, in response to the Chief Justice's argument that the Court's function should be limited to assuring governmental neutrality in regulating speech, *id.* at 561 (Burger, C.J., dissenting), the Court did not argue that even such content-neutral regulations could significantly impair first amendment interests. Rather, Justice White's plurality opinion merely noted that the traditional concern for neutrality was not "applicable to the facts of this case" because "San Diego has chosen to favor certain kinds of messages — such as on-site commercial advertising and temporary political campaign advertisements — over others." *Id.* 519. The dissent failed to explain, Justice White said, "why San Diego should not be held to have violated this concept of First Amendment neutrality." The decision, then, appears to be nothing more than another instance — like *Mosley* — in which the Court aberrationally decides to view subject matter categorization as a form of content regulation and therefore subject to a stricter form of scrutiny. *See* text accompanying notes 29-40 *supra*. *See also* Clark v. Community for Creative Non-Violence, 52 U.S.L.W. 4986 (1984).

realization principle, developed in Chapter I, as the exclusive rationale for free speech protection in order to reject the content distinction. Whatever rationale one adopts for the constitutional protection of speech,[103] the goals behind that rationale are undermined by *any* limitation on expression, content-based or not. For example, if one adopts the principle that the purpose of the first amendment is to facilitate the democratic process by making individuals better informed voters,[104] regulations that limit expression on content-neutral grounds should logically be as suspect as content-based regulations, since they may also undermine this value.

Letter Carriers illustrates this point. The Court upheld widespread but neutral federal restrictions on the political activities of federal government employees,[105] though the ultimate impact of the law was undeniably a significant decrease in the dissemination of political information. The restriction on partisan political expression at military bases upheld in *Greer* similarly undermines the goal of increasing political awareness.[106] The point of these examples is not necessarily to suggest that the questioned laws were unconstitutional. Rather, the point is that because the laws effectively reduced the flow of protected expression, the regulations deserved considerably greater scrutiny than they received from the Court.[107]

---

103. This is true with the one exception of Professor Karst's "equality principle." *See generally* Karst, *supra* note 1. However, as discussed later in detail, *see* text accompanying notes 129-162 *infra,* this principle, standing alone, is not an appropriate theoretical rationale for free speech protection.

It might be argued that the content distinction is also supported by theory that the purpose of the first amendment is to perform a "checking" function on the operations of government. *See* Blasi, *The Checking Value in First Amendment Theory,* 1977 AM. B. FOUND. RESEARCH J. 521. *See* Chapter I, *supra* at 41-45. Although governmental regulation of expression because of disagreement with its content is a classic method for governments to avoid criticism, to the extent that content-neutral regulations deprive a listening or viewing audience of information — an almost inescapable result of such restrictions on expression — the checking function will naturally be undermined.

104. *See, e.g.,* A. MEIKLEJOHN, POLITICAL FREEDOM (1960); Bork, *Neutral Principles and Some First Amendment Problems,* 47 IND. L.J. 1 (1971); Brennan, *The Supreme Court and the Meiklejohn Interpretation of the First Amendment,* 79 HARV. L. REV. 1 (1965); Meiklejohn, *The First Amendment is an Absolute,* 1961 SUP. CT. REV. 245. *See* Chapter I, *supra* at 14-15.

105. *See* text accompanying notes 86-89 *supra;* text accompanying notes 201-203 *infra.*

106. *See* text accompanying notes 93-95 *supra.*

107. This chapter will ultimately conclude that each of these regulations should have been held unconstitutional. *See* text accompanying notes 176-215 *infra.*

If we broaden the value of free expression beyond the purely political realm to include any expression that contributes to the so-called "marketplace of ideas,"[108] the situation is unchanged. Content-neutral restrictions like the prohibition of the distribution of all leaflets on street corners[109] or the requirement of disclosure of authorship on all handbills[110] may reduce the level and quality of contributions to the free exchange of ideas as significantly as any content-based regulation. Even if we accept the often compelling criticisms leveled at the "marketplace" model of expression[111] and adopt instead the so-called "liberty" model, premised on the preeminent value of individual self-fulfillment,[112] we still need not accept the content distinction. Here, too, content-neutral restrictions may significantly undermine the value of free expression by imposing limitations on the opportunity for individual expression. That the expression is regulated for reasons other than its content makes it no less an interference with expression.

In the light of the foregoing analysis, it is difficult to understand why content-neutral regulations should receive any less scrutiny than other types of restriction. Surprisingly, most commentators who have either recognized or urged such a distinction give us little theoretical support to meet this objection.[113]

---

108. *See* Red Lion Broadcasting Co. v. FCC, 395 U.S. 367, 390 (1969) ("It is the purpose of the First Amendment to preserve an uninhibited marketplace of ideas in which truth will ultimately prevail ...."); Abrams v. United States, 250 U.S. 616, 630 (1919) (Holmes, J., dissenting) ("[W]hen men have realized that time has upset many fighting faiths, they may come to believe ... that the ultimate good desired is better reached by free trade in ideas — that the best test of truth is the power of the thought to get itself accepted in the competition of the market. ... That at any rate is the theory of our Constitution."); *cf.* T. EMERSON, *supra* note 42, at 7 ("[F]reedom of expression is ... the best process for advancing knowledge and discovering truth."). *See* Chapter I, *supra* at 45-48.

109. Schneider v. State, 308 U.S. 147 (1939); *see* text accompanying notes 58-62 *supra*.

110. Talley v. California, 362 U.S. 60 (1960).

111. *See, e.g.*, Baker, *Scope of the First Amendment Freedom of Speech*, 25 U.C.L.A. L. REV. 964, 974-81 (1978) (arguing that the assumptions underlying the marketplace of ideas are almost "universally rejected" today).

112. *See id.* at 990-1009. Of course, in Chapter I, I develop my own theory of the value of free speech. The point to be underscored, however, is that the content distinction makes little sense, regardless of what value or values of free speech one adopts.

113. *See* Stone, *supra* note 1, at 100-01 ("Although there has been much discussion of the purposes underlying the guarantee of free speech, surprisingly scant attention has been paid to the related question why, within the realm of possible abridgements of free expression, we are so especially wary of restrictions based upon content. On the rare occasion when the question does come up, the answer is all too often taken for granted.") (footnotes omitted).

The most detailed attempt at constructing an analytical basis for the distinction comes from Professor Geoffrey Stone.[114] Stone puts forth two reasons supporting the special sensitivity afforded content-based restrictions. First, he claims that content-based restrictions distort the "marketplace of ideas" in a content-differential fashion, leaving the public with an incomplete and perhaps inaccurate vision of society.[115] Second, he argues that content-related regulations violate the principle that denies the government power to restrict speech because it disapproves of the message conveyed.[116] Neither of these reasons, however, justifies the use of differing standards of review for content-based and content-neutral regulations.

Professor Stone's first point — that content-based restrictions leave the public with a more incomplete and inaccurate perception of social reality than do content-neutral restrictions — is neither intuitively nor empirically supportable. There is no way of knowing that content-neutral restrictions will have an equally negative impact on all competing views. Individuals who have heard one side of an issue may well be precluded from learning the other by content-neutral restrictions. This is because we have no way of ascertaining in what ways and at what times individuals are exposed to different facts or opinions. While such regulations do not focus upon expression of a single opinion, or impede expression of the same viewpoint at all times, erratic and unpredictable distortion of the marketplace is no less a distortion.

More importantly, even if content-neutral restrictions equally affected all competing points of view, such restrictions may undermine the functioning of the marketplace by keeping the public equally ignorant of *all* positions on issues, rather than merely of one viewpoint. "Neutral" limits on campaign spending illustrate this point. Assume Candidate A has available substantial funds with which to purchase widespread advertising time and space. Assume further that Candidate B, his opponent, has extremely limited finances for such purposes. Such a disparity may arguably distort the marketplace, since

---

114. *Id.* Though Professor Stone puts forward justifications for the content distinction, at one point he openly questions the validity of his suggested analysis: "[A]lthough at first glance it seems self-evident that content-based restrictions are more threatening to the system of free expression than content-neutral restrictions, this proposition is, on closer examination, somewhat more difficult to defend than might be expected." *Id.* at 107. More recently, Professor Stone has reiterated his position. Stone, *Content Regulation and the First Amendment*, 25 WM. & MARY L. REV. 189 (1983). However, he adds little to his earlier arguments.
115. *Id.* at 101.
116. *Id.* at 103.

the public will presumably be less aware of Candidate *B*'s record and views than they will of those of Candidate *A*. But even under a law which limits both candidates' spending to a level approximately the amount available to Candidate *B* (a viewpoint-neutral limitation), it is not obvious that the marketplace functions any more efficiently, since the voting public may generally be ignorant of *both* candidates. Such a restriction would therefore be subject to the same attack Professor Stone levels against content-based restrictions.

Professor Stone's second point — the impropriety of governmental regulation because of government disagreement with speech — is no more convincing. To be sure, the philosophy of free expression is inconsistent with government prohibitions of speech because of disagreement with its content. Our fundamental assumption is that there is a need for free competition of ideas.[117] But this assumption neither explains why all content regulations should be subject to close scrutiny nor why content-neutral restrictions need not receive such scrutiny. Such a rationale, even if we were to accept it, logically applies to *any* regulation the ultimate motive for which is governmental disagreement with speech, even if that regulation superficially appears to concern something other than the content of the speech. Thus, if the government prosecutes an individual for burning his draft card in an anti-war protest because the government wishes to suppress dissent, Professor Stone's second goal is undermined even though the regulation does not appear to concern the content of any message conveyed by the act of draft card burning.[118]

Professor Tribe says, and I suppose Stone would agree, that when the government's goal is to suppress particular ideas, even content neutral regulations require closer scrutiny.[119] But drawing this distinction is easier said than done, as *O'Brien* demonstrates.[120] Could the judiciary realistically have investigated and ascertained the true governmental motivation for either the statutory prohibition of draft card destruction or (more significantly) the prosecution of *O'Brien*? Either the courts would have risked a crisis in separation of powers by probing deeply into the psyches of those responsible for instituting the prosecution (if indeed this is possible), or they would have had to remain satisfied

---

117. *But see* Baker, *supra* note 111.
118. *See* O'Brien v. United States, 391 U.S. 389 (1968); text accompanying notes 96-102 *supra*.
119. L. TRIBE, *supra* note 1, § 12-6.
120. *See* text accompanying notes 96-102 *supra*.

with the government's proffered explanation, virtually inviting governmental subterfuge.[121]

Professor Tribe believes that it would have been relatively easy to ascertain an improper congressional motive in enacting the prohibition of draft card destruction.[122] But if the *O'Brien* Court had been willing to examine legislative motive, it is not difficult to imagine future legislative history being prepared with the possibility of judicial review in mind. Moreover, it is not clear how the Court would handle a situation where several legislators supporting a facially content-neutral regulation expressed concern, presumably honestly, with factors other than content while several others referred to the desire to suppress dissent. Professor Tribe suggests that the complainant need only prove that the legislature was substantially motivated by an illicit purpose. The burden would then shift to the government to establish that the same law probably would have been enacted absent the impermissible purpose.[123] How in Heaven's name is a court going to be able to make such a finding? This fact might be established simply by showing a compelling, noncontent-related ground which could underlie such legislation.[124] But this would mean examining the legitimacy of the noncontent interest claimed to be served by the law, and would effectively mean abandoning the content distinction. In addition, Professor Tribe does not address problems such as prosecutions allegedly filed for improper reasons for violations of laws

---

121. When the prosecution is filed by state, rather than federal, officials, the added danger to federalism is present.

122. L. TRIBE, *supra* note 1, § 12-20, at 596-97. He cites "the striking omission from the legislative history of any explanation for protecting draft cards as such," even though "[t]he Court's opinion listed some possible uses which draft cards might serve ...." *Id.* at 597.

123. *Id.* at 596.

124. *See* text accompanying notes 176-215 *infra*. This appears to be what the Court did in Mt. Healthy City School Dist. Bd. of Educ. v. Doyle, 429 U.S. 274 (1977). There, an untenured teacher was dismissed in part because of the exercise of his first amendment rights. This fact did not automatically mean, however, that the teacher should be rehired. A faculty member, said the Court, "ought not to be able by engaging in [first amendment protected] conduct, to prevent his employer from assessing his performance record and reaching a decision not to rehire on the basis of that record, simply because the protected conduct makes the employer more certain of the correctness of its decision." *Id.* at 286. Therefore, once the teacher established that his constitutionally protected conduct was a "substantial factor" in the Board's decision, the Board had to show "by a preponderance of the evidence that it would have reached the same decision as to [the teacher's] reemployment even in the absence of the protected conduct." *Id.* at 287. While the Court did not explain how this was to be done, it is likely that the only conceivable means open to the Board would have been to demonstrate that the teacher's record was inadequate.

passed for proper reasons, or laws enacted by state legislatures which record little or no legislative history. The most effective means of avoiding indirect suppression of particular viewpoints, then, is closely to scrutinize *all* content-neutral regulations.[125] And the most appropriate method available to the judiciary to avoid indirect suppression of ideas is to assure itself of the compelling nature of the government's asserted noncontent-related justification of the restriction.[126]

On the other hand, government may attempt to regulate content for reasons wholly apart from disagreement with or distaste for the views expressed. This is true when it prohibits the Ku Klux Klan from conducting a rally next to a Communist Party demonstration. The government can persuasively argue that while it is regulating because of content, it is doing so solely to avoid violence. In such an instance, Professor Stone's second rationale is irrelevant.

But these disagreements with Professor Stone's second justification are secondary. The true fallacy in using this rationale for the content distinction is more fundamental: To say that it is inherently improper for the government to restrict speech because of disagreement with its content does not imply that it is appropriate for government to restrict expression for other reasons. It is true that the philosophy of the first amendment rejects governmenal regulation of expression based on disagreement with the expression's content. But, as the previous analysis of the variety of first amendment theories demonstrates,[127] that philosophy is equally undermined whenever expression is limited without a valid and compelling justification. Restricting expression because of governmental insensitivity to the importance of expression or preoccupation with the avoidance of the smallest administrative complication violates constitutionally protected interests. Indeed,

---

125. Professor Stone argues that on the whole, it is more likely that regulations aimed at content will have the ulterior motive of suppressing unpopular ideas. Stone, *supra* note 1, at 107. While this is probably correct, the example of the *O'Brien* case should underscore the fact that improper ulterior legislative motives are not limited to cases of blatant content regulations.

126. This discussion is not designed to suggest that judicial investigation of motive is *never* appropriate. When the alternative to investigating motive is an automatic finding of constitutionality, the plaintiff should be afforded the opportunity to prove such motive, despite the inherent difficulties in its proof. *See* Washington v. Davis, 426 U.S. 229 (1976); Brest, Palmer v. Thompson: *An Approach to Unconstitutional Legislative Motivation,* 1971 SUP. CT. REV. 95.

However, in the first amendment context, I do not believe a plaintiff should be *required* to prove improper motive before obtaining strict scrutiny of legislative interference with his or her opportunity for expression.

127. *See* notes 108-113 *supra* and accompanying text.

speech interests may ultimately be as greatly threatened by bureaucrats who simply do not wish to cope with the difficulties inherent in allowing free expression — whatever its content — as by governmental attempts to squelch the expression of particular viewpoints.

Of course, in some cases the government may be able to provide a compelling justification for content-neutral regulation,[128] while in many cases the government will be unable to justify content-based regulation since mere disagreement with content is not a sufficient justification. Thus, advocates of the content distinction may be correct in the narrow sense that, in terms of individual cases, content-based regulations will and should be overturned in more instances than content-neutral restrictions. However, this difference results not because the threat to first amendment values is any greater in one than in the other or because the level of judicial scrutiny given to one is more demanding, but because the asserted justification is more likely to meet a strict level of scrutiny in the former than in the latter.

Perhaps the best theoretical justification for the content distinction is what Professor Kenneth Karst calls the "equality principle" of the first amendment.[129] The theory proposes that "[t]he principle of equality, when understood to mean equal liberty, is not just a peripheral support for the freedom of expression, but rather part of the 'central meaning of the First Amendment.'"[130] Under this explanation, the primary concern of the first amendment is that government will deny equal opportunity to all views seeking expression.[131]

---

128. *See* text accompanying notes 177-181 *infra*.

129. Karst, *supra* note 1, at 29.

130. *Id.* at 21 (borrowing the phrase "central meaning of the First Amendment" from New York Times Co. v. Sullivan, 376 U.S. 254, 273 (1964); Kalven, *The New York Times Case: A Note on "The Central Meaning of the First Amendment"*, 1964 SUP. CT. REV. 191.

131. Professor Karst is unclear as to exactly how "primary" the equality principle is in the hierarchy of first amendment values. At one point, he states that it is "part of the 'central meaning of the First Amendment.'" *Id.* This statement would naturally lead one to believe that Professor Karst is suggesting an extremely important, if not primary, role for the equality principle. At another point, however, he suggests that realization of the traditional goals of free speech "implies realization of the first amendment's equality principle." *Id.* at 23. He later states that "[i]nsofar as a guarantee of free speech rests on a theory of self-government, ... the principle of equal liberty of expression is inherent in that guarantee." *Id.* at 25. These appear to be considerably more modest assertions for the role of the equality principle. Yet, at a still later point, he claims that "'equality of status in the field of ideas' is not merely a first amendment value; it is the heart of the first amendment." *Id.* at 43 (footnote omitted). He also expresses the belief that "the equality principle will turn out to be more

While Professor Karst believes that the equality principle properly underlies the constitutional prohibition of some seemingly content-neutral restrictions,[132] on the whole the principle dictates considerably closer judicial scrutiny of content-based restrictions than of those that are content-neutral. As Professor Karst states, "the principle of equal liberty lies at the heart of the first amendment's protections against government regulation of the content of speech."[133] The link is not difficult to comprehend: to the extent that government restricts only the expression of certain views, those wishing to assert those views receive unequal treatment. However, to the extent that governmental restrictions impinge equally on the expressions of all viewpoints — as is the case, at least theoretically,[134] with content-neutral restrictions — the equality principle is not undermined.

The equality principle lies behind the Supreme Court's use of both a high level of scrutiny for content-based restrictions and lesser scrutiny for content-neutral regulations. In *Mosley,* for example, where the Court struck down what it perceived to be a content-based restriction,[135] Justice Marshall's opinion emphasized the importance of maintaining "an 'equality of status in the field of ideas,'"[136] adding that government must allow all viewpoints an equal opportunity to be heard.[137] In contrast, those decisions employing only minimal scrutiny of content-neutral restrictions have emphasized the lack of discriminatory effect of the challenged regulations.[138]

Although the equality principle may provide a theoretical justification for the content distinction, it does not explain why society protects free expression in the first instance. The goals furthered by principles of equality are, both conceptually and practically, distinct

---

protective of speech than previously-established first amendment doctrines." *Id.* at 67. The assumption made here is that Professor Karst intended as his basic point the more sweeping claims for the equality principle.

132. *Id.* at 35-43. Karst distinguishes between discriminatory controls on citizen access to the public forum, or de jure content discrimination, and formally content-neutral restrictions which affect unequally, whether intentionally or not, various kinds of messages, which he refers to as de facto content discrimination. *Id.* He emphasizes, however, that "the very concept of the public forum is based in large part on the first amendment equality principle's central concern with avoiding content censorship." *Id.* at 37.

133. *Id.* at 21.
134. *Id.* at 35-43.
135. *See* notes 80-85 *supra* and accompanying text.
136. 408 U.S. at 96 (quoting A. MEIKLEJOHN, *supra* note 104, at 27).
137. *Id.*
138. *See* text accompanying notes 86-102 *supra*.

from the purposes thought to be served by freedom of expression, and sometimes actually conflict with first amendment principles.[139] The equality principle is fully satisfied when, for instance, the government effectively prohibits the expression of *any* views, since all viewpoints receive equal treatment. Whether one accepts the "self-realization" model, the "marketplace" model, the "liberty" model, or the "democratic process" model of free speech, free expression interests are undermined by such a total ban on expression.[140]

Mosley illustrates this point. If the Court's sole concern was the discrimination between labor picketing, which was allowed near the school, and nonlabor picketing, which was not, presumably the city could have satisfied the Court's "equality" concern simply by prohibiting *all* picketing. Professor Karst considers and rejects this argument.[141] He suggests that the equality principle would be undermined even by a total prohibition of picketing around the school, because those who wished to communicate with the school population would bear the greater burden of the restriction.[142] But the extent to which the equality principle prohibits equal governmental treatment which may have an unequal impact is subject to debate.[143] More importantly, Professor Karst fails to consider that the form of inequality he describes could just as easily be remedied by a total prohibition of *all* picketing for *any* purpose, *anywhere*. He might respond that such a restriction still violates the equality principle, since it discriminates against those groups who lack the financial resources to gain effective access to the media. Yet, this "equality" problem could be solved, simply by prohibiting *everyone* from having access to the media. Ultimately, the government could suppress "enough" expression by "enough" groups or individuals that the equality principle would be satisfied. In a perverse sense, then, it appears that the more expression we prohibit, the closer we come to attaining the goal of the equality principle.

---

139. *See* text accompanying notes 141-155 *infra*.
140. *See* texts accompanying notes 103-104, 108-112 *supra*.
141. Karst, *supra* note 1, at 37.
142. *Id*.
143. It certainly has not prohibited disparate impact with regard to the fourteenth amendment's equal protection clause. Washington v. Davis, 426 U.S. 229 (1976). Professor Karst acknowledges that "[i]n this dimension, the first amendment's equality principle may be more far-reaching than the equal protection clause in its present application to de facto racial discrimination." Karst, *supra* note 1, at 37 n.88. But most of the first amendment decisions involving facially neutral limitations on expression — such as *Greer, Letter Carriers,* and *O'Brien* — fail to look beyond facial neutrality.

Such total governmental prohibition is, of course, unthinkable. But the construct is no less relevant as a test of Professor Karst's theoretical rationale. Moreover, as both *Greer* and *Letter Carriers* demonstate, the Supreme Court has not engaged in the form of "impact analysis" suggested by Professor Karst in its use of the equality principle as a first amendment rationale. Instead, the Court has been satisfied if the restrictions on expression impose a prima facie form of equality.

Professor Karst argues further that the equality principle itself may control the extent of permissible limitations of expression.[144] In reaching this conclusion, though, Professor Karst effectively undermines his fundamental assumption that the equality principle represents part of the central meaning of the first amendment.[145] He suggests that an ordinance banning all picketing around the school in *Mosley* would violate the overbreadth doctrine, since it would not be sufficiently tailored to the state's interest in preserving the peace of the classroom.[146] Professor Karst fails to demonstrate, however, how the overbreadth doctrine — an established and essential tool of first amendment analysis[147] — is a manifestation of the equality principle. He reasons that the overbreadth doctrine serves the equality principle because of an overly broad statute's potential for selective enforcement.[148] While this is true, it is difficult to believe that the overbreadth doctrine is satisfied by the state's demonstrating a total and unwavering equal enforcement against all groups and individuals. By recognizing that the overbreadth principle serves as a "countervailing force"[149] to the unacceptable logical extension of the equality principle, Professor Karst implicitly acknowledges that important values other than equality are at work in first amendment analysis and that, on occasion, these values may even clash with the equality principle.[150]

The campaign financing example illustrates this clash.[151] The desire to reduce the significant advantages possessed by those with greater

---

144. Karst, *supra* note 1, at 38-39.
145. *See* text accompanying notes 129-131 *supra*.
146. Karst, *supra* note 1, at 38.
147. *See generally* Chapter V.
148. Karst, *supra* note 1, at 38.
149. *Id.*
150. Nevertheless, Professor Karst, like earlier commentators, *see* Note, *supra* note 52, at 918-20, argues that the overbreadth doctrine should apply more vigorously to a content-neutral law shown to contain hidden inequalities than to a content-neutral law that applies equally to all. Karst, *supra* note 1, at 39.
151. *See* text accompanying notes 116-117 *supra*.

financial resources was a major impetus behind the enactment of federal legislation limiting contributions and expenditures for political campaigns.[152] This goal manifests the equality principle since it aims at equalizing candidates' access to the electorate. But by limiting spending, such regulation decreases the flow of information which might produce better informed voters and thus undermines important first amendment values.[153] Of course, such restrictions are not necessarily unconstitutional, for the benefits of "purifying" political campaigns and equalizing candidate access to the public may outweigh the resulting harms to free speech interest.[154] The outcome of the conflict is, for present purposes, irrelevant. Whatever the outcome, the example demonstrates how the equality principle and the values furthered by free expression may directly conflict, for the equality principle is satisfied by — and, in fact, may dictate — reduction of expression to the lowest common denominator.[155]

The most strained use of the equality principle is perhaps the suggestion that it should be employed to invalidate subject matter categorizations for purposes of first amendment analysis.[156] When

---

152. *See* Fleishman, *Freedom of Speech and Equality of Political Opportunity: The Constitutionality of the Federal Election Campaign Act of 1971*, 51 N.C.L. REV. 389 (1973); Redish, *Campaign Spending Laws and the First Amendment*, 46 N.Y.U. L. REV. 900 (1971).

153. *See* Buckley v. Valeo, 424 U.S. 1, 19 (1976) (per curiam).

154. The *Buckley* Court felt that the first amendment harms resulting from the campaign expenditure limitations outweighed the dangers of unequal access and candidate dependence on large contributions. *See id.* at 55-57.

155. The logic of the equality principle need not be limited to the regulation of campaign financing. Our economic system gives rise to significant differences in the relative power and financial resources of citizens. Those with greater resources and more power will invariably possess greater access to the media, and therefore to the public, than will those less well situated. These factors may be cited as reasons why a seemingly neutral restriction on picketing should in reality be found to discriminate (and therefore, constitute a violation of the equality principle). Those with greater resources and power do not need to picket to express their views; those lacking such advantages do. But it would be absurd to think that allowing individuals to picket produces anything approaching equality. If equality were truly our goal, we could prohibit those with greater financial resources from ever taking advantage of them (by, for example, prohibiting taking out full-page newspaper ads) and leave such things as picketing as the *only* access for *everyone*. Of course, the equality principle would also be satisfied by legislation going to the other extreme, mandating access for all equivalent to that of the highest common denominator. But the important point for present purposes is that the equality principle is logically satisfied by either form of regulation.

156. *See* Karst, *supra* note 1, at 30-35.

distinctions are drawn between commercial and political speech,[157] or between fighting words,[158] libel,[159] or obscenity[160] and other forms of expression, it makes little sense to criticize the distinctions solely because different forms of speech are receiving unequal treatment. Such forms of expression do not compete with one another, as, for example, do opposite positions on the Vietnam War or the defense budget. Those who do not receive protection for their commercial or libelous utterances are no worse off because other forms of speech are protected, and would be no better off if the other forms were also denied protection. This is not true when government prohibits the expression of only one viewpoint on a particular issue. In that case, the prohibited expression *is* harmed, in an equal protection sense, because competing views are allowed to be heard, and *would be* better off if the competing views were also prohibited. There may well be valid reasons for attacking first amendment distinctions drawn between commercial and noncommercial speech, or between libel and other forms of expression.[161] But such attacks should be based on the theoretically artificial nature of the distinction, since the excluded forms of expression may also further first amendment values.[162] Emphasizing some notion of aesthetic inequality among wholly unrelated and noncompeting forms of expression only obscures the appropriate analysis.

IV. Practical Difficulties in Applying the Content Distinction

Even if the content distinction were theoretically valid, the distinction is still pragmatically unworkable. It invites governmental regulation that will significantly harm many of the interests supposedly protected by the content distinction even where such regulation can formally be defined as "content-neutral." In fact, the assumption that the courts can recognize and distinguish between these two kinds of regulations has proven incorrect in numerous instances. This danger must be distinguished from the fear that

---

157. *See* Valentine v. Chrestensen, 316 U.S. 52 (1942).
158. *See* Chaplinsky v. New Hampshire, 315 U.S. 568 (1942).
159. *See* Beuharnais v. Illinois, 343 U.S. 250 (1952).
160. *See* Miller v. California, 413 U.S. 15 (1973).
161. *See* New York Times Co. v. Sullivan, 376 U.S. 254 (1964) (libel); Redish, *The First Amendment in the Marketplace: Commercial Speech and the Values of Free Expression,* 39 GEO. WASH. L. REV. 429 (1971) (commercial speech). *See generally* Chapter I.
162. *See* Chapter I, *supra* at 60-86.

government will regulate in a superficially content-neutral manner with the motive of penalizing particular viewpoints.[163] That is, of course, a matter of serious concern. But the danger also exists that, because of the often unclear line between regulation of the manner of expression and regulation of its content, government may both purport and intend to regulate what it considers to be "manner" while in reality having a significant indirect impact on interests meant to be protected by close scrutiny of content regulation.

Cohen v. California[164] presented such a situation. Cohen had been convicted of "offensive conduct" for walking in a courthouse corridor while wearing a jacket with the words "Fuck the Draft" emblazoned on it. In overturning the conviction, Justice Harlan, speaking for the Court, emphasized that the conviction obviously resulted from the alleged offensiveness of the *words* Cohen used to impart his message.[165] The state, in Harlan's view, had no power to punish Cohen for asserting the position on the draft which the message conveyed.[166] Yet, one could argue that the state objected not to the content of Cohen's "commentary," but to the offensive "manner" in which he expressed it. The state was merely telling Cohen that he could not protest the draft in a manner offensive to viewers for reasons wholly apart from the "content" of his message. Under this theory, viewers would have been equally offended if his jacket had said, "Fuck Communism," or "Fuck Those Opposing the Draft." The "content" was, therefore, irrelevant. Moreover, the state could argue that it was not discriminating among various viewpoints, since it would take the same action against any individual sufficiently uncouth to employ the same terminology to express a viewpoint. That no one had expressed a viewpoint in the same manner is not the fault of the state; the state cannot be blamed if only those expressing one viewpoint use offensive language.

Justice Harlan persuasively responded that much verbal expression is chosen as much for its emotive force as for its cognitive meaning.[167] But this response does not turn on whether we categorize the regulation as affecting "content." If we apply the philosophy of the content distinction, we must first define the concept of content-based regulation. If we define the concept as any regulation directed to the communicative impact of expression,[168] it is still unclear whether the

---

163. *See* text accompanying notes 119-124 *supra*.
164. 403 U.S. 15 (1971).
165. *Id.* at 18.
166. *Id.*
167. *Id.*
168. *See* notes 22-28 *supra* and accompanying text.

regulation involves "communicative impact" since it concerns the "impact" of the words involved.[169] But one could also contend that the regulation is not so concerned, since it does not turn on the communication of any particular idea. Ultimately, applying the content distinction to the *Cohen* facts collapses into a hopeless battle of semantics. A more perceptive approach is that of Justice Harlan, who avoids semantics and instead examines the theoretical and practical considerations involved when the state acts to restrict expression — whether in a content-based manner or not.

The flag desecration ordinances raise even more confusing issues.[170] In *People v. Street*,[171] the New York Court of Appeals upheld application of such a law to an individual who had burned a flag as part of a political protest. In doing so, the court emphasized that the law regulated only the manner of expression.[172] Street was not prohibited from expressing the substance of his political views, but only from doing so in an offensive manner. The flag-burning cases do not involve the use of words, a factor stressed by Justice Harlan in *Cohen*.[173] Yet the arguments used in *Cohen* seem equally dispositive of the flag-burning cases: The chosen "manner" of expression often makes the substance of the message more powerful. Governmental interference with the method of expression, then, can prove as injurious to first amendment interests — particularly the value of individual self-fulfillment[174] — as regulation of content. One could fashion an argument that flag desecration ordinances do regulate content,[175] since they prohibit the destruction of one of the most powerful symbols of the United States and its government. The basic point is this: Why should we care whether, in some metaphysical sense, a regulation is "content-based" or "content-neutral"? In either event, the regulation undermines free expression. Using the content distinction only obscures the appropriate inquiry in a sea of semantics.

V. Abandoning the Content Distinction

Everything said to this point leads to one conclusion: The content

---

169. *Id.*
170. *See generally* Ely, *supra* note 1.
171. 20 N.Y.2d 231, 229 N.E.2d 187 (1967), *rev'd sub nom.* Street v. New York, 394 U.S. 576 (1969).
172. 20 N.Y.2d at 235-36, 229 N.E.2d at 190.
173. *See* 403 U.S. at 18.
174. *See* note 111 *supra* and accompanying text. *See generally* Chapter I.
175. Ely comments that state desecration laws, though facially neutral, effectively

distinction is conceptually and pragmatically untenable and should therefore be abandoned. To be sure, different approaches to first amendment analysis may develop for different types of regulations.[176] But the source for such approaches need not and should not turn on the content distinction. Instead, the courts should subject all restrictions on expression to the same critical scrutiny traditionally reserved for regulations drawn in terms of content.

Proponents of the content distinction may be concerned that increasing the level of judicial scrutiny for content-neutral restrictions may result in a generally reduced skepticism for all content-based classification. This need not be the case. First, even under the content distinction, content-based regulations are not automatically invalidated.[177] Those advocating the violent overthrow of the government may constitutionally be subjected to severe penalties,[178] the use of "fighting words" may be punished,[179] and the advocacy of unlawful conduct may be punished if it "is directed to inciting or producing imminent lawless action and is likely to incite or produce such action."[180] The Court has approved such regulations as necessary and appropriate, though each turns, in one sense or another, on the content of the communication. In each, the Court effectively concluded that the government had established a compelling justification for content-based regulation,[181] even though one might argue that some of these interests are not "compelling," or not sufficiently compelling to justify significant invasions of free speech interests. I suggest simply that the same question be asked of content-neutral regulations.

The question, however, cannot be that simple. The Court's initial inquiry — once it has assured itself that speech is impaired — should be the type of question asked in *O'Brien*:[182] Does the regulation, wholly

---

proscribe only those ideological outlooks that condone hostile treatment of the flag. *See* Ely, *supra* note 1, at 1502-04.

176. *See generally* Shiffrin, *Defamatory Non-Media Speech and First Amendment Methodology,* 25 U.C.L.A. L. REV. 915 (1978).

177. "The question whether speech is, or is not, protected by the First Amendment often depends on the content of the speech." Young v. American Mini Theatres, Inc., 427 U.S. 50, 66 (1976); *see* Shiffrin *supra* note 176, at 955 ("[A]ny assessment of the legal regulation of communication must begin with the recognition that government does have power to restrict expression because of its content.").

178. *E.g.,* Dennis v. United States, 341 U.S. 494 (1951).

179. Chaplinsky v. New Hampshire, 315 U.S. 568 (1942).

180. Brandenburg v. Ohio, 395 U.S. 444, 447 (1969).

181. According to Professor Strong, similar reasoning has traditionally provided a rationale for the "clear and present danger" test. *See* Strong, *Fifty Years of "Clear and Present Danger": From* Schenck *to* Brandenburg *— and Beyond,* 1969 SUP. CT. REV. 41, 68.

182. *See* text accompanying notes 96-102 *supra*.

apart from its effect on speech, purport to further a non-negligible (or what the Court misleadingly labelled "substantial") government interest? In the rare case of a negative response,[183] the answer is clear: The law is unconstitutional. If this hurdle is overcome, the court should inquire: (1) Whether the regulation accomplishes the asserted goal; (2) whether "feasible" less restrictive alternatives are inadequate to accomplish that end; and (3) whether the speaker will have available adequate means to express the same views to roughly the same audience. If the government satisfies the court that the first two factors are present, the court should balance the compellingness of the state interest served by the law against the availability of alternative means of expression to the speaker. The initial criterion and the final inquiry will work in a reverse correlation: The less likely it is that the speaker will be able to find acceptable alternative methods of expression, the more compelling must be the government's asserted justification. However, this sliding scale analysis is to become relevant only after the reviewing court has concluded that the state interest is truly "compelling" in the first place. Unless the state interest is found to meet a threshold level of "compelling" — a level far beyond the Court's minimal requirement of "non-negligible" — the interest of the speaker in choosing the manner and timing of expression is paramount, even if conceivable alternatives for expression might exist.

I admit there is nothing revolutionary in this analysis,[184] but applying it to content-neutral regulations would represent a significant change in the Court's attitude. Since the Court generally uses many of these factors in reviewing content-based regulations, it should have no greater difficulty in applying them to *all* regulations of expression.

It is important to establish two points in applying this analysis to content-neutral regulations. First, when the test asks whether the government interest is "compelling," it means exactly that — not in

---

183. *See* Ely, *supra* note 1, at 1486.
184. Professor Shiffrin, for example, suggests that courts employ an analysis somewhat similar to the approach suggested here in determining whether content may be regulated. According to Shiffrin, "[t]hat task necessitates a determination of: (1) the nature of the interest sought to be furthered by the state; (2) the extent to which the state must abridge the particular speech in order to further that interest; (3) the extent to which the abridgment will further the state interest; and (4) the impact of that abridgment on free speech values." Shiffrin, *supra* note 176, at 955. While not identical to the mode of analysis suggested in the text, Shiffrin's approach does ask many of the same basic questions. Note, however, that Shiffrin puts forward his test as a guide in determining when content can be abridged, a task he views as primary in first amendment adjudication. *Id.*

the sense that the term has been distorted in modern equal protection analysis effectively to mean a standard incapable of compliance,[185] but in the commonsense interpretation of the word: a matter of truly vital and important concern. Thus, mere government inconvenience or difficulty in dealing with certain kinds of expression is insufficient to justify regulation. The first amendment demands no less. Of course, how a court will define "compelling" in particular cases is, to a certain extent, unpredictable. For example, it is impossible to know the point at which a court will decide that government expenses to protect marchers become compelling.[186] But this difficulty is no different from that encountered in assessing content-based regulation.[187]

Second, the distinction between ad hoc balancing and a "definitional" or "categorization" approach may conceivably develop in the application of this test,[188] but it need not be associated solely with the content distinction, as leading commentators have suggested it should.[189] In some situations, using the suggested "balancing" analysis will lead to rules that will provide general guidelines applicable to specific cases. The "actual malice" rule of *New York Times Co. v. Sullivan*[190] and the modern version of the "clear and present danger" test in *Brandenburg v. Ohio*[191] illustrate this notion. In other situations, case-by-case balancing will be unavoidable, though the elements of the suggested analysis will still provide a guide as to the proper weight of various factors. But the need for this variety of approaches does not arise out of a content-based versus content-neutral distinction. *Schneider v. State*[192] may have involved a content-neutral

---

185. *See* Gunther, *The Supreme Court, 1971 Term — Foreword: In Search of Evolving Doctrine on a Changing Court: A Model for a Newer Equal Protection*, 86 HARV. L. REV. 1, 8 (1972) (use of this standard has been "'strict' in theory and fatal in fact").

186. It is not likely that use of the "compelling interest" standard will cause serious difficulty to a municipality intending to impose traditional "time-place-manner" regulations on the conduct of public demonstrations or rallies. This is because once the state can establish a threshold compelling interest in not having a particular demonstration held, under the "sliding scale" approach described in this chapter, the more alternative avenues of expression that are available, the less justification the state must provide for restricting expression.

187. *See* text accompanying notes 125-128 *supra*.

188. I have questioned the distinction between definitional and ad hoc balancing in first amendment doctrine in other portions of this book. *See, e.g.*, Chapter IV, *infra* at 193-201; Chapter V, *infra* at 255-57.

189. *See* L. TRIBE, *supra* note 1, § 12-2, at 582-84; Ely, *supra* note 1, at 1496-1502.

190. 376 U.S. 254 (1964).

191. 395 U.S. 444 (1969).

192. 308 U.S. 147 (1939).

regulation, but the rule established there invalidating anti-littering ordinances which prohibited handbill distribution does not require a future case-by-case analysis any more than does the rule of *New York Times*. In fact, it does so considerably *less* than does the *New York Times* rule, which still requires the courts to inquire whether, under the unique facts, "actual malice" has been established. The same could, of course, be said for cases applying the *Brandenburg* test.[193]

In contrast, the constitutionality of many content-based regulations will necessarily be decided with ad hoc balancing. Could we establish a categorical rule, for example, that will define the proper circumstances for invalidating a city's decision to prohibit or restrict a rally by an unpopular group? At what point is the danger of violence or the cost of providing protection so great that the city is justified in limiting such a rally? Determinations like these necessarily turn on unique facts, even though the regulations are clearly content-based.[194] In cases so dependent on specific facts, we cannot avoid some form of ad hoc balancing, whatever the regulation's relevance to content. A "thumb on the scales" in favor of free speech,[195] as articulated in the "compelling interest" analysis, is our only protection against abuse. If used properly and consistently, it should be enough.

I do not mean to suggest that the content factor is always irrelevant. In one sense, the content factor is relevant in an almost evidentiary way. If the government attempts to justify a regulation on a basis unrelated to content, that the regulation actually turns on content will effectively "tip the hand" of the government. It will reveal that the government does not really believe that its asserted content-neutral justification is valid; for if it were, the government would presumably not exempt anyone from the regulation.

Mosley illustrates this approach. If the city were truly concerned about the danger of classroom disruption from peaceful, quiet picketing, it could not logically exempt labor picketing, since such picketing presents the same dangers. That the city tolerated labor picketing revealed that the city was not really concerned with the supposed harms of picketing.[196] The same could be said of *Erznoznik*: That other possible cinematic distractions to drivers were not

---

193. *See* note 51 *supra* and accompanying text.
194. *See also* Brandenburg v. Ohio, 395 U.S. 444 (1969).
195. Kalven, *supra* note 57, at 28.
196. In *Mosley,* the Court rejected the city's specious argument that labor picketing was inherently less likely to produce violence. 408 U.S. at 100-01.

prohibited rendered questionable the government's assertion that the regulation of nudity was needed to avoid traffic hazards.[197] Moreover, when government regulates content because of disagreement with the views conveyed, even the initial requirement of a non-negligible governmental interest is not satisfied.

Examining specific cases involving content-neutral regulations in light of the proposed "unified" first amendment analysis should help in understanding how the test will function. Prime candidates for reexamination are the decisions in *Greer, Letter Carriers,* and *O'Brien.*

In *Greer,* the Court upheld the refusal of military authorities to allow a third-party candidate for president to conduct a rally and distribute literature at an army base. The Court emphasized the following factors: (1) the army did not discriminate among competing political views, since it had never allowed other candidates to appear on the base; (2) the military has a legitimate interest in limiting both disruption on the base and the "politicization" of the armed forces; (3) the political rights of servicemen may be curtailed more than can those of civilians; and (4) members of the armed forces and their dependents could easily attend rallies off the base.[198] Under a unitary "compelling interest" analysis, none of these criteria would justify a total ban on political activity on the base.

The initial hurdle is met in *Greer* since legitimate governmental interests are obviously involved. But under the unitary analysis that conclusion does not end the inquiry. Nor does the absence of discrimination among various viewpoints end the inquiry: While discrimination automatically renders the regulation unconstitutional, the absence of discrimination does not necessarily imply constitutionality, since important first amendment values may be undermined even though the equality concern is satisfied.[199] Because viewpoint discrimination was absent, the Court gave summary consideration to the availability of other means for the speaker to convey his message. The fact that soldiers and their dependents *could* attend off-base rallies was no answer to the candidate: His argument presumably was that until they heard the persuasiveness of his appeal, they would have no motivation to attend such a rally. In any event, the argument that a speaker need not be permitted to reach a potential audience because they could seek him out is simply unsatisfying.

At this point, the question the Court should ask is whether the governmental interest involved could be satisfied without such a total

---

197. *See* text accompanying notes 73-79 *supra.*
198. 424 U.S. at 838-40; *see* text accompanying notes 93-95 *supra.*
199. *See* notes 129-162 *supra* and accompanying text.

ban on political activity at the base. An affirmative answer seems inescapable since it would be easy to allow one scheduled on-based rally by any recognized presidential candidate or to schedule one forum at which all presidential candidates or their representatives would be allowed to make brief statements, answer questions, and make campaign literature available.[200] Either solution is preferable to a total ban, and neither disrupts the workings of the base to such a degree that the governmental interest in avoiding disruption becomes compelling. After all, as long as military personnel vote, it is absurd to suggest that the need to preserve the military's appearance of political neutrality is so overwhelming that it justifies a total ban of nondisruptive informational political gatherings.

Letter Carriers is a more difficult case, even under the unified analysis, because while the compelling nature of the government interest — avoiding corruption and undue political pressure on civil service employees — is obvious, less restrictive viable alternatives do not clearly exist. However, the vagueness difficulties emphasized by the dissent[201] should have at least given the majority greater pause,[202] and the Court could certainly have considered the viability of relegating the government to rigorous investigation and prosecution of actual corruption, rather than using the admittedly easier, but considerably more constitutionally doubtful, prophylactic measures of the Hatch Act. Even the lesser effectiveness of such measures may not be dispositive in light of such widespread (albeit content-neutral) limitations on political activity.[203]

---

200. It is generally agreed that, in employing a "less restrictive alternative" analysis, the Court need not elaborate upon the specific alternatives that are available; that is a decision to be made by the legislature. *See* United States v. Robel, 389 U.S. 258, 267 (1967); L. TRIBE, *supra* note 1, § 12-30, at 724. *But see* Gunther, *Reflections on Robel: It's Not What the Court Did But the Way That It Did It,* 20 STAN. L. REV. 1140, 1147-48 (1968). *See generally* Chapter V.

201. 413 U.S. at 595-96 (Douglas, J., dissenting).

202. The majority summarily disposed of the vagueness challenge by stating that while "[t]here might be quibbles" about the meaning of the statutory language, these were simply the result of "limitations in the English language ...." *Id.* at 577-78.

203. In dealing with the question of whether less restrictive means were available, the majority said, "The joint judgment of the Executive and Congress has been that to protect the rights of federal employees with respect to their jobs and their political acts and beliefs it is not enough merely to forbid one employee from attempting to influence or coerce another .... Perhaps Congress at some time will come to a different view of the realities of political life and Government service; but that is its current view of the matter, and we are not now in any position to dispute it." *Id.* at 566-67 (footnote omitted). *Letter Carriers'* application of overbreadth analysis is examined in Chapter V, *infra* at 232-33.

O'Brien is the easiest case to deal with under the unified analysis.[204] First, the government may not have met the threshold test of "substantiality" since the governmental interest was, at best, speculative.[205] Second, the government never established that O'Brien had other available means of expressing the same viewpoint.

Still, Professor Tribe argues that O'Brien failed to show that equally effective alternative methods of conveying his message were unavailable.[206] He suggests that O'Brien "could, after all, have burned a *copy* of his draft card in front of the very same audience, as a means of making precisely the same point."[207] The only reason this alternative might not be deemed as effective, according to Tribe, is the drama added by the illegal nature of burning the real card — grounds he deems logically questionable.[208] But it is unclear whether burning a copy of the draft card would have conveyed O'Brien's message as effectively, or that the effectiveness derived exclusively, or even primarily, from the illegal nature of the act. One could argue that by destroying the actual draft card, O'Brien was symbolically rejecting the moral authority of the United States government to use the draft as a means of world domination, or of suppression of dissent, or whatever it was O'Brien was complaining about. Merely destroying a copy of the card lacks the symbolism of authority rejection implicit in the destructive act. While the illegal nature of the act might add something to its intensity, even the legal act of card burning is likely to convey a powerful message.

---

204. The Court's unhelpful emphasis on the "conduct" element involved in O'Brien's actions requires some preliminary discussion. The point is misleading because it implies that speech and conduct come in neatly severable units — an obvious fallacy. Just as the newspaper boy's hurling a newspaper onto the front porch should not be subjected to regulation on the grounds that it is "conduct," not "speech," so too should the verbal command to "fire" in front of a firing squad not be deemed "speech" merely because vocal cords are utilized. The fact that O'Brien's actions had arguable harmful effects, unrelated to the communicative aspect of his message, means only that the regulation of the effects is content-neutral; it does not mean that "expression" is not being regulated. The same is true of a city's refusal to grant a picketing permit because of fear that the flowers will get trampled. The *O'Brien* Court's suggested analysis of how to decide free speech issues — the test it actually applied to the *O'Brien* facts — was not tied to the speech-conduct issue, however. Therefore, we can safely apply the unified analysis to the facts of *O'Brien* without further concern with the supposed content-expression distinction. *See* Ely, *supra* note 1, at 1491-96.

205. 391 U.S. at 378-80. The *O'Brien* Court did believe that the "substantiality" requirement had been satisfied, underscoring the limited character of judicial inquiry on this question.

206. L. TRIBE, *supra* note 1, § 12-20, at 686.

207. *Id.* (emphasis in original).

208. *Id.*

In any event, why is it an appropriate task for a law professor or for the Supreme Court to decide for Mr. O'Brien what increases or decreases the intensity of his message?[209] Is not this very inquiry an invasion of first amendment freedom? If not, why was the state or the Court prevented from telling the plaintiff in *Cohen v. California*[210] that he might gain more adherents to his cause if he chose not to use profanity? Surely Justice Harlan was not convinced that the use of four-letter words was essential to intelligent discourse on the subject of the draft; Justice Harlan simply concluded that the choice of how to make a message most effective belonged to the speaker.

Moreover, unless the government can establish that the means chosen by the speaker to convey his message impair a compelling interest, the speaker should not be required to establish that alternative avenues of expression are inadequate. The government failed to do this in *O'Brien*. Indeed, the government's proffered justifications for prohibiting draft card burning[211] were so dubious that Professor Tribe himself concludes that they could not have been the real reasons for the law's passage.[212] But one need not head into that political thicket; whether the legislators were actually motivated by the proffered content-neutral justification is irrelevant. Unless those reasons establish a compelling governmental interest furthered by the restriction on expression, expression may not be limited.

O'Brien illustrates how defining the relevant governmental interest can alter the mode of analysis. If the governmental justification is the need to assure that every registrant carries his draft card at all times, there can be no less restrictive alternatives.[213] But the government cannot be allowed to end the inquiry in this manner. In such an event, the court must ask whether that interest, standing alone, is compelling. The need to have registrants carry draft cards — unlike the need to avoid disrupting an army base in *Greer*, or the need to

---

209. It is true that under the analysis suggested here, if the state is able to establish a compelling interest for its regulation of expression, a court may well decide for the speaker that he has available adequate alternative avenues of expression. *See* text accompanying notes 182-184 *supra*. The important distinction between this analysis and that of Professor Tribe, however, is that Tribe would apparently allow the court to make such a determination for the individual, even absent any real showing of state interest for the regulation. He thus places the *initial* burden of proof on the speaker, rather than on the state.

210. 403 U.S. 15 (1971); *see* notes 164-169 *supra* and accompanying text.

211. *See* note 214 *infra* and accompanying text.

212. L. TRIBE, *supra* note 1, § 12-6, at 596-97.

213. 391 U.S. at 381 ("We perceive no alternative means that would more precisely and narrowly assure the continuing availability of issued Selective Service certificates than a law which prohibits their willful mutilation or destruction.").

prevent corruption among Civil Service employees in *Letter Carriers* — does not intuitively represent an end in itself. The court must ask *why* the government deems it necessary that all registrants carry their cards.

The reasons mentioned by the Court in *O'Brien* can best be described as strained.[214] At most, the Court established that a registrant's failure to carry his card pursuant to the law created a certain administrative inconvenience. Even this is unclear, since the overwhelming majority of young men probably would have voluntarily complied, if only for their own convenience. More importantly, once we acknowledge that *O'Brien's* actions contained a significant expressive element[215] and that the prohibition of his actions, even though seemingly content-neutral, must be measured by a compelling interest test, we must reject the asserted justifications. Moderate levels of administrative inconvenience can never constitute such a compelling interest; if they did, we would be authorizing sweeping governmental regulations of expression, since maintaining free expression often creates some administrative burden. This is a price that a democratic society committed to the integrity of the individual and the preeminent value of uninhibited discussion must be willing to tolerate.

VI. *Conclusion*

Both the Supreme Court and leading commentators have drawn a fairly strict dichotomy in the degree of judicial review given to content-based and content-neutral regulations of expression. This chapter has attempted to demonstrate the conceptual and practical awkwardness of this dichotomy. While governmental attempts to regulate the content of expression undoubtedly deserve strict judicial review, it does not logically follow that equally serious threats to first amendment freedoms cannot derive from restrictions imposed to regulate expression in a manner unrelated to content.

I have suggested that all governmental regulations of expression be subjected to a unified "compelling interest" analysis. To be sure, various types of expression often give rise to harmful consequences, and any judicial attempt to reconcile these competing interests will face a myriad of obstacles. In certain instances, the courts will mold the elements of the "compelling interest" analysis into general rules that provide some level of guidance to a reviewing court. In other cases the courts will be forced to apply the analysis in an ad hoc fashion. But this

---

214. *Id.* at 378-80.
215. *See* T. EMERSON, *supra* note 42, at 84-85.

distinction need not and should not turn on whether the regulation of expression is content-based or content-neutral. There are dangers of abuse inherent in any method of first amendment construction that turns heavily on the specific facts of a case. But as long as the courts begin each case with the premise that expression may be regulated only in the presence of a truly compelling governmental interest, the values of free expression will be appropriately served.

CHAPTER III

THE PROPER ROLE OF THE PRIOR RESTRAINT DOCTRINE IN FIRST AMENDMENT THEORY

I. Introduction

If one constant exists in Supreme Court first amendment theory, it is that "[a]ny prior restraint on expression comes to ... [the] Court with a 'heavy presumption' against its constitutional validity."[1] Under the prior restraint doctrine, the government may not restrain a particular expression prior to its dissemination even though the same expression could be constitutionally subjected to punishment after dissemination.[2] The doctrine thus turns not on the content or substantive character of the particular expression, but exclusively on the nature and form of governmental regulation of the expression. It assumes that prior restraints are more harmful to free speech interests than are other forms of regulation such as criminal prosecutions or the imposition of civil liability.[3]

Although the prior restraint doctrine pervades Supreme Court rhetoric, the Court's decisions reveal inconsistencies in the doctrine's application. On occasion the Court has condemned regulation solely because it came in the form of a prior restraint,[4] while at other times the Court has been surprisingly accepting of prior restraint despite the absence of any showing of need for this form of regulation.[5] More importantly, the doctrine's undue emphasis on the supposed harms of prior restraints in contrast to those of subsequent punishment schemes has often diverted judicial attention away from the significant substantive danger to first amendment rights posed by a particular regulation in question. Thus, reliance on the doctrine often has given rise to the inference that subsequent punishment in certain prior

---

1. Organization for a Better Austin v. Keefe, 402 U.S. 415, 419 (1971) (citations omitted). *See also* Bantam Books, Inc. v. Sullivan, 372 U.S. 58, 70 (1963).

2. According to Professor Thomas Emerson, "[R]estrictions which could be validly imposed when enforced by subsequent punishment are, nevertheless, forbidden if attempted by prior restraint." Emerson, *The Doctrine of Prior Restraint,* 20 LAW & CONTEMP. PROBS. 648 (1955). *See generally* O. FISS, THE CIVIL RIGHTS INJUNCTION 40 (1978) (an injunction against speech allowed only if speech is as clearly unprotected as that revealing troop movements during wartime); J. NOWAK, R. ROTUNDA & J. YOUNG, CONSTITUTIONAL LAW 886-94 (2d ed. 1983) (presumption against prior restraints). For a discussion of the doctrine's early development, see Emerson, *supra,* at 650-55.

3. *See, e.g., infra* text accompanying notes 25-49.

4. *See infra* notes 6, 163.

5. *See infra* text accompanying notes 92, 109, 116-117.

restraint cases would be permissible or has left that issue unnecessarily unresolved, causing a possible chilling effect.[6]

These apparent doctrinal ambiguities and inconsistencies result from the absence of any detailed judicial analysis of the true rationale behind the prior restraint doctrine.[7] Although several leading commentators have attempted to supply such an analysis, their arguments fail to justify the strong presumption against all forms of prior restraint, whether judicial or administrative.[8] Courts and commentators quick to invoke the doctrine mistakenly believe that in such cases first amendment interests can be discerned and protected with relative ease: if a prior restraint is involved, the presumption

---

6. Near v. Minnesota, 283 U.S. 697 (1931), and New York Times Co. v. United States, 403 U.S. 713 (1971), two classic prior restraint cases, illustrate this point. In *Near*, the Court struck down as an improper restraint a Minnesota statute that authorized judicial abatement of a "malicious, scandalous and defamatory newspaper." 283 U.S. at 701-02. The opinion focused exclusively on the harms of the prior restraint involved. One may ask, however, whether the true harm to first amendment rights actually was the prior restraint aspect of the regulation. Would the first amendment problems have been reduced or avoided if the legislature had instead made it a crime to publish such a newspaper? The Court's substantial emphasis on the evils of the prior restraint leaves such a conclusion an open possibility.

Similarly, in *New York Times* the Court invalidated judicial injunctions against the publication of the previously classified "Pentagon Papers" and in so doing generally emphasized the harmful nature of the prior restraint involved. 403 U.S. at 714. Yet, only Justices Black's and Douglas' concurrence in the per curiam opinion focused on the vitally important *substantive* first amendment issue of whether publication of supposedly secret documents that would have a possibly embarrassing impact on the government is fully protected by the first amendment. Ultimately, all that the Court held was that such publication could not constitutionally be subjected to prior restraint. *Id.* at 714. For all that most of the opinions reveal, someone who published these papers could have been convicted of a crime and given a life sentence. Professor Kalven has noted that use of the prior restraint doctrine in *New York Times* "left the Court free, if necessary, at some later time in a criminal prosecution to deal with the true and difficult merits." Kalven, *The Supreme Court 1970 Term — Foreword: Even When a Nation Is at War*, 85 HARV. L. REV. 3, 33 (1971). By emphasizing the supposed harms of the prior restraint, then, the decision diverted attention from the true first amendment issue and to this day has left a possible chill on anyone who might wish to publish similar documents.

7. As Judge Linde has written, "The rule against ... prior restraint entered modern Supreme Court doctrine under the aegis of history rather than logic or policy." Linde, *Courts and Censorship*, 66 MINN. L. REV. 171, 185 (1981).

8. *See, e.g.,* Blasi, *Toward a Theory of Prior Restraint: The Central Linkage*, 66 MINN. L. REV. 11, 93 (1981); Emerson, *supra* note 2, at 656-60. For a discussion of these arguments, see *infra* text accompanying notes 23-76.

against it is overwhelming. In reality, however, the first amendment interests are considerably more complex.[9] Try as the Court might, it cannot successfully substitute supposedly easily applied formulas for the careful balancing of interests necessary in first amendment analysis.[10]

Acceptance of these conclusions, however, does not necessarily lead to a total rejection of the prior restraint doctrine, for in certain instances prior restraints are appropriately disfavored. This is not because of most of the traditional judicial and scholarly arguments supporting the doctrine, but rather because of the coincidental harm to fully protected expression that results from the *preliminary* restraint imposed prior to a decision on the merits of a *final* restraint.[11] To be effective, a prior restraint must often restrict *all* relevant expression, whether or not fully protected, while the adjudicatory body determines whether the expression should be subjected to a final restraint. Such interim restraints present a threat to first amendment rights not found in subsequent punishment schemes — the threat that expression will be abridged, if only for a short time, prior to a full and fair hearing before an independent judicial forum to determine the scope of the speaker's constitutional right.

The requirement of a full and fair hearing before an independent judicial forum for the adjudication of constitutional rights is a widely accepted premise of modern constitutional thinking.[12] Somewhat

---

9. The prior restraint doctrine, like so many other code words of modern first amendment analysis discussed in other portions of this book, is premised upon a misleading simplicity that fails to comport with reality.

10. *See supra* note 6.

11. *See infra* text accompanying notes 25, 102-106, 119-127.

12. *See, e.g.,* Crowell v. Benson, 285 U.S. 22, 60 (1932) (Constitution requires a fair opportunity to submit the issue to an independent judicial tribunal); Battaglia v. General Motors Corp., 169 F.2d 254, 257 (2d Cir. 1948) (fifth amendment governs Congress' control over jurisdiction and requires independent judicial forum), *cert. denied,* 335 U.S. 887 (1948); D. CURRIE, FEDERAL JURISDICTION IN A NUTSHELL 37 (2d ed. 1981) (closing of the courts to any class of free speech claims is a deprivation of due process); C. WRIGHT, THE LAW OF FEDERAL COURTS 38-39 (4th ed. 1983) (Congress' power to alter federal courts' jurisdiction limited by due process); Hart, *The Power of Congress to Limit the Jurisdiction of Federal Courts: An Exercise in Dialectic,* 66 HARV. L. REV. 1362, 1371-72 (1953) (Congress' jurisdictional power is subject to all other portions of the Constitution); Redish & Woods, *Congressional Power to Control the Jurisdiction of Lower Federal Courts: A Critical Review and a New Synthesis,* 124 U. PA. L. REV. 45, 76-81 (1975) (recognizing a right to an independent judicial determination of all constitutional claims); Sager, *The Supreme Court, 1980 Term — Foreword: Constitutional Limitations on Congress' Authority to Regulate the Jurisdiction of the Federal Courts,* 95 HARV. L. REV. 17 (1981). *See infra* notes 76-82 and accompanying text.

surprisingly, however, the principle has received inconsistent attention in the Supreme Court's decisions applying the prior restraint doctrine.[13] Though the Court has, on occasion, recognized the absence of an independent judicial determination as a harm of prior restraint systems,[14] at other times the Court has disregarded this essential principle. A brief footnote in Justice Brennan's concurrence in *New York Times Co. v. United States*[15] provides a classic illustration of this disregard. While attacking the evils of the prior restraint in that case, despite the fact that they were issued by an independent judicial forum,[16] Justice Brennan attempted to distinguish the nonjudicial interim prior restraints that the Court had allowed in the obscenity area. He reasoned that "those cases rest upon the proposition that 'obscenity is not protected by the freedoms of speech and press.' ... Here there is no question but that the material sought to be suppressed is within the protection of the First Amendment ...."[17] The fallacy in Justice Brennan's logic is his assumption that the material restrained by the interim prior restraint in the obscenity area is necessarily obscene; such expression may ultimately be found to be protected. Yet it has been abridged for the time necessary to render that determination. Such interim restraints of speech — and *only* such restraints — present a threat not found in subsequent punishment systems.

Once we acknowledge that interim prior restraints are especially disfavored because they authorize abridgment of expression prior to a

---

13. To a certain extent, both the Supreme Court and certain commentators have recognized the advantages of judicial over administrative regulation of expression. *See* Freedman v. Maryland, 380 U.S. 51, 57-58 (1965); Jeffries, *Rethinking Prior Restraint*, 92 YALE L.J. 409, 416, 421-26 (1983); Mayton, *Toward a Theory of First Amendment Process: Injunctions of Speech, Subsequent Punishment, and the Costs of the Prior Restraint Doctrine*, 67 CORNELL L. REV. 245 (1982); Monaghan, *First Amendment "Due Process,"* 83 HARV. L. REV. 518 (1970). On a number of occasions, however, the Court has found no particular advantage or protection in judicial restraint. *See, e.g.*, National Socialist Party v. Village of Skokie, 432 U.S. 43 (1977); New York Times Co. v. United States, 403 U.S. 713 (1971); Organization for a Better Austin v. Keefe, 402 U.S. 415 (1971). Moreover, even the commentators who recognize the advantages of judicial over nonjudicial regulation (and many of the leading commentators do not; *see, e.g.*, Blasi, *supra* note 6; Emerson, *supra* note 2) fail either to view the distinction as a subpart of a broader due process concept of a right to an independent judicial forum for the adjudication of constitutional rights or to apply the principle consistently to reject any form of nonjudicial restraint not justified by a truly compelling governmental interest. *See infra* text accompanying notes 83-106.
14. *See supra* note 13 and *infra* text accompanying notes 88-89.
15. 403 U.S. 713, 726 n.* (1971).
16. Both restraints came in the form of judicially issued injunctions. *Id.* at 725.
17. *Id.* at 726 (citation omitted).

full and fair determination of the constitutionally protected nature of the expression by an independent judicial forum and because no other legitimate basis exists on which to disfavor prior restraints as compared to subsequent punishment schemes, certain conclusions logically follow. The validity of a prior restraint will be measured by comparison to the ultimate ideal of no abridgment prior to a full and fair judicial hearing. Most disfavored would be nonjudicial administrative licensing schemes, while the least problematic would be permanent judicial injunctions issued after trial.[18] Somewhere in between are judicially issued preliminary injunctions and temporary restraining orders.[19]

This suggested restructuring of the prior restraint doctrine does not alter most of the doctrine's traditional applications. Indeed, historically it was exactly such administrative licensing schemes at which the prior restraint doctrine was aimed and about which the first amendment's framers were primarily concerned.[20] The suggested alternative analysis, however, would alter the Supreme Court's[21] and commentators'[22] general failure to distinguish between *administrative* prior restraints on the one hand and *judicial* restraints on the other. In light of our accepted premises about both the constitutional necessity and sufficiency of an independent judicial forum, there is, on the whole, all the difference in the world between the two forms of prior restraint.

The full-and-fair-hearing rationale suggests that the prejudice against prior restraint results from lack of due process, a concern not met by traditional justifications of the doctrine. This chapter first considers and rejects the traditional arguments in support of the prior restraint doctrine, suggesting instead that the doctrine should strike down only restraints imposed prior to a full and fair judicial hearing. The chapter next examines what justifications should be accepted for the use of interim restraints which adversely affect protected expression. Analysis of these justifications reveals that, despite the Supreme Court's traditional reflexive rhetoric against prior restraints, the Court has improperly authorized certain forms of prior restraint — particularly in the areas of obscenity and demonstration regulation —

---

18. *See infra* text accompanying notes 106-110, 118-122, 128-130.
19. *See infra* text accompanying notes 102-106, 123-127.
20. *See* L. Levy, Legacy of Suppression 216-17 (1960).
21. *See supra* cases cited at note 13 and *infra* text accompanying notes 83-91. *See also supra* note 6 and *infra* note 163.
22. *See generally* Emerson, *supra* note 2 (distinguishing judicial from administrative prior restraints only by noting in passing that the latter is more egregious); Blasi, *supra* note 8 (distinguishing both administrative and judicial prior restraints from subsequent punishment schemes).

that are incompatible with the rationale and that cannot be justified by any legitimate compelling interest. The chapter then contrasts nonjudicial prior restraints with subsequent punishment schemes, particularly in light of Professor William Mayton's recent proposal that these two forms of speech regulation be viewed as equally threatening to first amendment values. Finally, the chapter examines the implications of the full-and-fair-hearing theory on the "collateral bar" doctrine, which prohibits an individual accused of violating an injunction from challenging the validity of that injunction in his prosecution for contempt. The full-and-fair-hearing rationale would allow both the collateral bar rule and the prior restraint doctrine to continue, but in considerably modified form. Under the suggested rationale, haphazard and incomplete development caused by uncertain theoretical bases would be replaced by a sure foundation allowing regular application in a form more sensitive to first amendment concerns.

II. The Traditional Justifications for the Prior Restraint Doctrine: Rationale and Critique

Respected commentators, notably Professors Thomas Emerson[23] and Vincent Blasi,[24] have offered several arguments favoring the presumption against prior restraint, judicial or nonjudicial. Their arguments assert the following reasons in support of the prior restraint doctrine: prior restraints (1) shut off expression before it has a chance to be heard, (2) are easier to obtain than criminal convictions and therefore are likely to be overused, (3) lack the constitutional procedural protections inherent in the criminal process, (4) require adjudication in the abstract, (5) improperly affect audience reception of messages, and (6) unduly extend the state's power into the individual's sphere. This section examines each of these proffered justifications and concludes that they are irrelevant to first amendment concerns, are equally true of subsequent punishment schemes, or are exclusively applicable to administrative rather than judicial restraints.

A. Inhibition of the Marketplace of Ideas

Commentators have argued that "[p]rior restraint limits public debate more severely" than does subsequent prosecution, because "[w]hile subsequent punishment may deter some speakers, at least the ideas or speech at issue can be placed before the public."[25] Prior

---

23. *See* Emerson, *supra* note 2.
24. *See* Blasi, *supra* note 8.
25. J. Nowak, R. Rotunda & J. Young, *supra* note 2, at 887.

restraint thus imposes a greater burden on the marketplace of ideas than does subsequent punishment.

This analysis contains a fundamental fallacy. The prior restraint doctrine as it traditionally has been formulated posits that expression which could be constitutionally subjected to subsequent punishment is immune from regulation by prior restraint. When the doctrine is cast in these terms, one can logically assume that the speech which the prior restraint keeps from the marketplace of ideas is speech which would not be found constitutionally protected in a subsequent prosecution. Therefore, the affected speech is presumably beneath first amendment protection. If this is the case, we may question whether any harm of constitutional magnitude occurs in preventing such speech from reaching the marketplace.

Professor Blasi, however, has argued that "once a communication is disseminated it becomes to some extent a *fait accompli.* The world is a slightly different place; perceptions regarding what is tolerable are altered.... This phenomenon ... may influence the formulation and application of doctrine in the direction of permitting more speech."[26] He is correct in suggesting that, at least in a technical sense, the world is in some way a "different place," but that difference is not necessarily of constitutional magnitude. Blasi's apparent assumption is that the public availability of the challenged expression may somehow influence the substantive judicial first amendment analysis, leading speech that would otherwise be unprotected to be held protected. Yet Blasi fails to support this assumption with anything more than speculation, and the point is by no means intuitively clear. For Blasi's assumption to be correct, public reaction to the challenged expression must be favorable, the judiciary must somehow be made aware of this reaction, and the judiciary must be sufficiently influenced by this reaction to reverse its decision on constitutionality. Though all three of these events could conceivably occur in the same case, it is at least doubtful.

Initially, the public would not likely react to particular expression with sufficient fervor and unanimity that the reaction would be widely noticed. Secondly, given generally accepted first amendment jurisprudence, speech that is both subject to serious governmental challenge and likely to be found unprotected by the courts is invariably going to be speech that would be *rejected* by the majority, not accepted with wild enthusiasm. Thirdly, even if the public did express a coherent and favorable opinion, it is doubtful that that view would

---

26. Blasi, *supra* note 8, at 51.

influence a court's substantive constitutional analysis. Moreover, it is arguable that it should not do so in any event because most would agree that generally a strong *negative* public reaction to challenged expression should have no influence on judicial constitutional analysis.[27]

B. Overuse

Similarly unpersuasive is the argument that prior restraints threaten first amendment rights because they are likely to be employed more often than subsequent punishment schemes. The overuse theory is premised largely on the ground that prior restraints are inherently easier to obtain than criminal convictions and are therefore likely to be employed more frequently to stifle expression. Professor Emerson has stated:

> A government official thinks longer and harder before deciding to undertake the serious task of subsequent punishment — the expenditure of time, funds, energy, and personnel that will be necessary. Under a system of prior restraint, he can reach the result by a simple stroke of the pen. Thus, in one case, the burden of initial action falls upon the government; in the other, on the citizen. Again, once a communication has been made, the government official may give consideration to the stigma and the troubles a criminal prosecution forces on the citizen.[28]

This analysis is fraught with assumptions that are neither empirically nor intuitively supported when applied to judicial restraints.[29] Initially, there is no reason to believe that a prosecutor "thinks longer and harder" about filing a criminal prosecution than about filing an action for an injunction. Although a criminal conviction may require more elaborate and stringent judicial process than would an injunction proceeding, the deterrent effect of a criminal conviction — indeed, of the very bringing of a prosecution — may be significantly greater than that of an injunction because the punishments involved differ

---

27. Of course, the arguable concern exists that prior to dissemination we cannot ascertain the possible harm speech may cause. This point is considered *infra* text accompanying notes 48-59. There also exists the underlying fear that the speech would have been found constitutionally protected in a subsequent prosecution, and the prior restraint would have thus impeded the dissemination of protected, rather than unprotected expression. Such a fear is well taken and forms the basis of my own rationale supporting a presumption against prior restraint in certain circumstances. *See infra* text accompanying notes 80-82, 91-106, 120-127.

28. Emerson, *supra* note 2, at 657.

29. Administrative restraints may well pose a danger of overuse. Most traditional justifications for the prior restraint doctrine, however, do not distinguish judicial from administrative restraints.

substantially in severity. Thus, the effectiveness of simply bringing a criminal prosecution may cause a prosecutor to file a criminal case rather than an action for an injunction, even though the chance of ultimate conviction is low and the proceeding requires greater effort than would an injunction.[30]

More importantly, those making the overuse argument fail to recognize the fundamental similarity in the proceedings: in each, assuming no interim prior restraint, no penalty or restraint is imposed absent a full and fair judicial determination that the challenged expression is not protected by the first amendment. Thus, even if it were true that authorities are more likely to attempt to obtain judicial prior restraints than they are criminal convictions, a fact far from established, it does not follow that the former present greater threats to first amendment interests than do the latter. Regardless of how many attempts are made, those attempts will prove successful only after a judicial body has concluded that the speech in question is unprotected.[31]

One might respond that the relative number of attempts to impose penalties on expression remains an important consideration, because the assumed deterrent to the filing of criminal prosecutions will mean that certain expression will not be restrained even though a court might have found it unprotected. Requiring state authorities to employ solely criminal prosecutions to penalize speech thus will have the ultimate effect of leaving more expression unrestrained. If this expression would ultimately have been judicially determined to be unprotected, however, first amendment interests are unaffected by either the allowance or the restraint of that particular expression.

One could further argue that an increased number of attempts to obtain judicial prior restraints will provide more opportunity for judicial mistakes in failing to protect expression that deserves protection. The argument raises an interesting if largely unresolvable question concerning the definition of a constitutional right: is it some abstract, preexisting notion that the courts merely attempt to decipher, or is it simply whatever the final adjudicator deems it to be? If the latter, the judiciary's interpretation of the first amendment could not be deemed a mistake, as a definitional matter. Whatever the

---

30. Professor Emerson argues that a prosecutor may wish to avoid the "stigma" on the citizen that will result from the filing of a prosecution. *See supra* text accompanying note 28. If a prosecutor has concluded that a citizen is violating the law, however, she is likely to pursue the course of action deemed to enforce that law most effectively. *See also* Jeffries, *supra* note 12, at 430 n.67; Mayton, *supra* note 12, at 257.

31. To the extent Professor Emerson's point is limited to *administrative* restraints, however, it is valid.

philosophical answer, as a purely practical matter the first amendment — and any other constitutional right — protects only what the judiciary deems it to protect. Academics may criticize one or more judicial first amendment interpretations, and appellate courts may reject or modify constitutional interpretations by the lower courts, but ultimately the first amendment has no legal force beyond what the highest court has held that it has. Thus, as long as the requisite judicial forum is provided before any penalty is imposed because of expression, it makes no difference whether the relative number of attempts to impose penalties is greater with one form of regulation than with another.

That judicial restraints will result in overuse of regulation when compared to subsequent punishment systems remains, then, far from clear. Even if such overuse were established, the relative difference should not have any constitutional consequences when the restraint follows a full and fair judicial determination that the challenged speech is not protected by the first amendment. In such cases the similarities between subsequent punishment and prior restraint override any differences in impact.

C. Difference in the Level of Procedural Protections

Closely related to the previous argument is the contention that subsequent punishment systems, criminal ones at least,[32] are preferable to prior restraint systems because they provide the defendant with both due process protections[33] and the right to a jury trial,[34] procedural guarantees that are presumably unavailable in even

---

32. A subsequent punishment scheme could take the form of civil damage liability as well as criminal prosecution.

33. "The presumption of innocence, the heavier burden of proof borne by the government, the stricter rules of evidence, the stronger objection to vagueness, the immeasurably tighter and more technical procedure — all these are not on the side of free expression when its fate is decided [under a prior restraint system]." Emerson, *supra* note 2, at 657. *But see* Mayton, *supra* note 12, at 277-78 (rejecting argument that "criminal procedures ... afford speech a protection superior to that of the civil procedures of injunctive relief").

34. Emerson, *supra* note 2, at 657. *But see* Blasi, *supra* note 8, at 63 (right to a jury trial in criminal proceedings is irrelevant because "all state constitutions guarantee civil defendants a jury trial"); Mayton, *supra* note 12, at 277 (stating that trial by jury "has generally been overly suppressive of speech"; hence, "scholars who have considered this problem are inclined towards a civil process that limits jury participation").

a judicial prior restraint proceeding.[35] One fallacy in this argument is that it confuses the mechanisms for finding guilt or innocence with those for determining the level of constitutional protection given to particular expression. Procedural guarantees may guard against an individual's conviction for a crime she did not commit, but the factual questions that must be decided to prove or disprove an offense are often irrelevant to the legal issue of whether the first amendment protects particular expression.[36]

If an individual is prosecuted for distributing leaflets in violation of a criminal statute, for example, the procedural protections required in a criminal prosecution will help assure that the defendant will not be convicted for illegally distributing leaflets when she has never done so. The first amendment, however, will only become relevant when the defendant acknowledges that her conduct violates the statute, but contends that as applied to her activity, the statute violates her free speech rights. Where the relevant issue is the substantive scope of the first amendment, due process and the right to a jury trial are of no significance to the judicial determination which is the same in both criminal and prior restraint proceedings.

Adjudication of the first amendment right may involve determination of various factual or semifactual issues, however. A first amendment determination in the hypothetical leafleting case might turn in part on whether the defendant was harassing passersby. Another case might raise the question of whether the advocacy of unlawful conduct presents a clear and present danger that harm will result. In such cases, procedural guarantees may well provide significant assistance or protection to a defendant asserting her first amendment rights. If these protections are essential to vindicate an individual's first amendment rights, however, they can be employed in a prior restraint proceeding. That such proceedings are purely civil in nature need not preclude the use of these guarantees if the first amendment requires them.[37]

---

35. Much of Professor Emerson's analysis assumes a contrast between an administrative licensing scheme and a criminal prosecution. Emerson, *supra* note 2, at 657-58. The argument that procedural protections are essential, however, could also be made in regard to a judicially imposed prior restraint.

36. Such guarantees, of course, are not required in a civil proceeding as a matter of procedural due process because the potential risk to the individual does not include criminal conviction.

37. Employing these procedural protections may be impractical in proceedings seeking a temporary restraining order or preliminary injunction against expression. The standard of protection employed in this Chapter, however, may not be completely satisfied in such proceedings because they may fail to provide the required full and fair adjudication. *See infra* text accompanying notes 119-127.

Thus, jury trials in a civil prior restraint proceeding could be employed if the first amendment required them.[38] Courts, however, need not necessarily impose such a requirement. Though Professor Emerson has argued that "[t]hose who framed the First Amendment placed great emphasis upon the value of a jury of citizens in checking government efforts to limit freedom of expression,"[39] Professor Monaghan has reminded us "that the famous free speech cases of the past were really part of a much larger conflict between a fairly homogeneous citizenry and an unrepresentative government."[40] Today, however, "[l]ike administrative agencies, the jury cannot be expected to be sufficiently sensitive to the first amendment interests involved in any given proceeding."[41] The jury's role in making first amendment determinations, even in subsequent punishment schemes, is erratic. For example, the Supreme Court has given the judge, rather than the jury, the authority to determine whether advocacy of unlawful conduct presents a clear and present danger.[42] Furthermore, though the Court has given the jury authority to make certain mixed law-fact first amendment determinations, it has severely restricted the scope of that authority.[43] Thus, the jury initially determines whether allegedly obscene material violates community standards,[44] but may not hold obscene a movie that did not "'depict ... patently offensive "hard core" sexual conduct.'"[45]

---

38. Such a requirement would render even more doubtful the constitutional validity of proceedings for temporary restraining orders or preliminary injunctions against speech.

39. Emerson, *supra* note 2, at 657. Justice Brennan has argued that prior restraints are constitutionally defective because of the lack of a jury trial. Kingsley Books, Inc. v. Brown, 354 U.S. 436, 447-48 (1957) (Brennan, J., dissenting). According to Professor Monaghan, however, Justice Brennan's opinion "fails to articulate any comprehensive conception of the role of the jury in the first amendment. Moreover, in *Freedman v. Maryland*, Mr. Justice Brennan seems to have abandoned his position because in *Freedman* he sanctions an administrative-judicial process without jury participation." Monaghan, *supra* note 12, at 527 (footnote omitted). For a discussion of *Freedman* and the general issue of prior restraints in the obscenity area, see *infra* text accompanying notes 83-95.

40. Monaghan, *supra* note 12, at 528.

41. *Id.* at 527.

42. Dennis v. United States, 341 U.S. 494, 513-15 (1951).

43. The Supreme Court has also significantly curbed the jury's factfinding authority in the determination of whether a defendant in a defamation action brought by a public figure has acted with reckless disregard of the truth or falsity of his statements. St. Amant v. Thompson, 390 U.S. 727 (1968).

44. Miller v. California, 413 U.S. 15, 26, 30 (1973).

45. Jenkins v. Georgia, 418 U.S. 153, 160 (1974) (quoting Miller v. California, 413 U.S. 15, 27 (1973)). *Jenkins* concerned the film *Carnal Knowledge.* Despite the jury's

As the use of the jury to define community standards in obscenity cases reveals, the jury's current rule in first amendment cases is to apply majoritarian values that *limit* expression, rather than to defend the expression of unpopular views. The Court's test for determining whether expression is obscene (and therefore beneath first amendment concerns) turns in part on "whether 'the average person, applying contemporary community standards' would consider [the challenged expression] ... 'prurient.'"[46] This determination of "contemporary community standards" is to be made by "lay jurors as the usual ultimate factfinders in criminal prosecutions."[47] In determining the governing standards of morality and good taste, the jurors act as society's representatives — hardly a role for a protector of minority or unpopular views. Thus, the use of a jury, like other subsequent punishment process protections, is not in any way dictated by the first amendment.

D. Abstract Determinations

Perhaps the strongest argument against judicial prior restraint is that because such a restraint is imposed prior to the actual dissemination of expression, a court's first amendment ruling will necessarily be made in the abstract and therefore without any knowledge of the actual effect of the challenged expression.[48] As a result, the court will be forced to determine whether expression is so dangerous that it may be suppressed, without knowing whether harm will actually ensue — a problem that arguably does not plague subsequent punishment schemes.[49]

Several answers can be made to this contention. First, even if substantive questions are decided more often in the abstract in prior restraint proceedings than in subsequent punishment proceedings, first amendment interests are not necessarily harmed as a result. The only way that the abstract nature of the determination could

---

contrary finding, the Court concluded that "[o]ur own viewing of the film satisfies us that [it] ... could not be found under the *Miller* standards to depict sexual conduct in a patently offensive way." 418 U.S. at 161.

46. Miller v. California, 413 U.S. 15, 30 (1973).
47. *Id.*
48. *See* Blasi, *supra* note 8, at 49.
49. "When adjudication precedes initial dissemination, the communication cannot be judged by its actual consequences or public reception. The adjudicative assessment of speech value versus social harm must be made in the abstract, based on speculation or generalizations embodied in presumptions." *Id. See also* F. Haiman, Speech and Law in a Free Society 404 (1981). Haiman noted that subsequent punishment systems avoid "penalties for defiance of authority per se — for instance, contempt of court — as contrasted with those which are responsive to the offense itself." *Id.*

undermine first amendment interests is if the court were to assume the possibility of more harm than would actually have occurred. No firm basis exists for assuming such judicial behavior.[50] Because generally expression may be regulated only in the presence of a truly compelling governmental interest,[51] courts will be slow to uphold any restriction on expression when the demonstration of harm flowing from the expression is purely speculative. Under properly applied first amendment standards, the harm's abstractness should actually aid free speech interests because the burden would always be on the government to demonstrate the existence of significant danger from the expression, not on the speaker to prove the opposite. A court could conceivably deny a prior restraint because harm is too speculative, but later allow a subsequent punishment because harm actually resulted from the speech.[52]

Two additional points demonstrate the inaccuracy of the abstractness argument. First, mere abstractness does not in itself render a regulation unconstitutional so long as regulation "in the abstract" means regulation based on potential rather than actual harm. Second, even if abstractness were generally deemed a constitutional defect, the problem may plague subsequent punishment schemes, just as it does prior restraints. Both points may be illustrated by examining *Dennis v. United States*,[53] in which the Supreme Court upheld criminal convictions of Communist Party leaders for conspiring to advocate overthrow of the government. Under the terms of the

---

50. *See* Jeffries, *supra* note 12, at 417 n. 57. Professor Jeffries noted two reasons for trusting judicial behavior. First he observed that "with every passing decade — not excluding the 1970's and the advent of the Burger Court — there is increasingly widespread acceptance of First Amendment claims that would have been thought fanciful only a few years earlier." Next he suggested that judges hostile to first amendment claims in general will not be more hostile in prior restraint proceedings than they would be in subsequent prosecutions.

51. NAACP v. Button, 371 U.S. 415, 438 (1963).

52. Of course, a court might disregard this fundamental first amendment directive and instead demand a showing of only remote danger. If so, the problem does not derive from use of a prior restraint but from misapplication of the law. The thrust of Supreme Court doctrine on the subject is clear. *See, e.g.,* Brandenburg v. Ohio, 395 U.S. 444 (1969) (per curiam). The standard is somewhat less rigorous when regulation does not turn on the content of expression. *See generally* Chapter II (advocating a unitary standard for all judicial review of governmental regulation of expression). To the extent that the standards differ for content-neutral regulation of expression, however, the difference flows from substantive first amendment doctrine and would therefore apply to either subsequent punishment or prior restraint. This doctrinal clarity suggests that many adjudicators would be unlikely to demand less than a showing of serious and imminent danger.

53. 341 U.S. 494 (1951).

indictment, the defendants had not even been accused of actually advocating overthrow; certainly, no evidence was presented that any harm had already occurred. On the contrary, the Court acknowledged that the government need not await any actual showing of damage before it could criminally prosecute.[54] Although the decision has been heavily criticized for effectively dispensing with any requirement of temporal relation between expression and harm,[55] such criticism does not imply that the only speech which could be punished is speech which has actually led to provable harm. In any event, such criticism underscores the point that abstractness, to the extent it is a constitutional problem, may plague subsequent punishment as well as prior restraint.

One can imagine numerous other situations in which regulation of expression would be permissible, even in the absence of a demonstration of actual harm. It is difficult to believe, for example, that a court would be constitutionally restrained from prohibiting the holding of a Progressive Labor Party rally adjacent to a Nazi or Ku Klux Klan gathering. Consider also the individual, prosecuted for solicitation to crime, who had said to another, "I will pay you $500 to kill my wife." Could one realistically argue that that individual's speech is protected absent a showing that it actually led to the murder of his wife?

The point may be further demonstrated by hypothetically transforming two classic modern prior restraint cases into examples of subsequent punishment: the Supreme Court's invalidation of a judicial prior restraint of publication of the Pentagon Papers in *New York Times Co. v. United States*[56] and a lower court's order enjoining the publication of a magazine article describing how to construct a nuclear weapon in *United States v. Progressive, Inc.*[57] If the two cases had arisen in the course of subsequent punishment proceedings, the publishers of the Pentagon Papers and of the how-to-do-it article on nuclear weapons would have been prosecuted for violation of hypothetical criminal statutes making such actions crimes. Is it likely that to defeat the free speech claims in both cases the government would have had to establish that actual harm had resulted? Would a prosecutor have had to establish that someone actually had built a nuclear weapon as a result of the magazine article before a court could have found the defendant's free speech claim outbalanced by the

---

54. *Id.* at 509-11.
55. I have been one of the strongest critics. *See* Chapter IV.
56. 403 U.S. 713 (1971).
57. 467 F. Supp. 990 (W.D. Wis. 1979), *appeal dismissed,* 610 F.2d 819 (1979).

danger the speech caused? Similarly, would a court in the Pentagon Papers case have to find that some measurable harm to American interests had resulted from the publication before a conviction could have been obtained?[58] Because the courts would presumably apply some form of clear-and-present-danger analysis to determine whether the speech in both cases was constitutionally protected, they would not likely demand such a concrete showing. The court also could conclude that the speech was constitutionally protected in both hypotheticals, but a finding that there had been no provable harm directly attributable to the challenged expression probably would not be either necessary or sufficient to reach that conclusion.

The abstract nature of harm thus does not distinguish prior restraints from many subsequent prosecutions, as *Dennis* and the two hypothetical prosecutions demonstrate, nor is abstractness an inherent constitutional defect. Although a court's ability to assess the actual harmful impact of challenged expression may sometimes affect the degree of constitutional protection it affords,[59] abstractness cannot justify a bright-line dichotomy between judicial prior restraints and subsequent punishments.

E. Impact on Audience Reception

Professor Blasi has correctly asserted that "[i]t should be a matter of doctrinal concern if certain laws or methods of regulation cause audiences to shrink, or individual listeners to respond less intently (pro or con) to the speaker's message."[60] It does not follow, however, that all prior restraints should therefore be disfavored.

Professor Blasi argued that "audiences may react less intently, perhaps less spontaneously, when they know that the speech has already passed through a regulatory filter."[61] They may or they may not; Blasi provided no empirical or psychological basis on which to rest such a conclusion. The issue will likely turn on what we allow the regulatory filter to filter. If we were in a totalitarian society that censored any statement critical of the government, an audience would likely be less than impressed with a speech staunchly endorsing the government.

Procedural issues of speech regulation must be distinguished from the actual *substantive* matters of what speech can be regulated. If prior

---

58. *See supra* text accompanying notes 53-54.
59. *See generally* Chapter IV (stating that any version of unlawful advocacy regulation that does not require courts to assess the individual facts of the case will offer either too much or too little first amendment protection).
60. Blasi, *supra* note 8, at 63-64.
61. *Id.* at 64.

restraints were not subjected to special disfavor, the substantive first amendment standards applied would presumably be no less protective than those used in subsequent punishment schemes. Under those standards, speech cannot be regulated merely because it criticizes the government[62] or because someone in authority disagrees with it[63] or because someone finds it distasteful.[64] Given the context of our constitutional system, prior approval of speech thus would not amount to a government stamp of approval on speech; rather, it would mean only that nothing contained in the expression falls within any of the narrowly drawn categories of expression that are unprotected by the first amendment. Though an audience may be less receptive to expression when it knows that the expression has met constitutional standards, it is doubtful that we should defer to such an audience's prejudices. In any event, an audience just as plausibly could be *more* receptive to speech when it knows that the speech is constitutionally protected, because that protection may well increase the speaker's legitimacy in the audience's eyes.

Professor Blasi has argued that when prior restraint systems are employed "audiences may wonder whether the communication that is transmitted represents the true message the speaker desired to convey. Did the speaker change a few passages in order to placate the censor or expedite the process of prior approval?"[65] Though some audience members might react in this manner to prior restraint systems, they could just as easily entertain similar doubts about the speaker's message if they knew that the speaker was subject to subsequent punishment.[66] Indeed, the fear that a speaker will exercise self-censorship to avoid a subsequent civil or criminal penalty provides the entire basis for the concept of an unconstitutional chilling effect, a concern which has substantially shaped much first amendment doctrine.[67] Thus, to the extent that audience reaction might actually be

---

62. *See, e.g.*, Garrison v. Louisiana, 379 U.S. 64 (1964).

63. Such a possibility represents the fundamental reason for the traditional disdain for content-based regulation of expression. *See, e.g.*, Police Dep't v. Mosley, 408 U.S. 92 (1972).

64. This is true as long as the expression in question is not deemed legally obscene. *See, e.g.*, Jenkins v. Georgia, 418 U.S. 153 (1974).

65. Blasi, *supra* note 8, at 67.

66. Schauer, *Fear, Risk and the First Amendment: Unraveling the "Chilling Effect,"* 58 B. U. L. REV. 685, 725-30 (1978).

67. New York Times Co. v. Sullivan, 376 U.S. 254 (1964), in which the Supreme Court invalidated the subsequent punishment system of civil damage awards for defamation against public officials, provides a classic illustration of this concern. The Court worried that fear of large damage awards in libel suits might cause public debate to become less "uninhibited, robust, and wide-open." *Id.* at 270. *See also*

altered as a result of some form of prior regulation, an unproven assumption, much the same problem plagues subsequent punishment systems.[68]

F. IMPROPER DIVISION OF STATE AND INDIVIDUAL AUTHORITY

Professor Blasi has written:

> An important reason for disfavoring injunctions and licensing systems as methods of speech regulation is that they rest on three objectionable premises: (1) that speakers and audiences are to be trusted less than regulatory processes; (2) that the act of speaking is an abnormally hazardous activity that warrants special regulation; and (3) that the integrity of the communication or the autonomy of the speaker is not undermined when government plays a large role in determining the details and timing of a communication.[69]

Dombrowski v. Pfister, 380 U.S. 479, 487-89 (1965); Jeffries, *supra* note 12, at 430 n. 67 (arguing that there can be no sharp doctrinal line between injunctions and subsequent punishment); Schauer, *supra* note 66, at 695-701 (subsequent punishment schemes may exert a chilling effect due to speaker's fear of an incorrect verdict or uncertainty about the protected status of the speech).

68. A number of years ago, Professor Kalven made a related but "mirror image" argument in regard to New York Times Co. v. United States, 403 U.S. 713 (1971). Unlike Professor Blasi's argument, Professor Kalven's point concerns the intended impact of the restraint on the speaker's words and actions, rather than its impact on the listener or viewer. Professor Kalven asserts, "It is ... reasonably clear that Daniel Ellsberg, and also the *New York Times* and *Washington Post,* were engaged in a kind of political action, akin to civil disobedience." Kalven, *supra* note 6, at 34. This fact led him to conclude that

> in this context prior and subsequent restraints are not coterminous. No politically tolerable scheme of subsequent restraints would have prohibited the principled disobedience of the newspapers. But presuming the papers were not ready to frontally defy an injunction, in forbidding the prior restraint, the Court can be seen as protecting the chance for civil disobedience.

Id. (footnote omitted).

Perhaps the simplest response to this argument is to express wonder at Professor Kalven's implicit assumption that the first amendment should be construed to protect intended violations of constitutionally valid statutes, which is what the concept of civil disobedience means. More importantly, Professor Kalven apparently has seriously mischaracterized the intent of both the newspapers and Mr. Ellsberg. Although they were clearly willing to risk subsequent prosecution, their goal was clearly not purposely to violate a law they deemed unjust and to suffer the consequences. Rather, they sought to disseminate the information contained in the Pentagon Papers, fully believing that what they were doing was protected by the first amendment. Thus, they wished to publish the material in spite of, not because of governmental regulation.

69. Blasi, *supra* note 8, at 91.

Blasi's rejection of these "unacceptable premises"[70] is based on the contention that prior restraints, more than subsequent punishment systems, improperly allocate authority between state and individual.[71] Closer examination reveals, however, that Blasi's objections do not lead to his conclusion that all prior restraints are to be specially disfavored.

First, he incorrectly suggests that prior restraints, more than subsequent punishment systems, reflect the view "that speakers and audiences are to be trusted less than regulatory processes." A subsequent punishment system that is premised on the assumption that certain expression is not constitutionally protected and therefore is subject to punishment necessarily presumes that the speaker and audience are not to be "trusted."[72] Otherwise, we would allow the speaker to communicate whatever she wished and trust the audience to reject any harmful or evil suggestions contained in the speech.[73] Blasi's argument, then, confuses substance and procedure: to the extent that failure to accord first amendment protection improperly reflects a lack of faith in individual judgment, this lack of faith is a problem derived from the substantive scope of first amendment doctrine, not from the regulatory method chosen.

Also puzzling is Blasi's belief that use of the prior restraint mechanism reflects the premise "that the act of speaking is an abnormally hazardous activity." If a system were established in which no one could speak, regardless of content, without first obtaining a license, Blasi's point might have validity. But at the very least that is not the manner in which judicially imposed prior restraints are employed.[74] Rather, the procedure is not even initiated without an allegation that the challenged expression actually is "abnormally hazardous" in some way, and presumably no restraint is issued unless an independent judicial officer determines that the expression presents

---

70. *Id.*
71. *Id.* at 93.
72. *See* Jeffries, *supra* note 12, at 431 n. 67.
73. The long history of unlawful advocacy regulation establishes that even subsequent punishment systems, in the form of criminal prosecution, are established for the very reason that we do not always trust either the speaker or the audience. The same is true of the imposition of civil damage awards for libel and privacy invasions; if we truly trusted both the speaker and the audience, deterrence of such conduct by the provision of such penalties would presumably be unnecessary. For a description of the history of advocacy regulation, see generally Chapter IV.
74. The analogy may apply to sweeping administrative licensing schemes for parades and obscene literature, but those forms of licensing are also rejected under the structure adopted in this book.

such a danger. Thus, judicial prior restraints do not rest on the assumption that Professor Blasi asserted.

Professor Blasi's final point was that individual autonomy is unduly undermined when "government plays a large role in determining the details and timing of a communication." His concern over timing is valid, but for reasons different from those he asserted.[75] His view that government is unduly involved in the details of the communication under a properly functioning system of prior restraint, however, is unacceptable. As long as the substantive first amendment doctrine applied in the prior restraint proceeding is valid (an issue distinct from the issue of regulatory method), the government will be unconcerned with details of communication that do not directly affect the speech's constitutionality. Blasi argued that inherent in prior restraint systems "is the ever present possibility, due to the phenomenon of adjudication prior to initial dissemination, that government officials may convince speakers to alter the details of their plans in order to conform to the government's preferences."[76] Yet unless the government's "preferences" derive from accepted first amendment doctrine, such pressure is not legal, need not be countenanced, and can be corrected by a judicial determination of constitutionality in a prior restraint hearing. Although government officials might use the threat of a prior restraint proceeding to achieve constitutionally impermissible ends, such a danger is likely to be as great or greater in the case of subsequent punishment where the speaker's fear of severe penalties may make her more susceptible to suggested governmental "preferences." These dangers do not affect judicial prior restraint because the court informs the speaker that her expression is or is not constitutionally protected before she disseminates it. Thus, the speaker need not risk severe criminal or civil penalties in order to obtain such a determination. Blasi's three unacceptable premises simply do not distinguish prior restraint from subsequent punishment systems. The argument that prior restraint, more than other means of regulation, improperly divides state and individual authority is therefore not supportable.

The six traditional justifications for prior restraint do not ultimately support the present strong distinction between the acceptability of all forms of prior restraint as opposed to subsequent punishment. These justifications are often irrelevant to first amendment concerns, confusing procedural issues with the substantive law of the first

---

75. For discussion of the free speech interest affected by delay, see *infra* text accompanying notes 96-106.

76. Blasi, *supra* note 8, at 80.

amendment. In addition, many of the justifications fail because the harms they seek to prevent are present in both prior restraint and subsequent punishment systems. Finally, some of the justifications apply only to administrative restraints. With the failure of these traditional justifications, a closer look at the proper role of the prior restraint doctrine and its true theoretical rationale becomes necessary.

III. Determining the Proper Role of the Prior Restraint Doctrine

A. Assessing the True Theoretical Rationale

Although none of the traditional rationales supporting mistrust of prior restraint justifies a sharp dichotomy between all forms of prior restraints and subsequent punishment systems, an alternative theoretical basis supports a doctrine mistrustful of some forms of prior restraint.[77] Such a doctrine specially disfavors prior restraint as a form of speech regulation when that restraint limits expression prior to a full and fair hearing in an independent judicial forum to determine whether the challenged expression is constitutionally protected. Such restraint is permissible only in the presence of a truly compelling interest.

In contexts other than the first amendment, the Supreme Court has long held that a person's constitutional rights are violated when she is subjected to the judgment of an individual or institution directly interested in the outcome of the case.[78] If the body or individual determining whether a governmental agency has violated a constitutional right is a part of or directly controlled by the agency, that governmental agency is effectively determining the constitutionality of its own actions. The institution simply cannot be relied upon in such cases because its interests, both practical and emotional, are so intertwined in the decisionmaking process that any judgment will be designed inevitably, if only inadvertently, to further those interests, and the constitutional right in question will be violated

---

77. *See infra* text accompanying notes 80-82, 125-127.
78. *See, e.g.,* Gibson v. Berryhill, 411 U.S. 564, 578-79 (1973) (holding that state board of optometry was so biased by pecuniary interest that it could not constitutionally conduct hearings to revoke optometrists' licenses); Tumey v. Ohio, 273 U.S. 510, 531 (1927) (holding unconstitutional practice whereby adjudicator's financial benefit from conviction greater than from acquittal). *Cf.* United States v. United States Dist. Court, 407 U.S. 297, 316-17 (1972) (holding that executive officers do not meet fourth amendment neutral-and-detached-magistrate requirement for issuing warrants); Coolidge v. New Hampshire, 403 U.S. 443, 453 (1971) (holding that search warrant issued by chief investigator violates due process).

for all practical purposes. Thus, for example, even though article III of the Constitution has been construed to provide Congress broad authority to limit the jurisdiction of the federal courts, courts have held that Congress may not close off all judicial forums from adjudicating the claim that congressional legislation unconstitutionally deprives individuals of their property.[79]

Applied to the first amendment context, this principle gives rise to several conclusions. Nonjudicial administrative regulators of expression exist for the sole purpose of regulating; this is their raison d'etre.[80] They simultaneously perform the functions of prosecutor and

---

79. *See, e.g.,* Battaglia v. General Motors Corp., 169 F.2d 254 (2d Cir.), *cert. denied,* 335 U.S. 887 (1948). *See also* Lockerty v. Phillips, 319 U.S. 182 (1943) (sustaining the Emergency Price Control Act of 1942, which restricted jurisdiction over the Act to an Emergency Court, because that court's decisions on the constitutional validity of the Act or regulations under it may be reviewed in specified article III federal courts). Perhaps partly because of these constitutional limitations, Chief Justice Hughes in Crowell v. Benson, 285 U.S. 22, 60 (1932), concluded that "[i]n cases brought to enforce constitutional rights, the judicial power of the United States necessarily extends to the independent determination of all questions, both of fact and law, necessary to the performance of that supreme function." According to Professor Jaffe, *Crowell* dictates that "[w]hen adjudication seriously touches property or interests traditionally of great moment, due process may require judicial process." L. JAFFE, JUDICIAL CONTROL OF ADMINISTRATIVE ACTION 388 (1965).

Although *Crowell* has largely fallen into disfavor, this is surely not because of the broad contours of this statement. *See, e.g.,* Associated Indem. Corp. v. Shea, 455 F.2d 913, 914 n.2 (5th Cir. 1972) (per curiam) (observing that Supreme Court has failed to follow *Crowell* by no longer requiring trial de novo on jurisdictional issues at appellate review); K. DAVIS, 4 ADMINISTRATIVE LAW TREATISE § 29.08, at 156-63 (1958) (noting that most courts reject *Crowell* doctrine that jurisdictional facts are subject to de novo review). *But see* Feinberg v. Federal Deposit Ins. Corp., 522 F.2d 1335, 1342 (D.C. Cir. 1975) (citing *Crowell* for the proposition that Congress may not exercise its power to limit jurisdiction so as to deprive any person of life, liberty, or property without due process); Cross v. United States, 512 F.2d 1212, 1217 (4th Cir. 1975) (citing *Crowell* for the proposition that judicial review is constitutionally required for administrative determinations of rights and privileges). Even dissenting Justice Brandeis agreed that when the potential loss of personal liberty was involved, "the constitutional requirement of due process is a requirement of judicial process." 285 U.S. at 87 (Brandeis, J., dissenting). Similarly, ten years prior to *Crowell,* Brandeis authored the Court's decision in Ng Fung Ho v. White, 259 U.S. 276 (1922), granting a writ of habeas corpus to an individual alleging that he was being deported by the executive branch despite the fact that he was a citizen. Noting that "[t]he difference in security of judicial over administrative action has been adverted to by this court," *id.* at 285 (citations omitted), Brandeis held that a court rather than an agent of the executive branch must have final say on the issue of citizenship. *See also* United States v. Woo Jan, 245 U.S. 552, 556 (1918).

80. Professor Emerson has observed, "The function of the censor is to censor. He has a professional interest in finding things to suppress." Emerson, *supra* note 2, at 659.

adjudicator and, if only subconsciously, will likely feel the obligation to justify their existence by finding some expression constitutionally subject to regulation. Such a systemic danger does not plague the functioning of a judicial forum.[81] In addition, the tradition of independence from external political pressure provides grounds for preferring judicial to administrative adjudication.[82] Thus, if the

---

See generally Jeffries, *supra* note 12, at 421-26 (asserting that administrative preclearance is the worst type of prior restraint system, but approving such a system if the statutory standards guiding administrators are narrowly drawn). Jeffries' conclusion, however, fails to come to grips with the underlying constitutional difficulty with administrative restraints of expression. Professor Mayton has argued that the most important difference between judicial and administrative licensing is that the latter "lends itself to a more pervasive censorship," because "[l]aws providing for administrative censorship are typically broad and vague, according the licenser wide discretion." Mayton, *supra* note 12, at 251. To the extent that this is true, however, the problem could be resolved as easily by narrowing the substantive statutory scope. *See* Jeffries, *supra*, at 425-26. This reason therefore cannot serve as a valid basis for preferring judicial to administrative restraints of expression.

81. Professor Monaghan has argued that the administrative censor does not play the role of "the impartial adjudicator but that of the expert — a role which necessarily gives an administrative agency a narrow and restricted viewpoint.... Courts, on the other hand, do not suffer congenitally from this myopia; their general jurisdiction gives them a broad perspective which no agency can have." Monaghan, *supra* note 12, at 523. Professor Monaghan's point, though perhaps a valid one, is distinct from the one in the text. The text's argument turns not on the administrator's limited perspective, but rather on his likely tendency to use his regulatory power because his sole reason for existence is to regulate.

82. I have argued previously that any state judiciary not provided the constitutional protections of salary and life tenure is insufficiently independent for purposes of due process in cases brought to challenge the constitutionality of state or local legislative or executive action. In effect, I proposed incorporating by reference into the due process clause the separation-of-powers protections of article III. Redish, *Constitutional Limitations on Congressional Power to Control Federal Jurisdiction: A Reaction to Professor Sager,* 77 Nw. U. L. Rev. 143, 161-66 (1982). This is a position to which I still adhere. Thus, under my previously developed analysis of due process independence, state judges lacking these protections are in certain senses not substantially more constitutionally acceptable than are nonjudicial administrators. Although the Supreme Court has held that due process requires an independent adjudicator, it has never construed the due process clause to require such a level of independence for state judges. *See, e.g.,* Palmore v. United States, 411 U.S. 389, 402 (1973). My due process analysis must therefore supplement everything I say about the need for an independent judicial forum.

Nevertheless, even if my due process analysis were rejected, the constitutional arguments for preferring even the less-protected state judges over administrators remain valid. State judges generally use more formalized adversarial procedures and have greater exposure to a broader spectrum of legal problems and concerns. In addition, state courts — unlike most administrative agencies— do not exist solely to regulate.

constitutional right to freedom of expression can be abridged only in the presence of a truly compelling governmental interest and if only an independent judicial forum can adequately decide whether particular expression is unprotected by the first amendment, it follows that any restriction of expression by an agency of government other than such a judicial forum is an unconstitutional abridgment of that expression except in the most extreme circumstances. We must conclude, then, that nonjudicial restraint of expression prior to ultimate judicial review is the only form of prior restraint appropriately subjected to a special negative presumption. This is true, even if the nonjudicial restraint is imposed merely on an interim basis pending ultimate judicial resolution. During that time period a prima facie abridgment of speech is taking place. As such, it can be permitted only in the presence of a truly compelling interest.

The Court appeared to accept the need for an independent judicial forum as an appropriate rationale for the prior restraint doctrine in *Freedman v. Maryland*,[83] but closer examination reveals that the Court's analysis ultimately failed to grasp the true justification for the principle and, as a result, failed to carry the principle to its logical conclusion.[84] The appellant had been convicted of exhibiting a movie without submitting it to the Maryland State Board of Censors for prior approval. The state conceded that the picture involved did not violate statutory standards and would have received a license had it been properly submitted.

In reversing the conviction, the Court held the Maryland censorship system to be unconstitutional, noting that "no time limit is imposed for completion of Board action"[85] and that "there is no statutory provision for judicial participation in the procedure which bars a film, nor even assurance of prompt judicial review."[86] Justice Brennan's opinion fully recognized the dangers of having obscenity determinations made by administrative censors rather than courts[87] and added that "if it is

---

83. 380 U.S. 51 (1965).

84. Recognition of the unique damages presented by such interim restraints has escaped not only the Court but also commentators acknowledging a preference for judicial over administrative action in restraining expression. *See, e.g.,* Jeffries, *supra* note 12; Mayton, *supra* note 12 (discussed *infra* text accompanying notes 97-106, 132).

85. 380 U.S. at 55.

86. *Id.*

87. "Because the censor's business is to censor, there inheres the danger that he may well be less responsive than a court — part of an independent branch of government — to the constitutionally protected interests in free expression." *Id.* at 57-58.

made unduly onerous, by reason of delay or otherwise, to seek judicial review, the censor's determination may in practice be final."[88] The opinion therefore established a set of criteria on which to judge the constitutionality of administrative licensing schemes for expressive activities:

> [T]he exhibitor must be assured, by statute or authoritative judicial construction, that the censor will, within a specified brief period, either issue a license or go to court to restrain showing the film. Any restraint imposed in advance of a final judicial determination on the merits must similarly be limited to preservation of the status quo for the shortest fixed period compatible with sound judicial resolution. ... [T]he procedure must also assure a prompt final judicial decision, to minimize the deterrent effect of an interim and possibly erroneous denial of a license.[89]

Upon superficial examination, Justice Brennan's opinion appears to be extremely speech-protective. The standards adopted are certainly more protective than those employed by the Maryland statute. Indeed, even commentators who generally decry the use of nonjudicial restraints of expression seem all too eager to accept the *Freedman* result as a satisfactory resolution of the problem.[90] Such an analysis, however, totally disregards the harm resulting from the *interim* invasion of the free speech right caused by an administrative restraint prior to even the promptest judicial review.[91] The fundamental defect in the Court's analysis is its unquestioned assumption that *any* form of administrative prior restraint for the distribution of films or books could *ever* be deemed constitutionally valid, at least when the asserted justification for such a system is to ferret out obscene films and publications.

---

88. *Id.* at 58.
89. *Id.* at 58-59.
90. *See, e.g.*, Jeffries, *supra* note 12, at 424-25; Mayton, *supra* note 12, at 252-53. Professor Mayton approvingly interprets the Supreme Court's decisions as declaring "that when bureaucratic censorship is attended by prompt judicial review, it is no longer part of the prior restraint doctrine — the idea being that judicial review eliminates the evils that give rise to a presumption against such restraints." *Id.* at 253. This view fails to grasp the dangers to free speech interests of *any* interim nonjudicial restraint, regardless of the supposed promptness of the subsequent judicial review, and the consequential need to subject all such restraints to a compelling interest test. *See infra* text accompanying notes 91-106.
91. *See infra* notes 97-106 and accompanying text. *See also supra* text accompanying notes 11-12.

At no point in *Freedman* did the Court explore the reasons for allowing even the most minimal form of prior restraint. Any societal harms caused by the distribution of obscenity are speculative at best[92] and in any event may be no worse than those caused by protected expression such as extremely violent but nonobscene books and movies. In fact, part of the accepted basis for excluding obscenity from first amendment protection is not its harm but its presumed worthlessness.[93] Even assuming that obscene speech can be regulated constitutionally,[94] the resultant harms of such speech are not so great or compelling as to justify even a temporary abridgment of nonobscene expression.[95] Yet no evidence was suggested in *Freedman,* and apparently the Court demanded none, to establish a need for *any* form of administrative screening, with its resultant interim restraints, prior to judicial intervention. The Court gave no indication why obscene expression could not be regulated adequately through prompt resort to judicial action. Because a judicial forum would issue the requested relief, the relief granted could conceivably come in the form of a civil restraint against further exhibition or distribution. Such relief would require, however, that the government establish a likelihood of success on the merits at an adversary judicial hearing and some form of compelling interest justifying resort to injunctive relief, as where minors are involved as viewers or performers.

One might argue that in most cases, the relatively limited time restrictions caused by administrative interim restraints on protected expression will be of little consequence to the speaker for two reasons. First, the time periods involved are likely to be so limited as to be de minimis. Second, as long as the relevant expression is not a news story about a current political event, one might think that the actual timing of dissemination is of little import and therefore a restriction on the timing represents only a minimal interference with first amendment freedom. Indeed, commentators concerned with the dangers of prior restraints have referred to such restrictions only when, according to

---

92. Comm'n on Obscenity and Pornography, The Report of the Commission on Obscenity and Pornography 32 (1970) ("empirical research ... has found no evidence to date that exposure to explicit sexual materials plays a significant role in the causation of delinquent or criminal behavior among youths or adults"); *see* Chapter I at 68-76.

93. As the Supreme Court stated in Roth v. United States, 354 U.S. 476, 484 (1957): "[I]mplicit in the history of the First Amendment is the rejection of obscenity as utterly without redeeming social importance."

94. I, however, have taken just the opposite position. *See* Chapter I at 68-76.

95. *Cf.* Jeffries, *supra* note 12, at 412.

some undefined external standard, timing was considered to be of the essence.[96]

Such an analysis, however, improperly shifts the burden of production in a first amendment case away from the government and onto the individual. Unless the government can establish a compelling interest to justify a restriction on any aspect of protected expression, the individual should be allowed to express herself in any manner deemed appropriate.[97] The choice of timing and manner of expression are themselves an integral part of the expression and thus intertwined with the exercise of first amendment rights. The Supreme Court has held, for example, that an individual's decision to express opposition to the draft by means of offensive language in a public place cannot be penalized.[98] Presumably the Court did not intend to express agreement with the individual that the use of obscenities was the most persuasive method of discourse about the draft. Rather, the Court was simply holding that — absent an overriding governmental interest — the manner of expression is for the individual to choose.[99] Similarly, the individual should make the decision as to timing because *when* she chooses to speak is as much a part of the individual's self-expression as is the substantive content of her statement.

Obviously, neither timing nor manner will always be within the total discretion of the individual, just as the actual substance of an individual's expression will not always be free from governmental regulation.[100] Unless a court finds that the government has met its initial burden of proof by establishing a threshold level of compelling interest in regulating the expression prior to its initial dissemination, however, the speaker should not be required under some externally devised standard to establish a reason for the importance of her chosen

---

96. *See, e.g.,* F. HAIMAN, *supra* note 49, at 404; L. TRIBE, AMERICAN CONSTITUTIONAL LAW § 12-33, at 730-31 (1978); Blasi, *supra* note 8, at 30-33; Emerson, *supra* note 2, at 657. Blasi noted, however, that "it is plausible that on some occasions, persons who lose control of the timing of their utterances thereby lose their desire to speak." Blasi, *supra,* at 33.

97. See the discussion in Chapter II, at 123-24.

98. Cohen v. California, 403 U.S. 15 (1971).

99. The Court arguably rejected the overriding governmental interest analysis in United States v. O'Brien, 391 U.S. 367 (1968), where it held constitutional a federal statute making criminal the destruction of a draft card even in protest against the Vietnam War. The Court, however, based its decision partly on the presence of what it found to be a legitimate governmental interest in preventing draft card destruction. *Id.* at 377-78. See the discussion of both *Cohen* and *O'Brien* in Chapter II, *supra* at 100-01; 114-16; 123-25.

100. I have consistently rejected any form of absolutism in my first amendment analysis. *See, e.g.,* Chapter I, at 52-55; Chapter II at 117-21.

timing. If the government cannot establish a compelling interest, even a minimal restriction on the timing of protected expression cannot be justified.[101]

Moreover, the interim restraint on protected expression may not always be as minimal as some might believe,[102] even under the seemingly speech-protective standards adopted in *Freedman*. *Freedman* requires that "[a]ny restraint imposed in advance of a final judicial determination on the merits must ... be limited to preservation of the status quo for the shortest fixed period *compatible with sound judicial resolution.*"[103] The final phrase ominously invites some degree of disguised manipulation. More importantly, even good faith efforts to obtain such a "sound judicial resolution" would require significant periods of time given current docket delays and potentially lengthy proceedings.[104] To be sure, the *Freedman* Court added that "the procedure must also assure a prompt final judicial decision."[105] In light of the Court's previously quoted statement, however, this statement does not appear intended to establish an objective promptness standard. Common sense dictates that promptness be defined in relation to the time period ordinarily required for such adjudications, even if we were to accept that a de minimis abridgment is allowable in the absence of a compelling interest.[106]

---

101. A proper first amendment analysis would look at the relatively short time period between initial dissemination of obscene matter and the opportunity of the government to obtain civil restraint at a full and fair judicial hearing and would conclude that the *government's* interest, rather than the speaker's, is de minimis.

102. Professor Blasi, for example, noted that under *Freedman*, "[T]he administrative censor's power is only to disallow speech pending expeditious adjudication." Blasi, *supra* note 8, at 33.

103. 380 U.S. at 59.

104. Recall that any judicial obscenity determination will probably be held to require the use of numerous procedural protections. *See supra* text accompanying notes 85-89.

105. 380 U.S. at 59.

106. A possible problem with my "interim restraint" analysis is that although due process may well require judicial process at some point, such process is not always deemed required at the very beginning of the governmental regulatory process. *Compare* Mathews v. Eldridge, 424 U.S. 319 (1976) (allowing termination of Social Security payments prior to the holding of a hearing), *with* Fuentes v. Shevin, 407 U.S. 67 (1972) (holding unconstitutional state statutes authorizing summary seizure of secured goods on ex parte application). Even when the Supreme Court has required a predeprivation hearing, that hearing often may be administrative, rather than judicial. *See, e.g.,* Bell v. Burson, 402 U.S. 535 (1971) (removal of driver's license). As a practical matter, however, the procedural requirements of due process will ultimately be the product of a balancing of competing interests. Our political and judicial traditions dictate that the first amendment right of free expression receive the greatest

A proper construction of the prior restraint doctrine, then, would focus exclusively on the issue of providing a full and fair judicial hearing prior to any abridgment. Thus directed, the doctrine would impose its heavy negative presumption against any form of administrative abridgment, no matter how temporary. Of course, the relatively limited nature of the temporal restraint might properly be included in the weighing necessary in virtually every first amendment case. Hence, if the government showed a compelling interest, the fact that the abridgment was strictly time-limited might influence a decision to defer to that interest. Absent such a threshold demonstration of a compelling interest, however, such abridgments should not be allowed, regardless of the supposedly minimal nature of the restraint.

B. Practical Implications of the Theoretical Rationale

Once we recognize the full-and-fair-judicial-hearing rationale as the sole basis on which to impose the prior restraint doctrine's negative presumption, we must determine under what circumstances, if any, interim restraints of expression should be allowed prior to a formal, adversarial judicial determination. First amendment interests may properly be forced to give way, but only in extreme circumstances. Interim restraints thus should be permitted only when a compelling emergency exists. The preceding analysis has made clear that the interest in regulating obscenity does not meet this standard.[107] The only other conceivable justifications for such interim restraints are the need for administrative screening of planned demonstrations and the concern for national security.

1. Demonstrations

Although the Court has imposed some restrictions on the administrative licensing of parades and demonstrations,[108] it has never

---

possible constitutional protection, a description which could not be made of the quasi-property interests involved in cases like *Mathews* or *Bell*. Moreover, as a purely conceptual matter an administrative restraint, on penalty of contempt for failure to comply, effectively abridges expression for however long that restraint remains in force. In light of the extremely strong constitutional interest involved, the need for such a system of administrative restraint, even for relatively limited time periods, must be justified by a truly compelling governmental interest. Because the *Freedman* Court concluded that the first amendment interest is fully satisfied by so-called "prompt" post-administrative judicial review, it never asked whether these interim administrative restraints are really necessary. The Court thus completely ignored the effective interim abridgment of expression.

107. *See supra* text accompanying notes 92-95.
108. *See, e.g.*, Thornhill v. Alabama, 310 U.S. 88 (1940) (holding unconstitutional statute prohibiting any picketing of businesses).

held the use of such nonjudicial screening of this fully protected form of expressive activity unconstitutional per se.[109] Yet in every sense, such systems present the core danger of a prior restraint: they limit speech prior to a judicial determination that the speech may properly be the subject of regulation. Despite this fact, the Court has never engaged in a detailed analysis to determine whether such prima facie abridgments are supported by a compelling justification.

Perhaps this failure can be explained by what many would consider the obvious practical need for such licensing; without it, total chaos might well result. Professor Baker argued in a recent provocative article, however, that administrative licensing of demonstrations effectively discriminates against expressive activity.[110] He correctly pointed out that on the night that the would-be demonstrators in the famed case of *Cox v. New Hampshire*[111] were arrested for marching down the streets of Manchester without a permit, many other individuals walked the streets of that city without any governmental interference. The only difference between the two groups, he noted, was that the former pedestrians were attempting to express a viewpoint, while the latter were not.[112] Therefore licensing requirements, he argued, seek out expressive activity for negative treatment. The point has considerable force: such licensing requirements deter spontaneous expressive activity. It does not necessarily follow, however, that there is no role to be played by administrative licensing of demonstrations; not even Baker's analysis goes quite that far.[113] The question is whether recognition of the constitutional dangers presented by licensing should require an adjustment in the scope of authority exercised by the licensers.

To prevent chaos when more than one group attempts to employ the same space at the same time, an administrative licensing system could function properly as a reservations service. One might argue that licensers should have no authority to deny a license on *any* ground other than the existence of a prior reservation. Yet demonstrations planned for 5 p.m. Friday evening on Chicago's Michigan Avenue obviously cannot be allowed. Thus, once we move beyond licenser as

---

109. *See, e.g.,* Poulos v. New Hampshire, 345 U.S. 395 (1953); Cox v. New Hampshire, 312 U.S. 569 (1941). *See generally* J. Nowak, R. Rotunda & J. Young, *supra* note 2, at 973-76 (stating that administrative licensing schemes are constitutional unless vague or overbroad).

110. Baker, *Unreasoned Reasonableness: Mandatory Parade Permits and Time, Place, and Manner Regulations,* 78 Nw. U. L. Rev. 937 (1983).

111. 312 U.S. 569 (1941).

112. Baker, *supra* note 110, at 992.

113. *Id.* at 969.

reservationist to licenser as protector of public order, the question becomes whether the licensing determination can be made by the administrator alone or whether she must instead seek a judicial order prohibiting the demonstration.

Because judicial injunctions are often employed to preserve the status quo in emergency situations of all types, the clear constitutional preference for a judicial rather than an administrative determination would seem to require the administrators to resort to the judiciary to restrain a proposed demonstration for reasons other than schedule conflicts. Though authorities not given notice of a planned demonstration obviously will have insufficient opportunity to seek a judicial order, most demonstration planners will wish to notify the authorities if only to reserve the exclusive opportunity to parade at their chosen time and place.[114] Thus, recognition that expression may not be abridged prior to a full and fair judicial hearing requires that the administrative role in the licensing of demonstrations be substantially reduced.

2. National Security

In *Near v. Minnesota*,[115] the classic expression of the presumption against prior restraints, the Court acknowledged that such restraints were permissible in certain situations. "No one would question," said the Court, "but that a government might prevent actual obstruction to its recruiting service or the publication of the sailing dates of transports or the number and location of troops."[116] From this statement has developed the accepted principle that national security stands as an exception to the presumption against prior restraints.[117]

---

114. Nevertheless, if individuals engage in a demonstration that presents a real threat to safety or order, without giving prior notice, the obvious recourse is to arrest them for breach of the peace, just as when a licensed demonstration gets out of hand. This method concededly carries with it the danger of police abuse of authority, an abuse that can only be remedied by overturning the arrest long after the demonstration has been disrupted. The danger of improper police disruption is always present, however, for either licensed or unlicensed demonstrations, and any would-be demonstrators seeking to reduce this risk may notify the authorities of their plans sufficiently prior to the demonstration date to allow a judicial ruling.

115. 283 U.S. 697 (1931).

116. *Id.* at 716.

117. Judge Linde has questioned this exception. Linde, *supra* note 7. He pointed to the important distinction "between breach of secrecy and publication." *Id.* at 196. Usually, the threat to national security will not come from the general *publication* of sensitive information, but from the simple act of privately passing the information on to our enemies. "It seems more likely," he argued, "that when the press has the information, its secrecy already cannot be relied on, and publication may only alert the

The use of any form of administrative restraint to effect this principle, however, can never be justified. Administrative authority to impose restraints on grounds of national security is especially harmful to free speech interests for two reasons. First, the definition of "national security" is likely to fluctuate with the contemporary political climate. Second, the incentive of nonjudicial regulators, as for any censor, is to use their authority to suppress.[118] Given the obvious political sensitivity of much information that a government might choose to consider secret, the need for a forum with a long tradition of independence from the political branches is overriding. The courts are therefore the only proper forum for restricting publication in the interests of national security.

C. Differentiating Among Forms of Judicial Restraint

Because of the concern that expression may be abridged prior to a full and fair judicial ruling on the protected nature of the challenged expression, the prior restraint doctrine appropriately should impose a strong presumption against any form of nonjudicial restraint. Though resort to a judicial rather than an administrative forum is a necessary condition for avoiding the negative presumption imposed by the prior restraint doctrine, it is not a sufficient condition. To meet the concerns of the prior restraint doctrine, judicial action must be preceded by a full and fair hearing; the mere presence of a judicial rather than an administrative officer does not by itself guarantee such a hearing.

Most suspect of the possible judicial actions is the ex parte temporary restraining order. In *Carroll v. President and Commissioners*,[119] the Court held unconstitutional an ex parte restraining order of a planned

---

government to that fact." *Id.* He further noted that "to suppress public reporting of government acts and policies in the name of security also means suppressing the political means of affecting those acts and policies." *Id.* at 197.

Judge Linde's position is, to say the least, a controversial one. His arguments, however, in no way turn on the method of regulation; they apply with equal force to subsequent punishments and prior restraints. Thus, we need not view the issue simply as a matter of the prior restraint doctrine. That doctrine comes into play only when a prior restraint would not be constitutional in a case in which subsequent punishment would be; otherwise, the constitutional issue is one of substantive first amendment analysis rather than of the manner of regulation. Because it is difficult to imagine that substantive first amendment doctrine would prohibit subsequent punishment of the revelation of truly sensitive military secrets, the analysis in this chapter suggests that judicially ordered restraints should in many instances be permitted with equal frequency. *But see infra* text accompanying notes 119-131.

118. *See supra* notes 80-82 and accompanying text.
119. 393 U.S. 175 (1968).

rally "because of a basic infirmity in the procedure by which it was obtained."[120] The Court noted that the order had been issued "without notice to petitioners and without any effort, however informal, to invite or permit their participation in the proceedings" and concluded that "there is no place within the area of basic freedoms guaranteed by the First Amendment for such orders where no showing is made that it is impossible to serve or to notify the opposing parties and to give them an opportunity to participate."[121] In this case the Court's treatment of prior restraint is beyond criticism.[122]

The situation is not so clear-cut, however, when temporary relief follows notice and some form of hearing. A temporary restraining order, for example, should usually issue only after notice and hearing.[123] The due process problems that plague hearings for temporary restraining orders similarly affect hearings on preliminary injunctions. Neither type of hearing provides all procedural protections afforded at a full trial.[124] Such temporary forms of relief fall into a "twilight zone" of prior restraint — not deserving of the strong negative presumption traditionally associated with the prior restraint doctrine, but also not deserving of treatment identical to that given to most subsequent punishment systems.

To a certain extent, these first amendment concerns are already accommodated by the nonconstitutional limitations traditionally imposed on these forms of relief. Purely as a matter of equity, injunctions cannot be issued without a demonstrated likelihood of

---

120. *Id.* at 180.

121. *Id.*

122. The issue of ex parte temporary restraining orders becomes more complicated, however, when a speaker defies such an order, even one improperly issued, and then attempts to defend against a contempt citation on the grounds that the order was improper. This question implicates the controversial collateral bar rule, discussed *infra* text accompanying notes 143-161.

123. *See* Fed. R. Civ. P. 65(b) advisory committee note ("In view of the possibly drastic consequence of a temporary restraining order, the opposition should be heard, if feasible, before the order is granted.").

124. As Professor Fiss has noted:

> Preliminary injunctions may be issued after a truncated presentation of the facts and law. The ordinary opportunities for discovery may be curtailed. The rules of evidence ... may be abandoned; heavy reliance is likely to be placed on documents rather than on live testimony to establish a factual point; the ordinary opportunities for cross-examination are curtailed; and often the judge must decide without adequate opportunity to study either the law or the facts.

O. FISS, *supra* note 2, at 28-29.

success on the merits and a threat of significant, irreparable harm if the injunction is denied.[125] In a sense, these requirements reflect the same concerns that are inherent in a "twilight zone" form of compelling interest analysis derived from the first amendment itself: because such prior restraints are imposed by a judicial officer following some form of adversarial judicial process, the heavy negative presumption traditionally associated with the prior restraint doctrine is inappropriate. Nevertheless, because prior restraints are issued following only an abbreviated judicial inquiry, they are properly employed only if the asserted governmental interest could not be adequately protected by regulation following a full adversarial trial and only if the court determines that a strong likelihood exists that the government will be able to establish that the challenged expression is regulable under substantive first amendment standards. Thus, substantial alteration of the traditional limitations on preliminary equitable relief may be unnecessary to meet first amendment standards under the revised version of the prior restraint doctrine.[126] The traditional equitable principle that the issuance of such preliminary relief is largely a matter of the court's discretion,[127] however, would have to change. Such broad discretion is not consistent with first amendment concerns, and any court issuing such preliminary relief against expression should expect no deference in the course of appellate review.

Most of the problems plaguing the use of preliminary injunctive relief against expressive activity are irrelevant to the issuance of permanent injunctive relief following a full trial because all of the procedural protections necessary for a full and fair adjudication are present. One might argue, however, even with all of these protections, that such equitable relief should nevertheless be presumptively invalid because the relief is issued prior to any appellate review. No doubt an opportunity for appellate review is important to the fairness of the

---

125. 11 C. WRIGHT & A. MILLER, FEDERAL PRACTICE AND PROCEDURE § 2948 (1973).

126. Many of the same equitable limitations, particularly the requirement that no adequate remedy exists at law, apply as well to the issuance of permanent injunctive relief after a full trial. In light of the theory of prior restraint advocated here, such requirements need not be imposed as a first amendment matter. No reason exists, however, to alter these traditional equitable requirements. The first amendment does not require them, but it in no way prohibits them.

127. *See generally* 11 C. WRIGHT & A. MILLER, *supra* note 125, at § 2948 (stating that trial court has discretion to grant or deny temporary restraining orders; standard of appellate review is abuse of discretion).

judicial process and may do much to preserve the legitimacy of that process in the eyes of the litigants.[128] Although provision of an opportunity for appeal may be advisable, however, the Supreme Court has unequivocally refused to recognize the right of appeal to have constitutional significance.[129] In light of this refusal, no basis exists for extending this principle in the first amendment context.[130]

The theoretical basis for the prior restraint doctrine is thus a question of process, not substance. A speaker must be afforded an opportunity in a full and fair judicial hearing to contest any restraint before it is imposed. To prove the speech constitutionally unprotected, the government must show a truly compelling interest that outweighs the first amendment right. This requirement parallels the requirements of likely success on the merits and irreparable harm that traditionally accompany temporary relief in nonconstitutional issues.[131] A judicial determination is necessary even when issues of national security are involved and when the licenser's duty passes beyond that of a reservations officer. A nonjudicial prior restraint, therefore, is seldom permissible. Contrasting nonjudicial prior restraints and subsequent punishment systems will make clearer the unique dangers of the nonjudicial prior restraint.

IV. Nonjudicial Prior Restraints and Subsequent Punishment Contrasted

In most instances, judicially issued prior restraints on expression are no more harmful to first amendment interests than are subsequent punishment systems and therefore do not deserve the traditional disdain imposed by the prior restraint doctrine. Only administrative restraints present problems unique to prior restraints and therefore should continue to receive the special disdain of the prior restraint doctrine. Professor Mayton, however, has gone considerably further, arguing that subsequent punishment systems are themselves an unduly invasive means of regulating expression and should be as suspect as nonjudicial restraints.[132] Under Professor Mayton's

---

128. I have made this argument in greater detail in a different context. *See* Redish, *The Pragmatic Approach to Appealability in the Federal Courts*, 75 COLUM. L. REV. 89, 96-97 (1975).

129. *See, e.g.*, Griffin v. Illinois, 351 U.S. 12, 18 (1956).

130. Of course, a trial court always has discretion to stay its order pending appeal, and in certain cases the appellate court itself may grant a stay. But it is difficult to see how these possibilities can be raised to the level of a constitutional right.

131. *See supra* text accompanying note 125.

132. Mayton, *supra* note 12, at 265, 281. Interestingly, although Professor Mayton was quick to condemn subsequent punishment systems, he accepted administrative

hierarchy, the most acceptable method of regulating expression is by means of judicial injunction, while subsequent punishment and administrative restraints are equally disfavored.[133] Such an analysis mistakenly disregards significant differences between subsequent punishment systems and nonjudicial prior restraints in both potential harm to free speech interests and potential benefit to society.

Mayton argued that both forms of regulation "effectively evade[] judicial review"[134] and that both "depend upon the threat of punishment and litigation costs to instill compliance."[135] It is clearly overstatement, however, to suggest that subsequent punishment schemes, as a general matter, effectively evade judicial review. In too many criminal prosecutions a first amendment defense has been raised, often successfully, for us to accept such a sweeping assertion.[136] Although administrative restraints may often restrain expression under penalty of contempt without opportunity for effective judicial review, at least no one may *formally* be penalized by a subsequent punishment scheme absent substantial judicial involvement.

The central difficulty with Mayton's equation of administrative restraint and subsequent punishment is that the former is virtually never necessary to protect a compelling governmental interest;[137] the

---

restraints when they are followed by some form of judicial process. *See id.* at 252-53. He thus completely ignored the danger of an unjustified interim restraint. *See supra* text accompanying notes 97-106.

133. "[A]s courts disapprove of schemes of ... administrative censorship, they should also disfavor systems of subsequent punishment." Mayton, *supra* note 12, at 281. Mayton recognized that, despite a general presumption against subsequent punishment, on occasion such a regulatory method may be employed. *Id.* at 273. He cited as an example federal laws limiting the amount of money that individuals and corporations may contribute to political campaigns. *Id.* This example of expressive activity which Mayton believed should be subjected to subsequent punishment is one that I believe should not constitutionally be subjected to *any* form of governmental regulation. *See generally* Redish, *Campaign Spending Laws and the First Amendment,* 46 N.Y.U. L. REV. 900 (1971) (arguing that proposals to limit campaign expenditures and to require disclosure of funds' sources violate candidates' and contributors' freedom of speech); Redish, *Reflections on Federal Regulation of Corporate Political Activity,* 21 J. PUB. L. 339 (1972) (suggesting that the Federal Corrupt Practices Act violates the first amendment by criminalizing corporate political expenditures). In any event, it is questionable why this activity is so much more threatening to societal interests than are other forms of expression that it should be subjected to what Mayton deems a more invasive regulatory method.

134. Mayton, *supra* note 12, at 281. Mayton argued that subsequent punishment systems exert a chilling effect that escapes judicial review.

135. *Id.* at 265.

136. *See, e.g.,* Wooley v. Maynard, 430 U.S. 705 (1977); Cohen v. California, 403 U.S. 15 (1971); Lovell v. Griffin, 303 U.S. 444 (1938).

137. *See supra* text accompanying notes 117-118.

latter often is. To the extent that pre-expression restraints are ever required, they usually can be as effectively invoked by judicial as by nonjudicial mechanisms. Attaining the legitimate goals of the criminal law, however, will often be impossible by any means other than the threat of subsequent prosecution. Thus, though Mayton has correctly pointed to the potential chill on protected behavior which subsequent punishment systems sometimes share with administrative restraints, he has ignored the fact that such a chill properly results from a compelling interest in *deterring,* not just punishing crime.

The presumably acceptable legislative goal of preventing solicitation of crime provides a clear example. Traditionally, this goal is attained by legislatively categorizing such conduct as criminal; someone soliciting a criminal act may be punished for doing so. Could one reasonably suggest that the same goal could be achieved by means of pre-expression restraint? Such a suggestion is, of course, absurd: a court or prosecutor could not know of the planned solicitation before it is spoken. Once the solicitation has been made, a court, instead of criminally prosecuting the speaker, could restrain her from soliciting again, under threat of a contempt citation. That individual, however, has absolutely no incentive not to solicit criminal conduct the first time if the worst that can happen to her is that she will be prohibited from doing it again. She may never be discovered, and if she is, she has lost little. The threat of a criminal sanction for that initial utterance, however, will presumably deter many people from the start, including a few whose behavior would have gone undetected.

Mayton acknowledged that this chilling effect of the criminal law is desirable for overt, physical crimes such as bank robbery.[138] He suggested, however, that "[i]t is quite another thing when the state seeks to define something not so readily perceived by the senses."[139] But the situation is different only if we have preliminarily concluded that the speech sought to be regulated is protected by the first amendment. Certain forms of expression in certain contexts have been found unprotected, presumably because the danger of this expression to society outweighs its benefits.[140] Once that decision about the substantive nature of the expression has been reached, the societal danger of the speech is of as much legitimate concern as is the bank robbery. True, statutes that criminally punish expression certainly

---

138. Mayton, *supra* note 12, at 254.
139. *Id.*
140. An example of this type of speech is advocacy of unlawful conduct. *See, e.g.,* Brandenburg v. Ohio, 395 U.S. 444 (1969).

may, through overbreadth or vagueness, spill over to chill fully protected speech.[141] This concern is admittedly unique to statutes regulating expression and one of which the courts must routinely be wary. But once we have concluded that certain types of expression are so dangerous as to be constitutionally regulable, to preclude the only method of regulation effective against such expression is nonsensical. Unless Professor Mayton believed than an injunction system can somehow effectively deter or remedy these forms of harmful expression, he would have to concede that subsequent punishment (usually of the criminal variety) presents the only viable regulatory option in certain contexts.[142]

Thus, Mayton's lumping together of administrative restraint and subsequent punishment as equally invasive means of regulating expression proves invalid. On balance, subsequent punishment systems provide greater access to a judicial forum prior to abridgment than do administrative restraints. Furthermore, though both remedies potentially chill protected behavior, that chill is a necessary adjunct to a subsequent punishment system which seeks to deter that which is illegal. Subsequent punishment systems, therefore, both protect first amendment activity by providing a full and fair trial to an accused speaker and protect society by chilling destructive behavior. Judicially imposed prior restraints, operating in a slightly different sphere, likewise provide a full and fair hearing and prevent destructive behavior but do so without the generalized chill, focusing instead on particular activities. Nonjudicial restraint on expression, on the other hand, is significantly more suspect as a constitutional matter than either of the other two forms of regulation, for it provides the benefits of neither and adds the danger of improper process.

V. Implications for the Collateral Bar Rule

The collateral bar rule provides that, with relatively rare but complex exceptions,[143] an individual who has knowingly violated an injunction cannot defend against a contempt citation on the ground

---

141. Mayton, *supra* note 12, at 254-57.

142. Mayton or other commentators could argue that such expression is not sufficiently dangerous to justify regulation or that the danger of expression should never be included in a first amendment calculus. Such an issue concerns the substantive scope of first amendment doctrine; it in no way turns on matters of regulatory form. In Mayton's analysis the real issue — the substantive reach of the first amendment — has become obscured by a debate about regulatory method, as so often happens in discussions of the prior restraint doctrine. *See supra* text accompanying notes 6, 69-76.

143. *See infra* text accompanying notes 150-154.

that the injunction was invalid. The doctrine has had a long history in contexts other than the first amendment.[144] When the rule has been applied to contempt for violation of injunctions against expressive activity, however, substantial controversy has ensued.

The Court applied the collateral bar rule in the first amendment context in *Walker v. City of Birmingham*.[145] Martin Luther King and a group of local Birmingham ministers planned to protest racial segregation in that city by picketing and parading. Informal attempts to obtain a permit required by a constitutionally dubious local ordinance were unsuccessful. On the basis of the ordinance, local authorities successfully obtained an ex parte temporary restraining order from the state circuit court against further mass demonstrations. Two days later, on Good Friday, Dr. King and his followers defied the injunction by holding a parade. Another demonstration was held on Easter Sunday, and Dr. King and other demonstration leaders were later convicted of criminal contempt for violating the injunction. A sharply divided Supreme Court upheld the contempt convictions on the basis of the collateral bar rule.

Use of this collateral bar rule for violations of injunctions stands in striking contrast to accepted procedure for violations of statutes, where an individual may first violate the law and then defend on the basis of the law's unconstitutionality.[146] If one seeks a justification for the collateral bar rule, one usually finds the argument "that in the fair administration of justice no man can be judge in his own case, however exalted his station, however righteous his motives, and irrespective of his race, color, politics, or religion."[147] The rule is thus thought to foster respect for the law and the legal system. This justification, however, appears embarrassingly inconsistent with the accepted practice for statutory violations.[148] Disrespect for the law is equally encouraged when we allow a defendant to challenge a law's constitutionality after he has violated it. We allow this practice perhaps because its costs are justified by the benefits of ferreting out unconstitutional laws. Yet, at

---

144. *See generally* Cox, *The Void Order and the Duty to Obey,* 16 U. CHI. L. REV. 86 (1948) (suggesting a rule that the duty to obey injunctions be qualified if the litigant has exhausted all normal methods of appellate review and will be irrevocably injured in some concrete way); Watt, *The Divine Right of Government by Judiciary,* 14 U. CHI. L. REV. 409 (1947) (criticizing the doctrine as repressive and reactionary in the context of injunctions issued against labor movements).
145. 388 U.S. 307 (1967).
146. *See infra* note 155.
147. *Walker,* 388 U.S. at 320-21 (footnote omitted).
148. O. FISS, *supra* note 2, at 73, noted that the *Walker* rule is at odds with the prior restraint doctrine because it makes injunctions more powerful than criminal statutes.

least in certain contexts, the same argument could be made about invalid injunctions.[149]

Certain judicially recognized exceptions to the rule seem to undermine the asserted rationale. In *Howat v. Kansas*,[150] one of the earlier Supreme Court decisions applying the rule, the Court impliedly recognized that a defendant could challenge the issuing court's jurisdiction in a contempt proceeding.[151] In *United States v. United Mine Workers*,[152] the Court appeared to limit the scope of this exception to cases not only in which the issuing court lacked jurisdiction, but also in which that court's assertion of jurisdiction was "frivolous and not substantial."[153] The *Walker* Court, however, seemed to expand significantly the *United Mine Workers* exception by applying the "frivolousness" criterion to the merits as well as to jurisdiction.[154] Yet if the rationale of the collateral bar rule is that one

---

149. Professor Blasi has argued that a speaker has an absolute duty to make an advance challenge to an injunction, no matter how obviously invalid, as long as time permits. First, he contends that legal obligations should be unambiguous and unequivocal. Second, self-help raises the risk of violence. Blasi, *Prior Restraints on Demonstrations*, 68 MICH. L. REV. 1481, 1558-59 (1970). Both of these reasons, however, could just as easily be asserted against the practice of allowing a challenge to a law's constitutionality as a defense against its violation.

150. 258 U.S. 181 (1922).

151. *Id.* at 189.

152. 330 U.S. 258 (1947). In *United Mine Workers*, the Supreme Court upheld the imposition of fines on a union and its president for willful violation of a judicial order restraining them from striking. The union defended against the contempt citation on the ground that the federal court lacked power to enjoin the strike because of the prohibitions contained in the Norris-LaGuardia Act. *Id.* at 269-72. Although the Supreme Court rejected this defense on the merits, *id.* at 282, the Court's decision is best remembered for the holding "that an order issued by a court with jurisdiction over the subject matter and person must be obeyed by the parties until it is reversed by orderly and proper proceedings. This is true without regard even for the constitutionality of the Act under which the order is issued." *Id.* at 293 (footnote omitted). The Court relied heavily upon the following language from Howat v. Kansas:

> An injunction duly issuing out of a court of general jurisdiction with equity powers upon pleadings properly invoking its action, and served upon persons made parties therein and within the jurisdiction, must be obeyed by them however erroneous the action of the court may be, even if the error be in the assumption of the validity of a seeming but void law going to the merits of the case. It is for the court of first instance to determine the question of the validity of the law, and until its decision is reversed for error by orderly review, either by itself or by a higher court, its orders based on its decision are to be respected, and disobedience of them is contempt of its lawful authority, to be punished.

258 U.S. 181, 189-90 (1922), quoted in 330 U.S. at 293-94 (footnote omitted).

153. 330 U.S. at 293.

154. 388 U.S. at 315.

should not be encouraged to act as a judge in his own case, recognition of *any* exception directly undermines that principle by encouraging defendants to decide for themselves whether a judicial order is frivolous.

Another argument justifying the rule is that an injunction, unlike a statute, is specifically designed to avoid irreparable injury in an individual case. Thus, society must discourage any attempt to circumvent an injunction's directive. The argument fails to persuade. Although a statute is generally not designed to prevent a specific harm in an individual case, it is difficult to believe that the harm which most criminal statutes are designed to deter could not be characterized as "irreparable." A statute making murder a crime, for example, surely is designed to deter conduct as harmful as that prohibited by any injunction, so it is unlikely we would wish to encourage such prohibited conduct any more than we would wish to encourage a violation of an injunction.

Despite the inadequacy of the traditional justifications for the collateral bar rule, however, it need not be abandoned in its entirety when applied in the first amendment context.[155] Use of the rule could

---

155. One commentator has suggested abolishing the rule to reduce the chilling effects of prior restraints. Barnett, *The Puzzle of Prior Restraint,* 29 STAN. L. REV. 539 (1977). An injunction would then be indistinguishable from a criminal statute which allows an individual first to defy a law and then to defend on the basis of the statute's unconstitutionality. *See, e.g.,* Shuttlesworth v. City of Birmingham, 394 U.S. 147 (1969); Lovell v. City of Griffin, 303 U.S. 444 (1938). As the Court stated in Thornhill v. Alabama, 310 U.S. 88, 97 (1940) (citation omitted): "One who might have had a license for the asking may ... call into question the whole scheme of licensing when he is prosecuted for failure to procure it." The Court has developed some limitations on the collateral bar rule, the contours of which are not entirely clear. *See, e.g.,* Poulos v. New Hampshire, 345 U.S. 395 (1953) (upholding conviction for conducting a religious service without a license because statute not facially void, even though defendant had been denied that license arbitrarily). *See generally* J. NOWAK, R. ROTUNDA & J. YOUNG, *supra* note 2, at 974-76 (explaining *Poulos* result by noting that the defendant had failed to show the lack of a prompt judicial remedy and that the statute was valid as interpreted by state courts). Regardless of these unclear limitations, it is safe to state that the collateral bar rule described in the text is by far the predominant rule.

If we were to dispense with the collateral bar rule entirely, however, those who have difficulties with judicially imposed prior restraints probably would not be satisfied. Even if a speaker were allowed to challenge the constitutionality of an injunction as a defense in a contempt proceeding, the speaker probably would not be as willing to defy an injunction as he would a criminal statute. A certain degree of chill undoubtedly exists when a speaker chooses to violate a criminal statute despite the ability to defend on the basis of the statute's unconstitutionality because the speaker risks criminal penalties if he guesses wrong. A considerably greater chill exists, however, when an individual is the subject of an injunction. An injunction is aimed directly at a particular individual and is issued only after the authorities have deemed it necessary

continue, but in a significantly modified form, by applying the full and fair hearing rationale to first amendment claims raised in collateral contempt proceedings.

The unique vice of prior restraints is that in certain instances they abridge expression that would ultimately be found protected in a judicial forum. Thus, if an individual violates a first amendment injunction issued after a full and fair hearing by a competent judicial forum, no constitutionally based reason exists to allow him to raise the first amendment issue a second time in a collateral contempt proceeding. To allow this issue to be raised would be to permit two bites at the judicial apple, a practice not required by either the first amendment or due process. Indeed, the logic of the rule of collateral estoppel suggests that a party should not be allowed to relitigate a factual or mixed law-fact question already litigated in a completed separate proceeding.[156] Thus, if after a full trial a court determines that challenged expressive activity is constitutionally regulable and enjoins that activity, no constitutional or common-law principle enables the losing party to relitigate those issues in a collateral contempt proceeding. This situation is very different from a case in which a defendant is charged with violation of a statute. There — unlike the case of an injunction — the defendant has not yet had a judicial hearing on his constitutional claim.

But most contempt proceedings in which the collateral bar rule is invoked probably do not follow an injunction issued after a full trial. Under the presently advocated criterion for measuring the constitutional validity of prior restraints,[157] ex parte temporary restraining orders such as those violated in both *United Mine Workers*[158] and *Walker*[159] are by far the most dubious of all judicially ordered restraints on expression because they are entered without either notice or opportunity for even the most basic form of adversary proceedings.[160] In such a case the defendant in the contempt proceeding

---

to invoke the judicial process. Contempt proceedings are thus highly likely to follow the violation of an injunction. Although the chill of a criminal statute may well be significant, the chill of a particularized injunction is likely to be even greater. Hence, even if the collateral bar rule were discarded, the dangers that some find in prior restraints would not necessarily be removed.

156. *See generally* F. JAMES & G. HAZARD, CIVIL PROCEDURE §§ 11.16-11.21, at 563-73 (2d ed. 1977) (stating that issues are precluded if they were litigated by the parties, determined by a tribunal, and necessarily so determined; modern tendency is to apply issue preclusion to matters of law as well as of fact).

157. *See supra* text accompanying notes 11-17, 80-82, 125-127.

158. 330 U.S. at 266.

159. 388 U.S. at 308-09.

160. *See supra* text accompanying notes 119-122.

is identical to the defendant in the criminal prosecution: neither has yet had a judicial hearing. This form of judicial restraint may be appropriate in a compelling emergency, but only for a highly restricted time period. If in such a case the traditional justifications for the collateral bar rule prove unacceptable, the government will never be able to establish a sufficiently compelling interest to prevent a defendant's collateral challenge at a contempt proceeding of the constitutionality of that restraining order. Though the government's interest may be sufficiently compelling to justify the initial issuance of the restraining order, as arguably was the case in *Walker*, that interest is satisfied by the court's issuance of the order; the interest does not justify insulating that order from any subsequent form of judicial review. Therefore, the *Walker* decision is clearly incorrect, at least under the narrow circumstances of that case.[161]

More complex is the issue of the collateral bar rule's validity when the judicial restraint is a preliminary injunction following an adversary hearing. Such orders fall into a constitutional twilight zone because they meet some but not all of the requisite constitutional criteria.[162] Thus, they should be measured by a sliding scale, compelling interest analysis. Though they need not be justified by a truly overwhelming emergency — the standard required for any form of nonjudicial prior restraint of expression — they do require at least some significant governmental interest to justify their use against expressive activity. A justification sufficiently compelling to authorize a preliminary injunction, however, does not necessarily justify use of the collateral bar rule in a proceeding brought to enforce that injunction. The same principle applies to statutes invoked against expressive activity: no one suggests that a justification sufficiently compelling to uphold such a statute would further justify a refusal to allow an intentional violator to challenge the statute's constitutionality as a defense to a prosecution. Because no strong

---

161. Professor Mayton, though recognizing the dangers of the summary process inherent in the preliminary injunction procedure, seemed to have no problem with the collateral bar rule in contempt proceedings for the violation of such an injunction. Mayton, *supra* note 12, at 278 n. 204. He reasoned that "[t]he Supreme Court ... by requiring that the duration of 'interim judicial orders' be 'limited to preserving the status quo for the shortest fixed period compatible with sound judicial administration' has diminished the problem." *Id.* at 278 n. 204 (citing United States v. Thirty-Seven Photographs, 402 U.S. 363, 368 (1971)). But Mayton's analysis misses the key point: the issue is not whether a sufficiently pressing emergency exists to justify dispensing with full adversarial judicial process prior to the issuance of a restraining order. The issue instead turns on whether that same emergency further justifies forbidding the defendant to challenge the validity of that order collaterally in a contempt proceeding.

162. *See supra* text accompanying notes 80-82, 125-127.

justification exists for the collateral bar rule in any context — at least as long as criminal prosecutions for violations of statutes are not deemed to require a similar rule — it follows that the collateral bar rule can never be justified in the enforcement of a preliminary injunction.

The collateral bar rules raises difficult questions in the first amendment arena. It need not, however, be totally abandoned to provide sufficient protection to speakers in the context of injunctions if the full-and-fair-hearing rationale for prior restraint is embraced. When a speaker receives adequate opportunity to litigate the constitutionality of the injunction, he does not need a second chance in a collateral contempt proceeding. When an individual does not receive such an opportunity, however, he should be put on the same footing as the defendant in a statutory violation proceeding. Both defendants should be allowed to attack the statute's or injunction's constitutionality when called upon to defend their violations.

VI. Conclusion

The prior restraint doctrine as it presently stands crudely sweeps within its reach all forms of direct governmental restraint of expression — those issued administratively and judicially, those issued prior to an adversarial hearing, as well as those issued following such a hearing.[163] Ironically, such an unbending, sweeping approach has led the Court both to condemn restraints when they perhaps should not have been condemned and to allow restraints, particularly in the areas of obscenity regulation and demonstrations, when they were actually harmful and could not be justified by truly compelling interests.

Most of the arguments traditionally employed to justify special mistrust of judicial prior restraints as a means of speech regulation are unacceptable for one reason or another. Prior restraints instead should be disfavored over subsequent punishment schemes when and only when they abridge expression prior to a full and fair hearing before an independent judicial forum. Only after such a hearing can we conclude with any level of confidence that the expression in question is unprotected by the first amendment. To be sure, a certain portion of the expressive activity swept within a prior restraint's dragnet will

---

163. One commentator has argued that the modern Supreme Court finds administrative restraints more egregious than judicial restraints. *See* Mayton, *supra* note 12, at 250. Nevertheless, in both New York Times Co. v. United States, 403 U.S. 713 (1971), and Organization for a Better Austin v. Keefe, 402 U.S. 415 (1971), the Court condemned the restraints issued even though they had been issued by courts, rather than by administrators.

ultimately be found unprotected. Only under the most extreme circumstances, however, should fully protected expression ever be restrained along with the unprotected expression even for a relatively limited time.

Hence, prior restraint terminology should not be used to avoid the hard questions that first amendment analysis invariably presents in individual cases. Use of the approach suggested here would often require careful and difficult balancing of competing interests. But first amendment interests are not served by attempts to avoid difficult questions by use of oversimplified formulas. Nowhere is this more evident than in the current structure of the prior restraint doctrine.

CHAPTER IV

ADVOCACY OF UNLAWFUL CONDUCT AND THE CLEAR AND PRESENT DANGER TEST

Since the early days of the twentieth century, theorists of free speech have grappled with the problem of determining how much protection the first amendment gives to speech which advocates unlawful conduct. On the one hand, speech urging criminal conduct appears to be of limited social value and may well lead to significant social harm. On the other hand, regulation of unlawful advocacy has often been employed as a means of suppressing unpopular social ideas and political groups, and attaching criminal penalties to such speech could substantially impair the flow of free and open discourse. In an effort to reconcile these competing concerns, various members of the Supreme Court have at different times suggested a number of constitutional tests. The test that has received the most attention from Justices and scholars is the so-called "clear and present danger" test, originated by Justice Holmes in his opinion for the Court in *Schenck v. United States*.[1] This first incarnation of the test provided that speech may be regulated if "the words are used in such circumstances and are of such a nature as to create a clear and present danger that they will bring about the substantive evils that Congress has a right to prevent."[2]

The clear and present danger test has, over the years, had its articulate advocates.[3] On the whole, however, both judicial[4] and scholarly[5] commentary has been quite negative. Virulent criticism has come from those who believe the test is insufficiently protective of free speech interests, and from others who find that the test unduly limits

---

1. 249 U.S. 47 (1919).
2. *Id.* at 52.
3. Perhaps the leading academic advocate of the test is Professor Chafee. *See generally* Z. CHAFEE, FREE SPEECH IN THE UNITED STATES (1941).
4. *See* Dennis v. United States, 341 U.S. 494, 517-56 (1951) (Frankfurter, J., concurring); *id.* at 567-70 (Jackson, J., concurring). Judge Learned Hand also expressed criticism of the test. *See* Gunther, *Learned Hand and the Origins of Modern First Amendment Doctrine: Some Fragments of History*, 27 STAN. L. REV. 719 (1975).
5. *See, e.g.*, T. EMERSON, TOWARD A GENERAL THEORY OF THE FIRST AMENDMENT 51-53 (1966); P. FREUND, ON UNDERSTANDING THE SUPREME COURT 27-28 (1951); Ely, *Flag Desecration: A Case Study in the Roles of Categorization and Balancing in First Amendment Analysis*, 88 HARV. L. REV. 1482 (1975); Kalven, *Professor Ernst Freund and Debs v. United States*, 40 U. CHI. L. REV. 235, 236 (1973). As Professor Strong wrote, "there are few who would grieve at [the test's] total demise." Strong, *Fifty Years of "Clear and Present Danger": From* Schenck *to* Brandenburg — *and Beyond*, 1969 SUP. CT. REV. 41.

legislative ability to protect society from the harm that unlawful advocacy may cause.[6]

The first chapter of this book considered whether advocacy of unlawful conduct is deserving of *any* level of constitutional protection. Here, we assume, as the Supreme Court has consistently done, that there properly exists at least some level of constitutional protection for at least some forms of unlawful advocacy. In light of this assumption, the chapter will examine the history, structure and theory of the clear and present danger test, the test most often discussed as a means of determining exactly when such unlawful advocacy will be protected. After resolving most of the ambiguities in the test's structure in favor of a protectionist approach and suggesting a reformulation of the test to reflect this, I consider and attempt to refute the criticisms which have been levelled over the years at clear and present danger. The consideration of the criticisms includes a demonstration of the inferiority of alternative ways of identifying the circumstances under which the free speech clause protects the advocacy of unlawful conduct from criminal sanctions. In so doing, I attempt to demonstrate that many of the criticisms aimed at clear and present danger are merely indicative of the general fallacies inherent in a rigid "categorization" approach to first amendment analysis.

My ultimate conclusion is that an examination of the test's scope and structure, as well as a comparative investigation of the alternative methods of determining the appropriate degree of protection for unlawful advocacy, reveal that, to analogize to Winston Churchill's famous comment about democracy,[7] the clear and present danger test is the worst method for determining the degree of constitutional protection of unlawful advocacy, except for all the other ways. The point, in other words, is that while the clear and present danger test is unfortunately subject to potential abuse in its application, no other suggested means of resolving the conflict inherent in regulating unlawful advocacy does a better job. Indeed, detailed examination of each of these alternatives establishes that they are either demonstrably inferior to clear and present danger, or represent merely minor variations or modifications of the clear and present danger test itself.

---

6. *See infra* at 193-211.

7. "No one pretends that democracy is perfect or all-wise. Indeed, it has been said that democracy is the worst form of government except all those other forms that have been tried from time to time." (Speech to the House of Commons, Nov. 11, 1947) (as quoted in THE OXFORD DICTIONARY OF QUOTATIONS 150 (3d ed. 1979)).

I. The Clear and Present Danger Test: History, Theory, Criticisms and Alternatives

A. History[8]

While the language of the clear and present danger test appears to express a judicial attitude that is highly protective of free speech, the test was originally used to justify results highly restrictive of free speech interests. Formulated initially by Justice Holmes in his opinion for the Court in *Schenck v. United States*,[9] the test was used to ratify suppression of speech that could hardly be said to create any actual danger to anyone. The defendants in *Schenck* had printed a circular opposing military conscription and had distributed it to persons accepted for military service. They were convicted for conspiring to violate the 1917 Espionage Act. The Supreme Court affirmed the convictions. Holmes conceded that the circular called for only peaceful measures against conscription, and that the sole unlawful advocacy it contained was a statement that those drafted should assert their rights and that everyone "must maintain, support, and uphold the rights of the people of this country."[10] But even such mild exhortations, the Court held, could be punished, because in the volatile atmosphere of wartime they could have had the effect of disrupting the war effort by convincing soldiers that their conscription was unlawful. No evidence was cited, however, to establish the threat of any actual, specific harm caused by the leaflet. While Holmes unveiled the clear and present danger test as a way of incorporating the circumstances surrounding speech into an evaluation of its claim to first amendment protection, in actuality he employed the test to suppress speech despite the absence of any showing that it presented a real threat in light of the surrounding circumstances.[11]

The newly devised test seemed to be immediately disregarded by the very Court that had created it. Two cases, *Frohwerk v. United States*[12] and *Debs v. United States*,[13] were decided virtually contemporaneously with *Schenck*, and like it upheld convictions for unlawful

---

8. The history of the clear and present danger test, particularly in its early stages, has been the subject of extensive scholarship. *See, e.g.,* J. Nowak, R. Rotunda & J. Young, Constitutional Law 873-85 (2d ed. 1983); S. Konefsky, The Legacy of Holmes and Brandeis: A Study in the Influence of Ideas 169-235 (Collier ed. 1961); T. Emerson, The System of Freedom of Expression 62-79, 101-29 (1970). The historical discussion in this chapter will therefore be limited to the essentials.
9. 249 U.S. 47 (1919).
10. *Id.* at 51.
11. *Id.* at 52.
12. 249 U.S. 204 (1919).
13. 249 U.S. 211 (1919).

advocacy, but did not even mention the clear and present danger test. *Debs* in particular presented a highly questionable approval of governmental suppression of unpopular advocacy. Debs, a popular socialist leader, was convicted under the Espionage Act of 1917[14] of attempting to cause insubordination in the military forces and obstructing recruiting and enlistment into the military. He had given a public speech praising socialism and decrying war and conscription. The speech ended with the exhortation, "[d]on't worry about the charge of treason to your masters; but be concerned about the treason that involves yourselves."[15] At no point did Debs openly advocate illegal activity, nor was any evidence presented that the speech had caused any noticeable insubordination or obstruction of the draft. Nevertheless, Holmes, writing again for the Court, upheld Debs' conviction. He found that while the main theme of the speech, the theory of socialism, was itself protected, the first amendment would not shelter Debs if he intended to encourage obstruction of the draft and if his remarks had the "reasonably probable" effect of doing so.[16] Holmes did not find free speech to be a central issue in *Debs*.[17] He never referred to the week-old clear and present danger formulation, seemingly leading to the conclusion that the test must at that time have been of little importance to its creator.[18]

Commentators[19] sense that Holmes dramatically shifted his emphasis with his dissent in *Abrams v. United States*.[20] The *Abrams*

---

14. Ch. 30, § 3, 40 Stat. 217, 219 (1917) (as amended by the Act of May 16, 1918, ch. 75, § 1, 40 Stat. 553).
15. As quoted in 249 U.S. at 214.
16. *Id.* at 216.
17. *Id.*
18. According to Professor Konefsky, "the author of the clear and present danger doctrine completely ignored his own brain child." S. KONEFSKY, *supra* note 8, at 183. In a letter to Pollack, Holmes wrote:

> I am beginning to get stupid letters of protest against a decision that Debs, a noted agitator, was rightly convicted of obstructing and recruiting service so far as the law was concerned.... There was a lot of jaw about free speech, which I dealt with somewhat summarily in an earlier case — Schenck v. U.S.

As quoted in id. at 182-83. Professor Kalven wrote that *Debs* "was for Holmes a routine criminal appeal." Kalven, *supra* note 5, at 238.

19. *See, e.g.,* A. MEIKLEJOHN, POLITICAL FREEDOM 46 (1960); Gunther, *supra* note 4, at 720. *But cf.* Nathanson, *The Communist Trial and the Clear and Present Danger Test*, 63 HARV. L. REV. 1167, 1174 n. 17 (1950) (later opinions "only spell[ed] out in greater detail what was implicit in the shorthand of Justice Holmes.") If this were correct, however, it is almost inconceivable that Holmes could have voted to uphold the convictions in *Schenck* and *Debs*.
20. 250 U.S. 616 (1919).

facts were similar to those in *Schenck* and *Debs*. Appellants had been convicted of conspiring to violate the amended Espionage Act, which prohibited speech that encouraged resistance to the war effort or reduction of production "with intent ... to cripple or hinder the United States in the prosecution of the war."[21] They had printed and distributed two circulars, written both in English and Yiddish, that denounced the sending of troops into Russia to oppose the Russian Revolution. While the circulars never explicitly called for law violation, they charged that capitalism is the "enemy of the workers of the world," and stated: "Workers in the ammunition factories, you are producing bullets, bayonets, cannon, to murder not only the Germans, but also your dearest, best, who are in Russia fighting for freedom."[22] Justice Clarke wrote the majority opinion, upholding the convictions on the ground that the defendants' purpose was "to create an attempt to defeat the war plans of the government of the United States by bringing upon the country the paralysis of a general strike, thereby arresting the production of all munitions and other things essential to the conduct of the war."[23] The Court never considered whether there was any real danger that the circulars would have any effect.

In dissent, Justice Holmes suddenly emerged as an eloquent champion of liberty: "It is only the present danger of immediate evil or an intent to bring it about that warrants Congress in setting a limit to the expression of opinion where private rights are not concerned."[24]

---

21. Act of May 16, 1918, § 1, 40 Stat. at 553.
22. 250 U.S. at 621.
23. *Id.* at 622. Justice Clarke faced a difficulty in bringing the appellant's conduct within the terms of the statute, since the Act prohibited efforts to undermine the war effort against Germany, while the circular had been directed only against American military activity in Russia. Clarke circumvented the difficulty by reasoning that

> [e]ven if their primary purpose and intent was to aid the cause of the Russian Revolution, the plan of action which they adopted necessarily involved, before it could be realized, defeat of the war program of the United States, for the obvious effect of this appeal, if it should become effective, as they hoped it might, would be to persuade persons of character such as those whom they regarded themselves as addressing, not to aid government loans and not to work in ammunition factories, where their work would produce ... munitions of war, the use of which would cause the "murder" of Germans and Russians.

Id. at 621.
24. *Id.* at 628 (Holmes, J., dissenting). Interestingly, Holmes reasserted his belief in the accuracy of the decisions in both *Frohwerk* and *Debs*. *Id.* at 627. Though he made no attempt to distinguish those cases from *Abrams*, at least *Debs* might be distinguished on the grounds that the defendant there, unlike those in *Abrams*, was far from "an unknown man," and therefore might be thought to have more influence on his listeners.

But while the *Abrams* dissent included some of the most famous words ever written about the importance of free speech,[25] it also contained several indications that Holmes' reading of the clear and present danger test was not all that protective of speech. Holmes argued that "nobody can suppose that the surreptitious publishing of a silly leaflet by an unknown man, without more, would present any immediate danger that its opinions would hinder the success of the government arms or have any appreciable tendency to do so."[26] The assertion that a "silly leaflet" would have no "appreciable tendency" to hinder the war effort may imply that had the circulars been less "silly," or had Holmes found some "appreciable tendency," he might have agreed with the majority that upheld the defendants' convictions. Moreover, Holmes noted that "[p]ublishing those opinions for the very purpose of obstructing ... might indicate a greater danger, and at any rate would have the quality of an attempt."[27] That is, while he did not find present the very specific intent that he thought was required for a violation of the statute,[28] Holmes' statement nevertheless reveals both his willingness to equate the exercise of pure speech with a criminal attempt and his unsupported equation of the presence of an intent to accomplish a harm with an increase in the likelihood of that harm. It would seem, then, that even after Holmes began to take seriously the meaning of the test he had formulated, he was willing to find clear and present danger in situations where the plain language of the test would seem to indicate otherwise. Holmes' *Abrams* dissent indicates a standard which would protect speech more often than the majority's rule, but which might allow widespread suppression on a showing of only the possibility of harm.

Holmes continued to adhere to a view that was more protective of free speech than the majority's. In *Gitlow v. New York*,[29] the majority upheld a conviction for unlawful advocacy without referring to the clear and present danger test. The Court found that the only issue was

---

25. "[W]hen men have realized that time has upset many fighting faiths, they may have come to believe even more than they believe the very foundations of their own conduct that the ultimate good desired is better reached by free trade in ideas — that the best test of truth is the power of the thought to get itself accepted in the competition of the market; and that truth is the only ground upon which their wishes safely can be carried out." *Id.* at 630.
26. *Id.* at 628.
27. *Id.*
28. *Id.*
29. 268 U.S. 652 (1925).

the constitutionality of a state statute which made it a crime to advocate violent or forceful overthrow of the government.[30] The majority applied a standard that was extremely deferential to legislative judgment,[31] and held that since it was reasonable that New York should protect itself from insurgency, and since defendants had clearly violated that statute, their conviction was constitutional.

The clear and present danger analysis did not assume a truly protectionist gloss until *Whitney v. California*.[32] The *Whitney* Court upheld defendant's conviction for helping to organize the Communist Labor Party in California. While Justices Brandeis and Holmes concurred in the holding, they did so only because Whitney had not made the argument that her activity was protected because it did not cause any clear and present danger of harm. Justice Brandeis' opinion, which Justice Holmes joined, laid out the protectionist analysis of the constitutionality of convictions for unlawful advocacy. As important as the rights of free speech and assembly are, Brandeis wrote, they are not absolute. "Their exercise is subject to restriction, if the particular restriction proposed is required in order to protect the State from destruction or from serious injury, political, economic or moral."[33] Citing *Schenck,* he asserted that a restriction cannot be imposed "unless speech would produce, or is intended to produce, a clear and imminent danger of some substantive evil which the State constitutionally may seek to prevent."[34] Brandeis' replacement of the word "present" by the word "imminent" reveals a clear intention to impose strict requirements concerning both the likelihood and timing of harm that would flow from any particular speech.[35] The Holmes-Brandeis stance was clear: only an emergency could justify repression.[36] Brandeis' incarnation of the test made its practical meaning for the first time consistent with its linguistic formulation.

---

30. The legislature had outlawed advocacy itself, rather than conduct of which advocacy could merely serve as evidence (as had been the Espionage Acts). The Court found that "[e]very presumption is to be indulged in favor of the validity of the statute." *Id.* at 668.
31. The *Gitlow* test has been referred to as the "bad tendency" approach. T. EMERSON, *supra* note 8, at 104.
32. 274 U.S. 357 (1927).
33. *Id.* at 373 (Brandeis, J., concurring).
34. *Id.*
35. *Id.*
36. The rationale for the "imminence" requirement — consistent with the "marketplace of ideas" concept — was that "[i]f there be time to expose through discussion the falsehood and fallacies, to avert the evil by the processes of education, the remedy to be applied is more speech, not enforced silence." *Id.* at 377.

Majority recognition of the clear and present danger test as a proper way of measuring the protection of free speech was some time in coming. Though by the time *Whitney* was decided the clear and present danger test had been the subject of fairly extensive discussion in Supreme Court opinions, that discussion had been carried on only in the minority opinions written by Justices Holmes and Brandeis. Just once had the test been used in an opinion that spoke for the majority of the Court, and that decision was *Schenck,* which upheld suppression without any real showing that the danger was either "clear" or "present." In fact, in *Fiske v. Kansas,*[37] its first decision to reverse a conviction for unlawful advocacy on first amendment grounds, the Court made no reference to the test. During the fifteen years following *Fiske,* however, the Court's acceptance of the clear and present danger test became increasingly clear,[38] although the Court never examined the theory or structure of the test in any detail.

The next stage of the Court's application of the clear and present danger analysis was characterized by a dramatic alteration in the test's scope. The case signalling the change was *Dennis v. United States.*[39] Defendants, leaders of the American Communist Party, had been convicted of violating the conspiracy provision of the Smith Act,[40] which made it a crime "to organize ... any society, group, or assembly of persons who teach, advocate, or encourage the overthrow or destruction of any government in the United States by force or violence." The Supreme Court upheld the convictions. Though Chief Justice Vinson's plurality opinion purported to adhere to the terms of the clear and present danger test,[41] the opinion so dramatically altered the test's structure that it effectively implemented a new analysis.[42]

---

37. 274 U.S. 380 (1927).

38. *See, eg.,* Thomas v. Collins, 323 U.S. 516, 530 (1945); Cantwell v. Connecticut, 310 U.S. 296, 308 (1940); Thornhill v. Alabama, 310 U.S. 88, 105 (1940). The test was also employed in Herndon v. Lowry, 301 U.S. 242 (1937), but, according to one commentator, "[t]he role which it played on this occasion was ... a minor and quite dispensable one." Corwin, *Bowing Out "Clear and Present Danger,"* 27 NOTRE DAME LAW. 325, 343 (1952).

The test was also relied upon in a series of decisions in the 1940's regulating the authority of a court to utilize its contempt power against commentary regarding the conduct of a trial. Craig v. Harney, 331 U.S. 367, 373 (1947); Pennekamp v. Florida, 328 U.S. 331, 350 (1946); Bridges v. California, 314 U.S. 252, 260-63 (1941).

39. 341 U.S. 494 (1951).

40. Ch. 439, § 2, 54 Stat. 670, 671 (1940) (current version at U.S.C. § 2385 (1976)).

41. 341 U.S. at 508.

42. *Cf.* T. EMERSON, *supra* note 8, at 114 ("On its face the Hand-Vinson formula [in *Dennis*] seems to emasculate the clear and present danger test"); Gunther, *supra* note 4, at 751 ("[t]he Vinson Court in *Dennis* restated clear and present danger in a manner draining it of most of the immediacy emphasis it had attained over the years").

Chief Justice Vinson cited the clear and present danger test as the proper one to apply in cases of suppression of unlawful advocacy. But in interpreting the test, he adopted the measure of the constitutionality of such governmental suppression developed in the lower court by Learned Hand.[43] Hand's formula, as quoted in *Dennis,* was this: "In each case [courts] must ask whether the gravity of the 'evil,' discounted by its improbability, justifies such an invasion of free speech as is necessary to avoid danger."[44] The difference between the two formulations is significant. The clear and present danger test featured two independent conditions: first, the threat that a substantive evil might follow from some speech, and second, the real imminence of that threat. Only the conjunction of the two conditions could justify curtailment of free speech. The Hand test, by contrast, made the variables dependent so that probability and gravity of harm would work in inverse correlation: the graver the evil threatened by speech, the less probable need be its occurrence before government is justified in suppressing the speech. The clear and present danger test did not allow either condition to mitigate or exacerbate the effect of the other, so that even if a threatened evil were great, a lack of true imminence would invalidate governmental suppression of its advocacy. The Hand test, in contrast, derives results by setting up and appraising such interaction: The threat of a great evil, even of a non-imminent one, would justify suppression of speech.

Under either test, the court had to identify and quantify both the nature of the threatened evil and the imminence of the perceived danger. The initial question was exactly what harm the defendant's speech might cause. If it was the actual overthrow of the government, the Court would have been justified in perceiving a significant evil. But the Court chose another course. Rather than finding a threat of actual overthrow, it declared that significant harm would result from even an unsuccessful attempt to overthrow the government.[45] The Court made no effort to describe that "significant harm"; it made only a

---

43. 183 F.2d 201, 212 (2d Cir. 1950). Interestingly, the approach adopted by Hand in *Dennis* is quite different from the test he created in the *Masses* decision many years earlier. *See infra* at 197-200.

44. 341 U.S. at 510 (quoting 183 F.2d at 212). The test is similar in structure to Hand's approach to the issue of negligence in tort law. *See* United States v. Carroll Towing Co., 159 F.2d 169, 173 (2d Cir. 1947).

45. "Certainly an attempt to overthrow the Government by force, even though doomed from the outset because of inadequate numbers or power of the revolutionists, is a sufficient evil for Congress to prevent. The damage which such attempts create both physically and politically to a nation makes it impossible to measure the validity in terms of the probability of success, or the immediacy of a successful attempt." 341 U.S. at 509.

vague allusion to the "physical and political" damage an attempted insurgency would cause.[46]

The next question was the imminence of the threat. The Chief Justice emphasized that the Smith Act, the indictment, and the jury instructions all referred to actual advocacy, not mere academic discussion.[47] He also noted that the jury had been instructed that it could not convict unless it found that the defendants intended to attempt to overthrow "as speedily as circumstances would permit," which the Court took to mean "that the revolutionists would strike when they thought the time was ripe."[48] Vinson found the "probability of success, or the immediacy of a successful attempt"[49] to be invalid measures of the legitimacy of suppression. Rather, the relevant "evil" was the attempt itself, because of the harm inherent in even an unsuccessful attempt. But the majority simply declined to make the detailed examination — seemingly required by the terms of the clear and present danger test — of whether the speech advocated an attempt to overthrow the government in the near future.[50]

Having diluted the requirement that there be some clear danger, and having dispensed entirely with the need for imminence, the Court supported the suppression of defendants' speech by supplying an introductory course in current events. Without ever alleging or proving any link between the defendants and any foreign power, the Court found justification for suppression in "the inflammable nature of world conditions, similar uprisings in other countries, and the touch-and-go of our relations with countries with whom petitioners were in the very least ideologically attuned."[51]

Even given the majority's adoption of the Hand sliding-scale test, its upholding of the convictions where the charge was not conspiracy to overthrow but merely conspiracy to advocate overthrow, and where no showing of imminence was made, was extraordinary. Perhaps the Court intended to establish the rule that the danger of harm created by

---

46. *Id.*
47. *Id.* at 501-02.
48. *Id.* at 509-10.
49. *Id.* at 509.
50. The only examination, if it can be called that, of the specific words and actions of the defendants appeared early in the opinion as a description of the court of appeals' findings on the issue of whether or not defendants actually advocated violent overthrow. *Id.* at 497-98. These findings were not necessarily relevant to the issue of the probability of an attempt. In any event, many of the findings (such as that the Party used aliases and "double-meaning language") were of little help, even to establish the existence of advocacy.
51. *Id.* at 511; *see* Filvaroff, *Conspiracy and the First Amendment,* 121 U. PA. L. REV. 189, 216 (1972).

an attempted overthrow is so great that there simply need not be a showing of *any* likelihood of its occurrence.[52] If so, the Court's *Dennis* test bears no relation whatsoever to the language or spirit of the test it purported to apply, and the Court's attitude becomes strikingly similar to the deferential standard applied in *Gitlow*.[53]

The Supreme Court made its next major statment on the clear and present danger test eighteen years later in *Brandenburg v. Ohio*.[54] The appellant, a leader of a Ku Klux Klan group, had arranged for a television station to cover his speech at a Klan rally. Appellant made the following statement: "We're not a revengent organization, but if our President, our Congress, our Supreme Court, continues to suppress

---

52. The Court noted that "[t]he situation with which Justices Holmes and Brandeis were concerned in *Gitlow* was a comparatively isolated event, bearing little relation in their minds to any substantial threat to the safety of the community. . . . They were not confronted with any situation comparable to the instant one — the development of an apparatus designed and dedicated to the overthrow of the Government, in the context of world crisis after crisis." 341 U.S. at 510.

53. *Cf.* M. SHAPIRO, FREEDOM OF SPEECH: THE SUPREME COURT AND JUDICIAL REVIEW 65 (1966) (*Dennis* "is simply the remote bad tendency test dressed up in modern style."). *See also* McCloskey, *Free Speech, Sedition and the Constitution*, 45 AM. POL. SCI. REV. 662, 668 (1951) ("These emendations, which reject time as a determinate factor in the equation, undermine the central premise of the clear and present danger principle."). The *Dennis* test has also been referred to as "a disguised balancing test which weighed the seriousness of the danger against competing interest in free speech." J. NOWAK, R. ROTUNDA & J. YOUNG, *supra* note 8, at 880. If so, the Court spent precious little time and effort in looking to the speech side of the balance.

After *Dennis*, the Court was faced with the great difficulty of distinguishing unprotected actual advocacy of overthrow, no matter how remote, from protected "abstract" discussion of the philosophy of violent overthrow.

Professor Walter Gellhorn has suggested the distinction is a relatively clear one:

> [O]ne can recognize a qualitative distinction between a speaker who expresses the opinion before a student audience that all law professors are scoundrels whose students should band together to beat them within an inch of their lives, and a second speaker who, taking up that theme, urges the audience to obtain baseball bats, meet behind the law faculty building at three o'clock next Thursday afternoon, and join him in attacking any professor who can then be found. The first speaker, in [the *Yates*] view, should not be prosecuted; the second has stepped over the line between advocating a belief and advocating an illegal action.

W. GELLHORN, AMERICAN RIGHTS 80-81 (1960). Far from illustrating the distinction, however, Professor Gellhorn's examples illustrate its murky nature. Why is not his first example also advocacy of action? True, it does not suggest a specific time or place. But it is at least as likely to induce relatively prompt action as the advocacy in *Dennis*. Furthermore, from a law professor's point of view, I can attest that I would far prefer a speaker to engage in the second type of advocacy described by Gellhorn, so that I could make sure that at three o'clock on Thursday afternoon I was downtown consulting.

54. 395 U.S. 444 (1969) (per curiam).

the white, Caucasian race, it's possible that there might have to be some revengeance taken."[55] He also suggested returning Blacks to Africa and Jews to Israel. The appellant was convicted under Ohio's Criminal Syndicalism statute of "'advocat[ing] ... the duty, necessity, or propriety of crime, sabotage, violence, or unlawful methods of terrorism as a means of accomplishing industrial or political reform' and for 'voluntarily assembl[ing] with any society, group, or assemblage of persons formed to teach or advocate the doctrines of criminal syndicalism.'"[56]

In a per curiam opinion, the Court invalidated the conviction and declared Ohio's law unconstitutional.[57] At no point did the opinion refer to the clear and present danger test by name, but it appeared to incorporate its meaning by finding the standard to be that "the constitutional guarantees of free speech and free press do not permit a State to forbid or proscribe advocacy of the use of force or of law violation except where such advocacy is directed to inciting or producing imminent lawless action and is likely to incite or produce such action."[58]

If the *Brandenburg* Court meant to implement the clear and present danger test, however, it appeared to be using a test very different from the *Dennis* standard. The Court mysteriously cited *Dennis* to support its understanding of proper analysis,[59] but the difference in the two decisions' treatments of the imminence requirement rendered it doubtful that *Brandenburg* followed the *Dennis* rationale.

Brandenburg, like the decisions before it, does not give an unambiguous explanation of the clear and present danger test, nor does it substitute some other standard for evaluating suppression of unlawful advocacy. The most important question left open by *Brandenburg* is exactly what the Court meant by requiring "imminent" lawless action. Did the Court intend to incorporate the temporal immediacy that Brandeis had emphasized in his *Whitney* concurrence? Surely the language would lead one to believe so. But placed in context, the answer is not so clear. The Court relied on the analysis it used in *Yates v. United States*,[60] in which it reversed Smith Act convictions on the ground that the advocacy that the defendant

---

55. As quoted in *id.* at 445-47. To the eternal question, asked by the famous Winston Cigarette commercial, "what do you want, good grammar or good taste?", Mr. Brandenburg apparently answered, "neither."
56. As quoted in *id.* at 445.
57. *Id.* at 449.
58. *Id.* at 448-49.
59. *Id.* at 447 n.2.
60. 354 U.S. 298 (1957).

Communists had engaged in was abstract in nature as such did not threaten any violent overthrow, and therefore did not violate the Smith Act at all. *Yates* did not call into question the *Dennis* holding that the Smith Act was constitutional; the only issue was whether appellants' advocacy fell within the type prohibited by the Act.[61] If the *Brandenburg* Court followed the *Yates* reasoning and struck down the Ohio statute on the ground that it was overbroad because, unlike the Smith Act, it sought to punish abstract advocacy, it had no need to adopt the Brandeis temporal imminence standard. This, in turn, would explain the Court's failure to distinguish *Dennis,* which turned on anything but temporal imminence. Thus *Brandenburg* left unresolved the question of whether it restored the clear and present danger test to its pre-*Dennis* state; the standard to be applied in unlawful advocacy cases remained uncertain.

Hess v. Indiana,[62] a 1973 Supreme Court decision, did little to clarify the issue. An antiwar demonstrator had been arrested for stating, "We'll take the fucking street later." A majority of the Court reversed his conviction. "At best," the per curiam opinion stated, the "statement could be taken as counsel for present moderation; at worst, it amounted to nothing more than advocacy of illegal action at some indefinite future time."[63] The *Hess* Court relied on the *Brandenburg* "inciting or producing imminent lawless action" language.[64] This may indicate that in *Brandenburg* it had indeed intended to adopt a standard of temporal imminence. The defendant's statement was so clearly not "advocacy" of anything, however, that it is difficult to be sure whether the Court believed that the lack of immediacy was dispositive.

Even if the Supreme Court's recent interpretations of the standard for unlawful advocacy cases resurrect the clear and present danger test from the ashes of *Dennis,* several important ambiguities remain. First, if the Court intended to be rigorous in requiring some "imminence," did it also intend to use this highly speech-protective test in cases that did not involve advocacy of "ideological" crimes? It is difficult to imagine that the Court intended to protect solicitations to ordinary murder, but the fact remains that the Court used no language that tended to limit the requirement of imminence.

A second ambiguity concerns the relevance of the specific words chosen by the speaker. A never-resolved question, first brought out in a battle between Learned Hand and Justice Holmes, was whether the

---

61. *Id.* at 318-19.
62. 414 U.S. 105 (1973) (per curiam).
63. *Id.* at 108.
64. *Id.*

first amendment ever allowed sanctions for indirect unlawful advocacy. In *Masses Publishing Co. v. Patten*,[65] Hand insisted that the only relevant inquiry was whether the speaker had directly and openly advocated unlawful conduct. Holmes, on the other hand, as *Debs* clearly shows, was more than willing to uphold convictions of those who never directly advocated unlawful conduct, so long as a finding of the requisite intent could be made. Despite the views of many to the contrary, *Brandenburg* does not seem to have resolved the question. It might be thought that the "directed to inciting or producing imminent lawless action" language represented adoption of the *Masses* requirement of direct advocacy.[66] But the Court's language should more likely be given a different interpretation. The Court's use of two words, "inciting" and "producing," seems to indicate that by the phrasing of the test itself it intended to make possible convictions for indirect ("producing") as well as direct ("inciting") advocacy. Illegal action may certainly be "produced" by indirect statements. The fallacy of equating *Brandenburg* with *Masses* lies in the confusion of the word "directly" in *Masses* with the words, "directed to" in *Brandenburg*. If a speaker so intends, advocacy which does not "directly" urge unlawful conduct may nevertheless be "directed" to bringing about such conduct. The statement before a mob, "the man in that jail tortured and killed my mother," does not directly advocate anything, but under the circumstances it might well be "directed" at bringing about unlawful conduct. Thus, the Hand-Holmes debate remains unresolved by the Supreme Court. The Supreme Court cases[67] decided after *Brandenburg* and *Hess* fail to shed substantial light on the proper resolutions of these ambiguities; they continue to plague the application of the clear and present danger test.

B. Proposed Structure

This chapter takes the position that the clear and present danger test is the most effective means of determining the level of

---

65. 244 F. 535, 540 (S.D.N.Y.), *rev'd*, 246 F. 24 (2d Cir. 1917).

66. *See, e.g.*, Gunther, *supra* note 4, at 722.

67. In addition to *Hess*, *Brandenburg* was relied on by the Court in Communist Party v. Whitcomb, 414 U.S. 441 (1974). There the Court struck down a state statute requiring a party seeking access to the ballot to subscribe to a loyalty oath stating that it did not advocate overthrow of the government by force or violence. The Court cited *Brandenburg, Yates* and other decisions as a basis for rejecting "a broad oath embracing advocacy of abstract doctrine as well as advocacy of action." *Id.* at 447. In one sense, this use of *Brandenburg* might be taken to support the view that the decision did nothing more than reiterate the *Dennis-Yates* distinction. It is difficult to draw a definitive conclusion on the point, however.

constitutional protection to be afforded advocacy of unlawful conduct. Before I articulate and defend that position, however, I include this section to perform the preliminary function of defining the particular version of the test I endorse. Since the process of definition involves the resolution of ambiguities, this section also undertakes analysis of the questions left open by past applications of the clear and present danger test.

The version of the clear and present danger test endorsed here favors a generally protectionist view of the right of free speech. On the whole, it validates the stringency that the language of the test imports "[t]o modern ears:" the phrasing of the test demands "a serious evil, a substantial likelihood that speech will cause the evil, and a close temporal nexus between speech and evil."[68] Because of the test's checkered history and the unclear nature of its current application, the version of the test advocated here is a product of theory, not of history or of the Supreme Court's most recent pronouncements. Therefore, my analysis of historical ambiguities is not bound by history; in general, I resolve those doubts in favor of protecting free speech. This rough formulation guides my approach to four ambiguities that should be resolved if future applications of the clear and present danger test are to rise above the confusion of past cases: first, the issue of intent as a substitute for the likelihood of harm; second, the need to distinguish direct from indirect advocacy; third, the type of threatened substantive evil that justifies suppression; and fourth, the degree of imminence required.

1. The Role of Intent

The early proponents of the clear and present danger test appeared to be willing to substitute a finding of the speaker's intent to bring about unlawful conduct for a showing of danger that the harm would actually come about. In other words, either clear and present danger of harm *or* intent to cause it would justify suppression. Given the rationale adopted in this book to justify constitutional protection for at least some kinds of unlawful advocacy,[69] it makes little sense to remove that protection solely because the speaker intended the result.[70] For it is only the actual harm that justifies suppression of speech. It is a hallmark of our free society that we tolerate all viewpoints, even those

---

68. Greenawalt, *Speech and Crime,* 1980 AM. B. FOUND. RESEARCH J. 645, 646.
69. *See* Chapter I, *supra* at 81-86.
70. It seems settled after *Brandenburg* that at the very least, a showing of intent is a necessary condition for loss of first amendment protection, even if not a sufficient one. *See* Shiffrin, *Defamatory Non-Media Speech and First Amendment Methodology,* 25 U.C.L.A. L. REV. 915, 947 n.205 (1978).

of "fringe" elements, who advocate illegal conduct, so long as they present no real threat to society. Only a danger of true harm justifies curtailing the flow of free and open discourse. Continued substitution of a finding of intent for a showing of a genuine threat to society would cause people to censor their thoughts and words. Such censorship is undesirable; avoiding it facilitates attainment of the goal of the free speech clause.

2. Direct v. Indirect Incitements

The Supreme Court has never faced the question of whether a distinction should be drawn between direct and indirect advocacy of unlawful action, but it is readily apparent that suppression of indirect advocacy should be very difficult to justify. While a showing of some real threat of harm should be necessary to justify suppression of even direct advocacy, courts should uphold punishment for indirect advocacy only in the most extreme circumstances. In other words, a court should be more willing to allow suppression of a statement that on its face urges another to commit a crime ("Let's overthrow the government," "you should kill that cop") than of statements that on their face urge no illegal act but which are assertions of fact or opinion that might lead another to commit a crime ("this government represses minorities;" "that cop harassed me yesterday"). I urge the distinction because failing to observe it, and demanding no greater justification for suppression of speech that does not advocate crime on the ground that it might lead to harm, would permit majorities to penalize unpopular minority views, ultimately for no other reason than dislike of or disagreement with those views.

Drawing a line between direct and indirect advocacy does not have the effect of totally preventing suppression of indirect advocacy. It is easy to imagine circumstances in which assertions of fact or opinion that do not advocate illegal conduct are sufficiently likely to cause immediate harm that society is justified in suppressing them in order to protect itself. To shout, "the man in that jail tortured and killed my mother" in front of an unruly mob outside a jail is a classic example.[71] But only such truly exacerbating circumstances, in which listeners' reactions are easily predictable, should justify upholding suppression of a statement which does not on its face urge unlawful conduct.[72]

---

71. It is primarily for this reason that the rigid categorical approach of Judge Hand in the *Masses* case is unworkable. *See* discussion *infra* at 197-200.

72. Thus, the government should not be allowed to suppress the depiction of violence in the movies because of the fear that such depiction will eventually lead to violence in society. *Cf.* Olivia N. v. National Broadcasting Co., 126 Cal. App. 3d 488, 178 Cal. Rptr. 888 (1st Dist. 1981), *cert. denied,* 458 U.S. 1108 (1982).

3. Types of Substantive Evil Threatened

As originally phrased, the clear and present danger test did not differentiate among various "evils;" the criterion was simply whether the evil threatened by some speech was one which Congress had the power to prevent.[73] If the goal of the test is protecting as much speech as possible without unduly endangering society, however, some rough demarcation is advisable.[74] Society's interest in suppressing speech is simply not as strong where the speech advocates only minor transgressions. In his *Whitney* concurrence, Justice Brandeis wrote that "even imminent danger cannot justify resort to prohibition of those functions essential to effective democracy, unless the evil apprehended is relatively serious."[75] This added consideration has the effect of making the test more protectionist in that it makes it more difficult for a government to justify suppressing the advocacy of some illegal course of conduct if the threatened evil is not deemed "relatively" or "extremely" serious.

Though it is difficult to predict exactly which harms will be so labelled, common sense indicates that the more "serious" crimes are those for which society has imposed the most severe penalties. Governments should be allowed more latitude in suppressing advocacy of the serious crimes than in punishing those who incite lesser offenses. While I do not suggest a strict rank-ordering of crimes according to their seriousness, I think that courts should take the seriousness of the advocated offense into account in applying the clear and present danger test.

At first blush, deciding whether to uphold some suppression of speech by balancing the imminence of the threatened harm against its seriousness makes perfect sense. After all, the clear and present danger test is really a balancing process which contrasts the need to protect expression with the danger of harm to the state. Thus, if the substantive evil involves violence to persons, it is only reasonable that society will be less willing to risk that ultimate consequence than when the "evil" in question is illegally walking on the grass. An analysis that takes the seriousness of the threatened harm into

---

73. Indeed, it appears that Congress need not have actually outlawed the evil; the only prerequisite is that the evil was one which Congress had a right to prevent. According to Professor Greenawalt, however, it is unclear whether in its origins the magnitude of the evil had any relevance. Greenawalt, *supra* note 68, at 696-99.

74. In Bridges v. California, 314 U.S. 252, 263 (1941), a judicial contempt case, the Court applied clear and present danger and stated that "the substantive evil must be extremely serious ... before utterances can be punished."

75. 274 U.S. at 377-78.

consideration is reminiscent of the "sliding scale" test invoked by Hand and Vinson in *Dennis*.[76] Ultimately, however, the *Dennis* Court's test effectively deleted the requirements that the danger be either clear or present when the potential harm was severe. If the clear and present danger test is to perform its function of assuring that speech is suppressed only when truly justified by societal need, courts must in every case require *some* showing that the danger is real. Even where the most serious substantive evils (such as murder or violent overthrow) are threatened, evidence should be required to show (1) that a specific crime has been advocated, (2) that the crime advocated is to be committed either at a specific time or within a specific range of time, (3) that the time occur within the not-too-distant future (usually within at most a period of months) and (4) that there is a clear likelihood that the advocacy would be acted upon.

4. Imminence

The Supreme Court has never explicitly laid out its understanding of the imminence required by the test. My interpretation of the "present" component of the test is very different from the Court's most recent permutation, the all-purpose "imminence" requirement used in *Brandenburg*, at least to the extent that the Court meant that danger must be "immediate."[77] In resolving this one ambiguity, I have chosen an alternative that is potentially less protective of speech interests.

My objections to the imminence requirement are both practical and theoretical. First, requiring true imminence in every case is unrealistic and unduly insensitive to society's legitimate interest in self-protection. Moreover, the theoretical underpinnings of a *Brandenburg*-style imminence requirement are weak.

The practical point is that a stringent imminence standard unduly restricts authorities' ability to deter criminal conduct. For example, what of the individual who urges another, "when your husband returns from Europe on the 11th of the next month, you should kill him"? Unless we deny the word "imminence" its legitimate meaning, we cannot say that such advocacy will produce "imminent" illegal conduct. Yet the language may well present a threat of violence that is sufficiently serious to justify society's desire to punish it.

One might be inclined to accept suppression of non-imminent criminal solicitation, but to stand by a strict imminence requirement where advocacy of ideological crimes is involved. But to do so would be to create an indefensible double standard, for it is easy to hypothesize

---

76. *See* discussion *supra* at 180-83.
77. *See* discussion *supra* at 184-85.

cases where advocacy of ideological non-imminent crimes is equally deserving of suppression. There is the example of a racist who, some time before the Bicentennial, urges other racists to select a black to execute in honor of that day when it arrives. Or what of the terrorist who persuades a comrade to plant a bomb in a public place next month to protest government policies? Both involve advocacy of purely political or ideological crimes that are not to be committed "imminently"; therefore, neither would be punishable if an imminence standard were strictly followed. Yet I have little trouble concluding that such advocacy may be punished, so long as it is clearly probable that it would be acted upon. By foreclosing such punishment, the all-purpose imminence requirement pushes first amendment protection to an impractical extreme.

My theoretical objection to the *Brandenburg*-style "imminence" requirement is that it harks back to the "marketplace of ideas" rationale for protecting unlawful advocacy. For it assumes that so long as there is sufficient time for rebuttal and reasoned consideration, we can rest assured that "truth" will best "falsity." Only when danger is so "imminent" that there is no time for response and discussion should suppression be upheld. However, there is simply no basis for the conclusion that the opportunity for reasoned response will always defuse unlawful advocacy. Requiring imminence in every case in the belief that if it is not present the advocacy will never lead to harm is unjustifiable.

My version of the test replaces the universal requirement of imminence with a flexible method of determining the level of immediacy needed in each case. The test should depend in part on the factors outlined above: the directness of the advocacy and the seriousness of the crime threatened. Where a very serious offense is directly and forcefully advocated, a lesser showing of imminence will justify suppression; at the other end of the scale, greater evidence of imminence would be required in the case of indirect advocacy of a less serious offense.

C. Defense and Criticisms

1. The Case for Clear and Present Danger

Having identified the test I am defending, it is appropriate here to make the general case for its use. Prior to doing battle with its attackers, then, I include this section to explain why the clear and present danger test is the most constitutionally sound way of dealing with the right of free speech and its limits.

The first amendment prohibits the government from making any law that abridges the freedom of speech. Given its phrasing, the only possible interpretation of the free speech clause is that the right to speak freely must be accorded high value. At the same time, common sense and practicality rebel at the notion of absolute protection for all speech, regardless of the harm to which it leads.

It is apparent that what is needed in cases where speech threatens to disrupt society is a balancing process that weighs the individual's right to free speech against society's interest in protecting itself. But the scales must be weighted in order to accord speech the dignity mandated by the Constitution. The clear and present danger test is a mechanism for solving the problem in a principled manner. Instead of giving equal weight to the competing interests, it engages in the presumption that free speech should generally prevail over attempts to silence it. In this manner, the version of the test that I have advocated partakes of the compelling interest approach that ideally guides courts in their interpretations of the first amendment. That is, because of the absolute language with which the Constitution shields free speech and the important role that free speech plays in society,[78] the test imposes a heavy burden of justification upon majoritarian branches of government that seek to suppress it. It is not enough that the majority is inconvenienced by, or has some distaste for, the views expressed; its interest in suppressing speech must be truly compelling.

A compelling interest test may at times be translated into a general rule of law that is to be applied to specific cases.[79] At other times, however, when the facts of a particular case are of special importance, it may be necessary to examine those unique facts without the benefit of a general rule, but still with use of the broad compelling interest test itself.

The clear and present danger test falls somewhere on the continuum between these two extremes. The test provides somewhat greater guidance than a bare-bones compelling interest test, yet it will of course call for a great deal of sifting and analyzing of the specific facts of the case.

When applied in the manner outlined above, then, the clear and present danger test gives considerable force to the language of the first amendment without neglecting society's reasonable desire to avert harm. Examination of the alternatives will demonstrate that using the weighted scale of clear and present danger is the best way to decide unlawful advocacy cases.[80]

---

78. *See generally* Chapter I.
79. *See* New York Times Co. v. Sullivan, 376 U.S. 255 (1964); Chapter II, *supra* at 119-20.
80. Measuring the legitimacy of unlawful advocacy regulation is probably the area

2. Ely's Search for a Categorical Rule: A Look at Brandenburg and Masses

John Ely has sharply criticized the clear and present danger test, suggesting that it should be replaced by a "categorical" rule that rigidly defines the kinds of speech that are not protected by the first amendment. Ely's general objection is that the clear and present danger test is insufficiently protective of free speech because it causes results to turn on the specific facts of each case. His concern is that

---

of first amendment interpretation that is best suited to use of the clear and present danger test. The test has on occasion been criticized for its inability to resolve all issues surrounding use of the first amendment, an attack comparable to criticism of Ryne Sandburg for an inability to play football. There exists no a priori reason why every first amendment issue must be resolved by means of the same legal formula; if clear and present danger does an adequate job of resolving the difficulties of unlawful advocacy, it will have more than justified its existence.

The Supreme Court has, in fact, employed the language of clear and present danger in a number of situations other than unlawful advocacy, without providing substantial guidance as to when the test will or will not be used. Historically, clear and present danger has been employed by the Court to measure the validity of restrictions on demonstrations and in cases in which speech has been held in judicial contempt. For a number of reasons, neither area seems ideally suited to use of the clear and present danger language. The demonstration area is a questionable object of the test, in part because the "danger" which the demonstration is likely to present will often derive more from a possibly violent reaction from opponents than from direct incitement by the demonstrators. In such a situation a strict burden must be placed upon the state to provide protection, lest individuals be given a *de facto* veto power over speech they dislike. The would-be speakers under these circumstances are deserving of greater protection than are those who advocate unlawful conduct. Also, since the issue in regulation of demonstrations will often be a question of the appropriate time and place, rather than the substance of the demonstration, a reviewing court should have the flexibility to measure the compelling nature of the state's justification for suppression by also examining the viability of alternative avenues of expression: the greater the availability of alternative means of expression, the less justification the state will need for its suppression. The strict wording of the clear and present danger test may not afford the court the requisite flexibility.

Similarly, in the area of judicial contempt, it would seem that the words of the clear and present danger formula do not lend themselves to a thorough analysis of all the competing factors. Perhaps a standard which asks whether the speech in question was highly likely to cause severe disruption of the judicial process or to the rights of the litigants to a fair trial would more accurately focus the court's attentions.

It is important to note, however, that the exact wording used is not of overwhelming significance, as long as the court applying the test recalls that its ultimate goal is to apply a form of compelling interest test in reviewing governmental suppression of speech. Clear and present danger is merely one manifestation of that broad test, one that is probably best suited to measuring the validity of suppression of unlawful advocacy.

where messages are proscribed because they are dangerous, balancing tests inevitably become intertwined with the ideological predispositions of those doing the balancing — or if not that, at least with the relative confidence or paranoia of the age in which they are doing it — and we must build barriers as strong as words are able to make them.[81]

In place of a balancing test, Ely prefers a form of "categorization," under which fairly rigid general guidelines are established to determine what is protected and what is not. The less a court has to examine the unique facts of a case to determine whether the speech in question is to be protected, the closer the rule applied is to being "categorical." Under such an approach, "the consideration of likely harm takes place at wholesale, in advance, outside the context of specific cases."[82]

The initial problem with Ely's analysis is that it fails to recognize that it is simply impossible to string together a group of words — with the possible exception of an unwavering absolutist approach (one that Ely obviously does not adopt) — that will remove from judges the ability to manipulate general rules when those rules are applied to specific cases. Even the classic categorical rule, *New York Times'* "actual malice" doctrine,[83] leaves a finder of fact room to maneuver in making a finding about the issue of actual malice. The same can be said of the approach to unlawful advocacy with which Ely is so enamored:[84] the "imminence" test of *Brandenburg*.

Initially, it is puzzling why Ely condemns clear and present danger as a balancing test while simultaneously lauding *Brandenburg* as an example of a categorical rule. "What distinguishes a categorization approach from 'clear and present danger,'" he argues,

> is that context is considered only to determine the message the defendant was transmitting and not to estimate the danger that the audience would react to the message by antisocial conduct .... [A] categorisation approach, in determining the constitutionality of a given restriction of expression, asks only "What was he saying?" — though admittedly a reference to context may be

---

81. Ely, *supra* note 5, at 1501. Ely argues:

> So long as the constitutional test is geared to the threat posed by the specific communication in issue ... courts will tend to be swept along by the same sorts of fears that moved the legislators and the prosecutorial authorities, and the First Amendment is likely to end up a very theoretical barrier.

J. ELY, DEMOCRACY AND DISTRUST 107 (1980).
  82. J. ELY, *supra* note 81, at 110.
  83. *See* New York Times Co. v. Sullivan, 376 U.S. at 279-80.
  84. Ely, *supra* note 5, at 1491-92.

needed to answer that question. A clear and present danger or ad hoc balancing approach, in contrast, would regard that question as nondispositive: a given message will be sometimes protected and sometimes not, depending on the actual or projected behavior of the audience in response to it.[85]

But certainly, the *Brandenburg* test does not ask *only*, "What was he saying?" While that is the first inquiry of the test, the second, very much like clear and present danger, looks to the impact of the words on the audience.[86] In fact, Ely's fundamentally negative reaction to clear and present danger and his positive reaction to *Brandenburg* are even more surprising in light of the fact that many have viewed *Brandenburg* — and it is a view that seems entirely correct — as simply a protectionist version of clear and present danger.[87] The difference is more a quantitative than a qualitative one.

Whether or not *Brandenburg* is nothing more than a protectionist version of clear and present danger, however, there can be little doubt that *both* halves of the *Brandenburg* test leave considerable room for flexibility, by either judge or jury, in their application to a particular case. How easy will it be to decide whether an individual's comments are "directed at inciting or producing imminent lawless action"? Certainly, Holmes in *Debs* believed that the jury had conclusively found that the defendant possessed the requisite intent, so the first part of *Brandenburg* would have been of little assistance in avoiding that travesty on the first amendment. To be sure, insertion of the word "imminent" might have provided *Debs* a somewhat greater degree of protection, but since the term is not self-defining we cannot even be sure of that, and in any event an imminence requirement is no more or less a "categorical" rule than is the requirement that the danger be "clear and present." Each employs general terms which will have to be

---

85. *Id.* at 1493 n.44.
86. The test's exact words are "where such advocacy is directed to inciting or producing imminent lawless action *and is likely to incite or produce such action.*" 395 U.S. at 447 (emphasis added: footnote omitted). Ely does acknowledge that in *Brandenburg* "the Court supplements its categorization test with a reference to likely effect." *Id.* at 1491 n.35. He does not seem to believe, however, that this turns *Brandenburg* into a test concerned with effect. It is true, as he asserts, that "in *Brandenburg* the danger question never had to be reached, since the speech itself did not fit within the category described by the Court." *Id.* But in a case in which the first portion of *Brandenburg* is met, the test turns entirely upon the likely effect on the listener. Thus, when, for example, a fringe political group directly advocates violent overthrow, the *Brandenburg* test would turn exclusively on an estimation of audience reaction to the advocacy, thereby inviting the very case-by-case manipulation Ely fears.
87. *See, e.g.,* Greenawalt, *supra* note 68, at 724.

applied to specific fact situations. Imminence may prove more protective, but not because it is more of a categorical rule.

While I share Ely's concern that courts should not become immersed in the "paranoia of the age," I do not share his belief that any phrasing of words in the form of a categorical test can avoid that danger. *Dennis* demonstrates this all too clearly. There can be little doubt that if the Court had applied the clear and present danger test as Brandeis had contemplated in *Whitney*, it would not have upheld the conviction. The Court therefore chose to bastardize the test beyond all recognition, while the more candid Justices openly advocated rejection of the test because it would not produce the desired conclusion.[88] A court caught up in the nation's paranoia could just as easily have shrugged off any categorical rule developed by Ely. Ultimately, if there is to be any protection against the courts becoming imbued with a "mob" psychology in time of crisis, it is the nation's long tradition of judicial independence and widespread recognition of the role of the courts as protectors of minority rights against majoritarian oppression.[89] If that fails, no grouping of words in the form of a constitutional test will help.

Perhaps anticipating this line of criticism, Ely argues: "One doesn't have to be much of a lawyer to recognize that even the clearest verbal formula can be manipulated. But it's a very bad lawyer who supposes that manipulability and infinite manipulability are the same thing."[90] This point is, of course, correct. But it should more properly be aimed at the limitless ad hoc balancing test advocated by Justices Frankfurter and Harlan[91] than at the clear and present danger test. Unlike undirected case-by-case balancing, which provides a court with absolutely no guidance in how to decide a particular case and ultimately degenerates into a means of condoning all legislative action, the clear and present danger test (at least once it is fleshed out)[92] provides a clear directive to the court in how to assess the various factual elements.

---

88. *See* Dennis v. United States, 341 U.S. 494, 542-44 (1951) (Frankfurter, J., concurring); *id.* at 568-69 (Jackson, J., concurring). *See supra* at 180-83.
89. *See generally* J. CHOPER, JUDICIAL REVIEW AND THE NATIONAL POLITICAL PROCESS (1980).
90. J. ELY, *supra* note 81, at 112.
91. *See* Barenblatt v. United States, 360 U.S. 109, 126 (1959) (Harlan, J.); Dennis v. United States, 341 U.S. 494, 543 (1951) (Frankfurter, J., concurring). *Compare* Mendelson, *On the Meaning of the First Amendment: Absolutes in the Balance*, 50 CALIF. L. REV. 821 (1962) *with* Frantz, *The First Amendment in the Balance*, 71 YALE L.J. 1424 (1962).
92. *See supra* at 186-91.

While no test removes all room for judicial manipulation, it is in fact possible to devise a test which will allow for less case-by-case flexibility than is permitted by either traditional clear and present danger or *Brandenburg*.[93] But there is a significant cost to any such test. For a decrease in flexibility is necessarily accompanied by an increase in the cumbersomeness of application. Because by definition an inflexible test cannot allow a court to fit its rule to the unique circumstances of a case, it is likely to become a procrustean bed that will often prove to be either overprotective or underprotective in individual instances. Given such a choice, as a practical matter a court is considerably more likely to choose a rule that will be underprotective than one that will be overprotective. The "fighting words" doctrine of *Chaplinsky v. New Hampshire*[94] provides a good illustration. There the Court established the categorical rule that "fighting words" were beneath first amendment protection. There may of course be debate as to whether specific statements are to be characterized as "fighting words" — again, no test is free of flexibility — but once that initial determination is made the court's function becomes automatic. An equally categorical rule, I suppose, would have been that "fighting words" are *always* to be protected. But given the choice between these two extremes, it comes as no great surprise that the Court opted for the less protective approach. It is debatable whether "fighting words" are ever worthy of first amendment protection.[95] But the important point for present purposes is that if the Court ever wanted to provide protection to such speech, under a strict categorical rule it simply could not take that option, for it would mean that "fighting words" would have to be protected in *all* instances. Use of a well-defined clear and present danger test, by contrast, would allow the Court the flexibility necessary to protect "fighting words" only when, in an individual instance, their use was not likely to give rise to violence. Thus, whatever one's feelings about the value of "fighting words," there can be no question that use of a categorical rule would result in far less protection than would the more flexible clear and present danger test.

In the area of unlawful advocacy the rule that is considerably more "categorical" than clear and present danger is the rule of the *Masses* case,[96] developed by Learned Hand in 1917. Interestingly, the test somehow manages to be simultaneously overprotective and

---

93. As noted previously *see* note 86 *supra*, the Brandenburg test is often likely to turn on the individual circumstances of the case.
94. 315 U.S. 569 (1942).
95. *See* discussion in Chapter I, *supra* at 55-57.
96. 244 F. 535 (S.D.N.Y.), *rev'd*, 246 F. 24 (2d Cir. 1917).

underprotective. The New York Postmaster had advised the plaintiff, publisher of a revolutionary periodical, that his publication would not be sent through the mail, pursuant to the Espionage Act, since it tended to hamper the United States in its war effort. The publisher sought a preliminary injunction against the journal's exclusion, which Judge Hand granted. Hand purported to interpret the language of the Espionage Act, but there has never been much doubt that the approach developed in *Masses* was intended to define the appropriate constitutional limitations as well. "One may not counsel or advise others to violate the law as it stands," Hand wrote.[97] "While, of course, this may be accomplished as well by indirection as expressly," he stated, "[i]f one stops short of urging upon others that it is their duty or their interest to resist the law, it seems to me one should not be held to have attempted to cause its violation."[98] He construed the Act to be limited to the direct advocacy of resistance to the recruiting and enlistment service,[99] which the journal in question had not done. Referring to the magazine's text, Hand said: "That such comments have a tendency to arouse emulation in others is clear enough, but that they counsel others to follow these examples is not so plain."[100] While Hand's decision was reversed on appeal,[101] his theory has withstood the test of time and has received plaudits from modern commentators as a viable, protectionist alternative to the clear and present danger test.[102]

It is true that, by requiring that the speaker have directly advocated unlawful conduct before speech is to be suppressed, the *Masses* test makes it difficult to employ the danger of speech as a guise for mere dislike. It is also true that the test seems to leave relatively little room for a judge or jury to manipulate it, a goal which Hand clearly sought.[103] For it would not seem to require the exercise of much case-by-case discretion to determine whether the speech in question directly advocated illegal action. Thus, it would appear that *Masses,* much more than *Brandenburg,* fulfills Ely's desire for a categorical rule. But as is the case with most such rules, by removing case-by-case flexibility

---

97. *Id.* at 540.
98. *Id.*
99. *Id.*
100. *Id.* at 541-42.
101. 246 F. 24 (2d Cir. 1917).
102. *See, e.g.,* Greenawalt, *supra* note 68, at 702; Gunther, *supra* note 4, at 729.
103. In a letter to Professor Chafee, Hand criticized Holmes' clear and present danger test, because "[o]nce you admit that the matter is one of degree, while you may put it where it genuinely belongs, you so obviously make it a matter of administration, i.e. you give to Tomdickandharry, D.J., so much latitude that the jig is at once up." Letter from Hand to Chafee, Jan. 2, 1921, *quoted in* Gunther, *supra* note 4, at 749.

the *Masses* test will often lead to justification of suppression of illegal advocacy that presents absolutely no danger of any harm to anyone. By definition, the test lets nothing turn on a showing of a likelihood of harm flowing from the challenged expression. Hence the test would allow authorities who dislike particular fringe or extremist groups or individuals to suppress them if they can find so much as one statement advocating illegal conduct, no matter how frivolous nor how unlikely it was to give rise to harm. Far from being the protectionist test which it has been portrayed to be,[104] then, the *Masses* test proves itself to be far inferior to a test, like a "fleshed-out" protectionist version of clear and present danger, which imposes a heavy burden on the authorities to demonstrate a real likelihood of harm, in each instance, before suppressing speech. We can, of course, borrow the better elements of *Masses*, so that a greater showing of likely harm should be required when a speaker does not directly advocate illegal action. But, taken as a whole, the categorical rule of *Masses* is just too clumsy a device to provide adequate protection to the interests of free speech.

At the same time, at least if taken literally, the *Masses* test is an inadequate protector of society's interest in maintaining order. For a literal reading of *Masses* would seem to protect those who urge unlawful conduct only by indirection. This is what has been labelled the problem of the Marc Antony funeral oration,[105] and has long been seen by critics as a defect in Hand's test.[106] Of course, the test could be modified to include within it an opportunity to demonstrate that in the particular context speech which did not directly call for unlawful conduct was actually so intended. But if this were done, the test would be deprived of one of its few advantages: its ease of application and limited potential for abuse. For if a court cannot be satisfied by a facial examination of the challenged speech and instead must look to the specific context to determine whether unlawful advocacy was the speaker's ulterior motive, the door is open to significant manipulation and abuse. Indeed, such a modification of *Masses*, if unaccompanied by a required demonstration of a real likelihood of harm, would produce disastrous results. For then the invitation to suppress unpopular groups would be tremendous; authorities would be freed from *both* the requirement that the speech advocate unlawful conduct on its face *and* that it present a real likelihood of harm. In light of these difficulties, it is indeed surprising that the *Masses* test continues to be championed as a protectionist device.

---

104. *See* Gunther, *supra* note 4, at 728.
105. *See* Greenawalt, *supra* note 68, at 704; Gunther, *supra* note 4, at 729.
106. *See, e.g.,* Z. CHAFEE, *supra* note 3, at 45.

This critique of *Masses* underscores another point in regard to Ely's desire to reduce emphasis on the effect of speech and to replace it with a detailed examination of what is actually being said. Ely believes that such a shift would reduce the danger of abuse and increase protection of first amendment interests. It should now be clear, however, that virtually the opposite is true. If we were forced to choose one or the other factor to be the sole criterion of first amendment analysis, I have no doubt that examination of effect would ultimately prove to be far more protective than examination of merely what is said. Ely's fear, and it is an understandable one, is that emphasis on effect and danger will get the court caught up in thinking about how dangerous everybody thinks the expression is. But, as already noted, no form of words will stop this if judges are so inclined, and an emphasis on danger and effect may well have the opposite effect. For if the courts are able to stand back and in each case demand a showing of a real likelihood of serious harm, crazed majorities will not be able to get away with vague or conclusory assertions about threats. Indeed, a full and honest emphasis on danger of harm would no doubt have led to reversals of the convictions in *Schenck, Frohwerk, Debs, Gitlow,* and *Dennis.* Instead, in each of these cases the Court emphasized what was said, rather than the danger of what was said, and in so doing upheld suspect convictions. The simple realities are that unlawful advocacy by fringe political groups rarely represents a real and immediate danger of serious harm. If, on the other hand, we were to look only to what is being said, the possibility of locking into the public's wild fears is significantly increased, since wild, fringe groups often say wild, fringe things.[107]

But of course, there is no reason to have to choose between one criterion or the other. Indeed, the *Brandenburg* test endorsed by Ely considers relevant both what was said and the likely effect of what was said. While I do not agree with all of the elements of that test, I wholeheartedly agree that examination of both factors is essential to the preservation of free and open discourse. But imposition of a stringent requirement that in each case a showing be made of real danger flowing from the challenged speech will ultimately prove to be the most effective safeguard of free speech. There are, to be sure,

---

107. *Cf.* Linde, *"Clear and Present Danger" Reexamined: Dissonance in the* Brandenburg *Concerto,* 22 STAN. L. REV. 1163, 1168 (1970) (footnote omitted) ("Examined simply for its content, the pyrotechnics of radical rhetoric in 1969 have escalated far beyond the dull and abstruse dialectics of the old Marxist sects. If 'advocacy of unlawful action' is the measure of illegality, it fits the content of contemporary rhetoric far more closely than it did that of the Communists against whom it has been traditionally employed.").

problems with its use, since it will always be applied by human beings who are capable of misapplying it. But it is, quite frankly, the best we have.

3. Professor Emerson and the Speech-Action Dichotomy

Like Ely, Professor Emerson thinks that the clear and present danger test is insufficiently protective of free speech. Emerson has criticized the test because it "assumes that once expression immediately threatens the attainment of some valid social objective, the expression can be prohibited."[108] The approach is fallacious, he argues, because "[t]o permit the state to cut off expression as soon as it comes close to being effective is essentially to allow only abstract or innocuous expression. In short, a legal formula framed solely in terms of effectiveness of the expression in influencing action is incompatible with the existence of free expression."[109]

Emerson's attack is both overstated and unfair, however, for it totally disregards the portion of the clear and present danger test that emphasizes the presence of a threat of serious evil. The test's concern is not with fear that speech will become "effective" but that *certain* speech — that advocating a serious evil — will become effective. The goal of clear and present danger — at least as described in this chapter — is not to protect merely innocuous speech. Rather, it is to protect as much speech as it possibly can without seriously endangering society, and it does so far better than do tests such as *Masses*.

But Professor Emerson presumably would not advocate a more categorical test such as that of *Masses,* either. To understand his approach to advocacy of unlawful conduct, it is first necessary to comprehend his broad approach to all questions of first amendment interpretation. "The central idea of a system of freedom of expression," Emerson states, "is that a fundamental distinction must be drawn between conduct which consists of 'expression' and conduct which consists of 'action.' 'Expression' must be freely allowed and encouraged. 'Action' can be controlled, subject to other constitutional requirements, but not by controlling expression."[110] The task of the judiciary under this system is not to balance free speech interests against competing social interests, but to define the words of the first amendment. Once particular activity is defined as falling within the bounds of the first amendment, it is to be fully protected.[111]

---

108. T. EMERSON, *supra* note 5, at 52.
109. *Id.* at 51.
110. T. EMERSON, *supra* note 8, at 17.
111. *Id.*

At least upon superficial inquiry, it appears that Professor Emerson has adopted a largely absolutist approach to free speech. However, Emerson never makes totally clear why his all-or-nothing interpretation of the first amendment is either necessary or appropriate. It certainly could not have been dictated by the intent of the framers, which, though shrouded in mystery, is sufficiently ascertainable to determine that absolute protection was not what they had in mind.[112]

While his definitional approach seems unwarranted by either language or history, Emerson's theory may also cause significant practical problems. One might wonder, for example, whether Emerson would provide absolute protection to such forms of "expression" as perjury or blackmail, since both may be transmitted by speech or in writing. But while he absolutely protects all that he defines to fall within the first amendment, the definitional inquiry may be a complex one. This is because it is often not easy to separate "expression" from "action." Close cases are to be decided, Emerson says, "by consideration of whether the conduct partakes of the essential qualities of expression or action, that is, whether expression or action is the dominant element."[113] This should already indicate, even to the uninitiated observer, that perhaps the test is not so clear cut as it first appeared. But the approach becomes even more confused when it is recognized that Emerson is willing either to exclude wholesale categories of pure speech from first amendment protection or reduce protection to accommodate competing needs:

> For reasons peculiar to each case, certain sectors of social conduct, though involving "expression" within the definition here used, must be deemed to fall outside the system .... The [cases] which must be excluded embrace certain aspects of the operations of the military, of commercial activities, of the activities of children, and of communication with foreign countries.[114]

It is natural to ask why Professor Emerson is apparently willing to "balance" out these broad categories of what admittedly is "expression," when he purportedly refuses to do the same in other instances. His only explanation is that "the functions of expression and the principles needed to protect expression in such areas are different from those in the main system ...."[115] But this makes Emerson's exclusions no less a balance. Thus, the principled consistency which

---

112. *See generally* L. LEVY, LEGACY OF SUPPRESSION (1960).
113. T. EMERSON, *supra* note 8, at 18.
114. *Id.* at 19-20.
115. *Id.* at 20.

seemed the greatest advantage of Emerson's rigid definitional structure is lost.

Even for expression which does not fall within the specific categories excluded, Emerson appears willing to come dangerously close to balancing while purporting to adhere to a definitional construct. His approach to the issue of illegal advocacy provides a good illustration. At one point, Emerson states that "[t]he issue should be resolved in terms of the usual rules for determining what is expression and what is action. Under these doctrines solicitation can be constitutionally punished only when the communication is so close, direct, effective, and instantaneous in its impact that it is part of the action."[116] This statement appears about as consistent with Emerson's speech-action dichotomy as one could get. It would seem to exclude from description as "expression" such statements as, "shoot him" said by one conspirator to another who is holding a gun on a potential victim, or "give me your money," said by a holdup person. But it would not seem to exclude from protection the statement, "when your wife returns from Europe next month you should kill her," or even, "I will pay you five hundred dollars to kill my wife when she returns from Europe next month." Certainly, these solicitations are not "so close, direct, effective, and instantaneous in [their] impact that [they are] part of the action," and under any common sense definition of the terms they certainly do not appear to be "action" rather than "expression."

But Emerson's analysis of illegal advocacy includes also the following:

> The more general the communication — the more it relates to general issues, is addressed to a number of persons, urges general action — the more readily it is classified as expression. On the other hand, communication that is specifically concerned with a particular law, aimed at a particular person, and urges particular action, moves closer to action. Communication also tends to become action as the speaker assumes a personal relation to the listener, deals with him on a face-to-face basis, or participates in an agency or partnership arrangement.[117]

So described, it appears that Emerson's approach *would* categorize the "wife-in-Europe" example as "action," rather than "expression." But such a conclusion destroys any credibility the dichotomy might have previously been thought to possess. For it is inconceivable that a discussion between two people about a possible action which is to occur in a month could conceptually be classified as "action." In fact, it is

---

116. *Id.* at 404.
117. *Id.* at 405.

difficult to understand how the factors mentioned by Emerson — the specificity of the communication, the number of individuals to whom the advocacy is addressed — are in any way conceptually relevant to the dichotomy between "action" and "expression." In effect, Emerson has introduced a form of balancing test — one quite similar to clear and present danger — under the guise of a strictly definitional approach.[118] He has done so, probably because there exists no viable alternative: the simple fact is that there are occasions when conduct that is inescapably classified as "expression" presents a serious threat to society.[119] But once this is acknowledged, there appears no longer to exist any reason to continue adherence to the definitional dichotomy. If a court is ultimately going to balance, it would seem far preferable for it to do so with the utmost candor.

4. *Alexander Meiklejohn and the "Absolute" Alternative*

One of the earliest of the protectionist critics of the clear and present danger test was Alexander Meiklejohn, who found that the test, by reducing public speech "to the level of 'proximity and degree'"[120] "ignored or repudiated" the concept of self-government.[121] Holmes' test,

---

118. Emerson's discussion of several state cases demonstrates that his definitional approach is, for all practical purposes, identical to clear and present danger. First, he notes that in State v. Quinlan, 86 N.J.L. 120, 91 A. 111 (1914), the defendant had said at a meeting of silk mill strikers, "I make a motion that we go to the silk mills, parade through the streets, and club them out of the mills; no matter how we get them out, we got to get them out." The strikers had in fact entered the mill and rioted after the defendant's statement. According to Emerson, "the treatment of the communication as part of a course of action, whether or not it came to fruition, would seem entirely justified." T. EMERSON, *supra* note 13, at 330 (footnote omitted). Yet it is only under a type of clear-and-present danger analysis that the *Quinlan* defendant's statements can be denied first amendment protection. Similarly, Emerson cites Kasper v. State, 206 Tenn. 434, 326 S.W.2d 664 (1959), *cert. denied*, 361 U.S. 930 (1960), where the defendant was convicted of inciting to riot. Emerson believes that "the result reached is probably correct" because "Kasper was urging immediate, specific acts of violence in a situation where violence was likely to occur." *Id.* at 333. This statement is, in effect, a slightly different means of describing the clear and present danger standard. For a perceptive critical analysis of Emerson's approach to this area, see F. HAIMAN, SPEECH AND LAW IN A FREE SOCIETY 247-50 (1981).

119. *See* Shiffrin, *supra* note 70, at 960 (footnotes omitted): "When as thoughtful a scholar as Professor Emerson slips into doctrines he denounces (*e.g.*, clear and present danger and balancing), there are grounds to conclude that a distinction between expression and action is not a workable basis upon which to base a general theory."

120. A. MEIKLEJOHN, *supra* note 19, at 55.

121. *Id.* at 76.

Meiklejohn wrote, operated to nullify the most significant part of the first amendment.[122] "Congress, we are now told, is forbidden to destroy our freedom except when it finds it advisable to do so."[123] Meiklejohn further attacked the test because, he alleged, it violates the language of the first amendment (which is absolute in its terms),[124] and because he claimed that there exists no historical basis to support it.[125] Meiklejohn advocated, instead of the clear and present danger test, what he termed the "absolute" approach to free speech.[126]

The first problem with Meiklejohn's criticisms is that they mischaracterize what clear and present danger does, or, more important, what it is capable of doing. The test has been misused in the past, and in some cases it seems to invite the interpretation "Congress ... is forbidden to destroy our freedom except when it is advisable to do so." But the protectionist version of clear and present danger I advocate here engages in a different presumption: Congress had better have an extremely good reason to justify its suppression of speech.

The second flaw in Meiklejohn's approach is that his "absolute" alternative provides no more protection for speech than the clear and present danger test does. While Meiklejohn enjoyed describing his approach as "absolute" it was far from it in any traditional sense of the term.[127] Speech that Meiklejohn found protected by the first amendment was "absolutely" protected in that society could never have a sufficiently compelling interest to control it. But Meiklejohn excluded wholesale from the first amendment all "non-political" speech.[128] Moreover, even purely political speech was not to receive

---

122. The test, Meiklejohn claims, "annuls the most significant purpose of the First Amendment. It destroys the intellectual basis of our plan of self-government. The Court has interpreted the dictum that Congress shall not abridge the freedom of speech by defining the conditions under which such abridging is allowable." *Id.* at 30.

123. *Id.*

124. *Id.* at 20 ("no one who reads with care the text of the First Amendment can fail to be startled by its absoluteness," "for our day and generation, the words of the First Amendment mean literally what they say").

125. *Id.* at 56.

126. *See generally* Meiklejohn, *The First Amendment Is an Absolute,* 1961 SUP. CT. REV. 245.

127. Meiklejohn's approach is not theoretically sound, as I have demonstrated. *See* Chapter I, *supra* at 14-15. *See also* Redish, *The First Amendment in the Marketplace: Commercial Speech and the Values of Free Expression,* 39 GEO. WASH. L. REV. 429, 434-38 (1971).

128. Even for political speech, Meiklejohn's protection cannot be deemed "absolute." *See* A. MEIKLEJOHN, *supra* note 19, at 21. Ultimately, Meiklejohn substantially expanded his concept of the types of expression thought to further the political process. *See* Meiklejohn, *supra* note 144, at 257-63.

total protection in every instance under Meiklejohn's scheme.[129] The meaning of "absolutism" becomes even less clear in the area of unlawful advocacy. At one point Meiklejohn suggests that "a person who successfully incites another to act must share in the legal responsibility for the consequences of the act."[130] "Words which incite men to crime," he wrote, "are themselves criminal and must be dealt with as such."[131] Perhaps Meiklejohn intended in these statements to refer only to non-political crimes, but neither the words themselves nor the context suggest such a limitation. And, if no such limitation can be read into his comments, it would seem that Meiklejohn may ultimately provide less protection to unlawful advocacy than does clear and present danger.[132]

5. Criticisms from the Opposite Direction: the Charge that Clear and Present Danger is Overprotective

The attacks on clear and present danger considered to this point all stem from the conclusion that the test, either inherently or potentially, inadequately protects the first amendment right of expression. Criticism has also come, however, from those who believe the test, in its protectionist form, provides insufficient concern for competing societal interests.

The source of most of these attacks are several of the opinions written in *Dennis.* The main argument deduced there against the requirement of a close temporal link between advocacy and action (which is, after all, the main import of the test) was that, at least for such major crimes as attempted overthrow, it was simply too risky to require the authorities to wait until the last minute. In Chief Justice Vinson's words, "[o]bviously, the words cannot mean that before the Government may act, it must wait until the *putsch* is about to be executed, the plans have been laid and the signal is awaited."[133]

---

129. A. MEIKLEJOHN, *supra* note 19, at 21.
130. *Id.* at 40.
131. *Id.* at 21.
132. The most puzzling aspect of Meiklejohn's attack on clear and present danger is his ultimate approval, or at least acceptance, of Justice Brandeis' elaboration of clear and present danger in *Whitney. Id.* at 48. Meiklejohn does argue that Brandeis had departed significantly from the origins of clear and present danger, and that is certainly true. But Meiklejohn's objection, then, is merely to certain methods of interpreting clear and present danger, not to the entire concept, for what is Brandeis' approach, but an extremely protectionist version of clear and present danger.
133. 341 U.S. at 509.

Justice Jackson, concurring, found clear and present danger woefully inadequate to deal with sophisticated revolutionary methodology.[134] While the test could be appropriately applied as a means of regulating the individualized instance of threatened violence, its use in the face of a widespread underground conspiracy plotting future overthrow would require that the Court "appraise imponderables, including international and national phenomena which baffle the best informed foreign offices and our most experienced politicians .... No doctrine can be sound whose application requires us to make a prophecy of that sort in the guise of a legal decision."[135]

To the extent the *Dennis* Court's criticisms are aimed at a rigidly imposed temporal "imminence" test, they are well-taken, for such an unbending formula cannot possibly provide the level of protection needed by society. But the opinions go much further in their critique. They ultimately challenge the imposition of any required temporal link between advocacy and the resulting proscribed action. In so doing, they create an impossible situation, for the opinions rightly acknowledge that if the first amendment means anything, it is that free and open philosophical discussion must be preserved.[136] Yet if such discussion is to be given the necessary freedom, it of course cannot be limited to neutral descriptions; much of philosophy's life's blood is the normative debate concerning the morality of various courses of conduct. Thus, if the Court is not to obliterate the first amendment, it must provide room for even normative discussions about competing political philosophies, even those that ultimately contemplate overthrow. It did just that in *Yates*.[137] But if no temporal relationship between advocacy and action is imposed, the distinction between protected philosophical discourse and proscribed advocacy is impossible to draw.[138] Attempting to distinguish between one who favors the ultimate overthrow of the government in the "abstract" and one who illegally advocates overthrow at some undetermined future time rivals the inquiry into the number of angels dancing on a pin's head for absurdity. More importantly, the requirement of showing a true temporal link between advocacy and harm is ultimately the only effective protection against allowing national hysteria to consume the judiciary with the public's dislike of and mistrust for different ideas.

---

134. *Id.* at 567-70 (Jackson, J., concurring).
135. *Id.* at 570.
136. Dennis v. United States, 341 U.S. at 502; Yates v. United States, 354 U.S. 298, 325 (1957).
137. Yates v. United States, 354 U.S. 298 (1957).
138. *See* Chapter I, *supra* at 180-83.

The *Dennis* Court, in other words, allowed itself to be trapped into focusing on what was said, rather than on the possible existence of a threat of real harm flowing from what was said.

It is likely that a real but moderately flexible temporal requirement, as suggested here,[139] would provide sufficient opportunity for authorities to prevent actual violence. Even if it were thought not to do so in the extreme situation of attempted overthrow, alternative avenues of protection remain available. It is inconceivable that anything above the level of a frivolous attempt would not require significant planning and effort well before the actual event. Such planning would necessarily consist of something more than sitting around a table advocating attempted overthrow. Weapons would have to be obtained; the groundwork for specific acts of sabotage would have to be laid. In other words, a true conspiracy, complete with countless overt acts, would have to be undertaken. With the proof of such acts, first amendment protection for the speech incident to those acts could well be lost; the speech would probably have become so intertwined with the acts themselves that the speech itself could comfortably be deemed action, and in any event punishment of the acts themselves should provide sufficient protection.[140] So construed, the "speech" could be penalized without a showing of a temporal link between that speech and the ultimate attempt at overthrow.

But the prosecutors in *Dennis* made no attempt to establish the existence of any such conspiracy. While the prosecution was for a form of conspiracy, it was conspiracy once removed. The defendants were charged only with conspiring to *advocate* attempted overthrow, not with conspiring actually to attempt overthrow.[141] Such a course of action may significantly ease the evidentiary burden on the prosecution, and it would quite probably increase society's ability to protect itself from such attempts, for it would allow prosecution of individuals who even hinted overthrow. But if we are to draw a balance consistent with recognition of the first amendment's existence, it is necessary to provide society only the level of protection it truly needs, not the prophylactic level that a nation caught up in a state of paranoia would desire.

---

139. *See supra* at 190-91.

140. Many conspiracy statutes require the performance of an overt act. *See, e.g.,* ILL. REV. STAT. ch. 38, § 8.2(a) (1981). For those conspiracy statutes which do not so require, the courts could read in such a requirement when first amendment interests are threatened.

141. 341 U.S. at 561 (Jackson, J., concurring).

In his concurring opinion, Justice Frankfurter voiced a different criticism of clear and present danger, one that runs more deeply than the others. Frankfurter assumed that in a democracy basic policy choices are to be made by the representative legislative bodies, rather than by the courts.[142] Hence a strong presumption of validity should be imposed on judicial review of all legislation. To the extent that the clear and present danger test undermined such a presumption or engaged in the opposite prescription, it represented improper judicial usurpation.[143] Frankfurter put forward one side of a seemingly never-ending argument about the role of the judiciary in a democratic society that goes well beyond the issues surrounding clear and present danger.[144] If one accepts Frankfurter's arguments, it is all but inconceivable that the generally protectionist version of clear and present danger urged here would be adopted. It therefore seems that my major goal here is to convince those — such as Ely and Emerson — who reject Justice Frankfurter's philosophy, that a protectionist version of clear and present danger is the most effective means of fulfilling the judiciary's obligation to protect individual liberty. But having said that, I must attempt to point out what I see as Frankfurter's fundamental mistake: equating "democracy" with total majoritarian rule. If they were identical, there would be little point in imposing supra-legislative constitutional limitations in the first place. The limitations of the Bill of Rights are by nature counter-majoritarian; it therefore makes little sense to entrust to the majoritarian branches of government virtually unreviewable authority to decide whether those limitations have been outbalanced. A strict clear and present danger test is premised on the theory that the very governmental bodies challenging individual liberties are in no position to draw the requisite balance.

---

142. "Free speech cases are not an exception to the principle that we are not legislators, that direct policy-making is not our province. How best to reconcile competing interests is the business of legislatures, and the balance they strike is a judgment not to be displaced by ours, to be respected unless outside the pale of fair judgment." *Id.* at 539-40 (Frankfurter, J., concurrring).

143. "It were far better that the phrase [clear and present danger] be abandoned than that it be sounded once more to hide from the believers in an absolute right of free speech the plain fact that the interest in speech, profoundly important as it is, is no more conclusive in judicial review than other attributes of democracy or than a determination of the people's representatives that a measure is necessary to assure the safety of government itself." 341 U.S. at 544 (Frankfurter, J., concurring).

144. "Civil liberties draw at best only limited strength from legal guaranties. Preoccupation by our people with the constitutionality, instead of with the wisdom, of legislation or of executive action is preoccupation with a false value." *Id.* at 555 (Frankfurter, J., concurring).

Even if one accepts Justice Frankfurter's philosophy of judicial review, however, at least a certain portion of his criticism of clear and present danger is unjustified. One of his objections to the test's use was that "[t]he complex issues presented by ... legislation prohibiting advocacy of crime have been resolved by scrutiny of many factors besides the imminence and gravity of the evil threatened."[145] In elaborating on the point, he quoted Professor Freund's well-known critique of the clear and present danger concept:

> The truth is that the clear-and-present danger test is an oversimplified judgment unless it takes account also of a number of other factors: the relative seriousness of the danger in comparison with the value of the occasion for speech or political activity; the availability of more moderate controls than those which the state has imposed; and perhaps the specific intent with which the speech or activity is launched. No matter how rapidly we utter the phrase "clear and present danger," or how closely we hyphenate the words, they are not a substitute for the weighing of values. They tend to convey a delusion of certitude when what is most certain is the complexity of the strands in the web of freedoms which the judge must disentangle.[146]

True, use of the clear and present danger approach is not a "substitute" for the weighing of values. Rather, it is the final product of such a weighing process. It represents the conclusion that the most appropriate method of reconciling the state's interest in preserving order and the competing interest in free expression is to require the state to demonstrate the existence of a real — not imagined or speculative — threat of harm flowing from speech to justify suppression of that speech. The test need not examine "the value of the occasion for speech or political activity," other than to determine whether the occasion is likely to give rise to danger or actual harm, for the occasion's value for speech is an issue for the individual speaker to decide. Intent of the speaker, another factor mentioned by Freund, has already been shown to be logically irrelevant. Finally, there is no reason why resort to clear and present danger may not be preceded by examination of the regulation of speech under the overbreadth doctrine, so that if the state's purpose can be achieved by the use of less drastic means or the regulation sweeps within its reach occasions where no danger exists, the regulation may be invalidatd without resort to clear and present danger. Hence Professor Freund's criticisms are unfounded. The test's words do not "convey a delusion of certitude."

---

145. *Id.* at 542 (Frankfurter, J., concurring).
146. *Id.* at 542-43 (quoting P. FREUND, ON UNDERSTANDING THE SUPREME COURT 27-28 (1949)).

Quite the contrary: they convey only enough "certitude" to provide sufficient general guidance to the courts, who then will have to apply those general terms to meet the unique circumstances of individual cases.

II. Conclusion

It seems to have become fashionable in modern times to attack clear and present danger on one ground or another. It is thought to be either too dependent upon individual factual circumstances and therefore too easily subject to manipulation, to be overly concerned with the ultimate danger of speech, or to lead illogically to the conclusion that only innocuous speech is to be protected. At the same time, it has been attacked by those who believe that it inadequately recognizes society's need to protect itself. Complicating the debate has been the ambiguity of the test's wording, which has resulted over the years in varying interpretations of the very same language.

It would be incorrect to suggest that clear and present danger is free from doubt or defect as a constitutional measure of regulation of unlawful advocacy. No matter how clearly one attempts to define the test's language, it remains inescapably subject to potential manipulation by a particular court desirous of reaching a certain result. But I have attempted to show that in a sense every constitutional test is subject to similar dangers of manipulation in individual instances, and that to the extent a test is made more automatic in its application, significant costs are incurred. For a test that is limited in its ability to deal with the unique facts of a case will invariably provide either too much or too little protection in individual instances, and courts as a practical matter are likely to choose the latter, rather than the former. Because of this, I believe that use of the clear and present danger test, once its terms are given both a common sense and generally protectionist interpretation, remains — even given its potential problems — the most appropriate means of compromising the right of society to protect itself against criminal conduct and the value of preserving free and open discourse. As our history has shown all too clearly, the first amendment could do a lot worse. More importantly, it appears that courts can do no better.

CHAPTER V

THE WARREN COURT, THE BURGER COURT AND THE FIRST AMENDMENT OVERBREADTH DOCTRINE

I. Introduction

There has been much discussion in the literature about the widely differing substantive principles and judicial styles of the Supreme Courts run by Chief Justices Warren and Burger.[1] To the casual — and perhaps cynical — observer, the Warren and the Burger Courts seemed equally willing to manipulate or abandon precedent and doctrine in order to achieve a particular type of result: in the case of the Warren Court, one that is "liberal", protective of individual liberty, and likely to favor federal over state adjudiciation;[2] in the case of the Burger Court, one that is "conservative," more reflective of the interests of the government than the rights of the individual, and invariably favoring state over federal adjudication, even of federal constitutional or statutory rights.[3]

As with many stereotypes, there is certainly more than a grain of truth in both of these characterizations. At least in the area of freedom of expression, however, the situation is somewhat more complicated. Perhaps in this area more than any other, the Burger Court has evinced a partially protectionist attitude,[4] which, though assuredly not applied with unwavering consistency, occasionally even surpassed the protectionist zeal of the Warren Court.[5]

Nevertheless, in some of their major opinions under one subset of freedom of expression, both the Warren and the Burger Courts have manifested all of the worst aspects of their respective stereotypes. The

---

1. *Compare* Kalven, *"Uninhibited, Robust and Wide-Open": A Note on Free Speech and the Warren Court,* 67 MICH. L. REV. 289 (1968), *with* Emerson, *First Amendment Doctrine and the Burger Court,* 68 CALIF. L. REV. 422 (1980).

2. *See, e.g.,* Dombrowski v. Pfister, 380 U.S. 479 (1965); Fay v. Noia, 372 U.S. 391 (1963).

3. *See, e.g.,* National League of Cities v. Usery, 426 U.S. 833 (1976); Stone v. Powell, 428 U.S. 465 (1976).

4. *See, e.g.,* Richmond Newspapers, Inc. v. Virginia, 448 U.S. 55 (1980); National Bank of Boston v. Bellotti, 435 U.S. 765 (1968); Hess v. Indiana, 414 U.S. 105 (1973).

5. One example of the Burger Court's relative protectionism is in the area of commercial speech, where the Burger Court has provided a level of first amendment protection far beyond the nonexistent protection during the Warren years. *See, e.g.,* Bates v. State Bar, 433 U.S. 350 (1977); Virginia State Bd. of Pharmacy v. Virginia Citizens Consumer Council, 425 U.S. 748 (1976). This is true even though the Burger Court's level of protection remains significantly below that given to non-commercial expression. *Compare* Ohralik v. Ohio State Bar, 436 U.S. 447 (1978) *with* In re Primus, 436 U.S. 412 (1978).

213

area in which these characteristics are exhibited is the first amendment "overbreadth" doctrine, which is designed, basically, to invalidate statutes that infringe on expression to a degree greater than that justified by legitimate governmental need, and are therefore "overbroad." In defining and delimiting the doctrine's scope, the Warren Court illustrated all that is harmful in the use of an unbending protectionist principle that remains unaffected by differences in the circumstances surrounding individual cases.[6] On the other hand, the Burger Court — quite probably in overreaction to the unbending and unthinking protectionism of the Warren Court — introduced stringent general principles of limitation on the doctrine's use that seem to have no rhyme or reason, other than that they limit the protective reach of the overbreadth doctrine, a result that the Court obviously considers to be beneficial.[7]

Underlying the difficulties in both approaches is, ironically, an identical flaw: a fruitless and counterproductive search for easily applied, largely unbending categorical principles of free expression, and a corresponding unwillingness to recognize the need for first amendment principles that can be molded to achieve the most appropriate resolution of competing interests in individual cases. Complicating the analysis of the overbreadth doctrine are the views of leading commentators,[8] who urge additional tenets of overbreadth theory that are designed to establish still more categorical elements and avoid virtually any degree of case-by-case flexibility.[9]

My ultimate conclusion is that, while no area of first amendment interpretation lends itself successfully to easily-applied general formulas that fail to take account of the specific circumstances surrounding each case,[10] the overbreadth doctrine is perhaps the least adaptable to such efforts. By its nature, overbreadth analysis purports to examine and weigh the circumstances of particular social problems and particular legislative attempts to meet those problems. It is, then, perfectly Orwellian to suggest that in applying the doctrine a reviewing court is somehow able to perform its function without fully examining and taking into account all of the unique ramifications of the surrounding factual context.

---

6. *See infra* text accompanying notes 74-113.
7. *See infra* text accompanying notes 149-180.
8. *E.g.*, L. TRIBE, AMERICAN CONSTITUTIONAL LAW 710-24 (1978); Karst, *Equality as a Central Principle in the First Amendment*, 43 U. CHI. L. REV. 20, 38 (1975). *See infra* text accompanying notes 114-137.
9. *See infra* text accompanying notes 74-84 & 115-138.
10. *See generally* Chapter II.

As will be seen,[11] this is my criticism of both the Warren Court's application of overbreadth analysis,[12] and the analytical elements suggested in the literature.[13] On the other hand, although the Burger Court reacted negatively to the analytical model of the Warren Court's overbreadth analysis,[14] I hope to demonstrate that it failed completely to grasp the true flaws in that earlier analysis, for despite its attempts to remedy the Warren Court's deficiencies, it continued the earlier Court's search for easily recognized, easily applied rules of analysis. Ultimately, then, both efforts fail to employ the overbreath doctrine as a useful tool of first amendment theory. This failure is truly unfortunate, for the doctrine potentially provides a most helpful means of articulating how competing social interests implicating first amendment concerns may be accommodated.

The problem with my critique is that if the easily applied "quick fixes" adopted by the Warren and Burger Courts are abandoned, the institutional difficulties inherent in the use of overbreadth analysis are rendered glaringly apparent.[15] Without the crutch of categorical rules, courts applying the overbreadth doctrine will be forced to weigh and compare social costs and benefits in individual cases, a process which many believe courts are structurally incapable of performing, or at least performing successfully.[16] To a certain extent, the criticism is valid. Nevertheless, there are important countervailing, or at least ameliorating, considerations.

First, to the extent that the criticism is accepted, it applies far more broadly than merely to overbreadth analysis, for the same critique could be made of any judicial invalidation, on first amendment grounds, of legislation that the collective deems essential to achieve accepted social goals. Yet, for obvious reasons, we might rightfully shudder at the suggestion that the courts be relieved of this task in favor of final legislative determination of constitutionality.[17] Second, and more importantly, as long as we do leave enforcement of the first amendment to the judiciary, their decisions will inescapably have an impact, in one way or another, upon the adjustment of social costs and values. It seems advisable, then, that the courts should perform their function with full and candid recognition of the social impact of their first amendment holdings, so that the task is performed with care and

---

11. *See infra* text accompanying notes 74-113.
12. *See infra* text accompanying notes 86-95.
13. *See infra* text accompanying notes 108-113.
14. *See infra* text accompanying notes 139-148.
15. *See infra* text accompanying notes 204-208.
16. *See infra* text accompanying notes 115-138.
17. *See* Chapter IV at 209.

common sense rather than with only a haphazard, or indirect and unstated, form of social policy analysis. Finally, certain helpful principles of overbreadth analysis are available that can provide at least some level of guidance to a court called upon to perform what may appear to be the impossible task of exploring all possible practical implications of its decision.[18]

The first section of this chapter attempts to define the concept of overbreadth, as it has been used in the first amendment context,[19] and to consider the procedural and substantive consequences of its use.[20] The second section explores the use and development of the doctrine in the Warren Court years, and critiques what I find to be the significant flaws in its approach.[21] In addition, it examines alternative means of applying the overbreadth doctrine in order to achieve its beneficial goals while reducing the problems resulting from the use of an individualized, case-by-case analysis.[22] The section following provides a critique of scholarly views that urge recognition of certain additional elements of overbreadth analysis, which, in my opinion, improperly prevent courts from conforming the doctrine's use to the unique circumstances of the individual situation.[23] The final section explores the Burger Court's reaction to what it perceived to be the excesses of the Warren Court's overbreadth analysis, and criticizes the broad criteria that the Burger Court imposed to confine the doctrine's reach.[24]

II. The Overbreadth Doctrine: Definition and Consequences

A. DEFINING THE DOCTRINE

Fundamentally, the overbreadth doctrine postulates that the government may not achieve its concededly valid purpose by means

---

18. *See infra* text accompanying notes 204-208.
19. Professor Monaghan has recently suggested that nothing inherently ties the overbreadth doctrine to first amendment cases, and that indeed the doctrine has been applied in many other areas of constitutional analysis. Monaghan, *Overbreadth,* 1981 SUP. CT. REV. 1, 4. While this suggestion is surely correct, use of the overbreadth doctrine has often been tied to the special need to avoid chilling the exercise of first amendment rights. *See, e.g.,* W. LOCKHART, Y. KAMISAR & J. CHOPER, CONSTITUTIONAL LAW: CASES — COMMENTS — QUESTIONS 733 (5th ed. 1980); Bogen, *First Amendment Ancillary Doctrines,* 37 MD. L. REV. 679, 706-07 (1978). *See also* Gooding v. Wilson, 405 U.S. 518 (1971); *infra* text accompanying note 60. This chapter will focus solely on the doctrine's use in the first amendment context.
20. *See infra* text accompanying notes 47-73.
21. *See infra* text accompanying notes 74-113.
22. *See infra* text accompanying notes 50-113.
23. *See infra* text accompanying notes 115-138.
24. *See infra* text accompanying notes 139-203.

that sweep unnecessarily broadly, reaching constitutionally protected as well as unprotected activity.[25] One commentator[26] has suggested that the doctrine applies in three fundamental circumstances: (1) when "the governmental interest sought to be implemented is too insubstantial, or at least insufficient in relation to the inhibitory effect on first amendment freedoms";[27] (2) when the means employed bear little relation to the asserted governmental interest and (3) when the means chosen by the legislature do in fact relate to a substantial governmental interest, but that interest could be achieved by a "less drastic means" — that is, a method less invasive of free speech interests.[28]

It does not appear that the first category is appropriately described as a branch of overbreadth analysis, although this point may ultimately prove to be merely a matter of semantics.[29] The essence of overbreadth, as the name implies, is that the government has gone too far: its legitimate interest can be satisfied without reaching so broadly into the area of protected freedom.[30] The first category described above, on the other hand, appears to concern a situation in which the state simply has an insufficient interest to justify invasion of free speech. Unlike overbreadth analysis, then, which assumes the validity of the

---

25. *See Generally* J. NOWAK, R. ROTUNDA & J. YOUNG, HANDBOOK ON CONSTITUTIONAL LAW 868 (2d ed. 1983).

26. Israel, *Elfbrandt v. Russell: The Demise of the Oath?* 1966 SUP. CT. REV. 193, 217-19.

27. *Id.*

28. *Id.* at 217. Some commentators have assumed that the overbreadth and "less drastic means" doctrines are conceptually distinct. *See* J. NOWAK, R. ROTUNDA & J. YOUNG, *supra* note 25, at 867; 873. The Supreme Court, however, appears to view "less drastic means" as merely one means of articulating the elements of overbreadth analysis. *See, e.g.,* United States v. Robel, 389 U.S. 258, 268 (1967); Shelton v. Tucker, 364 U.S. 479, 488 (1960). *Cf.* L. TRIBE, *supra* note 8, at 722 ("The conclusion that a statute is fatally overbroad ... is often accompanied by an assumption that legislatures possess the ingenuity needed to develop statutory schemes essentially as effective as, but less sweeping ... than, the law judged void. This presumption is often stated in the language of 'less restrictive' alternatives.") (footnote omitted).

29. In a sense, this conclusion often may inhere implicitly in the conclusion that certain legislation is overbroad. *See infra* text accompanying notes 47-73.

30. "A statute is overbroad in constitutional terms if it comprehends a substantial range of applications to activity protected by the first amendment, *in addition to the unprotected activities it legitimately prohibits* ...." Turchick v. United States, 561 F.2d 719, 721 (8th Cir. 1977) (footnote omitted) (emphasis added). *See also* J. NOWAK, R. ROTUNDA & J. YOUNG, *supra* note 25, at 868 ("[a]n overbroad statute is one that is designed to burden or punish activities which are not constitutionally protected, but the statute includes within its scope activities which are protected by the first amendment.").

state's goal, this category openly calls upon the reviewing court to examine the sufficiency of the state interest.

The second category appears to be nothing more than an extreme version of the third category,[31] for if the means chosen bear little relation to the asserted legitimate end, then it goes without saying that the end can be achieved, if at all, only by use of other, presumably less invasive, means. The focus of the overbreadth doctrine, then, is the third category. This category can be viewed from different perspectives, though under current Supreme Court standards ultimately the focus of the inquiry will usually amount to much the same thing. On the one hand, the overbreadth doctrine may be perceived to invalidate a law that includes within its sweep individuals or situations that do not present the threat that the government is attempting to avoid. On the other hand, as the "less drastic means" language implies, the doctrine may be thought to turn on the availability of means less invasive of first amendment rights that will accomplish the state's end. Under existing principles the two approaches are often mirror images of each other, since if the statutory sweep includes individuals who do not present the threat the state seeks to avoid, then the Court generally presumes that the state could accomplish its goal by acting only against those who do present the threat. Nevertheless, at different times the Supreme Court, in invalidating a law on overbreadth grounds, has emphasized one or the other of these views. For example, in *Keyishian v. Board of Regents*,[32] the Court held overbroad New York's law that made Communist Party membership, as such, prima facie evidence of disqualification as a teacher. The Court noted that "[m]ere knowing membership without a specific intent to further the unlawful aims of an organization is not a constitutionally adequate basis for exclusion ...."[33] This basis for

---

31. An example of this second category is thought to be NAACP v. Alabama, 357 U.S. 449 (1958). There the state had brought a suit in equity in state court to enjoin the NAACP from doing business in the state. The court granted a restraining order ex parte, and on the petitioner's motion to dissolve, ordered production of records, including membership lists, upon the state's request. The petitioner produced most of the data, but refused to provide its membership lists and was therefore held in contempt. In reversing, the Supreme Court stated: "[W]e are unable to perceive that the disclosure of the names of petitioner's rank-and-file members has a substantial bearing" on the issues of whether the NAACP's activities made it subject to the state registration statute, and whether the extent of petitioner's activities without qualifying should lead to permanent ouster from the state. *Id.* at 464.
32. 385 U.S. 589 (1967).
33. *Id.* at 606.

exclusion was inadequate because those members who did not share the unlawful goals of the organization posed no threat.[34] Thus, the Court viewed overbreadth in terms of an unnecessarily broad statutory sweep.

In *Shelton v. Tucker*,[35] on the other hand, the Court emphasized the availability of less drastic means. It invalidated an Arkansas statute requiring all public school teachers to disclose annually the name of every organization to which they belonged or had regularly contributed within the previous five years. The state's asserted purpose was to ascertain teacher fitness and competence. "Even though the governmental purpose be legitimate and substantial," responded Justice Stewart, speaking for the Court, "that purpose cannot be pursued by means that broadly stifle fundamental personal liberties when the end can be more narrowly achieved. The breadth of legislative abridgement must be viewed in the light of less drastic means for achieving the same basic purpose."[36]

Yet in a sense, each decision could have been characterized in the language of the other. In *Keyishian*, the Court could just as easily have reasoned that since the mere act of membership did not necessarily pose the threat about which the state was concerned, the state could have accomplished its end by use of "less drastic means" — that is, by prohibiting only those who did share in the organization's unlawful aims from holding state employment.[37] Similarly, in *Shelton*, the Court might well have reasoned that since the names of the specific organizations to which the teachers belonged were largely irrelevant to

---

34. *Id.* The Court also noted that the provision "blankets all state employees, regardless of the 'sensitivity' of their positions." Elfbrandt v. Russell, 384 U.S. 11, 17, 19 (1966).

35. 364 U.S. 479 (1960).

36. *Id.* at 488.

37. Of course, the state could argue that the total ban on all members was, in fact, necessary to achieve its goal, because while its goal could theoretically be accomplished by acting against only those members who share the organization's unlawful aims, as a practical matter it would be administratively burdensome, if not impossible, to separate those who do share the organization's aims from those who do not. This fact demonstrates a significant defect in the Court's interchangeable use of the two methods of characterizing overbreadth: a law may sweep within its reach protected conduct, only because no viable means of separating protected from unprotected conduct exists. Whether or not this argument is valid, however, the Court has consistently refused to consider the viability of specific alternative means, even when it explicitly employs the "less drastic means" analysis. This approach is critized *infra* text accompanying notes 93-107.

the goal of assuring teacher competence, the challenged statute reached situations that did not further the state's purpose.[38]

Later decisions of the Court expressly blended the two modes of analysis. In *United States v. Robel*,[39] the Court, employing an overbreadth analysis, invalidated section 5(a)(1)(D) of the Subversive Activities Control Act of 1950,[40] which made it a crime for a member of a so-called "Communist-action organization" to engage in any employment in a defense facility. First, the Court spoke in terms of sweeping within the statutory reach individuals or situations that did not pose the threat of harm that the government was attempting to prevent.[41] The statute, said the Court, "contains the fatal defect of overbreadth because it seeks to bar employment both for association which may be proscribed and for association which may not be proscribed consistently with First Amendment rights."[42] Yet at the same time, the Court, citing *Shelton,* concluded that congressional goals must be achieved by less drastic means.[43] Similarly, in *Village of Schaumburg v. Citizens for A Better Environment*,[44] the Court combined the two modes of analysis in invalidating a local ordinance that prohibited door-to-door or on-street solicitation of contributions by

---

38. In *Shelton,* the Court did note:

> The question to be decided here is not whether the State of Arkansas can ask certain of its teachers about all their organizational relationships. It is not whether the State can ask all of its teachers about certain of their associational ties. It is not whether teachers can be asked how many organizations they belong to, or how much time they spend in organizational activity. The question is whether the State can ask every one of its teachers to disclose every single organization with which he has been associated over a five-year period.

Shelton v. Tucker, 364 U.S. at 487-88. In many ways, this passage is an illustration of the "sweep-too-far" mode of analysis.
39. 389 U.S. 258 (1967).
40. 50 U.S.C. § 784(a)(1)(d) (1976).
41. The Court observed that "[t]he statute quite literally establishes guilt by association alone, without any need to establish that an individual's association poses the threat feared by the Government in proscribing it." United States v. Robel, 389 U.S. at 265. The statute, said the Court,

> casts its net across a broad range of associational activities, indiscriminately trapping membership which can be constitutionally punished and membership which cannot be so proscribed. It is made irrelevant to the statute's operation that an individual may be a passive or inactive member of a designated organization, that he may be unaware of the organization's unlawful aims ... that he may disagree with those unlawful aims ... [or that he] may occupy a nonsensitive position in a defense facility.

Id. at 265-66 (footnotes omitted).
42. *Id.* at 266.
43. *Id.* at 268.
44. 444 U.S. 620 (1980).

charitable organizations that did not use at least 75 percent of their receipts for "charitable purposes." On the one hand, the Court reasoned that the ordinance swept within its reach certain protected activities that did not present the asserted danger.[45] On the other hand, the Court noted that the village's interest could be achieved by other, less invasive means, and indeed that the ordinance arguably failed to achieved the asserted goal at all.[46]

B. Consequences of the Doctrine's Use

Traditionally, it has been assumed that the most distinctive consequence of the overbreadth doctrine's application is its significant departure from generally accepted principles of standing.[47] It is accepted doctrine that one may not invoke the constitutional rights of another.[48] Since as far back as its 1940 decision in *Thornhill v. Alabama*,[49] however, the Supreme Court has allowed an individual whose conduct might well be prohibited by a properly and narrowly drawn statute to object to an existing statute on the basis of first amendment overbreadth, or, in other words, because the existing law conceivably could be applied to another whose conduct would be protected by the free speech guarantee.[50]

---

45. In the words of the Court:

> Prevention of fraud is the Village's principal justification for prohibiting solicitation by charities that spend more than one-quarter of their receipts on salaries and administrative expenses. The submission is that any organization using more than 25 percent of its receipts on fund-raising, salaries, and overhead is not a charitable, but a commercial, for-profit enterprise and that to permit it to represent itself as a charity is fraudulent. But ... this cannot be true of those organizations that are primarily engaged in research, advocacy, or public education and that use their own paid staff to carry out these functions as well as to solicit financial support.

Id. at 636-37.

46. In the words of the Court:

> The Village urges that the 75-percent requirement is intimately related to substantial governmental interests "in protecting the public from fraud, crime and undue annoyance." These interests are indeed substantial, but they are only peripherally promoted by the 75-percent requirement and could be sufficiently served by measures less destructive of First Amendment interests. Fraudulent misrepresentations can be prohibited and the penal law used to punish such conduct directly.

Id. at 636-37.

47. *See* Bogen, *supra* note 19, at 705.
48. *See, e.g.,* United States v. Raines, 362 U.S. 17 (1960).
49. 310 U.S. 88 (1940). *See* Sedler, *Standing to Assert Constitutional Jus Tertii in the Supreme Court,* 71 YALE L.J. 599, 614 (1962).
50. *See, e.g.,* NAACP v. Button, 371 U.S. 415, 432 (1963) ("[T]he instant decree may be invalid if it prohibits privileged exercises of First Amendment rights whether or not

In a provocative article, however, Professor Monaghan has challenged the traditional view that the overbreadth doctrine is a procedural departure from standing requirements.[51] At the very least, there can be no doubt that in fashioning the overbreadth doctrine the Court adheres to the article III requirement of an existing case or controversy,[52] the source of the constitutional branch of the standing requirement. At least if overbreadth is asserted as a defense to a criminal prosecution, this requirement is easily satisfied, since the defendant stands to suffer or gain in a very real sense on the basis of the success or failure of the overbreadth argument, even though he or she may be asserting the interests of others. Professor Monaghan's argument, however, goes much further. His position is that the overbreadth doctrine has no procedural impact whatsoever.[53] While it is true that, under overbreadth analysis, a party may challenge a law's constitutionality even though his or her conduct could be punished pursuant to a validly drawn statute, Monaghan contends that "[u]nder 'conventional' standing principles, a litigant has always had the right to be judged in accordance with a constitutionally valid rule of law,"[54] and that, as a general matter, "a litigant could make a facial challenge to the constitutional sufficiency of the rule actually applied to him, irrespective of the privileged character of his own activity."[55] Under Monaghan's analysis, then, the overbreadth doctrine is simply a substantive first amendment principle,[56] and indeed is not necessarily limited to the first amendment context.

We need not explore the historical accuracy of Professor Monaghan's assertions, however,[57] for I am here primarily concerned with the

---

the record discloses that the petitioner has engaged in privileged conduct."). *See also* Kunz v. New York, 340 U.S. 290 (1951). This exception to normal standing requirements was reaffirmed in the Supreme Court's decision in Village of Schaumburg v. Citizens for a Better Environment, 444 U.S. 620, 634 (1980).

51. Monaghan, *supra* note 19.
52. *See* Golden v. Zwickler, 394 U.S. 103, 110 (1969); Olitsky v. O'Malley, 597 F.2d 295, 299 (1st Cir. 1979).
53. Monaghan, *supra* note 19, at 13.
54. *Id.* at 3.
55. *Id.*
56. *Id.* at 37-38.
57. Clearly, the modern Supreme Court has viewed the situation very differently from Professor Monaghan, believing that the procedural implications of overbreadth analysis are "strong medicine" that represent significant departures from traditional procedural principles. *See* New York v. Ferber, 458 U.S. 747, 769 (1982); Broadrick v. Oklahoma, 413 U.S. 601, 613 (1973).

substantive contours of overbreadth analysis, which Monaghan agrees represent the doctrine's central thrust.[58] Fundamentally, the overbreadth doctrine asks simply whether legislation that prima facie impairs speech has gone further than necessary to achieve a concededly valid legislative goal.[59] Whatever the procedural consequences of a finding of overbreadth, this inquiry will have to be made in each case in which a statute is challenged as overbroad, and it is the flaws in the Supreme Court's approach to this substantive inquiry that provide the focus of this chapter.[60]

Nevertheless, whether or not Monaghan's historical claims are correct, there exists no a priori reason — as the Burger Court has suggested[61] — why *any* litigant whose conduct could be constitutionally prohibited should be allowed to challenge a law merely because that law might be applied unconstitutionally to another. The reply of some that the overbreadth claimant "is asserting his own right not to be burdened by an unconstitutional rule of law ...."[62] is conclusory and unresponsive: the law may well be unconstitutional, but if so, it is only so in the abstract. The Supreme Court has quite rightly characterized this procedural effect as "manifestly, strong medicine."[63] The rule that "under our constitutional system courts are not roving commissions to pass judgment on the validity of the Nation's laws"[64] is a well-established precept of judicial restraint. A persuasive argument could be fashioned that there will be plenty of opportunity to invalidate a law when it actually is applied improperly.

The classic response to this contention is that the danger to first amendment rights[65] of an overbroad law is its potential to cause a chilling effect on the exercise of free speech rights by those who would be in a position to challenge the statute's constitutionality as applied to them.[66] The theory, in other words, is that such individuals will be

---

58. Monaghan, *supra* note 19, at 23-33.
59. *See supra* text accompanying notes 24-46; *infra* text accompanying notes 72-73.
60. *See infra* text accompanying notes 74-203.
61. Broadrick v. Oklahoma, 413 U.S. 601, 610 (1973).
62. Note, *The First Amendment Overbreadth Doctrine*, 83 HARV. L. REV. 844, 848 (1970).
63. Broadrick v. Oklahoma, 413 U.S. 601, 613 (1973).
64. *Id.* at 610-11. *See also* New York v. Ferber, 102 S. Ct. 3348, 3360 (1982).
65. As noted previously, *see supra* note 19, it has been argued that the logic and history of the overbreadth doctrine are not limited to first amendment cases.
66. *See, e.g.,* Ulster County v. Allen, 442 U.S. 140, 155 (1979); Dombrowski v. Pfister, 380 U.S. 479, 487 (1965); Sedler, *supra* note 49, at 615; sources cited *supra* note 19.

intimidated by the very existence of the overbroad law and thus will not engage in what would ultimately be protected conduct.[67] This reasoning, however, is not premised on any empirical basis, and the extent to which people actually base their conduct on knowledge of statutory content may be questioned.[68] More important, to the extent individuals are likely to be chilled in the exercise of their first amendment rights, it is possible that alternative methods might be made available to them to remedy the difficulty. Under the federal Declaratory Judgment Act,[69] an individual may seek an anticipatory determination of his or her rights prior to engaging in activity that might be thought to fall within a statutory prohibition.[70] Thus, in theory at least, an individual has available a procedural means by which to cut down the Damoclean sword of an overbroad statute. Such a procedure might well be a more appropriate means of reducing a chill on first amendment rights than allowing a person who could constitutionally be punished to gain by indirection the beneficial effects of the overbreadth doctrine.

On the other hand, the declaratory judgment device may not be as effective in practice as it seems in theory. Initially, the constitutional case-or-controversy requirement dictates that a real dispute exists; if an individual cannot demonstrate a significant likelihood of prosecution once the activity is undertaken, the court may not deem the dispute ripe for adjudication.[71] Moreover, the act of filing a declaratory judgment action will inescapably alert the authorities to the potential activity of the individual, so it is at least conceivable that

---

67. As Justice Marshall, dissenting in Arnett v. Kennedy, 416 U.S. 134, 231 (1974), reasoned, such overbroad laws hang like a sword of Damocles, and "the value of a sword of Damocles is that it hangs — not that it drops."

68. *See infra* text accompanying notes 86-95. *Cf.* Note, *Overbreadth Review and the Burger Court,* 49 N.Y.U. L. REV. 532, 546 (1974) ("Chilling effect decisions are often dependent on the fiction that people are aware of the content of the statutes under which they live.").

69. 28 U.S.C. § 2201 (1976).

70. The declaratory judgment action was developed to remedy situations in which "one of the parties to a dispute had no way to take the initiative to get it judicially settled and where he would be seriously prejudiced by the other party's delay in initiating proceedings for this purpose." F. JAMES, CIVIL PROCEDURE 26 (1965). *See also* Note, *Developments in the Law: Declaratory Judgments, 1941-1949,* 62 HARV. L. REV. 787, 788-90 (1949).

71. *See, e.g.,* Younger v. Harris, 401 U.S. 37, 41-42 (1971), in which the Court held that would-be-intervenors in a criminal prosecution based on a criminal syndicalism statute lacked standing, even though they asserted that the prosecution inhibited them in their teaching and political activities.

the chilling effect will be so great as to deter even the filing of such an action.

Ultimately, the procedural impact of the overbreadth doctrine seems justifiable, not so much on the basis of some firmly ascertainable chilling effect, as on the basis of the special position that first amendment rights have been thought to hold.[72] Because the right of expression is widely deemed to be fundamental to the conduct of a free society, the overbreadth doctrine is designed to ferret out laws that unduly impair the functioning of that right, whether or not a reviewing court has before it a case in which those laws are being unconstitutionally applied, and whether or not one can properly assume the existence of a significant chill. Given the importance of the constitutional interests involved, the mere possibility of invading the rights of one not before the court is a risk thought not worth taking. The only means by which a court can encourage a litigant to assert the rights of others is to reward the litigant with protection, even though that particular individual would fall within the reach of a properly drawn statute.[73]

It is important to understand, however, that the substantive inquiry of the overbreadth doctrine may be conceptually relevant even to cases in which the challenging party asserts that his or her own activity is constitutionally privileged. The essential inquiry of the overbreadth doctrine, it should be recalled, is whether the challenged statute impedes first amendment rights more than is necessary to achieve a legitimate legislative goal. There is no logical reason why this inquiry should not be relevant in cases in which the party asserts that the very conduct subject to attack under the statute is privileged. Indeed, the determination of whether that conduct is in fact privileged under the circumstances may turn on a determination that the legislative goal could have been attained through less invasive means.

---

[72]. One commentator sees the departure from traditional standing rules inherent in the overbreadth doctrine as "a manifestation of the favored status enjoyed by the first amendment ...." Note, *supra* note 68, at 532 (footnote omitted). As the Supreme Court stated in Young v. American Mini Theatres, 427 U.S. 50, 60 (1976), "The exception is justified by the overriding importance of maintaining a free and open market for the interchange of ideas."

[73]. The issue of power to assert the rights of another in the first amendment context will of course arise only when a law is challenged on overbreadth grounds, since if a law is found to be unconstitutional not because it sweeps both protected and unprotected behavior within its reach, but because the asserted governmental interest simply cannot justify its limitation on first amendment rights, the law will be unconstitutional in *all* of its applications. In that case, the standing issue presented in overbreadth analysis can never arise.

III. The Warren Court and the Overbreadth Doctrine: An Exercise in Balancing the Unbalanceable

A. Ad Hoc Balancing and Free Expression

Before we can understand the Warren Court's analytical approach to the overbreadth doctrine, it is necessary to comprehend that Court's general attitude toward the use of a case-by-case balancing process as a means of first amendment construction. One distinctive feature of the Warren Court's liberal branch, as well as of those traditionally protectionist of free speech interests,[74] was an aversion to a "balancing" process in the adjudication of first amendment rights. Thus, when Justice Harlan adopted such a procedure in *Barenblatt v. United States*,[75] dissenting Justice Black literally bristled with indignation.[76]

The protectionists' fear of such a weighing process was understandable, for an ill-defined and unlimited balancing test easily could be — and, in fact, openly was[77] — employed as a means of simply validating a legislative judgment that the competing governmental interest outweighed the interest in preserving free expression.

The problem with the protectionists' aversion to such a balancing process, however, was, and remains, their failure to provide a viable alternative method of reconciling competing interests in first amendment adjudication. Since much of the perceived difficulty with ad hoc balancing was its total absence of guidance, its substantial unpredictability, and a resultant gaping hole in the protective wall of free speech,[78] protectionists naturally have sought alternatives that are designed to provide significant guidance and predictability in future cases, and that simultaneously leave as little room as possible for case-by-case manipulability. Protectionists believe that it is only by means of such rigid rules that courts can be prevented from becoming caught up in the nation's paranoia in individual cases of governmental regulation of expression.[79]

---

74. *See, e.g.*, L. TRIBE, *supra* note 8, at 722-24; Ely, *Flag Desecration: A Case Study in the Roles of Categorization and Balancing in First Amendment Analysis*, 88 HARV. L. REV. 1482 (1975).
75. 360 U.S. 109 (1959).
76. *Id.* at 141 (Black, J., dissenting).
77. Justice Frankfurter in particular urged that in striking a balance, significant deference necessarily must be given to legislative judgment. Dennis v. United States, 341 U.S. 494, 539-40 (1951) (Frankfurter, J., concurring). *See also* Mendelson, *On the Meaning of the First Amendment: Absolutes in the Balance*, 50 CALIF. L. REV. 821 (1962); Frantz, *The First Amendment in the Balance*, 71 YALE L. J. 1424 (1962).
78. *See, e.g.*, T. EMERSON, TOWARD A GENERAL THEORY OF THE FIRST AMENDMENT 53-56 (1966); Ely, *supra* note 74.
79. *See, e.g.*, Ely, *supra* note 74, at 1501; L. TRIBE, *supra* note 8, at 722.

While the goals of the protectionists are laudable, they have proven unrealistic and unattainable. For example, Professor Emerson's attempt to develop a viable distinction between "expression," which is absolutely protected, and "action," which is never protected, has been demonstrated by me[80] and others[81] to be internally inconsistent and unworkable. Similarly, the supposedly rigid absolutism of Justice Black — who was for many years the leading judicial opponent of ad hoc balancing — broke down many years ago, revealing itself to be little more than a disguised form of balancing.[82] Even the more realistic views of the so-called "categorizers" — those who simultaneously reject absolutism and ad hoc balancing in favor of an a priori balancing process that is translated into easily-applied categorical rules[83] — have proven to be of limited value at best.[84]

The awkwardness of the protectionists' refusal to accept the need for an individualized weighing process has never been more apparent than in the developmental stages of the overbreadth doctrine. An examination of the doctrine's high water mark in the Warren years, the decision in *United States v. Robel*,[85] demonstrates this awkwardness all too clearly.

B. The Application of Overbreadth in *Robel*

In *Robel*, the Court invalidated, on overbreadth grounds, the provision of the Subversive Activities Control Act of 1950[86] that imposed criminal penalties on a member of a so-called Communist-action organization who "engage[d] in any employment in any defense facility," because the law unnecessarily impinged upon constitutionally protected rights of association. While the governmental purpose — "to reduce the threat of sabotage and espionage in the Nation's defense plants"[87] — was "not insubstantial,"[88] said Chief Justice Warren, "[t]he statute quite literally establishes guilt by association alone, without any need to establish that an individual's

---

80. *See* Chapter IV, at 201-04.
81. *See, e.g.,* Shiffrin, *Defamatory Non-Media Speech and First Amendment Methodology*, 25 U.C.L.A. L. Rev. 915, 960 (1978).
82. *See, e.g.,* Adderley v. Florida, 385 U.S. 39 (1966).
83. The leading modern advocates for this position are Tribe and Ely. *See* sources cited *supra* note 74. *See also* Frantz, *supra* note 77; Frantz, *Is the First Amendment Law? A Reply to Professor Mendelson*, 51 Calif. L. Rev. 729, 750 (1963).
84. I have made this point in detail in Chapter IV at 193-201.
85. 389 U.S. 258 (1967).
86. 50 U.S.C. § 784(a)(1)(D) (1976).
87. United States v. Robel, 389 U.S. at 264.
88. *Id.*

association poses the threat feared by the Government in proscribing it."[89] The opinion noted that the law "casts its net across a broad range of associational activities, indiscriminately trapping membership which can be constitutionally punished and membership which cannot be so proscribed, because "[i]t is also made irrelevant to the statute's operation that an individual may be a passive or inactive member of the organization's unlawful aims, . . . that he may disagree with those unlawful aims . . . [or that he] may occupy a nonsensitive position in a defense facility."[90] Thus, the statute was fatally overbroad, and therefore "Congress must achieve its goal by means which have a 'less drastic' impact on the continued vitality of First Amendment freedoms."[91]

In effect, the Court was saying that Congress had a legitimate interest in keeping subversives out of sensitive positions in defense plants, but that the interest extended only to those who presented a true threat; since a member of a Communist organization might be inactive or passive, Congress could not constitutionally equate such membership with the presence of a real threat to national security.[92] The Court's implication, then, seems to have been that Congress could accomplish its legitimate goal simply by excluding only active members and those who clearly shared the values and subversive goals of the organization. The Court failed to specify, however, exactly how Congress or its administrative delegates could be expected to perform this separating function in individual cases. Rather, consistent with

---

89. *Id.* at 265.
90. *Id.* at 265-66.
91. *Id.* at 268.
92. There was some confusion in the Court's opinion concerning the specific reasons that the law was deemed overbroad. On the one hand, the Court noted that an inactive member of the Communist Party would not present the threat of sabotage. On the other hand, the Court noted that under the statute "[i]t is also made irrelevant that an individual who is subject to the penalties of § 5(a)(1)(D) may occupy a nonsensitive position in a defense facility." *Id.* at 266 (footnote omitted). It is not entirely clear, however, how the Court viewed the interrelation of the two grounds of overbreadth. Consider, for example, an *inactive* Communist working in a *sensitive* position, or an *active* Communist working in a *nonsensitive* position. Implicitly, at least, it seems that the Court's reasoning would not allow Congress to prohibit flatly an inactive Communist from holding even a sensitive position, for the Court reasoned that the law's overbreadth derived from the fact that inactive Communists might present no threat if they disagreed with or rejected their organization's unlawful aims. *Id.* Given this logic, the conclusion seems inescapable that an inactive Party member could not automatically be barred from even a sensitive position, since if he or she rejects the Party's aims, the person presents no threat whatsoever.

the Court's traditional practice in applying the "less drastic means" test,[93] the Court in *Robel* refused to identify the possible less restrictive alternatives, much less consider their viability.[94] Presumably, the most logical alternative to the invalidated congressional scheme would have been an individualized governmental screening procedure used to determine whether a member of a Communist-action organization did in fact know of and share the organization's objectives. The Court, however, failed to consider whether the administrative burdens created by such a practice, combined with the danger of making an incorrect assessment in a particular case and the potentially grave risk to national security of incorrectly deciding that an individual member did not share his organization's objectives, justified Congress's equation of mere membership with a threat to security. Thus, the Court, in a manner somewhat reminiscent of the argument between Alice and the Mad Hatter concerning the availability of seating at the table, concluded that there were less restrictive alternatives available while at the same time it refused to consider whether such alternatives actually existed.

Although the Court's overbreadth policy in *Robel* might appear questionable to the casual observer, its logic derives from the Court's broader perceptions about the dangers to constitutional rights of anything approaching a detailed case-by-case balancing process. Ironically, the Court's refusal to consider the viability of specific alternative means of achieving the challenged regulation's legitimate goal has likewise been defended on the basis of the Court's institutional incompetence to perform such a "legislative" function.[95] The irony of these two arguments is that they appear to derive from totally opposite, or at least different, perceptions of the Court's proper role in reviewing legislation under the first amendment. As I hope to

---

93. *See* Gunther, *Reflections on Robel: It's Not What the Court Did But the Way That It Did It*, 20 STAN. L. REV. 1140 (1968).

94. The Court observed:

The Government has told us that Congress, in passing § 5(a)(1)(D), made a considered judgment that one possible alternative to that statute — an industrial security screening program — would be inadequate and ineffective to protect against sabotage in defense facilities. It is not our function to examine the validity of that congressional judgment. Neither is it our function to determine whether an industrial security program exhausts the possible alternatives to the statute under review. We are concerned solely with determining whether the statute before us has exceeded the bounds imposed by the Constitution when first amendment rights are at stake. The task of writing legislation that will stay within those bounds has been committed to Congress.

United States v. Robel, 389 U.S. at 267.

95. *See infra* text accompanying notes 105-107.

show, this schizophrenic theoretical defense of the Court's practice underscores its theoretical awkwardness, which in turn leads to practical chaos. Under the Court's approach, neither the goal of vigorous protection of constitutional rights against government intrusion nor that of avoidance of improper judicial interference with performance of the legislative function is achieved.

C. Reluctance to Evaluate Less Restrictive Alternatives as an Avoidance of Balancing

First, let us consider the contention of Chief Justice Warren that in undertaking overbreadth analysis the Court is not engaged in the process of "balancing," and the implication of this position in terms of the Court's willingness to consider the viability of specific possible legislative alternatives. In an extended footnote,[96] the Chief Justice vigorously denied that in invalidating the challenged law the Court was somehow balancing competing governmental and constitutional interests: "We recognize that both interests are substantial," he said, "but we deem it inappropriate for this Court to label one as being more important or more substantial than the other. Our inquiry is more circumscribed."[97] In a sense, of course, Chief Justice Warren was absolutely correct. Use of the overbreadth doctrine does not automatically imply a need to balance competing interests, since it generally assumes the validity of the state's asserted goal.[98] It turns not on the fact that the free speech interest outweighs the government's asserted interest, but rather on the availability of other means, less invasive of first amendment interests, to achieve the government's goal. The overbreadth doctrine, then, might be thought to deflect or avoid the need for a direct clash between the competing interests.

While the overbreadth doctrine does not require a direct form of interest-balancing, however, it is both incorrect and harmful to disregard the unique form of delicate balancing inherent in that doctrine's use. *Robel* itself presents a classic illustration.[99] In deciding that the government's concededly legitimate goal of keeping subversives out of sensitive positions in defense facilities did not justify a blanket exclusion of all members of Communist-action organizations, the Court was inescapably concluding that the constitutional interests

---

96. United States v. Robel, 389 U.S. at 268 n.20.
97. *Id.*
98. *See supra* text accompanying notes 25-46.
99. Professor Gunther was especially critical of the Court's denial in *Robel* that it was balancing. Gunther, *supra* note 93, at 1147.

of passive members excluded from such work justified whatever administrative burdens or risks of nondetection that resulted from forcing Congress to employ a less sweeping or less automatic method of exclusion. By its nature, the overbreadth inquiry asks whether the regulation has swept "too far," or has gone further than "necessary" to achieve the asserted legislative goal. One cannot answer that question affirmatively unless one has first concluded that the measure in question is not "necessary" to achieve that goal. There can be no question that, as drafted, section 5(a) (1) (D) provided executive officials a safer and more easily enforced mechanism to accomplish the goal of keeping subversives out of defense plants than any conceivable alternative. Therefore, the only means by which the Court could have concluded that such measures were not "necessary" was to conclude that the increased harm to constitutionally protected interests that flowed from the use of the more sweeping measures justified whatever additional risks and burden that the use of less sweeping alternatives imposed. To reach this conclusion, however, the Court must have engaged, at some level, in a sophisticated form of interest-balancing, and essential to that balancing process is a full understanding of the true nature of the added burdens and risks of the supposedly less restrictive alternative measures.

It might be thought that the Court's refusal to consider the viability of alternatives simply demonstrates the Court's unwillingness to "balance away" free speech interests. Under this analysis, the inquiry into the possible "necessity" of the additional risks and burdens of individualized screening would be irrelevant; whatever the increased danger, the first amendment right of association must remain absolutely inviolate. Yet such a mode of analysis would require the Court to state that no matter how significant the competing governmental interest, the free speech right must remain unimpaired. That statement, however, is simply not consistent with the overbreadth doctrine. By its nature, that doctrine purports to accommodate a competing governmental interest by assuming that it can be attained through other means. If the Court wished to conclude that the interests in free speech should prevail, even if the asserted governmental interest could not be accomplished by other means, then it should have said so, rather than assuming away any possible conflict by imagining — without necessarily any basis in reality — that no clash of interests existed. Indeed, if the Chief Justice had made such a candid acknowledgment, it is highly likely that he could not have obtained a majority for a proposition that effectively views the first amendment as a form of societal suicide pact. Of course, it might have been argued that permitting Communists to serve in defense plants in no way presented a real threat to society's continued existence, and the point might well have been valid. Yet this argument effectively brings us full circle, back to the initial inquiry into the "necessity" of sweeping prophylactic prohibitions, for such an argument effectively concedes the relevance of at least some form of balancing analysis.

Despite the numerous problems that plague the Court's analysis in *Robel,* it is easy to see why the Court refused to consider the viability of specific alternatives. To have done so would have been to concede that the Court was engaging in a form of case-by-case interest-balancing, a concession which, if openly acknowledged, the Court feared would have invited a return to the extreme deference of the early years of the use of balancing in first amendment cases.[100] By denying the existence of interest-balancing, however, the Court was not avoiding use of a balancing process; rather, it was turning the process into an unstated, and therefore likely unthinking and less refined, balance.

In light of the early anti-protectionist history of the balancing test, the Court's reluctance to use it openly is perfectly understandable. The Court's fallacy, however, was the belief that the only viable alternative to such a deferential standard is a search for categorical rules that are blind to the realities of the specific situation. The Chief Justice failed to recognize that a process of constitutional adjudication that openly balances competing interests need not engage in a strong presumption — or any kind of presumption — in favor of constitutionality. Indeed, as I have argued in other portions of this book,[101] both constitutional logic and history seem to dictate the opposite presumption.

Moreover, it is by no means clear that the Court's unwillingness to consider the viability of less restrictive alternatives will necessarily result in an increase, rather than a decrease, in the protection of speech interests. A classic illustration is the post-Warren Court decision in *United States Civil Service Commission v. National Association of Letter Carriers.*[102] In that case, the Court upheld against an overbreadth challenge a federal statute[103] that prohibited public employees from engaging in partisan political activity. Consistent with its policy in *Robel,* the Court refused to consider whether the government's goal of deterring corruption and undue pressure by superiors could be achieved by the less invasive means of case-by-case enforcement of anti-corruption legislation.[104] Of course, such a case-by-

---

100. *See supra* text accompanying notes 74-77.
101. *See* Chapter III at 118-20.
102. 413 U.S. 548 (1973).
103. The statute is § 9 (a) of the Hatch Act, 5 U.S.C. § 7324(a)(2) (1982).
104. The Court dealt with the possibility of less restrictive alternatives by stating:

case inquiry would undoubtedly impose a greater burden on government resources while simultaneously reducing the effectiveness of corruption avoidance, but much the same argument could have been adopted in *Robel*. The important issue, which the Court declined to consider in both *Robel* and *Letter Carriers,* is whether the available less invasive alternatives are so ineffective as to justify use of the more sweeping prophylactic measures. In one case the Court assumed that they were, and in the other it assumed that they were not, apparently without any examination of the likely realities. Thus, it appears that the Warren Court's reluctance to balance and, as a result, to examine the viability of alternatives is not inherently a speech-protective mechanism. Rather, because of its wholly illogical nature, this reluctance simply leads to significant unpredictability and potential chaos.

D. Reluctance to Evaluate Less Restrictive Alternatives as a Limitation of the Judicial Function

Although the Court's reluctance to balance and thereby undermine the court's function as protector of first amendment rights may not justify its refusal to consider the viability of specific alternative measures, it is nevertheless necessary to consider the arguments from the opposite side, that it is beyond the scope of the judiciary's province

---

> [T]he joint judgment of the Executive and Congress has been that to protect the rights of federal employees with respect to their jobs and their political acts and beliefs it is not enough merely to forbid one employee to attempt to influence or coerce another.... Perhaps Congress at some time will come to a different view of the realities of political life and Government service; but that is its current view of the matter, and we are not now in any position to dispute it.

United States Civil Serv. Comm'n v. National Ass'n of Letter Carriers, 413 U.S. at 566-67 (footnote omitted).

It is true that *Letter Carriers* and *Robel* might be distinguished on the ground that the former case involved merely what has been called "content-neutral" regulation, while the latter decision concerned a "content-based" regulation. *See generally* Chapter II.

I argue there that there is no valid justification for such a dichotomy in the level of judicial review applied in first amendment cases. *See id.* More important for present purposes, however, regardless of the classification of a regulation of expression in terms of the content factor, the Court's refusal to consider the viability of possible less restrictive alternatives could just as logically lead to the *Letter Carriers* conclusion that the alternatives are not viable as it could to *Robel*'s conclusion that they are. If the Court refuses to engage in such an examination, there is, of course, logically no basis on which to determine whether the challenged law is truly "overbroad."

and abilities to undertake such an inquiry in reviewing legislation. One commentator has phrased the argument this way:

> Since by definition an overbroad law extends to activity it did not have to reach in order to accomplish its valid goal, there are always less drastic alternatives to overbroad laws and the judiciary need not choose the appropriate ones for the legislatures. If there is no less drastic alternative there is no overbreadth problem, since the invasion of rights is necessary to the state's end.[105]

Yet this explanation is too facile; the first issue is to determine whether a law is in fact overbroad, but in doing so the Court has, by definition, concluded that there are less drastic means without ever considering the viability of those means. Other commentators have argued that the judiciary lacks the competence necessary to determine the legitimacy of alternative measures,[106] and can comfortably rely on the "reasonable presumption that legislatures possess the ingenuity necessary to fashion schemes to promote valid aims without bringing privileged conduct within the scope of the burdens."[107] Whether the former point is correct, however, it is clear that the latter comment paints far too rosy a picture of the realities. Overbreadth challenges generally arise in complex areas that require careful structuring of legislative schemes. Presumably the legislature enacted the challenged statute because it concluded that such a statute represented the best alternative. It is by no means clear, then — at least without detailed examination — that the legislature can be expected to devise an alternative scheme that will as effectively achieve its goals.

More troublesome are the doubts raised about the judiciary's ability to predict the viability of hypothetical alternative legislative measures. There can be little question that such a task would be difficult in a number of respects. First, the Court would not have before it a real situation with real facts. Second, the Court does not have the information-gathering resources of a legislature, so it could never be

---

105. Note, *supra* note 68, at 546.
106. Note, *supra* note 62, at 917.
107. *Id.* The same commentator argues that "[t]he overbreadth doctrine ... is concerned with the reach of a challenged statute rather than the effectiveness of alternative schemes. Statutory overbreadth represents a legislative failure to focus narrowly enough on evils which concededly justify some interference." *Id.* This analysis begs the question, however, for if there exists no effective alternative method of narrowing the statutory reach — as, arguably, was the case in *Robel* — it is no answer to suggest that the doctrine is concerned with statutory reach rather than with the effectiveness of alternatives.

certain that its estimates of the benefits and disadvantages of possible alternatives were accurate.

The best response to these arguments, however, is that the Court has no real choice in the matter. Common sense rebels against the Court's practice of deciding that there exist — or, as in *Letter Carriers,* that there do not exist — viable less restrictive alternatives without inquiring whether such alternatives actually do exist. Under this practice, the Court either will treat the asserted governmental interest unfairly by assuming possibly non-existent alternatives, or will give too little protection to free speech concerns by taking at face value the legislative conclusion that no viable less invasive alternatives exist. Neither result is pragmatically or conceptually satisfactory.

E. ANALYZING THE "RISK OF THE WRONG GUESS"

While the Court must inquire about the viability of suggested alternative means of achieving the asserted governmental interest when presented with an overbreadth challenge, in doing so it must be aware of the inherent limitations in the process. With this awareness, it may be able to perform its function of balancing competing free speech and governmental interests more effectively. In other words, the Court must take into account the possibility that it has either underestimated or overestimated the viability of alternative measures, and consider the potential risks and consequences of a mistaken judgment. Such a practice might be labelled, for want of a better phrase, an inquiry into "the risk of the wrong guess." If the asserted governmental interest is of overwhelming importance — such as national security — and there is serious doubt concerning the viability of less restrictive means of achieving that end, the risk of an overestimation of the viability of alternative measures might be significant, and might cause the Court to think twice before it invalidates legislation on overbreadth grounds. If, on the other hand, the government interest, while not insubstantial, is such that no overriding threat to physical safety or national security would result from failure to promote it, the Court might be more willing to take the risk of overestimating the viability of less drastic means.

Illustrative of the latter situation are the decisions in *Talley v. California*[108] and *Schneider v. State.*[109] In *Talley,* the Court held unconstitutional a city ordinance that prohibited distribution of any handbill that did not have printed on it the name of the individual who prepared, distributed, or sponsored it. In support of the ordinance, it

---

108. 362 U.S. 60 (1960).
109. 308 U.S. 147 (1939).

was argued that the identification requirement was designed to reveal those responsible for fraud, false advertising, and libel.[110] The Court responded that the ordinance was not limited to such situations, so it did not need to consider the validity of an ordinance so limited.[111] Yet the Court never stopped to consider that an ordinance requiring identification only on fraudulent, false, misleading, or libelous handbills would undoubtedly be unworkable. To remedy or deter the distribution of such handbills, the government would be relegated to individual enforcement of laws making such activity illegal, and without identification on the handbills in question such enforcement would undoubtedly be difficult, if not impossible. The Court never bothered to examine the likelihood that less sweeping measures might not achieve the admittedly legitimate governmental goals. Even if the Court had done so and had become aware of the risks of overestimating the viability of less drastic means, however, it could properly have concluded that the risk was worth taking, given the relatively limited nature of the resulting social harm (at least as compared to threats to physical safety or national security) and the significant negative impact of the ordinance on the interests in freedom of speech and association.

In *Schneider,* the Court was somewhat more candid in its analysis. The case involved local ordinances making it a crime to distribute handbills on public streets. The laws were justified on the basis that they deterred littering. The Court responded that to hold such ordinances unconstitutional "does not deprive a city of all power to prevent street littering. There are obvious methods of preventing littering. Amongst these is the punishment of those who actually throw papers on the streets."[112] Although such less restrictive alternatives would probably not be as effective deterrents to littering as the actual banning of handbill distribution, the Court bluntly concluded:

> the purpose to keep the streets clean and of good appearance is insufficient to justify an ordinance which prohibits a person rightfully on a public street from handing literature to one willing to receive it. Any burden imposed upon the city authorities in cleaning and caring for the streets as an indirect consequence of such distribution results from the constitutional protection of the freedom of speech and press.[113]

---

110. Talley v. California, 362 U.S. at 64.
111. *Id.*
112. Schneider v. State, 308 U.S. at 162.
113. *Id. See also id.* at 163.

The analysis suggested here may imply that at least a portion of the decision in *Robel* was incorrect. In cases such as *Talley* and *Schneider* an overestimation of the viability of less drastic means might not cause overwhelming social harm. On the other hand, if the Court's implicit assumption that individualized screening procedures could satisfactorily achieve the congressional goal were inaccurate, the risk of harm to the operation of national defense and security could be extreme. Perhaps the Court nevertheless could have concluded that the risk of individualized screening procedures was worth taking, but if so, it surely should have engaged in a detailed consideration of the likely effectiveness of such procedures or at the very least should have provided the government with an opportunity to demonstrate that the procedures were unworkable.[114] The "risk-of-the-wrong-guess" analysis, in other words, logically dictates that if the Court decides to take a substantial risk of societal harm for the benefit of free speech concerns, then it at least must first engage in as detailed and thorough an inquiry as possible, in order to assure itself that the risk is not truly prohibitive.

IV. Suggested Alterations of Overbreadth Analysis: The Continued Search for Categorical Alternatives

In the preceding sections I have attempted to establish that the Warren Court's reluctance to consider the practical viability of specific alternatives flowed from that Court's concern about the unpredictability and reduced protection of a case-by-case balancing process.[115] Commentators, concerned with much the same danger, have on occasion suggested alterations in overbreadth analysis in an attempt to confine even further the case-by-case flexibility and resultant unpredictability inherent in its use.

Professor Tribe in particular has suggested a limitation on accepted overbreadth analysis that is designed to reflect these concerns.[116] Traditionally, it has been thought that an overbroad law will not be invalidated if it is readily subject to a narrowing construction.[117] The rule is understandable, since if a court can avoid holding a statute unconstitutional while avoiding the dangers of overbreadth, it

---

114. Even if an inaccurate assumption would create an extreme risk, the Court might still correctly have concluded that the prohibition on employment of members of Communist-action organizations need not apply to nonsensitive positions at defense facilities.
115. *See supra* text accompanying notes 74-77.
116. *See* L. TRIBE, *supra* note 8, at 714-15.
117. *See, e.g.,* Gooding v. Wilson, 405 U.S. 518 (1972).

naturally should do so. Professor Tribe, however, has argued that an overbroad law may not be narrowed by a judicial appending of a construction that limits the statute's reach by means of a principle of first amendment interpretation, unless that principle constitutes a clearly defined, so-called "categorical" rule.[118] To illustrate, Tribe cites as an example of a proper limiting construction the judicial imposition of the constitutionally required "actual malice" standard of *New York Times Co. v. Sullivan*[119] on state defamation statutes.[120] Such a rule, Tribe believes, (echoing the earlier analysis of Dean Ely)[121] is preferable to a rule of first amendment construction that requires a case-by-case inquiry. The "actual malice" standard of *New York Times*, Tribe concludes, provides sufficient guidance to future courts and litigants, because its directives are encased in a rule that does not turn on the unique, specific facts of an individual case. Rather, the rule, general in its terms, only needs to be applied to specific cases in order to determine the result. On the other hand, when a suggested narrowing construction instead turns on a first amendment principle that is vague in its terms and difficult in its application in individual cases, Tribe believes that a narrowing construction is impermissible.[122] Such a construction, he asserts, would simply trade overbreadth for vagueness.[123] As examples, he cites the clear-and-present danger test, used primarily as a constitutional measure of law regulating advocacy of unlawful conduct,[124] and the fighting words doctrine of *Chaplinsky v. New Hampshire*,[125] which denies constitutional protection to words having "'a direct tendency to cause acts of violence by the persons to whom, individually, the remark is addressed.'"[126]

As a factual matter, Tribe appears to be incorrect when he states that the Supreme Court has declined to accept narrowing constructions by means of the clear-and-present danger and fighting words doctrines. He is clearly incorrect in his statement that "[b]ecause of the test's indefiniteness from any vantage point other than hindsight, the

---

118. L. TRIBE, *supra* note 8, at 714.
119. 376 U.S. 254 (1964).
120. L. TRIBE, *supra* note 8, at 715-16.
121. Ely, *supra* note 74.
122. L. TRIBE, *supra* note 8, at 715-16.
123. *Id.* at 716.
124. According to Tribe, use of the clear-and-present danger test "is indistinguishable in operation from the process of piecemeal, ad hoc excision and does not meet the need to restructure a substantially overbroad statute in order to dissipate its chilling effect." *Id.* at 889 (footnotes omitted).
125. 315 U.S. 568 (1942).
126. *Id.* at 573 (quoting State v. Chaplinsky, 91 N.H. 310, 313, 18 A.2d 754, 758 (1941)).

Supreme Court in *Gooding v. Wilson* ... has declined to reconstruct statutes punishing offensive speech by judicially limiting the reach of the statutes to 'fighting words.'"[127] This assertion is simply a misreading of *Gooding*.

In that case the Court declined to read *Chaplinsky's* "fighting words" doctrine into the challenged Georgia abusive language statute because

> [our own] examination brings us to the conclusion [that the Georgia cases have not limited the provision's] application, as in *Chaplinsky*, to words that "have a direct tendency to cause acts of violence by the person to whom, individually, the remark is addressed." ... [The statute], as construed, does not define the standard of responsibility with requisite narrow specificity. ... [128]

If, however, the Georgia courts had read the *Chaplinsky* standard into the statute, the decision might well have been different. Indeed, in *Chaplinsky* itself, the challenged law did not contain the test ultimately adopted by the Supreme Court; it had been read into the law by the New Hampshire Supreme Court.[129]

Furthermore, Professor Tribe's attitude toward the use of clear and present danger as a means of narrowing overbreadth is not consistent with that of the Supreme Court. In *Brandenburg v. Ohio*,[130] the Court established as the constitutional measure of laws regulating advocacy of unlawful conduct the principle that such advocacy may not be prohibited "except where such advocacy is directed to inciting or producing imminent lawless action and is likely to incite or produce such action."[131] The Court then reversed a conviction under Ohio's Criminal Syndicalism Act because "[n]either the indictment nor the trial judge's instructions to the jury in any way refined the statute's bold definition of the crime in terms of mere advocacy not distinguished from incitement to imminent lawless action."[132] The apparent implication was that a judicial construction that narrowed the overbroad statute to fit the terms of the Court's test would have been sufficient. Since the *Brandenburg* test is in many ways merely a strict form of the clear-and-present danger test,[133] it seems that,

---

127. L. TRIBE, *supra* note 8, at 715-16.
128. Gooding v. Wilson, 405 U.S. at 524, 527.
129. Chaplinsky v. New Hampshire, 315 U.S. at 573.
130. 395 U.S. 444 (1969).
131. *Id.* at 447 (footnote omitted).
132. *Id.* at 448-49 (footnote omitted).
133. Professor Ely has argued that the *Brandenburg* test is somehow fundamentally different from the clear-and-present danger test. Ely, *supra* note 74, at 1491-94. The terms of the *Brandenburg* test, however, are virtually as indefinite, and are likely to require almost as much individualized application as the somewhat broader terminology of clear and present danger. *See* Chapter IV at 193-96.

contrary to Professor Tribe's belief, the Court is willing to accept a narrowing construction employing such a test.

Moreover, Professor Tribe's suggested dichotomy is conceptually troublesome — indeed, unworkable. I have discussed at length in other portions of this book[134] the artificial nature of the categorical-balancing dichotomy, because any general principle — even the "actual malice" standard of *New York Times* — leaves significant room for manipulation when it is applied to specific cases; indeed, such a principle allows almost as much manipulation as do most of the supposedly individualized tests, such as the clear-and-present danger test. In addition, I have questioned whether the so-called "categorical" rules of first amendment construction championed by such scholars as Tribe and Ely are necessarily likely to be more protective than tests that turn more on the specific facts of a case.[135] Even more devastating to Professor Tribe's suggested analysis, however, is the problematical situation that would result from adoption of his position. Most obviously, his position would effectively prevent legislatures from outlawing even unprotected conduct if such conduct were to be measured by one of the first amendment tests that Tribe deems to be insufficiently categorical. How, for example, would Tribe recommend that a legislature draft a non-overbroad statute outlawing advocacy of unlawful conduct or fighting words? The Supreme Court has said that a legislature may properly prohibit fighting words or words advocating imminent lawless action if the words are likely to incite or produce such action, but may not prohibit words that do not fall within those categories. It seems reasonable, then, that a legislature that desires to prohibit as much conduct as is constitutionally permissible would draft statutes incorporating the language of the constitutional tests set out by the Supreme Court. Yet Professor Tribe says that such a law would effectively trade overbreadth for vagueness, and would therefore be improper.[136] But what alternative does the legislature have? Perhaps it could employ general breach-of-the-peace statutes. Even if the courts did not hold such laws to be unconstitutionally overbroad, however, because they primarily regulate non-speech activities,[137] there can be little doubt that as a practical matter such laws would present problems of vagueness considerably greater than would a statute that by its terms was confined to activity falling beyond the limits of

---

134. Chapter II at 119-120; Chapter IV at 193-201.
135. *Id.*
136. L. TRIBE, *supra* note 8, at 716.
137. This point concerns the controversial issue of "substantiality" in overbreadth analysis. *See infra* text accompanying notes 186-203.

protection set out by the Supreme Court. In any event, the constitutionality of individual convictions pursuant to a general breach-of-the-peace statute ultimately would be measured by the very same tests that Professor Tribe claims turn unduly on the individual circumstances of a case. Why, then, may not a legislature — or a court, attempting to narrow overbroad legislation — simply incorporate the language of Supreme Court constitutional tests, whether or not those tests could be deemed "categorical," as a limitation on statutory reach?

To be sure, Professor Tribe is correct when he argues that a legislature may not avoid overbreadth problems merely by inserting a provision stating that the law is not intended to apply in circumstances prohibited by the Constitution.[138] Yet such an insertion would be quite different from either a legislature or a court appending to a statute limitations that conform to a specific constitutional test set out by the Supreme Court: if a test could not be so appended, it is difficult to imagine how the state could legislatively prohibit only as much activity as the Court's constitutional tests have authorized it to prohibit.

V. The Burger Court and the Overbreadth Doctrine: Retrenchment and Reaction

The preceding discussions of the Warren Court and of the views of commentators have attempted to demonstrate the fallacies in the protectionist theories of overbreadth analysis. Equally unsatisfying, however, have been the reactions of those members of the Court who have sought retrenchment and limitation of the doctrine's scope. Whatever the merits of the arguments for and against broad use of the overbreadth doctrine,[139] there can be little doubt that the vague and illogical limitations imposed on the doctrine in the early years of the Burger Court give rise to considerably more and greater problems than they purported to resolve.

For several years[140] the watershed (or perhaps Waterloo) of modern overbreadth analysis appeared to be the 1973 decision in *Broadrick v. Oklahoma*,[141] in which the Court imposed limitations on the doctrine's

---

138. L. TRIBE, *supra* note 8, at 716.
139. *See supra* text accompanying notes 74-114.
140. In the last several years, there have been two Supreme Court decisions arguably modifying or extending the reach of *Broadrick*. *See* Village of Schaumburg v. Citizens for a Better Environment, 444 U.S. 620 (1980); New York v. Ferber, 458 U.S. 747 (1982). *See infra* text accompanying notes 172-185.
141. 413 U.S. 601 (1973).

use so sweeping in their logic that it might reasonably have been suspected that the Court was effectively doing away with the doctrine.

Signs that the doctrine might have been in trouble appeared shortly before *Broadrick* was decided. In both *Gooding*[142] and *Coates v. City of Cincinnati*,[143] which invalidated laws on overbreadth grounds, vigorous dissents were filed at one point or another by Chief Justice Burger and Justices White and Blackmun. *Coates,* in which the majority rejected an ordinance that made it a crime for three or more persons to assemble on a street and act in a manner annoying to passers-by, contained a dissent by Justice White that foreshadowed his majority opinion in *Broadrick*. He reasoned that

> [e]ven accepting the overbreadth doctrine with respect to statutes clearly reaching speech, the Cincinnati ordinance does not purport to bar or regulate speech as such .... Even if the assembled defendants in this case were demonstrating and picketing, we have long recognized that picketing is not solely a communicative endeavor and has aspects which the State is entitled to regulate even though there is incidental impact on speech.[144]

Aided by the additions of Justices Powell and Rehnquist, the dissenters in *Coates* and *Gooding* asserted new force in *Broadrick*. The case involved a challenge to section 818 of Oklahoma's Merit System of Personnel Administration Act, which restricted the political activities of the state's classified civil servants. Paragraph seven of the section provided that "'[n]o employee in the civil service [shall] in any manner be concerned in soliciting or receiving any assessment [or] contribution for any political organization, candidacy or other political purpose.'"[145] Justice White, noting that "appellants' conduct falls squarely within the 'hard core' of the statute's proscriptions,"[146] refused to apply the overbreadth doctrine. In so doing, he imposed far-ranging limitations on the doctrine's reach. White correctly noted that overbreadth generally is not applied to an ordinary criminal law that may incidentally have an impact on expression,[147] but he proceeded to add:

> [F]acial overbreadth adjudication is an exception to our traditional rules of practice and ... its function, a limited one at the outset, attenuates as the otherwise unprotected behavior that it forbids the State to sanction moves from "pure speech" toward conduct and that conduct — even if expressive — falls within the scope of

---

142. Gooding v. Wilson, 405 U.S. 518 (1972).
143. 402 U.S. 611 (1971).
144. *Id.* at 620 (White, J., dissenting).
145. Broadrick v. Oklahoma, 413 U.S. at 604.
146. *Id.* at 608.
147. *Id.* at 613.

otherwise valid criminal laws that reflect legitimate state interests in maintaining comprehensive controls over harmful, constitutionally unprotected conduct .... [P]articularly where conduct and not merely speech is involved, we believe that the overbreadth of a statute must not only be real, but substantial as well, judged in relation to the statute's plainly legitimate sweep.[148]

In this statement, the Court effectively required subsequent reviewing courts to determine (1) whether the unprotected behavior is "conduct," even if "expressive," and (2) if so, whether the overbreadth is "substantial." As will be seen, however, neither the rationale for nor the meaning of the former limitation, nor the proper scope of the latter limitation, are easily ascertainable.

A. The "Expressive Conduct" Limitation

The most natural question to raise about the Court's "conduct" limitation in *Broadrick* concerns the logical link between the speech-conduct dichotomy and the overbreadth doctrine. To be sure, the Court has long given reduced constitutional protection to what has been referred to as "speech plus," or speech that contains within it strong elements of action.[149] If reassertion of this distinction were all Justice White had in mind, it would be arguable that *Broadrick* imposed no special limitations on overbreadth analysis; rather, the decision could be viewed simply as the application of a wholly distinct principle of first amendment construction — as questionable as that principle might be —[150] to the overbreadth context.

Several aspects of Justice White's opinion, however, render it highly doubtful that this was all the Court intended.[151] First, it is clear from

---

148. *Id.* at 615.
149. *See generally* J. Nowak, R. Rotunda & J. Young, *supra* note 25, at 988-96.
150. Professor Kalven effectively attacked the artificial and unworkable nature of the "speech plus" doctrine years ago. Kalven, *The Concept of the Public Forum: Cox v. Louisiana,* 1965 Sup. Ct. Rev. 1, 23-25. Since the Court in *Broadrick* did not appear to focus on the doctrine, however, *see infra* text accompanying notes 152-153, a detailed critical consideration is beyond the scope of this chapter. I have briefly critiqued the doctrine in Chapter II at 123 and note 204.
151. If such a reassertion were in fact what the Court had intended, the result would have been similar to the Court's application of the overbreadth doctrine in the commercial speech context. The Court has indicated that, just as is generally true of constitutional protection for commercial speech, the level of first amendment protection in the case of overbreadth analysis is reduced in the commercial speech context. *See* Bates v. State Bar, 433 U.S. 350, 380 (1977) ("the justification for the application of overbreadth analysis applies weakly, if at all, in the ordinary commercial context"). Similarly, the Court has held that the overbreadth doctrine has considerably reduced force in the context of free speech in the military. Parker v. Levy, 417 U.S. 733, 760 (1974).

its overriding tone that *Broadrick* is an overbreadth opinion, not a "speech-plus" opinion. Missing from the opinion are relevant references to the traditionally cited "speech-plus" chestnuts: *United States v. O'Brien*,[152] *Cox v. Louisiana*,[153] and *Adderley v. Florida*.[154] In fact, in support of its assertion that the overbreadth doctrine has less force when used to regulate "expressive conduct," the Court cited several decisions that concerned what the Court in those cases deemed to be fully protected expression,[155] though in some, but not all, the expression might have been deemed to be something other than classic speech.[156] In contrast, the Court's serious concern with the dangers of overbreadth analysis is pervasive throughout its opinion.[157] These facts seem to lead to the conclusion that the "expressive conduct" limitation on overbreadth analysis contained in *Broadrick* is not confined to situations in which the relevant expression can be characterized as less-protected "speech plus." As dissenting Justice Brennan characterized the majority's test, "for purposes of overbreadth analysis, deterrence of conduct should be viewed differently from deterrence of

---

152. 391 U.S. 367 (1968).

153. 379 U.S. 559 (1965). *Cox* was cited, but not for its "speech plus" component. Broadrick v. Oklahoma, 413 U.S. at 613.

154. 385 U.S. 39 (1966).

155. The Court cited United States v. Harriss, 347 U.S. 612 (1954), and United States v. CIO, 335 U.S. 106 (1948). Broadrick v. Oklahoma, 413 U.S. at 615. In *Harriss*, the Court upheld a federal statute requiring designated reports to Congress from every person receiving any contribution or expending any money for the purpose of influencing the passage of legislation by Congress. In *CIO*, the Court held that publication and distribution of an issue of a union weekly newspaper urging union members to vote for a particular congressional candidate were not intended to be covered by the statutory prohibition on union expenditures for political purposes. The Court in *Broadrick* added "cf." cites to Red Lion Broadcasting Co. v. FCC, 395 U.S. 367 (1969) (upholding the Commission's fairness doctrine against constitutional attack); Pickering v. Board of Educ., 391 U.S. 563, 565 n.1 (1968) (holding unconstitutional dismissal of a public school teacher for writing and publishing in a newspaper a letter criticizing the school board's policies and practices; the cited footnote states merely that the Court need not reach the overbreadth challenge to the relevant statutory standard); and Eastern R. R. Conference v. Noerr Motor Freight, Inc., 365 U.S. 127 (1961) (holding that no violation of the Sherman Act can be predicated upon mere attempts to influence the passage or enforcement of laws).

156. The activity regulated in *Harriss* arguably might have been deemed to be something other than pure speech, though in upholding the regulation the Court in that decision at no point suggested that the nature of the relevant first amendment activity influenced its decision. *CIO* concerned federal regulation of financial expenditures, but the specific activity involved in that case amounted to pure expression. The activities sought to be regulated in *Pickering, Red Lion* and *Noerr*, however, could not reasonably be characterized as something other than pure speech.

157. *See* Broadrick v. Oklahoma, 413 U.S. at 610-16.

speech, *even where both are equally protected by the First Amendment.*"[158]

If, however, as argued here, the Court in *Broadrick* intended to limit the use of overbreadth analysis when it is applied to a category of fully protected expression designated as "expressive conduct," different in content from the classically less protected "speech plus" category, it is by no means clear how the Court intended to define the former category. Indeed, most confusing was the Court's application of its categorical rule to the facts of *Broadrick* itself. The activity regulated by the Oklahoma statute, it should be recalled, included "soliciting or receiving any assessment ... or contribution for any political organization, candidacy or other political purpose."[159] While both before[160] and after[161] *Broadrick* the Court has unambiguously asserted that such activity represents fully protected expression, it is conceivable that the Court in *Broadrick* had this type of "conduct" in mind when it set forth its categorical overbreadth limitation. On the other hand, the statute also prohibited civil service employees from "tak[ing] part in the management or affairs of any political party or any political campaign, except to exercise his right as a citizen privately to express his opinion and to cast his vote,"[162] although it was unclear what the legislature meant by the phrase, "right as a citizen *privately* to express his opinion." Presumably the qualification added by the word "privately" did not limit the exception to situations in which the employee spoke in an empty room. Perhaps the legislature intended to exclude from the exception statements made outdoors or in public buildings, though of course neither of these constructions makes much sense.

In any event, what the statute explicitly does prohibit is active participation in a political campaign, presumably including, in addition to fund raising, such activities as envelope stuffing, strategy planning, doorbell ringing, and leaflet distribution. It is difficult to understand how such actions can be deemed to be merely "conduct in the shadow of the First Amendment,"[163] in light of the Supreme Court's

---

158. *Id.* at 631 (Brennan, J., dissenting) (emphasis added).
159. *Id.* at 604 n.1.
160. *See, e.g.,* Jamison v. Texas, 318 U.S. 413 (1943); Schneider v. State, 308 U.S. 147 (1939); Lovell v. Griffin, 303 U.S. 444 (1938). *See Generally* Village of Schaumburg v. Citizens for a Better Environment, 444 U.S. 620, 628-32 (1980).
161. *See, e.g.,* Buckley v. Valeo, 424 U.S. 1 (1976) (per curiam).
162. Broadrick v. Oklahoma, 413 U.S. at 604 n.1.
163. *Id.* at 614.

long and unqualified recognition of such political associational activities as central to first amendment protections.[164] Indeed, the Court in *Broadrick* itself acknowledged that the Oklahoma statute "is directed, by its terms, at political expression which if engaged in by private persons would plainly be protected by the First and Fourteenth Amendments."[165] The fact that the regulated activity was to be engaged in by civil service employees may alter the relative balance of governmental and free speech interests,[166] but surely it in no way alters the conceptual characterization of the activity as expression. The Court in *Broadrick* did not even attempt to explain why the regulated conduct was classifiable as "conduct in the shadow of the First Amendment," rather than pure expressive activity. We therefore cannot be certain exactly how the Court intended to define this category, a problem which has continued to cause significant trouble for the lower courts.[167] Nevertheless, the only reasonable explanation of the Court's concept is that it is intended to include any form of expression — even though fully and equally protected by the first amendment — that is something other than the expression of words by mouth.

If this definition is, in fact, what the Court had in mind, one may question its logic. As long as the category does not consist of the less-protected "speech plus," why should non-verbal first amendment activity receive less constitutional protection than purely verbal communications? After all, the Court has gone to great pains over

---

164. *See, e.g.,* Buckley v. Valeo, 424 U.S. 1, 15 (1976) (per curiam) ("The First Amendment protects political association as well as political expression."). *See also* Citizens Against Rent Control v. City of Berkeley, 454 U.S. 290 (1981); Williams v. Rhodes, 393 U.S. 23 (1968); Shelton v. Tucker, 364 U.S. 479 (1960); NAACP v. Alabama, 357 U.S. 449 (1958).

165. Broadrick v. Oklahoma, 413 U.S. at 616.

166. The point is, of course, debatable. *See* Chapter II at 122.

167. *See, e.g.,* Gormley v. Director, Conn. State Dep't of Probation, 632 F.2d 938 (2d Cir.), *cert. denied,* 449 U.S. 1023 (1980). In that case, the court upheld Connecticut's telephone harassment statute against an overbreadth challenge. In so doing, the court, relying on *Broadrick's* dichotomy, noted that "[c]learly the Connecticut statute regulates *conduct,* not mere speech. What is proscribed is the making of a telephone call, with the requisite intent and in the specified manner." *Id.* at 941-42 (emphasis in original). It is unclear, however, why a telephone call — at least if words are used for purposes of communication — is conduct rather than merely speech. Is it because fingers are used to dial the telephone? If so, one may wonder what the court would say to a telephone that was activated by the use of voice messages. The distinction's absurdity is thus underscored in *Gormley.*

many years to underscore the constitutional values fostered by such non-verbal first amendment activity.[168] The Court's dichotomy, then, is one based solely on the most technical formalism, a ground entirely divorced from any rational first amendment policies or values. Moreover, we may question why such expressive activity is to receive reduced protection only in the case of the overbreadth doctrine. At no point does the Court explain why the dangers of overbroad legislation are somehow reduced when the regulated activity is non-verbal rather than verbal. Thus, the Court left us with a categorization without any rational foundation, as well as a set of legal consequences flowing from that characterization that are equally devoid of logic.

The Court's initial post-*Broadrick* statement on overbreadth tended to indicate that the Court meant business in drawing its "expressive conduct"-pure speech dichotomy. In *Lewis v. City of New Orleans*,[169] for example, the Court struck down a city ordinance that made it unlawful "to curse or revile or to use obscene or opprobrious language toward or with reference to any member of the city police while in the actual performance of his duty."[170] The Court, in an opinion by Justice Brennan, held that the word "opprobrious" was overbroad because it could be applied to statements that were not likely to give rise to an immediate breach of the peace. *Broadrick* was not mentioned. The decision, according to one commentator, "indicates very strongly that *Broadrick* will have little, if any, effect on overbreadth review of statutes directly aimed at regulating speech."[171]

More surprising than the decision in *Lewis* was the Court's failure to refer to *Broadrick*'s "conduct" limitation in its decision in *Village of Schaumburg v. Citizens for a Better Environment*.[172] That case involved an overbreadth challenge to an ordinance prohibiting door-to-door or on-street solicitation of contributions by charitable organizations that do not use at least seventy-five percent of their receipts for "charitable purposes." The Court's opinion, written by the author of *Broadrick*, Justice White, made only minimal reference to *Broadrick*[173] and absolutely no reference to the "conduct" limitation

---

168. *See* cases cited *supra* note 164.
169. 415 U.S. 130 (1974).
170. This ordinance is quoted in full in the Court's opinion. *Id.* at 132.
171. Note, *supra* note 68, at 544.
172. 444 U.S. 620 (1980). This case is discussed *supra* text accompanying notes 44-46.
173. The Court's only reference to *Broadrick* followed the statement that "[g]iven a case or controversy, a litigant whose own activities are unprotected may nevertheless challenge a statute by showing that it substantially abridges the First Amendment rights of other parties not before the court." Village of Schaumburg v. Citizens for a

imposed by that decision. Yet it would seem reasonable to expect that the Court would deem the activity protected in *Schaumburg* to be "expressive conduct" at least as much as was the activity regulated in *Broadrick*. The Court correctly noted that the first amendment has long been thought to protect on-street and door-to-door solicitation[174] and that "'[o]ur cases long have protected speech even though it is in the form of ... a solicitation to pay or contribute money ... .'"[175] Yet in *Broadrick,* the Court had referred to "conduct in the shadow of the First Amendment,"[176] and in support cited two decisions concerning regulation of financial expenditures for the purpose of expression.[177] Is not the on-street and door-to-door solicitation regulated in *Schaumburg* as much "conduct" as the gathering on street corners involved in *Coates,* in which Justice White, in dissent, first urged application of his "conduct" limitation?[178] Perhaps the Court in *Schaumburg* simply believed that the requirement of "substantial" overbreadth, imposed in *Broadrick* for cases involving regulation of "expressive conduct," was met. The Court appeared to make no such special finding,[179] however, and in any event it is clear that the Court did not preface its overbreadth analysis by recognizing the applicability of the *Broadrick* limitation.[180]

In sharp contrast to *Schaumburg* is a recent Burger Court decision that significantly expands the reach of *Broadrick*'s limitations on the use of overbreadth analysis. In *New York v. Ferber,*[181] the Court reversed the New York Court of Appeals's invalidation, on overbreadth

---

Better Environment, 444 U.S. at 634. After citing many of the classic overbreadth decisions, the Court added: "See also the discussion in *Broadrick v. Oklahoma* ... ." *Id.* While this statement does contain a reference to the "substantiality" requirement, the Court's inclusion of references to the traditional overbreadth decisions indicates that it was referring to the well-established *"de minimis"* form of substantiality noted by Justice Brennan in his *Broadrick* dissent. Broadrick v. Oklahoma, 413 U.S. at 614. *See infra* notes 186-188 and accompanying text.

174. Village of Schaumburg v. Citizens for a Better Environment, 444 U.S. at 628-32.

175. *Id.* at 633 (quoting Bates v. State Bar of Arizona, 433 U.S. 350, 363 (1977)).

176. Broadrick v. Oklahoma, 413 U.S. at 614.

177. United States v. Harriss, 347 U.S. 612 (1954); United States v. CIO, 335 U.S. 106 (1948). *See supra* text accompanying note 155.

178. Coates v. City of Cincinnati, 402 U.S. 611, 618, 620-21 (1971) (White, J., dissenting). *See supra* text accompanying notes 143-144.

179. The Court's conclusion was that "the Village's proffered justifications are inadequate and that the ordinance cannot survive scrutiny under the First Amendment." Village of Schaumburg v. Citizens for a Better Environment, 444 U.S. at 636.

180. *See supra* note 173.

181. 458 U.S. 747 (1982).

grounds, of a state statute that prohibited the knowing promotion of a sexual performance by a child under the age of sixteen by distributing material that depicts such a performance. The New York court had found the law to be overbroad, because it would have forbidden the distribution of material with serious literary, scientific, or educational value.[182] The state court had rejected applicability of the *Broadrick* exception, since it believed that "pure speech" was involved.

The Supreme Court stated that "[t]his case ... convinces us that the rationale of *Broadrick* is sound and should be applied in the present context involving the harmful employment of children to make sexually explicit materials for distribution,"[183] even though more traditional forms of expression were the subject of regulation.[184] The Court held that the special "substantiality" requirement of *Broadrick* was applicable because:

> the extent of deterrence of protected speech can be expected to decrease with the declining reach of the regulation. This observation appears equally applicable to the publication of books and films as it is to activities, such as picketing or participation in election campaigns, which have previously been categorized as involving conduct plus speech. We see no appreciable difference between the position of a publisher or bookseller in doubt as to the reach of New York's child pornography law and the situation faced by the Oklahoma state employees with respect to that state's restriction on partisan political activity. Indeed, it could reasonably be argued that the bookseller, with an economic incentive to sell materials that may fall within the statute's scope, may be less likely to be deterred than the employee who wishes to engage in political campaign activity.[185]

In *Ferber*, then, the Court seemingly abandoned the illogical distinction, for purposes of overbreadth analysis, between expressive conduct and pure speech. The *Ferber* decision does not mean, however, that the Court has abandoned its apparent fascination with easily-applied "code" words in overbreadth analysis in lieu of a more sophisticated and open interest-balancing process. Rather, the result of *Ferber* is, it would seem, that *all* overbreadth challenges will now be tested by the special "substantiality" requirement, which was devised originally in *Broadrick* only for regulation of "expressive conduct." To understand the difficulties with the use of such a requirement, it is necessary to explore both the application and the rationale of the

---

182. People v. Ferber, 52 N.Y.2d 674, 422 N.E.2d 523 (1981).
183. New York v. Ferber, 458 U.S. at 771.
184. *Id.*
185. *Id.* at 772 (footnote omitted).

"substantiality" principle as it was developed in *Broadrick* and elaborated upon in *Ferber*.

B. THE "SUBSTANTIALITY" REQUIREMENT

In *Broadrick,* it should be recalled, the Court held that when expressive conduct, rather than speech, is the subject of regulation, the challenged law can be held invalid only if overbreadth is found to be "not only ... real, but substantial as well, judged in relation to the statute's plainly legitimate sweep."[186] Though the statement is not free from ambiguity, it probably should be construed to dictate that if the majority of cases reached by the statute does not involve protected conduct, the statute's overbreadth will not be deemed "substantial," even though it might be "real."[187]

A puzzling aspect of the Court's emphasis on "substantiality" in *Broadrick,* in light of past precedent, was its implication that the requirement is somehow specially applicable to cases in which the protected activity is "expressive conduct" rather than pure speech. As Justice Brennan noted in dissent, "We have never held that a statute should be held invalid on its face merely because it is possible to conceive of a single impermissible application, and in that sense a requirement of substantial overbreadth is already implicit in the doctrine."[188] Thus, in a sense, the requirement of "substantial" overbreadth was nothing new, and had never been thought to be limited to regulation of "expressive conduct." On the other hand, the substantiality that had been required previously seemed to be almost a common sense type of *"de minimis"* requirement. While *Broadrick's* complete ramifications were far from clear, the Court definitely seemed to be referring to a much stiffer form of "substantiality."

Whatever the Court in *Broadrick* meant by "substantiality," however, serious questions remained as to why the justification for the requirement's use was somehow thought to turn on whether expressive conduct or speech was the subject of regulation. Since the Court made no attempt to explain why the special substantiality requirement was ever necessary, those questions remained unanswered.

In *Ferber,* however, the Court explained its imposition of the strengthened substantiality requirement in overbreadth analysis, and in so doing, apparently realized that its rationale in no way turned on the conduct-speech dichotomy. The explanation was, simply, that "the

---

186. Broadrick v. Oklahoma, 413 U.S. 615-16. *See supra* text accompanying notes 145-168.
187. Broadrick v. Oklahoma, 413 U.S. at 615-16.
188. *Id.* at 630 (Brennan, J., dissenting).

FIRST AMENDMENT OVERBREADTH DOCTRINE

extent of deterrence of protected speech can be expected to decrease with the declining reach of the regulation."[189] In support of this proposition, the Court cited the reasoning of a student comment that "[a] substantial overbreadth rule is implicit in the chilling effect rationale ... the presumption must be that only substantially overbroad laws set up the kind and degree of chill that is judicially cognizable."[190] If we recall, however, that the "substantiality" of overbreadth, as employed in *Broadrick* and *Ferber,* is apparently to be determined on a comparative or relative basis — that is, by comparing the number of instances of unprotected activity reached by the challenged statute to the number of instances of protected activity reached[191] — the Court's logic breaks down. There is no reason to assume that "the extent of deterrence of protected speech" somehow necessarily decreases when the number of instances of unprotected activity reached by the challenged statute increases, relative to the number of protected instances.

In other words, if statute A simultaneously reaches 5000 instances of unprotected activity and 50 instances of protected activity, the Court would presumably conclude that the law was not "substantially" overbroad, even though the overbreadth might be considered "real," because the statute reaches far more instances of unprotected than protected activity. This was, in effect, the Court's conclusion in *Ferber,* in which the Court cited the challenged child pornography law as "the paradigmatic case of a state statute whose legitimate reach dwarfs its arguably impermissible applications,"[192] and therefore one whose overbreadth was not "substantial." On the other hand, if statute B reaches 50 instances of unprotected activity, as well as 50 instances of protected activity, the Court would presumably find the statute's overbreadth to be "substantial" as well as "real."[193] In both situations, however, the chilling effect, in an *absolute* sense, is identical — that is, the same absolute number of cases of "chilling" would be found, or at

---

189. New York v. Ferber, 458 U.S. at 772 (footnote omitted).
190. Note, *supra* note 62, at 859 n. 61, cited in New York v. Ferber, 458 U.S. at 772 n. 27.
191. Recall that, as phrased in *Broadrick,* the test turns on whether the overbreadth is "substantial," *"judged in relation to the statute's plainly legitimate sweep."* Broadrick v. Oklahoma, 413 U.S. at 615 (emphasis added). This requirement is also true of *Ferber. See infra* text accompanying note 192.
192. New York v. Ferber, 458 U.S. at 773.
193. Of course, a construct which quantifies the number of instances of protected and unprotected conduct reached by a statute cannot be thought to comport with reality, since we can never predict exactly how many instances will be contained in either category. Nevertheless, I believe that the quantified construct is helpful as a means of underscoring the logical point I am making.

least there is no basis to believe that the absolute number of cases of "chilling" would be greater in one situation than in the other. How, then, can the Court assert, as it did in *Ferber,* that the less "substantial" the overbreadth in a *relative* sense, the less deterrence to the exercise of protected activity, presumably in an *absolute* sense?

Perhaps the Court's linguistic gymnastics were designed merely to indicate that if the number of instances of protected activity reached by a challenged statute is small in relation to the number of instances of unprotected activity, it is safe to conclude, on the basis of an implicit balancing process, that the need for the statute outweighs the harms it causes. Yet by applying its code word — "substantiality" — instead of engaging in a careful interest-balancing process, the Court disregards completely the essential function performed by the overbreadth doctrine in the first place: to determine whether a valid statutory goal can be achieved by means less invasive of free speech interests. If the valid goal of statute *A* in the hypothetical could be achieved by a less restrictive means, there is no state interest served by upholding the law's constitutionality, regardless of the fact that the number of unprotected instances reached by the law significantly exceeds the number of protected instances.[194] Under the analysis of *Broadrick* and *Ferber,* however, the Court will never reach this essential overbreadth inquiry.[195]

The Court's discussion of overbreadth in *Ferber,* like that in *Broadrick,* underscores the dangers of an overbreadth doctrine that fails to examine the specific circumstances of the individual situation. Whether the Court acknowledges the fact, a delicate balancing process

---

194. Even accepting this criticism of the "substantiality" requirement, the Court might still adhere to the traditional, *pre-Broadrick de minimis* type of substantiality imposed on overbreadth analysis. *See* Broadrick v. Oklahoma, 413 U.S. at 630 (Brennan, J., dissenting). *See also supra* text accompanying notes 136-138. For example, a broadly phrased breach-of-the-peace ordinance might not be held to be unconstitutionally overbroad, because the overwhelming majority of activities reached by the statute do not concern speech at all, much less speech that is arguably protected. Such a *de minimis* form of the "substantiality" requirement would seem to comport with the logic of the overbreadth doctrine, because it is difficult to imagine how a legislature could realistically be expected to achieve its valid goal through more narrowly-drawn legislation. This "substantiality" requirement, however, is quite different from the considerably broader one imposed in *Broadrick* and expanded in *Ferber.* Under the latter analysis, once the Court finds no "substantial" overbreadth, it precludes itself from engaging in the "less restrictive alternative" analysis, when the answer to that question — unlike the situation involving the breach-of-the-peace ordinance — is by no means self-evident.

195. *See supra* text accompanying notes 186-191.

is going on — or at least should be going on — when overbreadth analysis is employed.

It is both unfortunate and puzzling that the Court in *Ferber* deemed it necessary to include its questionable general discussion of overbreadth analysis, because earlier portions of the opinion admirably attempted to come to grips with the competing social policy considerations surrounding the New York statute, in much the way a proper overbreadth analysis should be conducted. This is so, whether or not one accepts the Court's substantive conclusions on the statute's validity.[196]

The logical question to be posed to the state under an overbreadth analysis is whether vigorous enforcement of the more narrowly drawn traditional obscenity statutes would inadequately achieve the state's goal. Though in section III of its opinion the Court declined to engage in an overbreadth analysis because of the lack of "substantiality," in section II the Court expended considerable thoughtful effort in explaining why it believed that the state's needs could not be achieved by use of the less restrictive means of obscenity regulation.[197] Thus,

---

196. It should be emphasized that recognition of the propriety of the Court's general mode of analysis does not necessarily represent agreement with the correctness of the Court's ultimate conclusion. In fact, it is highly likely that the use of traditional obscenity statutes as a method of regulating child pornography would have been more than adequate. *See* New York v. Ferber, 458 U.S. at 779 n.4 (Stevens, J., concurring) (citing S. REP. NO. 438, 95th Cong., 1st Sess. 13, *reprinted in* 1978 U.S. CODE CONG. & AD. NEWS 50).

197. The Court began its analysis by describing the unique nature of the state's interest in regulating the use of children in sexual performances:

> It is evident beyond the need for elaboration that a state's interest in "safeguarding the physical and psychological well being of a minor" is "compelling." ... "A democratic society rests, for its continuance, upon the healthy well-rounded growth of young people into full maturity as citizens." ...
>
> The prevention of sexual exploitation and abuse of children constitutes a governmental objective of surpassing importance. ...
>
> ... The distribution of photographs and films depicting sexual activity by juveniles is intrinsically related to the sexual abuses of children in at least two ways. First, the materials produced are a permanent record of the children's participation and the harm to the child is exacerbated by their circulation. Second, the distribution network for child pornography must be closed if the production of material which requires the sexual exploitation of children is to be effectively controlled.

New York v. Ferber, 458 U.S. at 756-59 (footnotes omitted). In direct response to the contention that the state's interest could be achieved through the narrower means of obscenity regulation, the Court stated:

> The *Miller* [obscenity] standard, like all general definitions of what may be banned as obscene, does not reflect the State's particular and more compelling interest in prosecuting those who promote the sexual exploitation of children. Thus, the question under the *Miller* test of whether a work, taken as a whole,

despite its subsequent refusal to invoke the traditional overbreadth inquiry, the Court effectively did so, and concluded that, as long as the New York courts gave the statute a reasonably limited interpretation,[198] the law simply was not overbroad: the state's valid goal could not effectively be achieved by less restrictive alternatives.

Perhaps the Court's subsequent overbreadth discussion was designed to recognize that the statute might conceivably have unconstitutional applications (such as to National Geographic or a medical textbook)[199] but that the few conceivable instances did not render the statute invalid. If so, the Court would then be leaving its options open in later cases. Yet such an escape hatch was unnecessary: to hold that a law is not overbroad is not to hold that it can never be applied unconstitutionally in individual cases (though in *Ferber,* much of the Court's earlier reasoning might well be taken to mean that the law could be constitutionally applied even to the National Geographic and textbook hypotheticals).[200] Thus, the Court need not have feared that a direct decision on the merits of the overbreadth challenge — without the procedural insulation of the strengthened "substantiality"

> appeals to the prurient interest of the average person bears no connection to the issue of whether a child has been physically or psychologically harmed in the production of the work. Similarly, a sexually explicit depiction need not be "patently offensive" in order to have required the sexual exploitation of a child for its production. In addition, a work which, taken on the whole, contains serious literary, artistic, political, or scientific value may nevertheless embody the hardest core of child pornography. "It is irrelevant to the child [who has been abused] whether or not the material ... has a literary, artistic, political, or social value." ... We therefore cannot conclude that the *Miller* standard is a satisfactory solution to the child pornography problem.

Id. at 761 (footnote omitted). Finally, the Court noted that the competing first amendment interest was not overwhelming, because

> if it were necessary for literary or artistic value, a person over the statutory age who perhaps looked younger could be utilized. Simulation outside of the prohibition of the statute could provide another alternative. Nor is there any question here of censoring a particular literary theme or portrayal of sexual activity. The First Amendment interest is limited to that of rendering the portrayal somewhat more "realistic" by utilizing or photographing children.

Id. at 763 (footnote omitted). In this carefully reasoned passage (whether or not one accepts its conclusion), the Court decides that the state's valid goal of preventing sexual abuse to children *cannot* be achieved by the less drastic means of obscenity regulation. The Court, then, was effectively deciding that the New York law simply was not overbroad.

198. "Nor will we assume that the New York courts will widen the possibly invalid reach of the statute by giving an expansive construction to the proscription on 'lewd exhibition[s] of the genitals.'" *Id.* at 773.
199. *Id.*
200. *See supra* note 197.

requirement — would necessarily have precluded it from invalidating specific statutory applications.

Ferber, then, is in many ways a Jekyll-Hyde decision that simultaneously demonstrates all the worst and all the best in overbreadth analysis. On the one hand, the Court exacerbates the harm caused by *Broadrick* by expanding that decision's artificial and specious "substantiality" requirement, thus establishing a most troublesome precedent for future overbreadth cases. Use of code words like "substantiality" — as much as the refusal in *Robel* to examine the viability of allegedly less restrictive alternatives[201] — effectively prevents the overbreadth doctrine from performing the valuable function of accommodating competing social and constitutional interests. On the other hand, despite the Court's suggestion in *Ferber* to the contrary, the case also engaged in a careful, reasoned analysis of the competing concerns,[202] in much the way traditional overbreadth analysis — freed from the artificial constraints of *Broadrick* — should be conducted.[203]

VI. Conclusion: The Overbreadth Doctrine and the Categorization Debate in First Amendment Analysis

As I noted at the outset of this chapter,[204] my primary goal in critiquing the versions of overbreadth analysis that the Warren and the Burger Courts have employed was to demonstrate the unworkability of unbending categorical rules, and supposedly easily-applied "code words" and principles, in development of the overbreadth doctrine. Particularly with regard to my critical examination of the Burger Court's decision in *Broadrick,* I may be open to attack by the "categorizers," who could rightfully point out that the mere fact that a court has developed an absurd categorical rule is not necessarily an indictment of the categorization process, and that it is therefore unfair for me to saddle them with the silliness of the *Broadrick* decision. To a certain extent, of course, the point is valid. In a broader sense, however, I believe that the fallacies of the *Broadrick* categorizations, almost as much as the Court's stubborn refusal in *Robel* to consider the

---

201. *See supra* text accompanying notes 91-95.
202. *See supra* text accompanying note 196.
203. The Court's discussion in *Ferber* of the law's merits perhaps could be translated into a form of the "risk-of-the-wrong guess" analysis suggested earlier, see *supra* text accompanying notes 108-114: because of the great significance of the relevant state interest, the Court is unwilling to take the risk that it might be underestimating the effectiveness of allegedly less restrictive alternatives.
204. *See supra* text accompanying notes 11-14.

viability of arguably less restrictive alternatives in individual cases, tend to underscore the general unworkability of rigidly defined categorical rules in overbreadth analysis in particular, and first amendment analysis in general. Attempts at categorization such as the ones in *Broadrick* seem to represent a yearning for a simplicity and ease of application that just does not comport with reality.

It is true that a total abandonment of any attempt at categorization in favor of a wholly directionless ad hoc balancing test would be disastrous in its impact on the protection of first amendment rights, for the very reasons noted by the categorizers.[205] Yet the fundamental fallacy in the view of the strict categorizers is their desire to view the situation as almost an all-or-nothing proposition: any principle of first amendment construction that does not impose a priori-developed, rigid categories of protected and unprotected activity is viewed as a manifestation of ad hoc balancing, with all the evils that the concept conjures in the minds of those of us who consider ourselves to be protectionists.[206] In reality, however, the situation should be viewed as being on a continuum, rather than viewed in the strict lines of demarcation urged by the categorizers. Principles of first amendment construction that provide courts with some level of guidance as to how to weigh respective factors in individual cases are far preferable to such a totally standardless balancing test, and should be adopted whenever feasible.[207] Indeed, the overbreadth doctrine itself, especially when combined with the "risk-of-the-wrong-guess" analysis,[208] provides at least some degree of guidance to a reviewing court, by directing the court to ask whether the state's goal could be achieved by means less invasive of free speech interests. The conceptually troubled history of the overbreadth doctrine, however, demonstrates that a rigid refusal in the use of overbreadth analysis to recognize the need for a sophisticated form of interest-balancing on the basis of the individual

---

205. Primarily, these reasons include the dangers of abuse, manipulation, and unpredictability, and the great likelihood that such a test will lead to an automatic affirmation of the legislative judgment. *See* Ely, *supra* note 74, at 1506; Frantz, *The First Amendment in the Balance*, 71 YALE L. J. 1424, 1435, 1443 (1962).

206. Illustrative is Professor Tribe's discussion of the legitimate grounds for narrowing overbroad laws, L. TRIBE, *supra* note 8, at 714-15 (discussed *supra* text accompanying notes 116-138), and Professor Ely's attack on the clear-and-present danger test, *see* Ely, *supra* note 74, at 1501; Chapter IV at 193-96.

207. In another chapter, however, I have pointed out that a number of first amendment problems — for example, the danger of harm from a particular planned demonstration — are so individualized that it is unlikely that even the loosest form of categorization, other than simply a broad "compelling interest" or somewhat narrower "clear and present danger" analysis, will be possible. *See* Chapter II at 120.

208. *See supra* text accompanying notes 108-114.

circumstances of a case benefits neither the concerns of free speech nor the competing governmental interests in regulation. To be sure, the performance of such a delicate task by a fallible judiciary is plagued with risks. Yet, if the first amendment is to function effectively, there seems to be no realistic alternative.

CONCLUSION

Though in preparing the preceding essays I have attempted to develop certain underlying themes which link the examination of these seemingly distinct first amendment issues, it is quite conceivable that one could accept the analysis in one essay while rejecting it in another. For example, a reader might be unpersuaded by my argument that the value of free expression should be deemed to apply to all forms of purely communicative activity,[1] yet still accept my argument that there exists no rational basis on which to distinguish content-based regulation from content-neutral regulation, at least as applied to whatever expression the reader deems worthy of constitutional protection.[2] Similarly, one who is unconvinced by my attack on the content distinction might nevertheless be persuaded by my contention that not all forms of prior restraint are deserving of an equally negative presumption.[3] Thus, the essays do not necessarily build on assumptions made or conclusions reached in the remaining essays.

Nevertheless, when read in combination, the five essays represent applications of a unified approach to questions of first amendment interpretation. For in these essays, I attempt to stake out a position that is in many senses unique among those expressed by the modern contributors to the rich and varied literature on the subject of free speech. My approach adopts a strongly protectionist philosophy that

---

1. *See* Chapter I. It should be noted that certain activity may conceivably be "communicative", in the sense that it conveys some sort of message, yet nevertheless be found unworthy of first amendment protection, because it simultaneously has direct and immediate physical consequences unrelated to the communication. For example, an individual may assassinate a political leader, in order to communicate displeasure with that leader's policies. Obviously, such activity cannot rationally be classified as "speech". Drawing the necessary lines, however, will not often prove to be an easy task. This problem has particularly plagued application of Professor Emerson's strict dichotomy between absolutely protected "speech" and unprotected "conduct." *See* T. EMERSON, THE SYSTEM OF FREEDOM OF EXPRESSION 17 (1970). *See* Chapter IV at 201-04. However, to one who openly recognizes the need to balance free speech interests, the problem is somewhat less severe. For while we may still categorically eliminate from the contours of the first amendment many activities on the basis of common sense — for example, the assassination illustration — more difficult conceptual distinctions between "speech" and "conduct" need never be drawn. Rather, we may assume that the activity's communicative aspect brings it within the broad boundaries of the free speech guarantee, but nevertheless conclude that the significant negative immediate physical consequences of the activity justify its regulation. On the other hand, to the extent the communicative activity, even though it does contain non-communicative elements, presents no serious danger of negative physical consequences, and is not overwhelmed by its non-communicative aspects, there is no reason not to protect it.
2. *See* Chapter II.
3. *See* Chapter III.

simultaneously recognizes the need for a significant degree of judicial discretion in balancing competing social interests, often in individual cases. Traditionally protectionist theorists have considered such a possibility a frightening prospect, and have urged various forms of so-called "absolute" protection or, at the very least, relatively rigid forms of categorization, so that courts will have little discretion in individual cases. Thus, in the early years of modern free speech theory, Alexander Meiklejohn bitterly decried any form of judicial balancing and in its place suggested a type of absolutism premised on his own analysis of the relative values of different forms of expression.[4] Thomas Emerson expressed similar concerns over case-by-case judicial discretion, and adopted a definitional approach that purported to determine protection exclusively on whether the challenged activity could be characterized as "speech" or "conduct."[5] Even the more recent theorists, like Tribe[6] and Ely,[7] who acknowledge, either implicitly or explicitly, the difficulties involved in any absolutist approach, nevertheless urge use of predetermined categorizations to determine protection, at least when regulation is premised on the content of the communication.[8]

Admittedly, modern judicial history does not give substantial comfort to a protectionist who recognizes the need for substantial judicial flexibility in guarding the right of free expression. The Supreme Court of the 1950's often employed the balancing rhetoric as simply a means of validating legislative judgment.[9] But any attempt to establish an inherent linkage between case-by-case judicial flexibility and virtually total judicial deference to legislative judgment amounts to a non-sequitur: courts could just as logically combine wideranging judicial discretion with a form of strict scrutiny of legislative incursions on expression (as, indeed, I urge throughout the book).[10] Moreover, there is no logical reason why the judiciary could not adopt strict categories of protected and unprotected expression that provide relatively little protection and instead provide the legislature with

---

4. A. MEIKLEJOHN, POLITICAL FREEDOM (1960). *See* the discussion in Chapter I *supra* at 17-18.

5. T. EMERSON, *supra* note 1. *See* the discussion in Chapter IV *supra* at 201-04.

6. L. TRIBE, AMERICAN CONSTITUTIONAL LAW §§ 12-2, 12-10 (1978). *See* the discussion in Chapter II *supra* at 93-94.

7. Ely, *Flag Desecration: A Case Study in the Roles of Categorization and Balancing in First Amendment Analysis,* 88 HARV. L. REV. 1482 (1975). *See* the discussion in Chapter II *supra* at 93-94.

8. *See* Chapter II *supra* at 90-94.

9. *See* Chapter IV *supra* at 209; Chapter V *supra* at 226-27.

10. *See,* particularly, Chapter II *supra* at 117-20; Chapter IV *supra* at 191-92; Chapter V *supra* at 227.

substantial power to regulate expression in the presence of only minimal governmental interests. In fact, this is exactly what the Burger Court did in its limitation of the protective impact of the overbreadth doctrine.[11] In addition, Learned Hand's categorical test for requiring advocacy of unlawful conduct, developed in *Masses*,[12] lends itself to substantial and unjustified inroads on free speech, since it would logically lead to regulation of any speech that directly advocates unlawful conduct, even though no real danger of harm exists.[13]

The point, in other words, is that there is no magical protectionism in the categorization concept, and there is no inherent reason for a protectionist to fear judicial flexibility. Indeed, as I argue at various points,[14] reduction of case-by-case flexibility may often undermine the interest in free expression, since use of unbending categorical rules may often require adoption of a standard that is going to be either overprotective or underprotective in individual cases, and if so, as a practical matter there is a strong likelihood that a court will err on the side of the societal interest.

It should be emphasized that belief in some degree of case-by-case judicial flexibility does not imply acceptance of completely unguided, virtually emotive and unprincipled judicial decision-making. At the very least, the court should be directed to begin its analysis with a strong presumption in favor of expression and accept regulation only in the presence of a compelling governmental interest. There may well be ambiguities and uncertainties in deciding exactly when a compelling interest is present, but a healthy judicial skepticism of asserted justifications for regulation and a requirement that all conceivable less invasive means of satisfying the governmental interest be fully explored should provide a safety net for protection of the speech interest. In certain instances, the broad contours of the compelling interest analysis may be translated into more narrow formulations for specific situations. The "clear and present danger" test in the area of unlawful advocacy regulation is one illustration, and what I label the "risk-of-the-wrong-guess" analysis in the use of the overbreadth doctrine is in some senses another.[15] In appropriate instances, it is even conceivable that tests approaching true categorizations may work

---

11. *See* the discussion in Chapter V *supra* at 240-55.
12. 244 F. 535 (S.D.N.Y.), *rev'd*, 246 F. 24 (2d Cir. 1917).
13. *See* the discussion in Chapter IV *supra* at 197-200.
14. *See* Chapter IV *supra* at 197-200; Chapter V *supra* at 255-57.
15. *See* Chapter V *supra* at 234-36.

effectively. The "actual malice" test of the defamation doctrine of *New York Times Co. v. Sullivan*[16] illustrates. But this fact merely underscores the need for flexibility: in certain instances, we may safely employ categorical rules[17] while in others the interests of free speech call for greater case-by-case discretion. The problems inherent in the process of defining the outer perimeters of free speech protection are generally too complex to lend themselves to all-encompassing, rigid lines of demarcation.

It is true that the approach adopted here places considerable faith in the ability of the judiciary to provide correct solutions in individual cases, and it might be suggested that such faith is unjustified. The problem is one I candidly acknowledge. Indeed, it is sensitivity to this very concern that has significantly influenced my thinking in other writings on the interrelation of due process and formalized protections of judicial independence.[18] But ultimately, use of rigid categories — even largely protective ones — cannot effectively guard against a judiciary either insensitive to free speech concerns or caught up in a nation's paranoia.[19] More importantly, as I have attempted to demonstrate,[20] in many situations we simply have no choice; as well intended as they obviously have been, attempts to replace judicial flexibility with more automatic definitional or categorical approaches have generally proven unworkable in individual instances, or have merely disguised what is in reality a form of flexible balancing process. If the judiciary is to be able to develop workable and effective principles of free speech protection, its balancing of competing interests must be done openly and candidly, rather than indirectly or surreptitiously.

Despite the substantial power which I believe the judiciary must exercise in individual first amendment cases, there is one area of first amendment construction where I would remove all judicial flexibility: the gradating of free speech protection on the basis of the relative

---

16. 376 U.S. 254 (1964).

17. It should be emphasized, however, that even these so-called categorical rules leave a not-insignificant degree of case-by-case flexibility. In the "actual malice" example, a court or jury must still apply that broad terminology to specific factual situations, and it is likely that in many situations reasonable people could differ on the appropriate characterization of those facts.

18. *See* Redish, *Constitutional Limitations on Congressional Power to Control Federal Jurisdiction: A Reaction to Professor Sager,* 77 Nw. U.L. Rev. 143, 161-66 (1982).

19. *See* Chapter IV *supra* at 196.

20. *See,* particularly, Chapter IV *supra* at 197-200; Chapter V *supra* at 255-57. *See also* Chapter II *supra* at 120.

value of the speech being regulated. There is no inherent inconsistency in recognizing substantial judicial flexibility to determine first amendment protection on the basis of danger to accepted societal interests, but to reject such flexibility in determining the value of different subjects of expressive activity. As I established in Chapter I,[21] ultimately the same values served by protecting the traditionally exalted political expression[22] are fostered by any communicative activity[23] that aids individual intellectual self-fulfillment or facilitates life-affecting decisions. There is therefore no legitimate basis on which to distinguish protection of political expression from other forms of expression, including literature, scientific inquiry, commercial speech, or even pornography. Moreover, any attempt by the judiciary to determine for the individual that one form of expression fosters the values of intellectual development or facilitates life-affecting decisions more than another is inherently violative of the value of individual integrity intertwined in both constitutional democracy and the first amendment, functioning as a catalyst in the workings of the democratic process.[24]

Those who find these assertions intuitively troubling should ask how they would react to a court — or any governmental body, for that matter — deciding that one novel or film is more "valuable" than another, and therefore more deserving of first amendment protection. My own reaction to such a process is that it is simply none of the government's business to decide for the individual that certain novels or films are better for him than are others; that is a decision our constitutional values leave to the individual. Much the same reasoning presumably lies behind the strong presumption against governmental regulation of viewpoint:[25] in a democracy, it is not for the government to decide that one normative view of the world is somehow "better" than another. If we do not allow governmental agencies to have this power, there is no reason to believe the judiciary should be able to render similar judgments: the thought of a court providing greater first

---

21. Chapter I *supra* at 19-29.
22. *See* A. MEIKLEJOHN, *supra* note 4; Bork, *Neutral Principles and Some First Amendment Problems,* 47 IND. L.J. 1 (1971). *See* the discussion in Chapter I *supra* at 14-19.
23. *But see* note 1 *supra*.
24. *See* the more detailed discussion in Chapter I *supra* at 19-29.
25. It should be emphasized that while in Chapter II I argue that content-neutral regulations should be subjected to as strong a negative presumption as that imposed on content-based regulations, I in no way intend to imply that the presumption against the latter should be decreased, but only that the presumption against the former should be increased.

amendment protection to a viewpoint with which it agrees than one with which it does not, is no doubt frightening to many.

Once it is acknowledged that in some sense *all* communicative activity[26] fosters the same ultimate intellectual values embodied in the first amendment, a judicial determination that one broad subject of expression does so more than another differs little from its conclusion that one novel does so more than another. Expression of a political viewpoint that is deemed by many to be illogical or repulsive is protected as much as one that is thought to be cogently reasoned; the works of Shakespeare are no more protected than are the critically attacked novels churned out for mass consumption. Similarly, the logic of the first amendment precludes any judicial determination that one form or subject of expression is more valuable than another.

In summary, under the broad guidelines described here and applied in specific areas in the book's five essays, the judiciary is provided flexible authority to regulate expression, but only in the presence of a significant danger to a truly compelling societal interest.[27] In the large majority of cases, this determination is to be made without the use of rigid formulas or unbending categorizations. However, the judiciary should be denied all authority to make judgments about the moral, social, literary or political value of expression in determining the level of constitutional protection it is to receive. Acceptance of these conclusions, I submit, would do much to provide an appropriate level of protection to freedom of expression.

---

26. *See* note 1 *supra*.

27. In Chapter II, I discuss in some detail a proposed "sliding scale" analysis: the more feasible alternative avenues of expression that are open to the speaker, the less compelling must be the governmental interest. *See supra* at 118. It is by this means that I believe most acceptable regulations of time and place may be justified. However, it should be emphasized that this sliding-scale analysis becomes relevant only if the asserted governmental justification passes a threshold level of significance. If it fails to do so, the conceivable availability of alternative modes of expression is irrelevant, for choice of time and place for expression are presumptively to be made by the individuals themselves. It should also be noted that this threshold must be considerably higher than the traditional "non-negligible" level required by the Supreme Court in cases of content-neutral regulation. In other words, minimal governmental inconvenience is insufficient to reach even the threshold level of compelling interest. *See* the discussion in Chapter II *supra* at 118.

TABLE OF CASES

A

Abrams v. United States, 1, 10, 46, 81, 176-78
Adderley v. Florida, 227, 244
Arnett v. Kennedy, 224
Associated Indem. Corp. v. Shea, 148

B

Bantam Books, Inc. v. Sullivan, 127
Barenblatt v. United States, 196, 226
Bates v. City of Little Rock, 94
Bates v. State Bar, 213, 243, 248
Battaglia v. General Motors Corp., 129, 148
Bell v. Burson, 154
Beuharnais v. Illinois, 55, 114
Book Named "John Cleland's Memoirs of a Woman of Pleasure" v. Attorney Gen., 68
Brandenburg v. Ohio, 71, 95, 117, 119-20, 140, 163, 183-86, 190-91, 193-200, 239
Bridges v. California, 180, 189
Broadrick v. Oklahoma, 100, 222-23, 241-57
Buckley v. Valeo, 90, 102, 113, 245, 246

C

Cantwell v. Connecticut, 180
Carey v. Population Servs. Int'l, 61
Carroll v. President and Comm'rs, 158-59
Central Gas & Elec. Corp. v. Public Serv. Comm'n, 63
Chaplinsky v. New Hampshire, 55-56, 69, 114, 117, 197, 238
Citizens Against Rent Control v. City of Berkeley, 246
Clark v. Community for Creative Non-Violence, 102
Coates v. City of Cincinnati, 242, 248
Cohen v. California, 58, 115-16, 124, 153, 162
Coolidge v. New Hampshire, 147
Cox v. Louisiana, 96-97, 244
Cox v. New Hampshire, 156

Craig v. Harney, 180
Crowell v. Benson, 129, 148
Curtis Publishing Co. v. Butts, 77

D

Debs v. United States, 175-76, 195, 200
Dennis v. United States, 54, 71, 117, 138, 140, 142, 180-86, 190, 200, 206-11, 226
Dombrowski v. Pfister, 144, 213, 223

E

Eastern R.R. Conference v. Noerr Motor Freight, Inc., 244
Elfbrandt v. Russell, 219
Erznoznik v. City of Jacksonville, 87, 89, 92, 97-100, 120

F

Fay v. Noia, 213
FCC v. Pacifica Found., 12, 58
Feinberg v. Federal Deposit Ins. Corp., 148
First Nat'l Bank of Boston v. Bellotti, 30
Freedman v. Maryland, 130, 138, 150-54
Friedman v. Rogers, 61, 63
Frohwerk v. United States, 175-77, 200
Fuentes v. Shevin, 154

G

Garrison v. Louisiana, 76, 143
Gertz v. Robert Welch, Inc., 37, 64, 79-81
Gibson v. Berryhill, 147
Gitlow v. New York, 1, 178, 183, 200
Golden v. Zwickler, 222
Gooding v. Wilson, 237, 239, 242
Gormley v. Director, Conn. State Dep't of Probation, 246
Grayned v. City of Rockford, 99
Greer v. Spock, 87, 92, 94, 97, 102, 111-12
Griffin v. Illinois, 161

TABLE OF CASES

H

Hague v. CIO, 95-96
Hess v. Indiana, 185-86, 213
Howat v. Kansas, 166
Hudgens v. NLRB, 97

I

In re Primus, 213

J

Jamison v. Texas, 245
Jenkins v. Georgia, 138-39, 143
Julian Messner, Inc. v. Spahn, 77-78

K

Kasper v. State, 204
Keyishian v. Board of Regents, 100, 218-19
Kingsley Books, Inc. v. Brown, 138
Kingsley Int'l Pictures Corp. v. Regents, 92
Kovacs v. Cooper, 60, 97
Kunz v. New York, 222

L

Lehman v. City of Shaker Heights, 102
Lewis v. City of New Orleans, 247
Linmark Assocs., Inc. v. Willingboro, 61
Lochner v. New York, 62, 68
Lockerty v. Phillips, 148
Lovell v. Griffin, 162, 167, 245

M

Masses Publishing Co. v. Patten, 81, 186, 188, 193-201
Mathews v. Eldridge, 154
Metromedia, Inc. v. City of San Diego, 102
Miami Herald Publishing Co. v. Tornillo, 49
Miller v. California, 68, 71, 91, 114, 138, 252-53
Mills v. Alabama, 34, 101

Monitor Patriot Co. v. Roy, 33
Mt. Healthy City School Dist. Bd. of Educ. v. Doyle, 107

N

NAACP v. Alabama, 246
NAACP v. Button, 94, 140, 218, 221
National Bank of Boston v. Bellotti, 213
National League of Cities v. Usery, 213
National Socialist Party v. Village of Skokie, 130
Near v. Minnesota, 128, 157
New York v. Ferber, 37, 222-23, 241, 248-49, 251-55
New York Times Co. v. Sullivan, 57, 65, 76-81, 93, 109, 114, 119-20, 143, 192, 194, 238, 240, 262
New York Times Co. v. United States, 128, 130, 141, 144, 170
Ng Fung Ho v. White, 148

O

O'Brien v. United States, 106-07, 111, 117, 121-25
Ohralik v. Ohio State Bar Ass'n, 61, 63, 65, 213
Olitsky v. O'Malley, 222
Olivia N. v. National Broadcasting Co., 188
Organization for a Better Austin v. Keefe, 127, 130, 170

P

Palmer v. Thompson, 108
Palmore v. United States, 149
Paris Adult Theatre I v. Slaton, 68, 70-71
Parker v. Levy, 243
Pennekamp v. Florida, 180
People v. Ferber, 249
People v. Street, 116
Police Dep't v. Mosley, 60, 87-89, 92, 97-98, 110, 120, 143
Poulos v. New Hampshire, 156, 167

R

Red Lion Broadcasting Co. v. FCC, 49, 104, 244

TABLE OF CASES

Richmond Newspapers, Inc. v. Virginia, 213
Rosenbloom v. Metromedia, Inc., 79
Roth v. United States, 68-70, 91, 152

S

St. Amant v. Thompson, 138
Schacht v. United States, 97
Schad v. Borough of Mount Ephraim, 72, 89
Schenk v. United States, 1, 173, 175-80, 200
Schneider v. State, 34, 96, 104, 119-20, 235-37, 245
Shelton v. Tucker, 217, 219-20, 246
Shuttlesworth v. City of Birmingham, 167
Spahn v. Julian Messner, 78
State v. Chaplinsky, 238
State v. Quinlan, 204
Stone v. Powell, 213

T

Talley v. California, 104, 235-37
Thomas v. Collins, 94, 180
Thornhill v. Alabama, 155, 167, 180, 221
Time, Inc. v. Hill, 77-78
Tinker v. Des Moines School Dist., 94
Tumey v. Ohio, 147
Turchnik v. United States, 217

U

Ulster County v. Allen, 223
United Public Workers v. Mitchell, 89
United States Civil Serv. Comm'n v. National Ass'n of Letter Carriers, 87, 89, 92, 97-100, 102, 111-12, 121-22, 125, 232-33
United States v. Carroll Towing Co., 181
United States v. CIO, 244, 248
United States v. Harriss, 244, 248
United States v. O'Brien, 87, 97, 100-01, 153, 244
United States v. Progressive, Inc., 141
United States v. Raines, 221
United States v. Reidel, 68
United States v. Robel, 122, 217, 220, 227-33, 237, 255
United States v. Thirty-Seven (37) Photographs, 68, 169
United States v. United Mine Workers, 166, 168
United States v. United States Dist. Court, 147
United States v. Woo Jan, 148

V

Valentine v. Chrestensen, 61, 114
Village of Schaumberg v. Citizens for a Better Environment, 220-21, 241, 245, 247-48
Virginia State Bd. of Pharmacy v. Virginia Citizens Consumer Council, Inc., 61-63, 67-68, 91, 213

W

Walker v. City of Birmingham, 165, 168
Washington v. Davis, 111
Watts v. United States, 85
Whitney v. California, 1, 16, 179-80, 184, 189, 196
Williams v. Rhodes, 246
Wooley v. Maynard, 162

Y

Yates v. United States, 184-86, 207
Young v. American Mini Theatres, Inc., 68, 71-72, 89, 102, 117, 225
Younger v. Harris, 224

INDEX

A

Absolutism, 53-54, 201-206, 260

Advocacy of Unlawful Conduct
  see also Clear and Present Danger Test
    generally, 6, 173-211
    absolutist approach to, 54, 85-86, 201-206
    and balancing, 193-204
    and categorization, 119, 193-201, 239-240
    and dangers of abstract determinations, 140-141
    Dennis test, 180-183, 184-185, 196
    distinction between direct and indirect incitement, 197-200
    distinction between ideological and non-ideological, 83-84
    implications for, on basis of self-realization theory, 36, 57, 81-86
    and marketplace-of-ideas theory, 81-82, 191
    and overbreadth, 210
    and "safety-valve" theory, 82

"Actual Malice" Test, 119, 240, 262

Administrative Agencies, 131, 138, 148-158

Autonomy
    and prior restraints, 144-147
    as value of free speech, 11, 43

B

Baker, C. Edwin
    as absolutist, 85
    attack on marketplace-of-ideas theory, 48-49
    critic of self-realization theory, 30-36, 49-50
    development of "liberty" model, 12, 49-52
    and protection for advocacy of unlawful conduct, 54
    views on commercial speech, 51
    views on demonstrations, 156
    views on speech-conduct dichotomy, 38

Balancing
    generally, 226-227, 260-262
    and advocacy of unlawful conduct, 193-204
    and content distinction, 93, 96, 119-120
    and overbreadth doctrine, 213-216, 226-227

Blasi, Vincent
    "checking value" theory, 10, 36, 41-45
    and prior restraints, 133, 142-147
    views on balancing, 52

INDEX

Bork, Robert
    "democratic process" theory, 10, 15-19, 22-23, 25, 34, 36, 38
    views on protection of unlawful advocacy, 17

Brandeis, Louis D.
    concurring opinion in *Whitney v. California,* 16, 179-180, 189, 196
    as first amendment authority, 1

C

Categorization
    generally, 2, 54, 260-262
    and "actual malice" rule, 81
    and advocacy of unlawful conduct, 95, 119, 193-201
    and content regulation, 119-120
    and overbreadth doctrine, 7, 213-216, 237-241, 255-257

Censorship
    see Prior Restraint Doctrine

Chafee, Zechariah
    and advocacy of unlawful conduct, 173
    as first amendment authority, 2

Checking Value
    generally, 41-45
    and content regulation, 103
    and democratic theory, 44-45
    implications for, on basis of self-realization theory, 36

Chilling Effect
    and overbreadth doctrine, 222-225
    and prior restraints, 143-144, 167

Clear and Present Danger Test
  see also Advocacy of Unlawful Conduct
    generally, 6, 173-211
    and balancing, 192, 193-197
    and compelling interest test, 192, 261
    and content regulation, 117
    criticism of, 173, 193-211
    defense of, 174, 191-192
    and direct-indirect incitement distinction, 188
    history of, 175-186
    and imminence, 184-185, 190-191
    and intent, 187-188
    proposed structure of, 186-191
    use of for areas other than unlawful advocacy, 192-193

Collateral Bar Rule, 164-170

Commercial Speech
    generally, 4
    history of, 61-63
    and overbreadth doctrine, 243
    and protection for false advertising, 63-65
    and self-realization theory, 36, 60-68

INDEX

Compelling Interest Test, 8, 55, 117-125, 140, 153, 191-192

Conduct
    distinguished from pure speech, 4-5, 18-19

Content Distinction
  see also Content Regulation
    generally, 5, 87-126, 257
    and balancing, 93, 119-120
    and campaign financing regulation, 105-106, 112-113
    and categorization, 119-120
    and "communicative impact", 116
    and draft card burning, 100-101, 123-125
    different standards of review under, 93-95
    and flag desecration, 116
    and governmental motivation, 106-108
    and "manner" regulation, 115-116
    and *O'Brien* test, 100-101
    practical difficulties in applying, 114-116
    and subject matter categories, 91-92
    Supreme Court development of, 95-101
    theoretical critique of, 102-114
    unitary standard of review, 117-125

Content Regulation
  see also Content Distinction
    and clear and present danger test, 117
    and "communicative impact", 91
    definition of, 88-92
    and governmental motivation, 90, 107-108
    and profanity, 91
    and time-place-manner regulation, 88-89

D

Dahl, Robert, 26-27

Defamation
    and jury's role, 138
    and self-realization theory, 36, 37, 76-81

"Democratic Process" Theory of Free Speech
    generally, 14-36
    and content regulation, 103

Democratic Theory
    and checking value, 44-45
    classical version of, 21, 22, 29
    and efficiency, 20
    elitist version of, 22, 26-29, 44

Demonstrations, 119, 155-157

Due Process
  see Right to Independent Judicial Forum

INDEX

E

Ely, John Hart
    theory of content regulation, 90, 93-94
    views of advocacy of unlawful conduct, 95, 193-197

Emerson, Thomas I.
    and advocacy of unlawful conduct, 201-204
    analysis of free speech values, 9
    as first amendment authority, 2
    and speech-action dichotomy, 201-204, 259
    views on prior restraints, 134-138, 148

Equality, 103, 109-114

Equity, 159-160
  see also Injunctions

Espionage Acts, 176-177

F

"False Light" Tort, 77-78

"Fighting Words", 55-56, 197, 239

Flag Desecration, 116

Frankfurter, Felix, 209-210

Freund, Paul, 210

G

Greenawalt, Kent, 83-84

H

Hand, Learned
    and *Masses* test, 186, 188, 197-200
    and "sliding scale" test, 181-182

Hatch Act, 99-100, 122, 232-233

Holmes, Oliver W.
    and advocacy of unlawful conduct, 173, 175-180
    as first amendment authority, 1
    and marketplace-of-ideas theory, 10, 45-46, 176

I

Injunctions
  see also Equity
    and collateral bar rule, 164-170
    and prior restraints, 134, 158-161

Intent of the Framers
    generally, 13, 18, 41
    and absolutism, 85-86
    and advocacy of unlawful conduct, 83
    and obscenity, 69

INDEX

J

Judicial Review
    as limit on majoritarian will, 209
    and prior restraints, 150-154

Jury Trials, 136-139

K

Kalven, Harry
    criticism of "speech plus" doctrine, 243
    views on prior restraints, 144

Karst, Kenneth, 103, 109-114

L

Less Drastic Means Test
    See generally Overbreadth Doctrine

"Liberty" Model, 49-52, 104

Licensing
    see generally Prior Restraint Doctrine

Linde, Hans, 157-158

Locke, John, 23, 45

M

Majoritarian Principle, 23-24

Marketplace of Ideas
    generally, 45-48
    and advocacy of unlawful conduct, 81-82, 191
    and content regulation, 104
    and prior restraints, 132-134
    and self-realization theory, 36, 47-48

Mayton, William, 151, 161-164, 169

Meiklejohn, Alexander
    and absolutism, 82-83, 85
    and advocacy of unlawful conduct, 204-206
    and "democratic process" theory of free speech, 10, 14-15, 19, 20, 22, 23, 24, 25, 28, 36, 43, 45
    as first amendment authority, 2
    and *New York Times Co. v. Sullivan*, 76, 78

Military
    free speech in, 121-122
    and overbreadth doctrine, 243

Mill, John Stuart, 21, 31, 46-47

Monaghan, Henry, 138, 222-223

INDEX

N

National Security
    and overbreadth doctrine, 227-229, 237
    and prior restraint doctrine, 157-158

Neutral Principles, 15, 16

O

Obscenity
    generally, 4, 7
    and balancing, 7
    as conduct, 72-76
    rationale for exclusion from first amendment, 68-76
    and self-realization theory, 36, 68-76

Overbreadth Doctrine
    generally, 7, 213-264
    and advocacy of unlawful conduct, 210
    and balancing, 7, 213-216, 227-233, 255-257
    and categorization, 213-216, 237-241, 255-257
    and chilling effect, 222-225
    and commercial speech, 243
    consequences of use, 221-225
    and declaratory judgments, 223-225
    definition of, 216-221
    "expressive conduct" limitation, 243-250
    and military, 243
    and "risk of the wrong guess" analysis, 235-237
    and standing, 221-223
    "substantiality" requirement, 250-255
    and vagueness, 239

P

Prior Restraint Doctrine
  see also Injunctions
    generally, 5-6, 127-171
    and abstract determinations, 139-142
    and audience impact, 142-147
    and autonomy, 144-147
    and demonstrations, 155-157
    interim-final restraint distinction, 129-132, 152-154
    and judicial review, 150-154
    and jury trial, 136-139
    justifications for, 132-147
    and marketplace of ideas, 132-134
    and national security, 157-158
    and obscenity, 152-155
    and overuse, 134-136
    and procedural protection, 136-139
    and subsequent punishment, 127-164, 170-171

"Public Figure" doctrine, 79-80

Public Forum, 94, 96

INDEX

R

Right to an Independent Judicial Forum, 129-132, 147-155, 170-171

S

Schauer, Frederick
    and "expression", 1
    and "free speech principle", 38-40, 74
    and obscenity, 72-76
    and self-realization theory, 36-40

Self-Development, 20-21, 31-32

Self-Fulfillment
  see Self-Realization Theory

Self-Realization Theory
    generally, 5, 11-13, 19-40, 263
    and balancing, 52-55
    and children, 59
    criticism of, 29-40
    implications for types of expression, 56-89
    intrinsic value, 20-21, 27
    instrumental value, 20-21, 27
    and marketplace of ideas, 47-48

"Speech Plus" Doctrine, 243-244

Stone, Geoffrey, 104-109

Subject Matter Categorizations
  see Content Distinction

Subsequent Punishment, 161-164
  see also Prior Restraint Doctrine

Supreme Court
    and clear and present danger test, 175-186
    and content distinction, 95-101
    and free speech theory, 9
    and overbreadth doctrine, 213-214, 227-233, 241-257
    and prior restraint doctrine, 127-130

T

Temporary Restraining Order, 158-159

Time, Place and Manner Regulation
    and content regulation, 88-89
    and demonstrations, 119
    manner regulation, 115-116, 123-124, 153
    and obscenity, 58, 152-153

Tribe, Laurence
    and content regulation, 90, 93, 94
    and overbreadth doctrine, 237-241
    and *O'Brien* case, 106, 123-124
    "track" analysis, 93, 94

"Two-Level" Theory of Speech, 55-56

INDEX

V

Value of Free Speech, 4, 9-86, 262-264

Vagueness
   see Overbreadth Doctrine

Vietnam War
    impact of free speech on, 42, 45

Voting Studies, 27